# English Drama Since 1940

*Longman Literature in English Series*

General Editors:
David Carroll, University of Lancaster
Chris Walsh, Chester College of Higher Education
Michael Wheeler, University of Southampton

*For a complete list of titles, see back of book*

# English Drama Since 1940

David Ian Rabey

*An imprint of* **Pearson Education**

London · New York · Toronto · Sydney · Tokyo · Singapore · Hong Kong · Cape Town
New Delhi · Madrid · Paris · Amsterdam · Munich · Milan · Stockholm

PEARSON EDUCATION LIMITED

Head Office:
Edinburgh Gate
Harlow CM20 2JE
Tel: +44 (0)1279 623623
Fax: +44 (0)1279 431059

London Office:
128 Long Acre
London WC2E 9AN
Tel: +44 (0)20 7447 2000
Fax: +44 (0)20 7447 2170
Website: www.history-minds.com

First published in Great Britain in 2003

© Pearson Education Limited 2003

The right of David Ian Rabey to be identified as Author
of this Work has been asserted by him in accordance
with the Copyright, Designs and Patents Act 1988.

ISBN 0 582 42372 4

*British Library Cataloguing in Publication Data*
A CIP catalogue record for this book can be obtained from the British Library

*Library of Congress Cataloging in Publication Data*
A CIP catalog record for this book can be obtained from the Library of Congress

10 9 8 7 6 5 4 3 2 1

Typeset in 10/12pt Sabon by Graphicraft Limited, Hong Kong
Printed in Malaysia

*The Publishers' policy is to use paper manufactured from sustainable forests.*

To my students
And my countries
As an act
Of
Aggressive
Love . . .

# Contents

# Editors' Preface

The multi-volume Longman Literature in English Series provides students of literature with a critical introduction to the major genres in their historical and cultural context. Each volume gives a coherent account of a clearly defined area, and the series, when complete, will offer a practical and comprehensive guide to literature written in English from Anglo-Saxon times to the present. The aim of the series as a whole is to show that the most valuable and stimulating approach to literature is that based upon an awareness of the relations between literary forms and their historical context. Thus the areas covered by most of the separate volumes are defined by period and genre. Each volume offers new and informed ways of reading literary works, and provides guidance to further reading in an extensive reference section.

As well as studies on all periods of English and American literature, the series includes books on criticism and literary theory, and on the intellectual and cultural context. A comprehensive series of this kind must of course include other literatures written in English, and therefore a group of volumes deals with Irish and Scottish literature, and the literatures of India, Africa, the Caribbean, Australia and Canada. The forty-seven volumes of the series cover the following areas: Pre-Renaissance English Literature, English Poetry, English Drama, English Fiction, English Prose, Criticism and Literary Theory, Intellectual and Cultural Context, American Literature, Other Literatures in English.

David Carroll
Chris Walsh
Michael Wheeler

# Author's Preface

Dates assigned to plays refer to the year of first British production unless otherwise stated. My text identifies the place of a play's first performance with the following abbreviations, where relevant: (RC) = Royal Court; RSC = Royal Shakespeare Theatre; (R)NT = (Royal) National Theatre. This is not to suggest the exclusive pre-eminence of work premiered at these theatres, but will serve to indicate the importance of these three English theatrical institutions in presenting new writing, and the recurrent importance of their patronage in persuading publishers to consider plays for the historical record and wider availability of publication. Inevitably, this is far from being the full story of drama of the period, but reflects the most ready availability of material to read and study.

Bear in mind that I believe that some or all of the inevitable shortcomings in this book could have been overcome by my having at least half as many words again to play with. My editors, Mina Gera and Chris Walsh, very reasonably attempted to persuade me otherwise, and magnanimously countenanced a slight overspill from my 100,000 word limit. Chris also provided very valuable comments, annotations, enthusiasm and encouragement; so did Peter Thomson, whose scrutiny of the first nine draft chapters was a pleasure and a privilege. An award by The Arts and Humanities Research Board permitted me to augment my departmental study leave to write most of the manuscript; and, in the current academic climate, the writing of a book such as this would have been impossible without such study leave allowances; Peter, Ioan Williams and Martin Banham supported my successful application for this award. My most directly helpful Aberystwyth colleagues were Michael Mangan, who provided generous and supportive comments on, and ideas for, the Introduction and Chapters One and Nine; Jamie Medhurst, for information on television drama; and Roger Owen, who provided good sparring, and kept the faith. Brendan Kennelly's poetry and ideas provided insights and resonances of strong mischievous wisdom. Helen Iball graciously permitted my quotations of her splendid but as yet regrettably unpublished thesis. Ken Rabey shared valuable memories of British society and theatregoing in the 1940s, 1950s and 1960s; he and Roma Rabey (who died just before my completion of this book) instigated, encouraged and facilitated my own theatregoing, and look what happened. Roger, Sally Bartholomew-Biggs, Eric Schneider and Charmian Savill contributed vitally to the furtherance of my own theatrical activities with Lurking Truth Theatre Company/Cwmni'r Gwir sy'n Llechu, and John O'Brien moved some mountains. The title of my Epilogue is from Alan Halsey, via Nigel Wells. Charmian, Isabel Morgana Rabey and Ryan Jack Rabey have provided enthusiastic company on theatre visits and good discussions afterwards.

David Ian Rabey
Machynlleth, 2002

# Acknowledgements

We are grateful to Manchester University Press for permission to reproduce copyright material from Howard Barker's *Arguments for a Theatre* (third edition, 1997).

# Introduction: How Should We Live?

## Political determinism: 'either/or'

The creation and management of public order through shared meaning is in itself profoundly dramatic. Clarke notes how Churchill's wartime speeches (like those of Shakespeare's Henry V) appeal to a sense of performance which constitutes history in the making: 'Rather than minimising the threat of invasion, he dramatised it', projecting himself into the future and flattering by association his fellow members of 'the British Empire and its commonwealth' that this would stand as 'their finest hour'.[1] British history has often dealt with challenges to homogeneous national identity by 'ignoring' them and marginalising dissenting voices into ultimately supportive foils for the dramatic advancement of self-styled protagonists: 'Churchill and Orwell slipped into a well-established convention of illicitly, implicitly conscripting all Britons into a pageant of English history, with a few tartan-clad spear-carriers and Celtic bystanders, presumed to be muttering the Welsh for "rhubarb"'.[2]

However, drama also importantly provides cues for occasions and experiences which *speculate* in the *reversibility* of all power. In this study, I will principally identify what I consider to be important instances of fictional drama which interrogates the conventional notions of *social consensus* – a political reading of general opinion which presumes and claims to represent unanimous consent – and *determinism* – a political reading of all social manifestations of the human will as tending towards a single authoritative outcome, out of deference to 'realism', 'inevitability' or 'responsibility'. I readily acknowledge, and moreover argue, that drama has often deliberately worked, or been annexed and invoked, for both social consensus and social determinism. The 'mega-musical' of the 1980s and 1890s is a particularly consensual form: it offers an audience the chance to buy into a reassuringly predetermined experience, in which extravagant spectacle reflects the supposedly triumphant marriage of enterprise materialism and populist sentimentality. Less obviously, stage adaptations of novels have offered a readily consumable experience which also nostalgically invokes Leavisite values of cultural improvement, presenting themselves as attractively justifiable to the most benign terms of social control. Even tragic drama may be interpreted as bearing out a sense of deterministic inevitability: the post-war form of 'modern classic drama' is frequently identified with Chekhov's ironic tragedies, which sympathetically observe lost chance, missed opportunity, the sterility of self-defeating self-preoccupation and entropy (the irreversible decline of a system, in which energy exists only

1

residually and is lost for the purpose of doing work; a situation in which both fixity and fluidity imply a sense of everything running down into inertia). Whilst Chekhov's drama responds to the mood of Russia at a particular moment, British and Irish neo-Chekhovian drama claims for itself an authoritative timeless wisdom (or even absolution) in renunciation of resistance to 'inevitabilities'.

All drama involves a public choreography of crisis, constructed around a fictional confrontation: even the narrative of the musical *Oklahoma!* presents and exacerbates a social crisis, but in order to resolve it reassuringly. Drama may, as in that instance, mediate crisis through formal aesthetic resolution. Often, it stages an oscillation between containment and transgression, between convention and curiosity, rather than the (untheatrical?) presentation of a simplistic choice: *either/or*. But not always.

Interrogatory drama may subvert the conventional assumptions of its medium. It is these resonant occasions which Hare identifies with effects which can make the theatre, above all dramatic media, into 'the place to go for something you do not expect'; 'It is the theatre's aim to draw forth from people some of their most private and intimate emotions. But – and here is its governing paradox – it asks of its audience that these most private feelings be summoned up in a public place'.[3] It is a place where private and secret feelings may have public consequences; and *vice versa*. Within a frame of imaginative possibility and fictional analogy, particular characters, attitudes and actions may be dramatised from a perspective which makes them more appealing, dignified, admirable or alluring than the prevalent generalisations of social meaning would admit. This is an art form which involves and extends into moral enquiry: the insistence that there is an identifiable but not exclusive set of factors which have determined the terms of what is currently recognisable as dominant; and the restless manifestation of a shared question: *how should we live?*

Theatre can demonstrate the unique power of the fully articulate physical presence. Unlike poetry and fiction, drama calls for the physical mediation of the performer between author and audience. And, unlike dramatic forms which depend on electronic recording (radio, film, television), theatre assembles audiences and performers in an *event* of specific *location* and *duration*, all of which are to some extent shared by both the performer and the audience member. They may find themselves becoming sites of unrepeatable, simultaneous and different experience, in ways which dislocate them from social and/ or personal conventions.

A questioning theatrical drama offers, and fleshes out, speculation of a fleeting, artful possibility (if only for the duration of the drama): *both/and*. It may simultaneously delineate and delimit terms of power. In defiance of the emotive generalisations of social consensus, it may offer an *erotically specific* experience which is profoundly political: the surprising closeness of an approach – albeit one which is metaphorical or incomplete – may question the reasons why we hold ourselves back.

English Drama from 1940 to the Present may well provide us with the most conspicuous and confrontational emergences of interrogatory drama since the English Renaissance. Elsom suggests that, before our period, nineteenth-century British theatre challenged the terms of respectability through seeming to be 'without status, inherently useless, falsely alluring and, above all, licentious', deriving a marginal appeal from its apparent circumscription: 'By being the very opposite of what middle-class society was supposed to admire, the theatre came to represent an [acceptable because limited] alternative to bourgeois standards'.[4] Sinfield traces this *significant suggestiveness* into the early twentieth century:

> From J. M. Barrie's *Admirable Crichton* and Maugham's *Jack Straw* in the first decade of the century, through to Coward's *Relative Values* and Rattigan's *Separate Tables* in the 1950s, respectable characters meet a threat to the security of their group. Either a plausible impostor is making his or her way into Society, or one of their own number has 'gone wrong'. More challenging authors suggest that the intruder or misfit manifests a superior ethic or wisdom. Consider *Lady Windermere's Fan*, Shaw's *Saint Joan*, Coward's *Easy Virtue*, *The Chalk Garden* by Enid Bagnold. . . . But usually . . . the danger is adequately, though perhaps not entirely, contained at the final curtain.[5]

## Dramatic dayenglish and nightenglish: 'both/and'

I suggest that interrogatory drama offers an erotic (usually nocturnal) dialogue between *dayenglish and nightenglish*, between different liberties, of inclusion and distinction, of containment and transgression. My terms here are drawn from Brendan Kennelly's distinction between 'the English of explanation' and 'the calmly ecstatic, dreamenergised English of pure being which has little or nothing to do with the English of good behaviour'.[6] In the interests of communication, education, analysis and justification, Reason seeks to 'explain the dream beyond its reach' ('a civilised process, honest, heartwarmingly ludicrous, and necessary'), to (re-)establish a coherence even as it contemplates the meaning of the surprising presence, which invites 'a process of complete dreamsurrender to another's emotional and intellectual reality at its most articulate and vital'. Kennelly describes poetry as a passionate dialogue between these conditions and forces, worked out in combative rhythm: 'What is beautifully, restlessly and irrationally vivid in this rhythm is the strange, persistent sense of choice which exists like music in it despite the knowledge that darkness and light are locked in each other. Choose, the rhythm says. Choose, in spite of knowledge. When I dare to choose, I choose to begin'.[7]

Similarly, but with even more emphasis on physical confrontation and existential choice, a performance of interrogatory drama invites *presence and speculation*, in a ritualised suggestion of surprising interdependence and surprising reversibility. It asks its audience members to sit with unconventional proximity, stillness and duration amongst strangers, before the ritualistically and artificially highlighted and foregrounded active presence of freely moving,

3

unconventionally expressive bodies (other proximate strangers), who may extrematise, rather than simply comment upon, experience with surprising freedom. The objective is not a calm balance of opposing forces, but a creatively volatile disequilibrium which questions every perspective on every thing; and redefines choice, which is the precursor of change.

Iball calls these events of deliberate (if metaphorical) amplification of experience 'theatre of excess'; it offers a drama which makes things extreme and draws attention to this deliberate activity, and 'thus proclaims its separation from (the myth that is) daily life'[8] in order to indicate further possibilities. This drama should be distinguished from a conventional 'mainstream striving constantly for representational verisimilitude and struggling to counter suspicions of artifice';[9] rather it offers a disorganisational structure which demands audience recognition of an imaginative (but not literal) 'enabling space' rather than comparative restrictions of the literally 'escaping, entertaining or explaining space';[10] in this 'enabling space', the habitual 'inscription of bodies with socially specified meanings is brought into question, or is exploited'.[11] As noted, the theatrical performance (unlike the recorded one) is irrevocably specific in place and time,[12] proposing a beauty in its very transience, and its choice to go beyond what is necessary in terms of conventional social utilitarianism, and to argue with the morality of those terms. This choice of demonstrative commitment to the demands of artificiality may even energise the spectator's speculation about the 'complex cohabitation of actor and role', to know 'just how much the actor as "site of experience" is indeed experiencing'.[13] The purposefully excessive theatre experience stands in for contact by suggesting and prolonging imaginative consequences.[14] It may even suggest that being specifically artificial is what human beings do best.

The theatre event does not carry the same significance for everyone, but may show how sharing some space (or portion of it) with others can do more than we would expect or even like it to do (it can remind us of possibilities and opportunities forgotten or dismissed). The self-consciously presented fiction that is drama is particularly well placed to extend the peculiar power of theatre: the friction between the *artificial* and the *consequential*.[15] The mutually questioning mechanisms of convention and curiosity (the most familiar masks of dayenglish and nightenglish) can be amplified explosively, polarising associations and uniting polarities (or threatening to do so) by questioning the conventional terms of separation: spatially, temporally, realistically, imaginatively. This resonant drama of re-designation invites the audience to provide analogy, in terms of the rules and situations of their lives. It emphasises individual experience within a collective context, and the power of the moral imagination to renegotiate all limits. Social and educational organisation, as well as personal inclination, are factors influencing the amount of people who will respond to this invitation to renewal, identified by Kennelly as the insistence on forever beginning.[16] But, at best (when its choreography of physical presences purposefully exceeds the inarticulate and tokenistic), theatrical performance of interrogatory drama offers the discovery, challenge and demonstration – not just the description – of freedom.

# Notes

1. Clarke, *Hope and Glory: Britain 1900–1990* (1996), p. 197.
2. Ibid., p. 2.
3. Hare, *Writing Left-Handed* (1991), p. 44.
4. Elsom, *Erotic Theatre* (1973), p. 14.
5. Sinfield, *Out on Stage* (Yale, 1999), p. 167.
6. Kennelly, *The Man Made of Rain* (Newcastle, 1998), p. 7. Subsequent references in this paragraph are from the same page. I would not suggest that drama always favours nightenglish; nor even interrogatory drama. Shaw's heroes are often admirable spokes(wo)men for dayenglish, though often intriguingly susceptible to, or challenged by, representatives of nightenglish (Tanner in *Man and Superman*); so are Brecht's and Bond's.
7. Kennelly, *Begin* (Newcastle, 1999), p. 13.
8. Iball, *Mess en Scène* (PhD thesis, University of Wales, Aberystwyth, 2000), p. 4.
9. Ibid., p. 3.
10. Ibid., p. 26.
11. Ibid., p. 55.
12. Blau notes 'the one inalienable and arcane truth of theatre, that the living person performing there in front of you may die in front of your eyes and is in fact doing so': *Blooded Thought* (New York, 1982), p. 105.
13. Iball: 'a burning question particularly in situations of sexual contact and violence on stage', op. cit., 32. The formulation, 'site of experience', is interrogatively developed from E. Diamond's *Unmaking Mimesis* (1997).
14. Iball notes how, in Barker's *The Bite of the Night*, Helen of Troy's persisting sense of her amputated limbs ('Armless I reach out') serves as a metaphor for audience experience: 'Through the conventionality of the auditorium, spectators' bodies are expected to remain docile until the hands are permitted to rematerialise, hands clapping recognition at the close of play'; ibid., p. 30.
15. Thanks to Roger Owen for assisting in this formulation.
16. Kennelly, *Begin*, p. 104.

# Chapter 1

# 1940–56: Reconciliation and Dissociation

The watershed status of 1956 for English drama has been compounded and recognised as a critical cliché. Rebellato notes the frequent identification of this historical pivot in terms of 'an image of a repressed force bursting out' on 8 May 1956, with the premiere of Osborne's *Look Back in Anger* at London's Royal Court Theatre: 'Consequently, the old era becomes exclusively characterised by the absence of Anger, and the new era by its presence'.[1] My chapter divisions reflect that cliché, but in order to examine it.

Significantly, Morgan entitles his historical impression of the period 1943–45 in Britain 'The Façade of Unity'. After World War One, a sense of disillusionment and class betrayal had followed Lloyd George's post-war election pledges in 1918. Chamberlain's Britain in the 1930s was governed through polarisation, social division and economic segregation of the southern English Conservative ascendancy from the North of England, Wales and Scotland. In the 1940s, 'there was now a genuine sense of unity rooted in the social and cultural realities of wartime', but Attlee's Labour government of 1945 characteristically invoked the past to address a nation celebrating victory 'not in terms of a triumph of the will' but of suspicion and defiance of external change.[2]

In the immediate post-war period, most of the population continued to experience rationing, queues for food and buses, and a more general sense of restriction and drabness, but remained docile and accepting. Labour policies invoked the principle of universality, rather than the Conservatives' emphasis on selectivity.[3] The welfare state's new provisions of social welfare included increased access to medical and educational facilities; more generally, however, the governing ethos was 'vaguely socialist in theory while becoming individualistic and statist in practice',[4] depending on a presumed public morality of control based on the disciplined consumer. The wartime emphasis on thrift and deferral became subsequently equated with patriotism and responsibility. Morgan: 'The government relied, it seemed, on promoting a kind of secular religion in dictating the public's response'.[5]

Morgan's description of appetite *sublimated* through neo-religious preference for control might be juxtaposed provocatively with Peter Brook's description of late 1940s theatre in his popularly authoritative study, *The Empty Space* (1968): 'theatre of colour and movement, of fine fabrics, of shadows, of eccentric, cascading words, of leaps of thought and of cunning machines, of lightness and of all forms of mystery and surprise' but also 'the theatre of a battered Europe that seemed to share one aim – a reaching back towards a memory of lost grace' (p. 48). Here Brook seems to have Christopher Fry's drama particularly in mind. The first half of his description might, nevertheless, so nearly be a litany of positive qualities (befitting his favourite play, *The Tempest*), when opposed, say, to a theatre of drab literalism.

Whereas in the 1940s, theatre and cinema shared claims on the popular imagination, the war years had elevated the social focus of the dance hall at the expense of the theatre (but not of the cinema). In the post-war period, theatre had to win back an audience in the face of a passive consumerist consensus (the isolating terms of which would extend through subsequent leisure activities, such as television in the 1950s, bingo in the 1960s, video in the 1980s, and computer games and 'virtual reality' in the 1990s).

In 1940, the Council for the Encouragement of Music and Art (CEMA) was created to sponsor amateur, touring and regional drama. However, Rebellato has identified how three emphases were, in the next ten years, 'successively abandoned, and turned towards their precise opposites: professionalism, buildings and London',[6] under the aegis of the Arts Council, from the mid-1940s onwards; and how the altitudinal images and pyramid structures so dominant in Arts Council policy rhetoric reflect an anxiety about the increase in leisure time for the properly obedient and sexually puritan consumer. The 1945 promotion of the model of the Arts Centre was designed to channel its audience into a regular location for a variety of presentations (plays, opera, ballet, concerts, films, galleries, restaurants), whilst the pyramid structure of centralising excellence (and subsidy) is 'a mechanism to inscribe everyone into the values embodied at the peak by the prestigious national companies'; the Local Government Act accorded with this centralising strategy: 'By empowering local authorities to fund arts locally, it relieved the Council of the need to fund regional theatre projects, and allowed them to concentrate on the capital'.[7] The playwright Terence Rattigan publicly maintained the importance of never upsetting or alienating the contemporary middlebrow theatregoer, whom he dubbed 'Aunt Edna'. After the war, English theatre not only stood still but harked back, in all but London. If the rest of the country became identified with the tastes of 'Aunt Edna', that was not through regional choice, but reflected the narrowness of the theatrical options, and lack of alternatives, on regional offer.

English theatre of the 1940s was led by actors rather than dramatists. Olivier, Gielgud, Ashcroft, Redgrave, Edith Evans played in Shakespeare, Ibsen, Chekhov. As the Forties turned into the Fifties, there was a vogue for French drama as purveyed by Anouilh (perhaps the leading example of highbrow theatre in Britain at the time, as championed by the Francophile critic Harold Hobson), Giraudoux and Betti; in the mid-Fifties, the London debuts of Beckett, Brecht, Genet and Ionesco claimed attention, and directors such as Brook and Peter Hall made their names. The theatre which toured English regions relied heavily on author-based revivals (Shakespeare, early Shaw, adaptations of Brontë and Dickens) or domestic plays which could serve as star vehicles, such as N. C. Hunter's depictions of 'sad gentility mouldering away in country houses or hotels', which could pass for 'realism' in the 1940s.[8] Rodgers and Hammerstein's *Oklahoma!* arrived at Drury Lane in 1947, and its celebration of energy, expansiveness and simplicity proved popular and profitable, opening the door of the West End for other successful American musicals (including *Annie Get Your Gun*, 1947; *South Pacific*, 1950; *Guys and Dolls*, 1953). The London premieres of Tennessee Williams's *A Streetcar Named Desire* (1949) and Arthur Miller's *Death of a Salesman* (1950) suggested alternatives to English restraint in terms of social enquiry and theatrical performance.

The Irish drama developed by Yeats and O'Casey looks particularly foreign to the Britain of this era. Yeats's symbolic plays of Irish national regeneration were increasingly based on the Japanese principles of Noh drama – sparse events suggesting an ominous supernatural current and resonance beneath apparently simpler and more prosaic encounters – yielding a hellish sense of inescapable re-enactment and repetition in the traps of the past, best exemplified by *The Words upon the Windowpane* (1930) and the murderously involuted world of *Purgatory* (1939). O'Casey's plays similarly suggest a supernatural patterning, but more usually as a benign force, favouring and inspiring those who struggle for social equality and against capitalism, imperialism and a repressive clergy: *The Star Turns Red* (1940), *Purple Dust* (1945), *Red Roses for Me* (1946), *Cock-a-doodle Dandy* (1949) and *The Drums of Father Ned* (1959).

The early 1950s marked the start of the British television era, and many people purchased sets in order to watch the 1952 Coronation.[9] The artistic highlight of the television week was usually the Sunday Night Play, often a 'tried and trusted' theatrical success, purporting to (re)establish, (re)educate and (re)introduce an interest in drama. O'Casey's *Juno and the Paycock* was produced for television in 1938, as were adaptations of W. P. Lipscomb and R. J. Minney's *Clive* (a successful West End play, televised as *Clive of India*) and W. H. Auden and Christopher Isherwood's *The Ascent of F6*. Jacobs notes how *Clive* and *Ascent*, despite differences in style and address, both present psychological studies of one 'great man', and how part of the project of *Ascent* is to dramatise visually 'the process of mediation whereby [the protagonist's] heroic struggle with his psychology is distorted and trivialised through its state and media appropriation, and through its reception by the bourgeois listeners'.[10] However, 1954 saw the most unsettling example of television drama prior to the discoveries of Osborne and Sandford: Nigel Kneale's adaptation of Orwell's novel *1984*, produced by Rudolph Cartier. Cartier was significantly aware of how a television broadcast might bypass the reassurance which a film viewer might derive from an awareness of a mass audience in a modern cinema: 'in the TV viewer's own home ... cold eyes stared from the small screen straight at him, casting into the viewer's heart the same chill that the characters experienced whenever they heard [Big Brother's] voice coming from *their* "watching" TV screens'.[11] Such was the impact of Cartier's film that some viewers suspected their own new television sets to be *threateningly* intimate, latently interactive devices of authoritarian control.[12] 'If the Coronation proved that television had access to a mass national audience, *1984* demonstrated that television could also frighten and perhaps harm that audience',[13] by the subversion of conventions to suggest the reversibility of the viewer's presumed control of the medium, and to question the benign assumptions and promises supporting technological progress, social visibility and consumerist integration.

## Patterning poetics

> That's not the language
> I choose to be talking. I will not choose yours
>
> (T. S. Eliot, *The Family Reunion* (1939))

T. S. Eliot provided, not drama in the style of Yeats, but a poetic verse drama which was anchored in recognisably or ostensibly English senses of preoccupation with style of being. Whether anchored in a fictionalised exemplary history (*Murder in the Cathedral*, 1935) or the drawing room mystery, adultery drama or comedy (*The Family Reunion*, 1939; *The Cocktail Party*, 1949; *The Confidential Clerk*, 1953), Eliot's drama often sought to imbue the settings and plots of contemporary commercial theatre with the intellectually respectable fatalism associated with Greek tragedy. This represented an unfortunate turning away from the disturbing originalities suggested by Eliot's 1920s work on the uncompleted *Sweeney Agonistes*, which blends jaunty, rhythmical, repetitive colloquialism with the imperfectly articulated menace of blackly humorous amorality (where normal terms 'don't apply' to dead men or murderers, who nevertheless have 'gotta use words when [they] talk to you', adding 'But if you understand or if you don't / That's nothing to me and nothing to you'). Rather, Eliot concentrated on self-consciously elevated matters (locating a sense of supernatural truth behind the everyday experience of country and town house owners) – couched in elevated speech (intensified yet acceptable to the widest possible section of the currently defined theatregoing audience) attractive to classically trained actors and audiences of the day. In *The Cocktail Party*, the protagonist self-consciously reverses Sartre's epigram, 'Hell is other people', to suggest 'Hell is oneself, / Hell is alone, the other figures in it / Merely projections. There is nothing to escape from / And nothing to escape to. One is always alone'. Finally he suggests 'I think, that every moment is a fresh beginning; / And . . . that life is only keeping on; / And somehow, these two ideas seem to fit together'. The 'think' and 'somehow' testify to the sense of imaginative strain here. Eliot seeks to hint at redemption for the shriven, yet also the inescapability of listless *ennui* defined in terms of 'suffering' that is 'part of the design'. Poetic expression (striving for the cadence of divine inspiration) constitutes the tenuous spiritual (and theatrical) compulsion, and potential for redemption, of otherwise dully material characters. Thus, Eliot struggles to suggest the possibility of a compulsive, elevating nightenglish, associated with Greek ritual tragedy, exploding out of the banal dayenglish of the cocktail party. Contrastingly, Christopher Fry offered a poetic drama predicated on a sense of ultimately spiritually benign playfulness, perceiving a source of light behind each shadow: 'Poetry is the language in which man explores his own amazement. It is the language in which he says heaven and earth in one word. It is the language in which he speaks of himself and his predicament as though for the first time'.[14]

Leeming notes how Fry's early work was nourished by 'three historic movements or tendencies: the religious drama movement, the poetic drama movement, and the postwar hunger for lightness and expansiveness'; thus his ultimately positive philosophy contrasts with Eliot's suggestion that 'the world is to be endured rather than enjoyed'.[15] E. Martin Browne, a director and promoter of poetic and religious drama (who had directed work by Yeats and Eliot), discovered Fry and commissioned him to write plays for the English church, where pageants and holidays were sometimes marked at this period by dramatic presentations (the plays themselves frequently involving a church setting, reflecting the ready access of amateurs to a public space, albeit one specifically inflected in terms of belief). Whatever Eliot's literary ambitions, it is important to remember that his early drama (*The Rock, Murder in the Cathedral*) was dependent on the unpredictable and often uneven abilities of *ad hoc* amateur companies. Leeming observes: Shaw was 'as it were putting new wine in old bottles and insinuating his message under the guise of established comic forms', and so could 'rely on his company's training in such forms'.[16] So could the later Eliot, who chose religious enfusals of West End theatre's established paradigms. Fry's early work is part of this popular community (if specifically oriented) movement in religious drama and suggests a continuity and order at work behind human destructiveness, with time as a medium of fulfilment rather than decay. Nevertheless, the recurrent presence of (ex-)soldiers in all but two of his plays suggests a constant awareness of war's potential for mass destruction, and its problematic aftermath. A speech in Fry's *The Firstborn* (1948) succinctly reflects bewilderment as well as appreciation at the apparently chaotic movement of an ultimate order: 'What is this divinity / Which with no more dexterity than a man / Rips up good things / To make a different kind / Of good'. By the time of *Curtmantle* (1961), Fry's Thomas Becket play, a central character urges 'Consider complexity, delight in difference'. This is an apt keynote for Fry, who chooses comedy as a form through which to reveal a sense of mysterious but ultimately benign spiritual order triumphing through human muddle and malice, and in doing so discovers a dramatic style which has more in common with Shaw's comic moral pragmatism than Eliot's religious fatalism. Leeming's description of Fry's drama, in which 'the characters give their own points of view with a dazzling effect that is momentarily convincing, and at the same time the audience applies the more conventional or normal standards to what is said and done and laughs at the perceived incongruity',[17] might also serve to point up the affinity with Shaw's method. The anti-heroic extravagance expressed in *The Lady's Not for Burning* (1948) revolves around an attempted reconciliation to continued life. However, the surface vitality of the play might need a directorial restitution of shadow to keep its more serious preoccupations in focus for the audience. The dangers of *Venus Observed* (1950) resolve themselves with the Duke, a character of irrepressible appetite, exulting at the prospects of age: 'Shootings, stabbings, lynching of the limbs, / A sudden illumination of lumbago. / What a rich world of sensation to achieve'. This sense of an u̶ and self-conscious human comedy – that 'groaning as we n the figure of a dance'[18] – almost foreshadows Peter Barnes's ludicrousness of human social posture, but replaces Barnes view of an ultimately corrupting social authority with a sens redemptive divine authority.

The wintry comedy, *The Dark Is Light Enough* (1954, ̶ ̶ ̶ ̶ by Peter Brook), offers a nocturnal dream-like rhapsody of post-war refuge and atonement, revolving around an idealised matriarch: a nineteenth-century Austrian Countess, protected, isolated, affected by but somewhat spectrally detached from the action (like Catherine in Whiting's *Marching Song* in that same year). Her friends gather, in infantile dependence upon her, for a weekly salon, even as the Hungarian forces of revolution approach. Gettner, the first husband of the Countess's daughter Gilda, appears, a deserter from the Hungarian army. The Countess shelters him, and refuses to relinquish him even in a trade for her more recently acquired son-in-law. Gettner's deliberately irritating assaults on all forms of tolerance extend to rekindling some affection in Gilda before the eyes of her current husband, and even to proposing marriage to his former mother-in-law (he confesses to his ex-wife he married her in order 'to root [him]self' in the Countess's 'radiance'). The Countess admits that she has never loved him, and dies. Gettner decides to confront Austrian soldiers at the door, defending an enemy refugee rather than escape. Thus, the deliberately irresponsible Gettner repeatedly tests the Countess's divine generosity. He delights in his own 'infectious' status ('I carry the war with me') whilst maintaining 'I'll not die to oblige anybody; / Nor for the sake of keeping up / Decent appearances'. However, he finally applies himself to the task of 'making himself exist' by existentially inventing and choosing terms of good and evil (and certain death) for himself. Thus, redemption and reconciliation occur, with conscious unlikeliness, on the brink of death, transcending ironic egoism. The Oedipal terms of Gettner's individuation will be apparent, and the surface charm of witticisms in luxury is shadowed by events of warfare, treachery and conscious cruelty, though again Fry's tone tends to mitigate their severity. Problems of masculine self-definition through choice (or invention) of fundamental principles of appropriate action (often in relation to martial hostility) recur for more thorough exploration in Whiting's drama.

E. Martin Browne's 1945 season of New Plays by Poets, at London's Mercury Theatre, included Anne Ridler's *The Shadow Factory*. Ridler's play is a shrewd and resonant allegory of 1940s paternalism, in which the Director of a factory hires an Artist to illuminate the workplace and reconcile the workers to their routine tasks. The Director is keen to boost efficiency through the inclusive promise of a factory which not only focuses effort but also manages its workers lives, providing 'recreation', 'satisfying art' and 'philosophy' for leisure hours ('Leading industrialists today. . . . Aim to get the best from a worker. / Nerves, glands, arteries, all must be in order. / And that in turn means minds at rest'). The Artist recognises the ominous possibilities of this well-meaning but reductively totalitarian cultural ethos: 'You've taken the

*y* of Strength through Joy / And worked it out to its utmost limit'. Nevertheless, the Artist agrees to 'Live in this place and learn its secret', in order to
reveal its secret determination of imaginative identity ('Human hand, machine's
skeleton – / What is the true articulation?'). He paints murals which depict the
Director as a grotesque agent of monstrous control, manipulating his workers
towards their surrender of responsibility and response: their shadows expose
their degeneration into bestialised pawns. However, the Parson quells the
Director's outrage, recommending the Factory accept the murals: 'Don't you
see? / Your position would be stronger than ever. / Finding the courage to
leave them there – / Showing the factory rich to afford it – / Sturdy enough
to contain such satire / Right at its heart – what a display!'. Thus the Director
agrees on a plan to keep 'Position safe, all / sensible yet. Prestige – some little
loss, / Quickly retrievable'. The Artist is informed that 'after due consideration', the artistic merit of his murals is too great for them to be sentenced to
their destruction; however, he is to be commissioned to produce 'a more
flattering picture of factory life' to 'balance this one'. Ridler's play also suggests how the factory's incorporation of Christmas decorations and a Nativity
play can also be instruments of reconciliation and social control. The rather
generalised characterisations of the factory workers permit no major surprises:
they remain docile in their faith and optimism. However, *The Shadow Factory*
questions the location of this faith and optimism through its darkly fantastic
presentation of the confrontation between the Artist and the Director, which
identifies the connections between emergent notions of artistic terms of permission and deeper forms of imaginative and social control. Ridler's observation of how contemporary totalitarianism reclaims critical art significantly
anticipates Howard Barker's 1985 play *Scenes from an Execution*. She also
purposefully exposes the Platonic conjunction of industrial and spiritual terms
in the post-war social construction of human identity: terms which share
some resonances with those identified in David Rudkin's 1975 play *The Sons
of Light*.

The theological determinism of Eliot is echoed more prosaically in the plays
of Graham Greene, another author for whom artistic and intellectual respectability could be claimed primarily through his achievements in another genre.
*The Living Room* (1953) and *The Potting Shed* (1958) recall J. B. Priestley's
*An Inspector Calls* (1946) in suggesting a sense of concealment and malaise at
the heart of contemporary situations in which *something has to be admitted*
(allowed to be acknowledged, verbally or physically, within the tidy compartmentalisation of the domestic respectability). Such plays owe as much to popular
melodrama and mystery forms as to forensic Ibsenism. Ultimately a Christian
Socialist homily, Priestley's *Inspector* indicted the upper classes' aloofness
from, and refusal of kinship with, those less fortunate, through the agency
of an apparently unremarkable titular character who may be an agent of
God. Greene's *Living Room* similarly suggests that the egoism enshrined at
the heart of social convention represents a tragic turning away from divine
charity and forgiveness; *The Potting Shed* seeks to unravel 'the dark secret' at
the core of a family house and an individual psychology, and finally suggests

a God Himself devoid of choice. Greene's plays – like those of Eliot, Fry and Priestley – are often less concerned with dramatic conflict and character than with demonstration of a pattern, but give classically trained actors opportunities to strike attitudes of tragic dignity and display linguistic virtuosity in more contemporary vehicles (Redgrave in *The Family Reunion*, Gielgud in *The Potting Shed*, Olivier in *Venus Observed*, Evans in *The Dark Is Light Enough*). Again, the theatrical appeal lies in the *demonstrative*, and the plays call for a 'renewal' of fundamentally traditional values. They acknowledge the shadowy dream-like intimations of an instructive spiritual agency, in order to demonstrate and reinforce an ultimate loyalty to the dayenglish of explanation and good behaviour.

Two poetic radio plays provide informative contrasts, through being less traditional in location, tone and values. Louis MacNeice's *The Dark Tower* (broadcast 1946) reanimates Browning's nightmare ballad of Childe Roland, but characterises the hero as 'always asking questions' even when schooled in the socially deterministic 'necessity' of the quest to fight a dragon, from which none of his brothers returned. Whilst Roland's mother is simply and proudly instructional, his tutor identifies paradoxes involved in the task: opposing the dragon is both doomed and a crucial test of self-definition for men to 'be themselves'; shirking the task would make for 'a degraded life'. In an odyssey which MacNeice consciously compares to that in *Peer Gynt*, Roland meets a conciliator: a blind man who spent the dragon's time of dominion 'acquiring riches', until the beast infiltrated and changed people's appearances, the government, and even mirrors, which now accuse their owners of being 'informers'. A conventional sweetheart proposes Roland's individuation from his domineering mother but also rural retreat; he subsequently encounters a *femme fatale* who (like *Gynt*'s She-in-the-Green) may be a portrait-in-reverse of the same girl; and an Old Soak, presiding over a 'tavern of subjectivity' who claims to be making up the story, prompting dissolution into alcohol and luxury. Finally Roland resolutely prepares to confront the dragon, embracing and embodying the very paradox he earlier questioned ('I . . . Who never did anything of his free will – / Will do this now to bequeath free will to others'). The play remains artfully ambivalent regarding the fulfilment of the quest in this hallucinatory, post-war wasteland: is Roland, like Shakespeare's Coriolanus, ultimately subservient to the demands of tradition and authority as represented by his mother (who, rather than or as well as the Soak, may be controlling him like a puppet)? Or does he fulfil the quest on his own terms and thereby remake land, self and mission through just opposition to an invasive moral degradation? MacNeice leaves the audience with a mythic structure, and 'questions', rather than a didactic answer; he offers no interpretation of, or waking from, the dream.

Dylan Thomas's radio 'play for voices', *Under Milk Wood* (1954), is an even more striking example of distinctive use of the new medium's possibilities for imaginative agility. Voices tell the listener what 'Only you can hear and see' within both the houses and inhabitants of a Welsh coastal town. The boundary between imagination and reality is sympathetically dissolved so

13

that, for example, the surprising, eliding nightenglish of the drowned revenants of Captain Cat's dreams can sound as real and immediate to the listener, as to him, as the dayenglish of his neighbours' quotidian routines. Thomas's quasi-musical composition may be presentational (rather than plot-driven like MacNeice's), but is richly suggestive in calling into question rigours and divisions, by tracing 'the movements and countries and mazes and colours and dismays and rainbows and tunes and wishes and flight and fall and despairs and big seas' of his characters' dreams. Rev. Jenkins's reference to the Welsh cliché, 'we are a musical nation', takes on a new resonance, as consciousness and perhaps being in an apparently unremarkable town are presented as compulsively, playfully associative in both form and content: fragments of song jostle with murderous impulse, enactments of wild fantasy, compulsive expressions of sexual appetite, memories and voyeurism. Time (as exemplified by Lord Cut-Glass's 66 clocks of 'different times'), place and personality are shown to be kaleidoscopic rather than single, and surrounded by voices of sympathetic projection:

> GOSSAMER BEYNON: I want to gobble him up. I don't care if he *does* drop his aitches,
> SECOND VOICE: she tells the stripped and mother-of-the-world big-beamed and Eve-hipped spring of her self,
> GOSSAMER BEYNON: so long as he's all cucumber and hooves

The effect of opening a row of doll's-houses, a licensed panorama of conventionally separated perceptions, is extended into the release of the characters' conventionally separated compartments of thought, feeling and being, in compulsively and pleasurably associative terms, culminating in a sense of the surprisingly various within the apparently familiar: effects which will be developed in the 1980s and 1990s by Jim Cartwright (particularly in *Road* and *Bed*).

However, all the plays considered in this section propose a conscious address to the theme of community and individual, not just as a dramatic theme, but through the playwright's (self-)conscious *choices* in *mediating* (or even imposing) a vision of the 'deep structure' of reality, and relating to the playwright's relationship with his audience. These plays reflect a bid to keep at bay crises of faith: not only religious, but regarding the efficacy of language, theatre and communication. Eliot, Fry and MacNeice address and arguably depend upon an audience which is culturally literate, mythopoeically sophisticated and paralytically bewildered by a sense of isolation in existential nausea. Thomas does not so much *expose* as *present* ('Listen!') the complexities of his Welsh community (with its indigenous network of connections and isolations), via the national institution of the British Broadcasting Company, for the isolated radio listener who is offered a new but technologically-dependent intimacy. Some irony may be apparent in Thomas's bathetically reversible name for his apparently organic but highly artificial Welsh town; his working title 'The Town that Was Mad' hints at a potentially unmanageable marginality.[19] The problematic 'nature' of the playwright's topography is negotiated for the audience in terms which formally manifest and replay thematic concerns: perhaps most immediately in Ackland's initially enciphered drama, and in Rattigan's ambivalent appeasement of Aunt Edna.[20]

## *Absolute Hell* and *The Deep Blue Sea*

The murderousness of orthodoxy and the vain desperation of post-war hedonism are reflected in two plays, both directed by the gay director Frith Banbury but both forced to encode their concerns in order to avoid being censored by the Lord Chamberlain (and in the second case, to conceal the author's sexual orientation from his popular public and his ageing mother). Rodney Ackland's play *The Pink Room* was presented at Hammersmith Lyric in 1952 in an early, encoded form, and condemned by the powerful theatre impresario of the day, Binkie Beaumont (himself a closeted purveyor of high-budget escapism) as 'a libel on the British people'; not just because Ackland's play is set in 1945 London at a drinking club which is tolerant of a gay clientele, but because of how it shows the 'phony peace' of continued food rationing, governmentally prescribed austerity and complacent self-congratulation to be 'as sentimental and as hypocritical as anything else in the typical West End play'.[21] This is a particularly trenchant comment given the continued criminalising legislation and strenuous public silence surrounding homosexuality in the 1940s and 1950s, and the promise offered by theatre as a relatively tolerant profession for gay men who were nevertheless prepared to 'play straight' habitually.[22] Ackland revised the play, as *Absolute Hell*, for the 1980s (it was thus performed at The Orange Tree Theatre, Richmond, 1988, and the Royal National Theatre in 1995). Set on the eve of Labour's election victory, the play shows the landlady, Christine, frantically serving the riotous regulars of her club, 'La Vie en Rose', the symbolic epicentre of which is an artificial Magicoal fire, exuding a comforting pink glow (but no heat) even in sultry summer. Amidst the false alcoholic camaraderie, disintegrating artist Michael surveys the sheltered securities of non-combatants, able to continue their smoking and drinking 'while [he] was rotting in a German prison camp'. The recurrent cycle of false cheerfulness and dashed hopes is most painfully exemplified by the struggling writer, Hugh (whose gay relationship had to be rendered as heterosexual in *The Pink Room*). Hugh is wretchedly closeted to maintain the mutually dependent support offered by his ageing mother, and chided by his fickle lover Nigel for failing to live in 'reality'. Hugh ineffectually seeks to question the terms of that 'reality' as he backslides into pathetically desperate gratitude for advances from non-existent films and alcoholic sentimentality (another character pertinently mocks the myth of the work ethic: 'work's just as much escaping from reality as anything else is'). Ackland delineates his thirty self-contradictory characters through many telling interactive exchanges, which suggest the club members' general sympathy towards a Labour Party that offers some prospect of change from their current strenuous posture; however, the play suggests that then (as now) the sympathy will be only

15

selectively reciprocated by self-congratulatory politicians, indifferent to the minority interests they are supposed to represent. Ackland's historical perspective on 1945 sharpens the social ironies inherent in the myths of supposedly equalising post-war solidarity. Particularly notable scenes include the rampage of American GIs wearing animal masks, bellowing for 'a piece of ass' and welcomed by Christine tearing off her clothes and giving them freedom of the bar; Hugh telling Nigel that Nigel's bid to marry a woman is as much a bid to escape reality through respectability as is Hugh's through drunken bohemianism and casual sex; Michael's drunken terrorisation and disclosure of a tyrannical critic, culminating in pistol shots and her death; Hugh's bid to make his home in the club, as managerial assistant to Christine, who is increasingly wracked with the pain of alcohol-related arthritis, which she attempts to alleviate with whisky when the club is condemned as dangerous and 'unsafe'. Nigel provocatively returns to report the 'impossibility' of heterosexuality to Hugh, and plans to leave for Germany to assist with the organisation of 'displaced persons'; a good brave cause which is parodied by an evangelist's militant nonconformism, which attracts at least one supporter in its promise of company and purpose. The reality of the systematic process of 'displacement' exemplified by Nazi Germany is shockingly revealed by harrowing photographs of 'The Living Dead' from a concentration camp, envisaged by a soldier as part of a published montage contrasting with photographs from 'La Vie en Rose'. However, one club member recognises a former friend in the camp photographs, now dead. This confrontation with the essence of massacre, defined in ethnic, political and sexual terms, is sharpened by the earlier irreverent references to more immediate examples of 'horror camp', likely to have been as blackly amusing for the audience as for the characters up to this moment. There is also the growing sense that 'everyone in the club is a displaced person, and the club itself a concentration camp',[23] in the sense that they are compulsively self-deluding as to their ultimate disposability: Hugh goes back to live with his fussing, infantilising mother, as the club literally collapses on top of Christine whilst 'The Red Flag' is sung loudly outside by indifferent drunken celebrators.[24]

Hugh's anguished plea for the recognition of equality in the pain of rejection, in which 'the emotion's the same – the unhappiness, the misery, the *hurt*'s the same whether one's' gay or straight, might provide an epigraph for Rattigan's *The Deep Blue Sea* (1952). Rattigan's popular invocations of 'Aunt Edna' contrast with Ackland's revelatory initiatives (notwithstanding Rattigan's admiration and support for *The Pink Room*, which opposed Beaumont and assisted its premiere). However, the lost first draft of *The Deep Blue Sea* may have depicted a young man's addictive obsession for a fickle and frivolous wartime pilot hero.[25] In deference to the Lord Chamberlain, Beaumont and his own public reputation, Rattigan ultimately designated the doomed lover a female character suitable to be played by Peggy Ashcroft, and excised references to the homosexuality of a supporting character, Miller. The resultant play is a good example of what David Rudkin has observed in Rattigan's drama, when 'craftsmanship' is invested with 'deep psychological necessity, a drive to organise the energy that arises out of his own pain. Not to batten it down but to invest it with some expressive clarity that speaks immediately to people, yet keeps itself hidden', whilst generating a 'resonance of existential bleakness and irresoluble carnal solitude'.[26]

After its 1952 London premiere, *The Deep Blue Sea* was in regional performance by 1956–7, thus providing a more challenging and discomforting theatrical fare than Hunter's *The Waters of the Moon*. Rattigan here demonstrates how passion calls into question the terms and promises of socially normal, and continued, existence. The pilot, Freddie, is resentful of the demands for reciprocity made by former judge's wife, Hester; he claims she unreasonably expects a man to be 'a ruddy Romeo all the time'. Like several denizens of 'La Vie en Rose', the supposedly exemplary male national hero Freddie seeks to avoid monogamous commitment ('I hate getting tangled up in people's emotions') in a way which makes him an *'homme fatal'*. The neighbouring discredited doctor Miller recognises Hester's awareness of Freddie's shallowness as well as her continued craving for him (exemplifying the difficulty of 'loving with one's eyes open'). Hester repudiates attempted reconciliation from her former husband, whose English literary-genteel images of love based on Austen and Trollope are no imaginative equipment with which to recognise the depths and complexities of her consciously irrational passion: 'It's all far too big and confusing to be tied up in such a neat little parcel and labelled lust. Lust isn't the whole of life – and Freddie is, you see, to me. The whole of life – and of death, too, it seems. Put a label on that, if you can' (Act II). Another neighbour, a conventionally married man, attempts advice, recalling his own infatuation with an actress, and how he told himself 'on the physical side, she's everything in the world you want. On the other side – what is she? Nothing . . . I mean, without trying to be preachy or anything, it *is* really the spiritual values that count in this life, isn't it? I mean the physical side is really awfully unimportant – objectively speaking, don't you think?' (Act III). Rattigan's play, like Ackland's, forms a fiercely, engagingly and proudly subjective riposte to the promises of English quasi-objective spiritual transcendence of the physical self (such as preached by Eliot and Greene), by pushing (even obliquely, in Rattigan's case) towards the ultimate release of a forced self-discovery, which confronts the totality of the body and the self. Hester consciously and explicitly discards spiritual values, her word of honour, and traditional national assumptions of 'the pettiness of the physical'; Miller further counsels 'Get beyond hope. It's your only chance'. Indeed, it is regressions into doomed romantic and sentimental hopes which make Hester, Hugh and other denizens of 'La Vie en Rose' pathetic, or even doomed. Miller's Act III confrontation of Hester is particularly eloquently direct: 'Why should you accept the world's view of you as a weak-willed neurotic – better dead than alive? What right have they to judge? To judge you they must have the capacity to feel as you feel. And who has? One in a thousand. You alone know how you have felt'. Hester asks Miller (perhaps provocatively) to find 'one single reason why I should respect myself', before the final entrance of Freddie prompts further regressive impulses. Rattigan ends the play on Hester's lighting the gas fire, which raises the possibility of a repeated bid for suicide; however, her lighting the flame may suggest that she chooses to persist with a life of hopeless isolation, and thereby live with her eyes open. Thus, Rattigan suggests that the supposedly tragic attraction of suicide is understandable, given the falsity of social promise and the loss of desire; however, it also reflects an internalisation of *socially defined* worthlessness which perpetuates rather than challenges society's terms. Related issues of terms of social continuation and dissociation, and self-transcendence versus self-definition, are considered with particularly unEnglish intentness in the plays of John Whiting.

## John Whiting: learning how to die

The purpose of art is to raise doubt: the purpose of entertainment is to reassure.

(Whiting[27])

Whiting's plays are existential in an anti-ideological (non-Sartrean) way, depicting men aware both that their lives have to be imbued with meaning by their actions, and also that the rules for conventional masculine behaviour refute the possibility of individually generated meaning and insist on predetermined death to appease the controlling mythology of the social collective. His compulsively dissociative drama distinguishes him from 1940s and 1950s verse dramatists; in contrast to Eliot's insistence on the inadequacy of the individual consciousness ('a great barrier to creating interesting personalities in his characters'[28]), Whiting makes his characters surprisingly (if tragically) decisive, articulate and self-conscious. They are forced to operate in a semi-expressionistic landscape of socially consistent but nightmarishly burgeoning and resonating visual and aural images. Whiting presents deliberately anti-empathetic 'heroic and ennobling views of nihilism'[29] which confront and examine the impulse towards self-destruction. He is thus opposed both to Osborne's fundamental if vague empathetic veneration of emotion and to Wesker's faith in social improvement. Trussler suggests the social and theatrical circumstances in which *Saint's Day* was first produced – 1951, 'the year in which the British people were preparing to shake off the trappings of austerity in that gesture of touching if misplaced self-confidence that was to culminate in the restoration of Churchill and the Conservatives to power' – accounts to some extent for the 'puzzled fury' which greeted the play.[30]

Whiting's first play, *Conditions of Agreement* (written in 1948–9, but not staged until 1965), anticipates Pinter's *The Birthday Party* by ten years, but similarly deals with the location, separation and elimination of a victim through the form of a birthday party at which he is the chief guest. Whiting's play, however, proceeds from the points of view of the terrorisers rather than the victim. It also features a neo-Jacobean sense of the grotesque and macabre in its revenge plans, foreshadowing the suburban surrealism of Angela Carter's early novels (specifically her 1960s 'Bristol Trilogy'): a one-eyed clown returns, apparently from the dead, to wreak vengeance on a man who once cried at his act (because it was the occasion of his wife's ludicrously undignified death), and is assisted by the son of the man's impoverished neighbour, a one-legged giant determined to punish imperviousness to desperation for money. Trussler pithily notes the frequent manifestations of 'sick cheerfulness' and bathos, 'a collapsing inwards towards the dense core of the play, and this at once exemplifies and predicts the manner in which its every vital action resolves, ultimately, into childishness'.[31]

Whiting's *A Penny for a Song* (Theatre Royal, London, 1951; RSC, 1962, Whitehall Theatre, 1999) satirises the acceptance of warfare in an occasionally farcical, occasionally Shavian comedy, a precisely 'sentimental' play from a characteristically unsentimental writer. I use the term 'sentimental' here in the manner of Laurence Sterne: not a maudlin self-indulgence, but a sensory apprehension of others' behaviour, attempting a sympathy with other persons, notwithstanding the impossibility of full communication when social life is constructed from habitual actions which create a narrowness of perception, a monotony of being, and ultimate pervasive loneliness (the name of one of the characters, Edward Sterne, further suggests this lineage). Like Shaw's *Heartbreak House*, Whiting's *A Penny for a Song* assembles representative social types at an English country house for a diagnosis of national characters that is alternately absurdist, elegiac and abrasive. The outsider Edward is significantly worldlier than the ridiculous patriarch Sir Timothy and his brother, who swap bizarre theories and constant preoccupations with war; they and the shambolic local defence volunteers are depicted as squabbling cartoons which nevertheless represent national forces in emergency strategy. Edward, a former mercenary turned radical reformer, has found the Boy – a French, ostensibly 'enemy' child – deserted by his parents on a battlefield. At Sir Timothy's, they encounter the knight's enthusiastic but naïve daughter Dorcas and the self-proclaimed Christian Tory, Hallam, who takes refuge in hedonism and irony. The Boy is not depicted with stereotypical sentimentality, but he brings out a gentleness and directness in the otherwise self-absorbed characters although he is a racial representative of their enemy. Edward observes how he and the Boy represent the experience, rather than the theory of warfare:

> For the last four years I've been walking about Europe. I've seen such horrible things that it broke my heart. Poverty and disease, love and friendship ruined by war, men and women living like animals in a desperate attempt to stay alive. I was one who sold himself for war so that their children could eat . . . there's a cause for all this. And the cause is laziness and indifference. There are only a handful of tyrants at any one time, but there are millions who don't care . . . at last I decided to fight.
>
> (Act I)

However, Edward's new-found radicalism is a prescriptive ideology, and thus another theoretical release from complexity: early in their first meeting he instructs Dorcas to repeat 'Revolution is a good thing' and 'All my kind must go down before the scythe of history' more for his benefit than for hers. Whiting establishes some critical distance from his holy simplicities when Dorcas counters 'Don't become one of those men for whom the idea of people gets to be more important than people themselves'. She also mocks Hallam's hedon-istic inertia: 'the marvels of science and art can threaten us all with destruc-tion, but none of it matters so long as Hallam Matthews gets through luncheon without indigestion'. Yet in tune with the play's striving towards tolerant, wry sympathy, Hallam achieves a surprising and poignant breakthrough when the boy laughs at Hallam's French quotation '*On n'est jamais si heureux ni si malheureux qu'on s'imagine*', which might be an epigraph for the whole play. The Englishmen's discovery of the Boy's nationality prompts their recoil ('French! . . . I'd never have known it. There are children in the village who look just like that'), which in turn prompts Dorcas's rebuke: 'That boy has stood on battlefields, he's walked continents, he's been threatened and survived, he's seen the dead, he's swum rivers and gone hungry. My God, he makes you look innocent. He makes you look – like children.' Such moments add reverber-ative sonorities to the predominant comedy of English bumblings. Elsewhere, the Chekhovian quasi-allegorical group, house and garden lurch towards Shavian expressionism: the horseplay with an air balloon is a more ludicrous reminder of the plane which crashes into the world of *Misalliance*; and the entreaty and threat that the heaven pour destruction on Heartbreak House seems corrected by Dorcas's deduction that the skies will not fall in apoca-lyptic judgement: despite Edward's warning that 'War, revolution, famine, some horror, is going to bring them down, I think they'll stay up there. And so do you. Go on, admit it'. Dorcas ends the play alone, even more so than Shaw's Ellie; the romantic convention of a partnership with Edward is refused and she relinquishes romantic illusion even as, in the candlelit dusk, she enfolds into memory her initial first-hand emotional experiences.

Whiting chooses another microcosmic country house in which to set his next play, *Saint's Day* (1951), but on this occasion the apocalypse is man-made, immediate and invasive, as the Anglican landscape of village, church and big house becomes a place of abomination and terror. The play was a winner in the Arts Theatre's play competition to celebrate the Festival of Britain; its poor critical reception, notwithstanding this, might be at least partially attributed to the play's refusal of celebration or reconciliation. E. R. Wood notes that the play enjoyed a better reception from critics and public at Birmingham Repertory Theatre ten years later, suggesting 'in 1951 audiences were accustomed to plays which took little account of the immense changes in values and beliefs that the war years had brought . . . theatregoers were still enjoying plays that could have been written thirty years before':

> Even an iconoclastic writer like Shaw, who had once shocked and annoyed audi-ences by his paradoxical and sometimes heretical ideas, had left them in no doubt about which character was the author's spokesman or about what conclusions he was putting before them at the end . . . Whiting belongs to a different age, when the very solutions of the old problems seem to have produced new and more difficult ones; when the playwright does not claim to 'know the answers'.[32]

Robinson notes how 'Wavering between heroism and hysteria, merging the mystical with the banal, echoing Shaw and Eliot and foreshadowing Pinter,

*Saint's Day* upset expectations in every way';[33] moreover, she identifies how this effect continues: present-day playgoers may seek to explain or understand the irrationality of *Saint's Day* in terms of absurdism, but 'Whiting uses volatility and sudden turnabouts in apparently ordinary situations and without formalising them into a new dramatic system, which makes them even more frightening and ominous.'[34]

*Saint's Day* shows an ageing patriarch, poet and polemicist Paul Southman, presiding over a house containing his granddaughter Stella and her artist husband Charles, in a landscape charged from the outset with psychological anxiety and desperation rather than hierarchical security. Paul's manservant, Winter, has to haggle for food in the village and run a gauntlet of resentful threatening. The household is dominated by fear that anticipates and attracts ridicule and hostility. Its details singly and initially seem evidence of paranoid insecurities (Paul's cleaning a pistol, Stella's tales of planned attacks by drunken villagers, Winter's preparedness to fight for his master against 'his own kind', and the alleged poisoning of Paul's dog). However, the non-naturalistic development of the play mitigates any sense of a stable norm against which such suspicions might be judged, and incorporates sudden swings into irrational destructiveness which will make any catastrophe frighteningly possible. Paul himself bitterly dismisses Stella's sense of his 'integrity and saintliness' as a writer exiled by critical and political populism, and anticipates his own drunken regression into infantilism at the dinner to which he has been invited as guest of honour. As they await the arrival of Paul's escort to the event, the contrastingly polished modern poet Procathren, Winter bring news of three soldiers on the rampage, looting and terrorising the village. Paul takes the soldiers to be anti-populist allies, 'although ignorant of our aims and even of our existence', and considers support for their violent marauding by offering them the house. Stella reinforces the gravity of her fears to Charles: 'When Paul came here – when he withdrew himself from the world that attacked him – he chose the village to be his butt . . . he had no quarrel with them but for their sanity and security. Soon they felt – under his attack – they felt their security gone and with it their sanity.' The situation inside the house mirrors that outside: Stella has become neurotically flayed into a frantic spectre, carrying 'a child conceived in violence' and abjectly yearning for escape from the house, perhaps by prostrating herself before Procathren as 'his servant': the house and characters are stretched increasingly into the most bleakly Dickensian and gothic postures and moods, and a trumpet sounds offstage, as if a summons to judgement. Paul reflects viciously on his artistic career, when he went 'straight into my Lady Society's chamber and lifted the skirts of the old whore' in a bid to 'be a man – deliver the goods'; 'And when I had performed the obscene gesture what a rush there was to restore the disarray of the filthy old bag'. Having considered himself exiled as a 'rapist' ever since, Paul discovers a '*clear and forceful*' manner loading his pistol to plan 'as direct and cruel an act' as the poisoning of his dog. The play's most brittle moment is a piece of sub-Eliot foreboding voiced by Stella, awkwardly portentous unless startlingly directed and performed. After Stella has attempted to half-seduce,

21

half-mesmerise Procathren into complicity with her, he watches Paul dismiss the local vicar by pointing the pistol at him and saying 'Bang!'. Then, Paul, Charles and Procathren discover a form of ease and camaraderie through specifically male regression in their movement and speech around the pistol: '*PAUL savagely and in great exaltation: CHARLES amusedly and lightly, foreseeing towards what they are moving although not the actual event: ROBERT through fear, attempting to join in the fantastic jollity as he attempted to join in games and horseplay when a schoolboy*'. The fooling becomes devastatingly real when Robert accidentally fires the pistol and kills Stella. The implication is that such an event is symptomatic of the wider nation state which is darkly poeticised by Paul's wasteland palace of embittered, involuted barrenness. Procathren is riven by the experience, although partly relieved at the removal of the challenging obligations of her sexual and generative power: he tells the soldiers 'She was horrible – she was pregnant – but it was an accident'. Initially unmoved, the soldiers' leader, the ironically named Christian, becomes protective of Procathren, intrigued by the spectacle of his disintegration. Procathren degenerates into grotesque, childish spite at Paul's bid to offer the dignity of forgiveness. The Third Act pushes further into semi-expressionistic experience of nightmare, where what began in apparent paranoid fantasy becomes uncontrollable and envelopingly malevolent: refugee villagers, clutching objects and wearing a jumble of clothes, salvaged tokens of their desperation, watch Charles complete an unfinished mural by painting in the corpse of Stella, whilst a Child plays with contrasting animation. The vicar has been driven by Procathren – now a wild, self-appointed totemic prophet of destruction – to burn his books, ring his bells, then burn himself 'like a roasted potato' as the villagers refuse to aid him. The soldiers subjugate themselves mechanically to the Procathren's programme of chaotic destruction through which he seeks to express the shattering of his own faith in all form of defence against horror. Christian interprets this as a 'dare', challenging Procathren to smash all appeals to reason, plan and order by hanging Paul and Charles. Christian focuses the murderous impulse to reflect his own class antagonism, insisting Paul and Charles have brought this retribution on themselves, through being the supposedly aloof and immune 'people who live away out there with women and music'. Indeed, the grim irony of self-fulfilling prophecy chimes discordantly through the broken landscape of *Saint's Day*, from Paul's self-isolation above his neighbours, to Stella's near-hysterical fatalism, to the flippant gunplay, to the invitation to the soldiers into the house which they then subject to rule of terror. Paul crumbles into madness with a Lear-like address to the child, whom he calls Stella, and with whom he joins in a dance to mark his birthday, prompting the momentarily enraptured villagers' appreciation and congratulations. Undeterred, Christian initiates the hangings, if only – and apparently only – to prove to Procathren that 'If you want to order people like me around you've got to take the responsibility'. Procathren, now a terrifying shaman preaching the sole freedom of chaotic death, presides, with a sermon of nihilistic determinism, emphasising the essential and crucial inheritance of having to learn how to die. Finally, as the executions occur offstage, the

Child's mother does indeed call the Child Stella, attempting to limit her curiosity: the final stage direction deserves full quotation:

*The child takes up the copy of 'Alice in Wonderland' from the table. The trumpet suddenly sounds from the garden: a raucous tune. The CHILD, with the book in her hand, performs a grave dance to the music. As abruptly as it began the trumpet stops. The CHILD's dance continues for a little but she hesitates, listening. There is no sound. Dropping the book to the floor she runs to her MOTHER and hides her face in the woman's lap. There is no sound and everything is still: quite still.*

CURTAIN

This demonstrates Whiting's mastery of disturbingly tenacious scenic effect, as well as of the unsettling verbal language of skewed rationality. The use of the Boy in *A Penny for a Song* is here developed into a startling and resonant stroke of anti-sentimentality as the Child, unlike the cowed adults, ritualistically acknowledges catastrophe with a Dance of Death, which falters into the significantly appalled and appalling lack of closure which characterises so much of this bleakly resounding play. Whiting's 'ironic and fantastically melodramatic statement of doom'[35] anticipates Rudkin's *Afore Night Come* in demonstrating the awful facility with which rural England can upend itself into apocalypse and rites of sacrifice; Arden's *Serjeant Musgrave's Dance*, in which mutineer soldiers join those who would be conveniently separate from wartime ravages in a dance of death; Bond's self-consciously and savagely socially typified characters who find grim satisfaction in playing out the doom of others and themselves; and Barker's catastrophism, which refuses all forms of reconciliation to characters and audience alike. Its prophecy of postwar Europe erupting into the Cotswolds even foreshadows Sarah Kane's anticipation of Bosnian atrocity erupting into Leeds in *Blasted*.[36] Thus, *Saint's Day* is more revolutionary in form and drive than supposedly 'social-realist' 1950s drama, through extrapolating the expressionistic tendencies of Shaw into an unforgiving bleakness more reminiscent of post-1970s drama. Its appalling momentum, which refutes conventional resolution, is a major riposte to drama that makes (essentially conventional) sense through confirming predictable expectations. As Wood observes, its questions of responsibility for violence and suffering are posed in the wake of the first atom bomb being dropped on Hiroshima (August 6, 1945) and killing 78,000 people; 'The "well-made play" makes its calculated effect in the theatre, and that is all; but plays like *Saint's Day* haunt the imagination much longer'.[37] And they do so by calling controllability and calculation into question.

*Marching Song* (1954) is a more linear play, austerely rational: set in a somewhat futuristic stone, glass and steel fortress '*above a capital city in Europe*', it depicts judgement on Forster, a war hero redesignated criminal for his massacre of children who mounted an organised opposition to the tank force he commanded. In peacetime, he is separated and isolated as a suitable sacrificial scapegoat to placate national doubts and conscience. Forster's bleak frankness is contrasted to the opportunistic manoeuvring of the characters who surround him: a former lover who attempts to return to a past whose

23

innocence Forster knows to be lost; a drunken filmmaker who proposes to portray the characters of his own earlier, idealistically propagandist film in an entirely cynical light; a young girl, self-conscious representative of a younger generation which seeks to avoid entanglement in emotional commitment or idealism, who somewhat fantastically finds herself drawn to Forster; a young soldier who proposes to outdo Forster in ruthlessness, believing that reflection, not action, was his former hero's weakness; and Cadmus, the babyish father-figure who maintains government through strategic inertia and refusal to accept responsibility, in a populist authoritarianism which masquerades as democracy through a public address system. Wood notes explicit and implicit references in the text to Shakespearean Roman tragedies, particularly *Coriolanus*;[38] Forster claims a distinction in that, unlike Coriolanus, he is no tyrant (though Shakespeare's play can be directed to collapse that distinction). However, like Coriolanus, he has embarrassed his country through playing out its paradigms of masculinity with unforgivable, destabilising thoroughness, for which it now seeks to abject him. Cadmus, returned (like Churchill) from retirement to lead the country, holds fast to his conviction that 'The way to prevent revolt is to stop men living in the present time', through the specifically 'modern' appeal to pseudo-'democratic' emotionalism:

> For seven years we've been able to refer our major problems to foreigners. Now, once again, as in the war, we're on our own. We have to make up our minds about bigger things than the city drainage. One of the bigger things, my opposition tells me, is to find out who was responsible for this country losing the war. . . . They can't put Bad Luck in the dock, Forster, but they can put you there.
>
> (Act I)

Thus, *Marching Song* artfully conflates a vanquished country's recourse to show trials with the regressiveness of 1950s British populism in a parable akin to Kafka's *The Trial*. Its gambit is played out by all, including Forster, like a chess match, in full cognisance of significantly limited option and consequence. Forster holds fast to accepting responsibility for his actions. Accordingly, he accepts the proffered exit route of suicide, which earns him Cadmus's eulogy: 'He was a great soldier. Learn from him' (Act III). The chessgame atmosphere of *Marching Song* seems as deterministic and anti-climactic as the operation of an infernal machine. Whiting's implicit anger is focused on the manipulative apologist Cadmus, more so than on the 'acceptance' by which Forster capitulates and permits his own instrumentality. Robinson notes how Whiting characteristically suggests love is a distraction or snare for the hero, 'the female way of waging war' which 'becomes another invasion of man's privacy'.[39] Consequently the play lacks passion (the pain of wanting) or surprise, perhaps because Forster, however austere, is surrounded by manifestly lesser characters, deprived even of a partial equal like *Coriolanus*'s Aufidius.

*No Why* (written 1957, staged 1964) depicts the attempts to induce an admission of guilt from a child, Jacob, who has committed an unspecified crime. As elsewhere in Whiting's work, the self-possessed silence of the child makes the adults more volubly scandalised. The mother ostentatiously transfers affection to a cousin, whilst the scolding father criminalises the boy for his wilful independence, and in so doing discovers an inner voice (non-naturalistically amplified) compounding his antagonism, finally expressing a wish for Jacob's extermination. Jacob silently but decisively hangs himself – in compliance with, or in defiance of, parental authority and specifically masculine resentment? His silence represents an eloquently indeterminate void amidst the verbal bids for control, and Whiting is again startling in his use of the child actor, here the would-be 'little man', to repudiate the social control at the heart of adult language, whose meaning is interrogated by his refusal to participate in it. The Manichean bid to extract confession from a determined interrogator of social meaning (as well as the Father's discovery of a strange, horribly urgent 'inner voice') anticipates Whiting's next major play. After years of disheartening hack work on filmscripts, Whiting was invited by Peter Hall (who had directed productions of *Saint's Day* and *A Penny for a Song*, 1952–3) to write a new play for the RSC's first London season at the Aldwych, and produced *The Devils* (1961), based on Aldous Huxley's 1952 book *The Devils of Loudon*, a retelling of alleged possession of seventeenth century Ursuline nuns as a parable of the rival impulses towards self-transcendence and self-assertion. Whiting's version represents a movement towards a sparer, more fluid dramatic style which decisively breaks with drawing room drama to depict a panoramic vista of urban social hierarchies which accumulates into a profound sense of claustrophobic pressure. The often brief episodic scenes resemble film narrative[40] and Brecht. However, their characteristic alighting upon a short, decisive exchange which nevertheless generates precisely cumulative social effect is more tautly distinctive than these comparisons suggest, as is the way that almost every scene ends on a line or move or silence which evokes a resonant bleak irony: this foreshadows the tone of Bond's *Lear* (1971) and *The Fool* (1975), but also the actual technique of Churchill's *Vinegar Tom* and *Light Shining in Buckinghamshire* (both 1976, which in turn influence Wertenbaker's *The Grace of Mary Traverse*, 1985).

*The Devils* continues Whiting's enquiries into what might (un)make a man, and what might make him more than a man. The opening scene shows a chemist and a surgeon observing a corpse on the municipal gallows, whilst a sewerman works in a nearby drain. The surgeon wonders 'What resides' beyond death; Grandier, a priest, is distinguished from 'a man' by the sewerman, but Grandier discloses an awareness of the paradoxes of male pressures and impulses in the tale of a young man's confession of how 'Manhood led him into the power of the senses'. Grandier is suspected by the town governors of having highly developed 'secular senses' ('He fondled a rose as if it were the secret part of a woman'), and seeking to climb in political power on a 'ladder of doubt and laughter', heretical irreverencies. Grandier privately admits the wearying effects of his philandering ('time taken up with being that nothing, a man'), and prays to be released from such needs. His student Phillipe becomes infatuated with him, and during confession she discloses her hunger for him to 'take – no, possess – no, destroy' her. The deformed nun Jeanne becomes fixated by Grandier, and gives a rapturous commentary on the juxtaposed scene of Grandier and Phillipe's naked lovemaking, a perspective of convulsive, envious voyeurism, mixing excitement with jealous disgust, which the audience are required to share. Jeanne becomes 'possessed' and indicts Grandier.

Grandier confronts his fate with the fatalistic stoicism visible in other Whiting protagonists, 'I am a dead man, condemned to live'. He nevertheless does not suspect the depth and pitch of Jeanne's project, which she justifies as the mockery, not of God, but of Man, to show 'the glory of mortality, the purpose of man: loneliness and death'. Grandier is momentarily encouraged by a priest who bids him to will his own suffering: 'Offer God pain, convulsion and disgust.' He is faced with torture to instil despair and extract confession; significantly, he dreads humiliation in specifically public terms: 'A man is a private thing. He belongs to himself. The two most intimate experiences, love and pain, have nothing to do with the mob. How can they concern it? For the mob can feel neither.' When tortured, crippled, and carried to execution as a specimen of physical debasement, Grandier nevertheless insists on his paradoxical status as triumphant abject – 'Look on this thing which I am, and learn the meaning of love' – which even Jeanne finds beautiful, and therefore unforgivable. The Governor and Magistrate of Loudon appear drunk, vaguely conscious that as 'the rational, forward looking men of our age' they should be taking a stand against the mob's ecstasy in destruction, but cannot formulate what they believe when confronted by moral panic. So they go home, as do the theatre audience, whose faith in utilitarian social promises to extirpate all problem and contradiction is similarly challenged by Whiting's scenes of dionysia and machination: forces which are both exposed as tending towards social unification by different means. *The Devils* replaces *Marching Song*'s deficiency of passion with striking soundings of repressed and released longing, and desecratory cruelty, as well as showing the disturbing ways in which these two forces can answer and further excite each other. The agility and bleak ironies of the narrative are further charged by scenes of startling explicitness: not only of nakedness, copulation and torture, but of Jeanne riven into a dialogue between her own malice and that of apparent demonic possession, and the apocalyptic inversions suggested by the Boschian cavorting of the crazed nuns and the mob who encourage and mimic them: these are deliberate and conscious ripostes to the limitation and restraint of much English drama, and of English vocabularies of existence and possibility. Dramaturgically, it paves the way for Peter Barnes's *The Bewitched* (1974), which partly parodies and partly develops Whiting's play to create a more luridly fantastic and more precisely indicting anatomy of social authority.

Trussler summarises Whiting's theme: 'Through the sum of a man's actions he creates himself', a proposition which gives the work 'both its potential optimism and its potential pessimism. . . . If the circles of the plays are closed, the options for humankind are always open'.[41] However, the abiding impression is likely to be a 'collapsing inwards towards the dense core of the play', by protagonists who demand witness as they insist upon their own crucifixion, on crosses they have fashioned from the broken jetsam of conventional heroism and masculinity.

Whiting's plays are particularly stark and striking dramatisations of the 'Coriolanus complex' which is repeatedly fought out in drama of this period: post-war decay and populist masquerade prove unsatisfying and ultimately hostile towards the male character who partly reflects its edicts in unacceptable terms. That character is directly or indirectly termed and/or rendered *abject*, some*thing* to be isolated and severed from the sentimentalised body politic because it refuses to subordinate itself to that society's paternalistic promise (frequently *maternalistically* visaged, perhaps reflecting the 1952 accession of a well-meaning but ultimately separate, unworldly and protected monarch, marking a 'New Elizabethan' era). This ambivalent *indigestibility* is developed and played out differently in the drama of John Osborne.

# Notes

1. Rebellato, *1956 and All That* (1999), p. 4.

2. Morgan, *The People's Peace: British History Since 1945* (Oxford, 1999), pp. 3, 28. Morgan also observes that the Second World War 'marked the last effective gasp of the late-Victorian and Edwardian economy, given deceptive vigour after 1945 because economic rivals such as Germany and Japan were defeated', p. 10.

3. Marwick, *British Society Since 1945* (3rd edition, Harmondsworth, 1996), p. 46.

4. Donesky, *David Hare* (1996), p. 30.

5. Morgan, op. cit., p. 67.

6. Rebellato, op. cit., p. 41.

7. Ibid., p. 50.

8. Worth, *Revolutions in Modern English Drama* (1972), p. 19.

9. 'At least two million people turned out to watch the coronation procession; but the new twist was that almost 20,500,000 people, 56 per cent of the adult population, could watch, and did watch, the entire proceedings on television', Marwick, op. cit., p. 105.

10. Jacobs, *The Intimate Screen* (Oxford, 2000), p. 64.

11. Cartier, 1958, quoted in Jacobs, ibid., p. 153.

12. As recalled by my father, Ken Rabey.

13. Jacobs, op. cit., p. 155.

14. Fry, BBC talk printed in *The Listener*, 23 February 1950; quoted in Hinchcliffe, *British Theatre 1950–70* (Oxford, 1974), p. 40.

15. Leeming, *Christopher Fry* (Boston, 1990), p. 1.

16. Leeming, *Poetic Drama* (1989), pp. 78–9.

17. Ibid., p. 51.

18. Fry, 'Comedy', *Tulane Drama Review*, 4, no. 3 (1960), pp. 77–9 (77).

19. Thomas's original plan was that the community should be visited by bureaucratic political inspectors who want to cordon off the town and put it on trial for 'madness'; but when the inhabitants hear what the prosecution defines as its norms for 'sanity', they decide to put things in reverse and volunteer to cut themselves off from a 'sane' world. Thanks to Walford Davies for this information.

20. Thanks to Michael Mangan for assisting me towards some observations in this paragraph.

21. Dromgoole, Introduction to Ackland's *Absolute Hell* (1990), p. 10.

22. See Rebellato, Chapter 6, and particularly his list on p. 163 of homosexual and bisexual men visibly active in 1940s and 1950s British theatre, almost 'a roll-call of one generation in British theatre'.

23. Francis King, *Sunday Telegraph* review quoted on the back cover of *Absolute Hell*.

24. Ackland frequently delineates a regressive group, and the bid of one or more characters to individuate themselves from its inertia; however, this initiative is often crippled by an admitted weakness. *The Dark River* (1941) shows a meeting in support of the radical forces in the Spanish Civil War broken up by fascists; on the opposite riverbank, several relatively privileged characters refuse to believe that a war will occur, or that the world and warfare might have altered from their past; an actress backslides into sentimental affection for her ex-husband, and so she loses her new love through her inability to sever herself from the past, deducing 'We're both weak characters' as guns boom in the distance.

25. The theory of the lost homosexual draft is advanced by M. Darlow and G. Hodson's *Terence Rattigan: The Man and His Works* (1979), but opposed by Rebellato in notes to the 1999 NHB edition of *The Deep Blue Sea*. There is broader agreement that the play was inspired by the suicide of Kenneth Morgan, an actor with whom Rattigan had an on-off relationship 1939–45. Sinfield adds: 'The play still features sexual dissidence. It was scandalous for a woman to leave her husband, outrageous for her to declare that she had done so because of an overwhelming sexual passion, and courageous for her to relinquish both men for an independent life', op. cit., p. 160.

26. Quoted in Darlow and Hodson, op. cit., p. 15.

27. Whiting, *At Ease in a Bright Red Tie*, ed. Hayman (1999), p. 94.

28. Hayman, *Contemporary Playwrights: John Whiting* (1969), p. 3.

29. Ibid., p. 96.

30. Trussler, *The Plays of John Whiting* (1972), p. 17.

31. Ibid., p. 30.

32. Wood, Introduction to John Whiting's *Saint's Day* (London, 1963), pp. vi–vii.

33. Robinson, *A Private Mythology* (1988), p. 64.

34. Ibid., p. 73.

35. Robinson, op. cit., p. 80.

36. A comparison made by Michael Mangan on reading a draft of this chapter.

37. Op. cit., p. xxxii.

38. Wood: 'Pride and ambition were the most powerful motives in Coriolanus as in Forster; both did the state great service but incurred the hostility of the representatives of democracy; and both owed their defeat to allowing human feelings to temper military ruthlessness', Introduction to Whiting's *Marching Song* (1956), pp. viii–ix. *Marching Song* works as a more politically precise updating of the themes and issues of *Coriolanus* to post-war Europe than Osborne's linguistically slackened attempt, *A Place Calling Itself Rome* (1973).

39. Robinson, op. cit., p. 24.

40. Ken Russell's sensationalistic 1971 film version of *The Devils* draws all too briefly on Whiting's text.

41. Trussler, op. cit., p. 162.

# Chapter 2

# Out of 1956: A Rising Generation

In Chapter 1, I noted how the drama of Eliot and Greene attempts similar traditional (specifically religious) interpretations of experience, whereas Ackland, Dylan Thomas and Rattigan's *The Deep Blue Sea* emphasise an unruly physicality which defies the traditional terms of social generalisation, and Whiting represents compulsive dissociation. The rarely challenged securities of the early 50s New Elizabethan Age gave way in 1956 to the fracture of hegemony and the myth of British coherence. This was exposed by the division of public opinion over the Suez crisis, in which the authority of British imperial impulses was judged, globally and domestically, to have overstepped its political mark.

Also in 1956, the Hungarians rebelled against their apparatchik government of Kremlin-controlled secret police and, after several days' stand-off, Russian tanks invaded. Whilst the Suez crisis had an obvious effect on British conservative self-esteem, these events caused great difficulties for the British Left, and its tenacious holding to the myth of Soviet utopianism. Khrushchev suppressed the Hungarian Uprising ruthlessly; for all his talk of supplanting the 'cult of personality' which he critically associated with the Stalin era, Khrushchev promoted himself as an avuncular figure, but seemed one who might nevertheless suddenly say 'Off with his head'.

The widespread purchase and availability of televisions for symbolic participation in the Coronation ironically permitted a wider audience for John Osborne's *Look Back in Anger*, which attacks the vicariousness of English life (an extract of the Royal Court production was shown on BBC on 16 October 1956, reaching an estimated audience of 5 million, with ITV televising the play in full at peak viewing time on 28 November). The success of *Look Back* is also significant for the cultural placement of the theatre, specifically of The Royal Court, and the relationship of both to Arts Council policy. As Lacey observes, the arts, like much else in post-war reconstruction, were subjected to the economic theories of John Meynard Keynes, which rationalised State intervention not only in market forces but also in cultural issues: 'the arts were considered as the spiritual wing of the Welfare State, administering to the nation's psychic health as the NHS administered to its physical well-being. In this way, the Arts Council was a visible expression of consensual assumptions translated into the cultural sphere'.[1]

*Look Back in Anger* was not revolutionary in form. It was, in many ways, formally conventional, directing attention to its disturbing content.[2] The curtain rises on a striking contrast to the smart, charming drawing room usually depicted: '*a one-room flat in a large Midlands town*', which moreover contains an ironing board, and a woman standing ironing in her petticoat: all likely to be startling novelties to the mid-1950s London theatregoer. Moreover, whilst the curtain falls on a scene of regressive tenderness, this is not a conventional sentimental or melodramatic resolution: regressive tenderness is questioned *as a conventional resolution*, with Jimmy Porter unpunished for his unrepentant compulsion to cause pain, slighting the ideal of poetic justice. Indeed the play is an energetic celebration of the articulation of suffering which might have been more acceptable in a Russian play, but which most English drama of the time was concerned to tame, limit or redeem. London theatregoers were also used to a different theatrical voice, that of standardised, pseudo-public-school 'received pronunciation'. Unusually, Osborne dared to associate a 'non-BBC' accent with articulate intelligence. The 1944 Education Act had provided Osborne and Porter's generation with free education; a regional accent no longer automatically implied a lack of education, and the slackening of the pressure on younger people to hide behind 'public school' accents was indicated and intensified by the example of Osborne's protagonist.

Osborne was willingly labelled as a vanguard of the 'Angry Young Man' conglomeration of male artists who assumed a confrontational attitude towards the platitudes of the older generation, with particular attention to the question of social purpose in the wake of World War Two. Britain was not rebuilding as promised, and the continuity offered by comfortable stagnation was questioned by a generation who felt that conventional life offered little excitement. The war had demanded conformity for a larger purpose, but 1950s Conservatism emphasised the passive goal of 'affluence' – the dubious analogy between social progress and the growth of material wealth, extension of leisure and consumerist choice – rather than honourable conflict or release of energy. Osborne and Wesker attack 'the deadening effects of prosperity'[3] more frequently than the uncomfortable confines of poverty. There were other breaks in continuity in the experience of generations, with the disappearing tradition of job transition from father to son, and the emergence of rock'n'roll as a youth-based street culture which embraced some spirit of provocation and disturbance. Nevertheless, the hegemony – the mutually supporting and confirming series of practices and expectations, meanings and values – of early 1950s England was highly *consensual*, that is, it emphasised the management of consent as a way in which subordinate groups might understand their relationship to, and position within, society through the definitions of its dominant group. Lacey identifies how hegemony attempts to interpret 'new' social experiences in terms of 'traditional' values: for example, by attempting 'to persuade women to return to traditional roles in the family, establishing a kind of "domestic consensus", once their presence in the labour market was apparently no longer "necessary" for the national economy'.[4]

Whilst *Look Back* is anti-consensual, and remains challenging to English theatrical convention, its success constituted a necessary mutual vindication for the Royal Court and the Arts Council. It foregrounded and asserted the independence of English writing and professional theatrical practices at a time when British stages were dominated from abroad. The triumphalism of Martin Esslin's 1971 rationalisations is significant: 'In a period of steady decline of British power British artistic achievement has played an important part in keeping the country's prestige high. And in this area British playwrights have been of paramount importance. In the development of these playwrights the Royal Court played a decisive role.'[5] But Rebellato makes important distinctions:

> The great play made of 'regional accents' should be set against the metropolitanisation of culture; that the Court is considered to have forced regional accents onto the stage, thus ignoring (most immediately) all the community work of the forties and early fifties, is a talisman of the way that London became a focus for displaying the nation. Stephen Joseph [in 1957] complained that those who are searching for new playwrights are simply ignoring the work of the regions and the little theatres. But by now 'new writing' is a construct of Arts Council policy, and therefore pivoted on the metropolis.[6]

The English Stage Company at the Royal Court, under George Devine, emphasised its policy of foregrounding, attracting and assisting new writers. Whilst Devine's personal enthusiasm extended to presenting the work of Ionesco and Beckett in order to educate the parochial writer and public to more ambitious theatrical possibilities (and present 'the whole range of contemporary drama'[7]), the press releases of the Court proclaimed 'we are not avant garde, or highbrow, or a coterie set. We want to build a vital, living, popular theatre'.[8] This rhetoric of 'vitality' has been identified as according with attacks by Leavis, Hoggart and Raymond Williams upon the mechanical and debasing quality of mass culture and materialism;[9] it also appeals to the contemporary ideological and commercial construction of 'Youth' as something problematic (antagonistic towards the opportunities and benefits bestowed by the loosening of established values, their 'ingratitude' and dissociation being a source of general moral anxiety), yet commercially (and therefore ideologically) reclaimable as a 'market' to be exploited. Kenneth Tynan's famously significant and commercially crucial review of *Look Back* is not the only review to make much of 'youth',[10] but it most effectively associates youth with vitality and directness of feeling ('I doubt if I could love anyone who did not wish to see *Look Back in Anger*. It is the best young play of its decade'[11]) in a way which claims for the play both a divination of the *Zeitgeist*, and a general emotional respectability, ushering in an age of specifically English indigenous theatrical dominance. If, in the mid-1950s, 'young people had virtually no relationship with the theatre', a Court Stage Director claims that after the televised extract, the theatre became filled with people 'in their later teens and early twenties'.[12] The previously identified sensed crisis of faith and relation between playwright and audience, which emphasised *mediation* (albeit problematisingly, by Ackland and Whiting at their most unreclaimable), becomes replaced by a valorisation (and commercialisation) of communicative and intuitive *directness*, and emotional accessibility.

# John Osborne: just like a man

A theatre audience is no longer linked by anything but the climate of dissociation in which it tries to live out its baffled lives. A dramatist can no longer expect to draw many common references, be they social, sexual, or emotional. . . . He must be specific to himself and his own particular, concrete experience.

Osborne, 1967[13]

Thus, *Look Back* has been read as anti-hegemonic social realism, and subsequently as a precisely culturally manufactured example, in its 'success', of cynical (specifically, misogynistic) repressive tolerance and the adaptability of commercialism, responding to offset a fear of national decline. It also continues to exert a fascination and provoke voluble and impassioned responses in present-day teaching sessions in ways which earlier and later twentieth-century playtexts fail to do. This may be provoked by the insistently restless, confrontational energy of the play and its unusual acknowledgment of the appeal, and even eroticism, of eloquent hatred. Jimmy Porter explodes (out of) a stage tradition of terse, stoic English suffering, the first of many Osborne protagonists who are passionate, rhetorical, racked by self-doubts, often beset by marital or sexual crisis, but who are – unusually for the mid-1950s – actively and articulately exploring the impulses and consequences thereby generated. Jimmy seeks to goad the surrounding characters, and by implication, the theatre audience, into some form of response. His wife Alison acknowledges how Jimmy and his friend Hugh 'both came to regard me as a sort of hostage from those sections of society they had declared war on' (Act II), confirming the impression that Porter and, arguably, Osborne have displaced their sense of class antagonism onto a sense of heightened sexual antagonism, so that Alison represents both the promise and the inertia of the *status quo* which Jimmy suspects to be emasculating even as he finds her enticing. Sinfield observes that, in 1950s 'angry' literature as a whole, 'the destructive and unjust operations of power that its male protagonists identify and attack in society at large are reproduced and sanctioned (more or less unconsciously) by those protagonists in their personal lives and relationships'.[14]

Compared to the plays of Eliot, Greene and Fry, *Look Back* increases opportunities for either physical activity or significantly loaded contact, such as the 'horseplay' between Jimmy and Cliff which knocks Alison into the hot iron, and prompts both of them in turn to express protective affection, which she in turn plays up to. Cliff is a male, but often sexually 'neutral', friend to whom Alison can confess the mesmeric destructiveness of the relationship she remains in. Jimmy apologises yet cites the maddening power of his sexual dependence on her ('There's hardly a moment when I'm not – watching and wanting you. I've got to hit out somehow'); he ingratiates himself back with her by appealing to her sense of her own power – part sexual, part maternal – which he resents (perhaps envies) for its addictive subordination of him. Their brief truce is overshadowed by the news of an impending visit by Helena, described by Jimmy as one of Alison's 'old friends. And one of my natural enemies'. Semi-seriously, Jimmy despairs to Cliff of the pressures and manipulations involved in active heterosexuality,[15] but he is also resentful of the sexual power which the more independent and worldly Helena will bring into the household, his own susceptibility to it, and Alison's naïve obliviousness to it, or preference to ignore the danger. Jimmy attacks her avoidances with astonishing sexual viciousness, wishing that Alison would have a child, and it would die, so that she might thereby become more humanly 'recognisable'. This foreshadows later developments. Nevertheless, he goes on to associate her sexual power with an oppressive, suffocating maternity ('That bulge round her navel – if you're wondering what it is – it's me. Me, buried alive down there, and going mad, smothered in that peaceful looking coil. . . . She'll go on sleeping and devouring until there's nothing left of me'). Like Cliff, the audience can only look on and imaginatively formulate Alison's torrent of emotions as her *head goes back as if she were about to make some sound. But her mouth remains open and trembling* (end of Act I).

On Helena's arrival, the same postures are ostentatiously reiterated. Alison confides about the sentimental escape into the game of bears and squirrels, a 'cosy zoo' of 'silly animals', 'all love and no brains', for 'people who couldn't bear the pain of being human beings any longer' – significantly developed after Jimmy's friend Hugh 'went abroad'. Jimmy, as if obscurely guilty about an aspect of his own feelings he has buried or betrayed, clownishly strikes an attitude of *ennui* with the monotony of conventional sexuality ('I'm tired of being hetero / Rather ride on the metero. . . . So avoid that old python coil / And pass me the celibate oil'). Reminiscences about the start of his relationship with Alison prompt Jimmy's vehement dismissal of her family, whose controlling disapproval he incurred, even courted, in order to prove his own points about their social snobbery. His admission that 'brawling' is the 'only thing left I'm any good at' suggests his own conscious deterioration in a social climate which (like most others) presents few choices in masculine self-definition beyond repetition, conformity, and the strategic adoption of half-heartedness (what Cartwright in *Road* calls 'dying by instalments'). The momentum of Jimmy's invective drives him to include Helena in the charge of aloof escapism, but it is not until the next scene that she permits herself to be drawn in. When Jimmy dismisses the affection in Alison's farewell note to him as 'phoney' sentimentality, Helena divulges the detail that Alison is pregnant. Jimmy is unmoved and studiedly callous, driving Helena to slap him by calling her an 'evil-minded little virgin'. But even as he dissolves into pain and despair, Jimmy's seductive power is compounded, not broken: Helena finds herself suffused by her own erotic pity for him, generating an excitement (she *kisses him passionately, drawing him down beside her*) stimulated by the prospect of her own power to relieve his suffering and make him feel differently. Again, Jimmy appeals in part to women's vanity, in such a way as to consolidate his own, and thus vindicating his strategies from his own position of power.

The opening of Act III resembles the development of a Pinter play, specifically the frequent conflation of the sexual and territorial imperatives, in which one character ousts another from a room in order to occupy their position.

Helena has displaced Alison at the ironing board, and moreover '*wears an old shirt of Jimmy's*'. The mood is, however, little altered. Cliff and Jimmy persist in the opportunities for rapport provided by casually misogynistic music-hall routines and Jimmy proclaims his sense of purposelessness '*semi-seriously*'. Again he suggests that social complicity is underpinned by, and in turn reinforces, sexual complicity: 'If the big bang does come, and we all get killed off, it won't be in aid of the old-fashioned, grand design. It'll just be for the Brave New nothing-very-much-thank-you. About as pointless and inglorious as stepping in front of a bus. No, there's nothing left for it, me boy, but to let yourself be butchered by the women.' This part of the speech is probably more the heart of the play than the more frequently cited line lamenting the lack of 'good, brave causes' from which it develops. When Alison appears, having lost the child, she claims no intention of coming between Helena and Jimmy: or such are the terms of her own successful seduction. Helena is wrong-footed ('You should have been outraged, but you weren't. I feel so *ashamed*'). Perhaps Alison's meek exterior conceals a shrewd strategist who knows intuitively the power to be gained by robbing Helena's action of its transgression and brevity: after all, Helena seems to be reduced to a domesticated copy of Alison, rather than a sexually liberated woman, in the presence of Jimmy. Helena leaves, claiming to have satisfied her curiosity: 'I have discovered what is wrong with Jimmy. . . . There's no place for him any longer – in sex, or politics, or anything.' She regains her sense of independent status, turning her back on the lingering irrational temptation which Jimmy stirs in her. Alison and Jimmy are left together in their joint awareness of their *addiction* to suffering, which Jimmy equates with 'the pain of being alive' and 'love'. Jimmy's mixture of complaint, appeal and self-romanticizing assertion triggers Alison's performance of self-abjection, which in turn arouses his pity by flattering his power. This restores her to her choice of a relationship founded on the mutual dependency of regression, that ensures they remain 'a poor squirrel' and a 'poor bear' through the joint attitudes they agree to confirm.

*Look Back* was, and still is, a bold and discomforting play, in its convincing proposition that relationships can often be predicated on 'challenge and revenge', and that the recognition of this can serve to stimulate and intensify. It demonstrates dramatically how people frequently dislike the people they fall in love with, and can become sexually fascinated and subordinated by people they in many ways despise. It dramatises masculine capacities for resentful sadism, childlike impotence, self-compounding viciousness, and exultance at the momentary relief from self-loathing that is afforded by destructiveness. It also dramatises feminine capacities for the moral superiority of self-effacing martyrdom, the satisfied vanity in subordinating both another and oneself, a desperate but powerful indirectness in the resurgent appetite for ousting rivals, and the willingness to settle for an abusive familiarity. And it challenges its audiences to find these observations irrelevant or entirely alien to both genders.

Whereas *Look Back* associated Osborne with an innovative emotional directness, and capacity to articulate emotion in ways his relatively youthful audience found recognisable, his subsequent plays portray an aggressively ambivalent indifference on the parts of both speaker and audience. Language becomes a medium of expression, rather than of communication. His subsequent drama is frequently reiterative, and associates the audience with *surveillance* by representatives of traditional conformity, rather than with an emotionally liberated and expressive youth. The music-hall routines of *Look Back*, and the ritualised opportunities for interaction they afforded, are developed into the central motif of *The Entertainer* (RC, 1957), but the routines are flagging, a theatrical experience symptomatic of an age too prurient to permit, or too apathetic to express, contact. Osborne's lament for a fading theatrical form romanticises a lost ritual of communion (compare Jimmy's *Look Back* remark, 'If you've no world of your own, it's rather pleasant to regret the passing of someone else's'). Kennedy notes how the central Osborne activity is that of rhetorical self-dramatisation: 'At certain emotional climaxes, the central character . . . will dramatise, but not rationalise, his self-awareness (usually an ambivalent awareness of being both "exceptional" and exceptionally inadequate).'[16] *Inadmissible Evidence* (1964) dramatises abortive contact with an indifferent audience in a series of dream-like monologues and one-way telephone conversations which '*trail off into a feeling of doubt that there is anyone to speak to at all*'; '*the telephone is stalked, abused, taken for granted, feared*' – much like any Osborne supporting cast and audience: '*Most of all the fear of being cut off, no sound from either end.*' The protagonist's impulses towards contact are contradicted by the outburst: 'I'm tired of being watched by you, and observed and scrutinized and assessed and guessed about' (Act III). Osborne's dramatisation of resentful unease with an audience he ostensibly courts flourishes fully in the petulance and throwaway irony of 1972's *A Sense of Detachment*. The weight of scrutiny provides the keynote for *A Patriot for Me* (1965), in which Austro-Hungarian officer Redl attempts to avoid exposure as a homosexual, and is blackmailed into becoming a spy.[17] Redl's *reluctance* to be explicit makes him an unusual Osborne protagonist, but unusually engaging in his awareness of the contradiction between his reticence and his compulsion, which *admits* the audience sympathetically, rather than view them antagonistically. Redl tries to find a niche in social situations in which he is inevitably a misfit (including a drag ball), wrestles with jealousy and self-loathing, and finally accepts his society's verdict on him and commits suicide: the man initially assessed and nominated for success ends up condemned and vilified (perhaps reflecting Osborne's own fear).

*Déjàvu* (1991) reanimates the characters of Jimmy and Cliff 35 years on: the new Alison is the self-styled JP's daughter by a failed second marriage, to whom he cannot bring himself to speak when she leaves (possibly to have an abortion); the new Helena is Alison's youthful friend with whom JP manages a dalliance. However, JP seems most affected by the news of Hugh's death, even as he celebrates his own darkened, mangy solitude in a way which paradoxically demands an audience for him to bait. JP/Osborne (deliberately and selfconsciously conflated) proclaims himself 'a spokesman for no one but myself' and mocks a social (and theatrical) climate in which 'Everyone demands solutions, like happiness, as their right', resisting 'piety' and 'the noise and clamour of those who would impose their certainties upon us'. Osborne's equation of certainty with mediocrity concludes the play and his dramatic work ('Mediocrity is a great comforter. . . . And very democratic. It's all yours. Oh, *lucky* bears!'). His distinctive mixture of melancholy and spite is latterly best represented in his two volumes of autobiography (partly revelatory, partly self-dramatising, disarmingly seductive) which records contempt for a modern age in which 'Reticence is called elitism and priggishness passes for compassion. . . . Is it all to do with hatred of the past?';[18] and a 1991 ITV *South Bank Show* television profile in which he damns 'pressure from mealy-mouthed people who say "Oh don't be offensive" – Life *is* offensive, for God's sake'.

Osborne also acted in a 1956 Royal Court production of Brecht's *The Good Person of Setzuan*, the same year that the Berliner Ensemble visited London with three productions (up to this point, London audiences had been ignorant of Brecht). The German company demonstrated ensemble acting and a belief in theatre as a way of life for the players which was salutory but alien to the British professional theatre (as did a mid-1950s visit of a Russian production of *The Cherry Orchard*). Devine admired the principle of the state-funded permanent company, but not its political definiteness; similarly, Brook, Tynan, Hobson and Esslin were commentators who popularized the name of Brecht as a reference point for 'committed' theatre whilst being wary if not dismissive of his political theories and objectives. Some influence on dramatic tone and devices was apparent in Osborne's *Luther* (1961) and Robert Bolt's *A Man for All Seasons* (1960), but these works fall short of Brecht's *Verfremdungseffekt*, being ultimately historically situated empathetic dramas of individual temperament. Despite, or perhaps because of this, Osborne was enshrined as a representative of vigorous immediacy to be associated with the Court and distinguished from poetic drama, with which Whiting was tenuously grouped by Devine and thereby dismissed. But Osborne's increasing hostility towards scrutiny and expectation, and compulsive association of these with oppression, highlights the irony of this foregrounding: a 'certainty' to some extent imposed upon him.

## Arnold Wesker: melancholy optimism

Wesker wrote his first play, *The Kitchen*, in 1956, and the Royal Court production of *LBIA* inspired him to write his second, *Chicken Soup with Barley*, which opened at Coventry Belgrade Theatre, directed by John Dexter, before transferring to the Royal Court. The Court initially rejected *Roots*, but another Dexter production at Coventry overcame George Devine's misgivings, and the Court presented both plays in tandem with *I'm Talking about Jerusalem* in 1960 to form what became known as the Wesker Trilogy. The Wesker/Dexter/Court partnership subsequently scored their largest success, *Chips with Everything*, in 1962. Wesker then spent the rest of the 1960s as director of Centre 42, a project named after a Trades Union Conference resolution to promote the cultural enrichment as well as the material prosperity of working people.[19] In 1972, Wesker found himself in dispute with both the Royal Shakespeare Company (over *The Old Ones*, which Dexter instead directed once more at the Court) and with the National Theatre (over *The Journalists*). *Caritas* premiered at the National Theatre in 1981, but Wesker's other 1970s and 1980s plays have since mainly received first performances overseas, and other performances at provincial repertory theatres such as Birmingham. His late 1980s and 1990s drama mostly awaits production (he made a brief foray into community drama in 1989 with *Beorhtel's Hill*).

I condense Wesker's career thus in order to illuminate the significant professional vicissitudes of an essentially consistent yet exploratory dramatist. In contrast to articulately (Whiting) and intuitively (Osborne) dissociative writers, Wesker's characters and plays are – both formally and thematically – social and dialogic, verbally and physically expressive. However, *The Kitchen* and *Chips with Everything* both present intensified critical images of British society: hierarchical, compartmentalised and dehumanising through purposeful narrowness of focus. *The Kitchen* shows how pressured and hierarchically separated working conditions intensify resentments and lead workers to drop standards in ways which are apparently acceptable to industrialised consumerism. One cook reflects that 'when the world is filled with kitchens you get pigs' on either side of the serving hatch. *Chips* develops this theme through an image of national service – compulsory until 1959 – as a microcosm of, and preparation for, English social life, and specifically how the national hegemony absorbs potential dissenters to bolster the propagation of its own structure. The Trilogy develops *Look Back*'s theatrical discovery of feisty lower-class vernacular into sympathetic presentations of a family who are unashamed: of their working-class socialism, their Jewishness, and their compulsion to be argumentatively articulate and emotionally demonstrative (in contrast to conventional stage images of repressed, understating, control-orientated Englishness). However, Wesker's argumentative drama seeks to avoid static didacticism through dramatising contrapuntal physical activity (cooking, building, the teamwork of fuel-stealing in *Chips*) in ways which are simultaneously realistic, representational and thematic. In his manifestation of the active dialectic of 'tension between opposites',[20] Wesker is more formally ambitious and varied than Osborne. This physically contrapuntal technique reflects conceptual antithetical debate. Whilst *Chicken Soup* characteristically brings the curtain down on a negative image of 'disorder or humiliation', 'almost every scene of *I'm Talking About Jerusalem* ends with a ritual of reconciliation, which answers conflict and disappointment not with verbal argument but with physical gestures of human solidarity and understanding'.[21] And, whilst his characters frequently define themselves through explanatory language and their faith in it, Wesker is also concerned to test the limits of language (and thereby of the characters' faith in their definitions) in collision with the unruliness and complexity of experience. Wesker himself notes how 'the cut and thrust of domestic polemic' should take place 'in the midst of physical action',[22] as *Chicken Soup* follows the Kahn family's experiences. These encompass a naïve 1930s

37

optimism about the odds in favour of the struggle against racism and fascism, a 1940s Labour triumph which nevertheless breeds suspicions that the industrial apparatus has merely been transferred from one political party to another without its values being fundamentally questioned, and 1956 disillusionment at Russian repressions. *Roots* shows how Ronnie Kahn's girlfriend Beatie finds her family insists that discussion of ideas and politics 'only cause trouble' (they are later embarrassed by her emotional explicitness, 'the world don't want no feelings'). As Beatie acknowledges English acceptance of, and complicity in, third-rate commercial consumerism, she tries to discover her own rhetoric distinct from her previous quotations of Ronnie – but probably further isolates herself within the immediate social context. *Jerusalem* follows Dave and Ada's bid to 'live' rather than 'talk' socialism by withdrawing from industrialised values and society in favour of a more traditional rural craftsmanship. Ronnie initially exults at how Dave and Ada's new location permits him to shout without incurring complaint: 'No one argues with you. No one says anything. Freedom!' However, response is a particularly vital factor in Wesker's work, to permit the chance of progression through contraries. Ada's mother notes 'a cold English you-go-your-way-and-I'll-go-mine' in their distrust of, and retreat from, talking; and their bid to change social life through morally superior isolation, which achieves no real dialogue with local people, is more generally questioned. By 1959, their initiative has floundered in disillusion: Ada maintains 'We put a Labour Government in power', but Dave counters 'Hurrah! . . . They sang the Red Flag in Parliament and then started building atom bombs. . . . Raving Lunatics! And a whole generation of us laid down our arms and retreated into ourselves'. Ronnie's final shouted, defiant optimism is significantly conducted in, and implicitly interrogated by, surroundings which permit no response or argument: a momentarily impressive, but ultimately dubious freedom.

The impact of time upon idealism (and the possibilities of life itself) is also considered in *The Four Seasons* (1965), *Their Very Own and Golden City* (RC, 1966) and *The Friends* (1970), with the recurrent question as to whether the complication of idealism involves its inevitable *invalidation* or its necessary *transformation*. *Golden City* seems the most rueful, perhaps reflecting Wesker's own bruised stand down from Centre 42, and suggesting 'where previously it was personal weakness or dishonesty which had threatened ideals and the vision, now it is the vision itself which undermines and *isolates*'.[23] *The Old Ones* (1972) constitutes a characteristically irrepressible reassessment of this conclusion, in striking recapitulation and distillation of Wesker's formal strengths, whilst continuing his confrontations with the processes of mortality. In preparation for a Jewish festival, Sarah asks her daughter Rosa and nephew Martin to build a *Succah* (a symbolic tent partly roofed with branches) on the roof of her council flat. Meanwhile, Sarah's brothers Manny and Boomy engage in a long-running war of quotations proposing cosmic optimism and pessimism respectively. Significantly, Manny is more upset when his waking cries are unanswered: 'There should be an echo, a coming back or something'. Boomy's bleak pronouncements galvanise Manny into articulating faith against his own intimations of encroaching desolation ('With his philosophy of doom he keeps me alive'). The events of the play dramatise crises of purpose in the contemporary social experiences of a large group of characters, whilst the ritualised quarrel of Manny and Boomy acts as a choric counterpoint. The play ultimately brings together most of the characters in the physical activities of building the *Succah* and participating in the celebratory meal, observing the form of social comedy through a ritual designed as a reminder that the security and durability of life are delusions. Thus, the play parallels *Twelfth Night* (one character, Jack, seems an awkward Feste-figure) in highlighting both social harmony and its limits in a land where, too often, 'No one makes an answer', and there is evidence to support Teressa's observation 'People close their ears anyway so it's necessary to keep talking or you'd forget language. . . . Without language men think with their fists'. Manny claims a victory over Boomy by coining his own optimistic assertions (transcending quotation of others), but Boomy continues his deterministic litany of doom: whilst Manny exults at the centre of the festival, Boomy's wife is bandaged after a mugging, and his son's involvement in student politics has led to a schism with his father and the prospect of prison; 'Manny's breakthrough to articulateness is a merely personal victory that does not constitute an unassailable refutation of his brother's pessimism'.[24] In its active continuation of debate of purpose, *The Old Ones* is a particularly artful address to considerations which loom large in Wesker's *oeuvre*, expressed in Rosa's quotation of the proposition that 'It is not the number of years but rather the quality that determines whether life is transient or permanent'.

Wesker identifies a 'melancholy optimism' to be a recognisable (and recognisably Jewish) colour in his work,[25] and the melancholia becomes more apparent in later work, which often depicts the disastrous consequences of polarisation, (self-)isolation and marginalisation (and is thus diametrically divergent from Whiting and Osborne's increasingly extreme identifications with the unassimilable and dissociative). *The Merchant/Shylock* (1976) reorientates the story of Shakespeare's *The Merchant of Venice* so that the central bond is designed as a mockery of the stupidity of a society which insists trust cannot exist between Jew and Gentile. However, the precarious Jewish community insist on the inviolability of all bonds, and the young Venetians relish the opportunity to visit a neo-Maoist infantile violence upon Shylock by seizing the library (rather than the wealth) which he counts as his crucial possession. The rise of the independent woman Portia constitutes some hope for the future, but Shylock fades, tragically dispirited, whilst the young aristocracy and upwardly mobile mercantile citizens of Venice congratulate themselves on their 'heroic' contempt for the conservation of traditions which they do not understand (including the 'blinding questions and succulent doubts' collected in Shylock's library). *Caritas* (NT, 1981) tells the story of a fourteenth-century anchoress who seeks silence and dark out of devotion to a Christian ideal, and thereby forfeits her chances to teach the illiterate but searching youth of her home village, and to experience the confusion of physical eroticism: Wesker introduces it as another parable about the anti-humanity of 'capitalist or socialist or religious

is also a further example of the regressive, warping and ultimately
's of placing oneself beyond contact and dialogue. Here, the neo-
__ttrian deprivation and concentration of theatrical detail indicates a spiritu-
ally barren isolation which is demanded by ideological literalism, rather than
any metaphysical indifference. Wesker further characterises his work as starting, not with ideas, but 'with people I meet who are driven by ideas. I can't
imagine anything more extraordinary than [that which] I experience. It's a
fatal limitation';[26] more accurately, it reflects the importance of reciprocal
definition for Wesker and his characters.

## Theatre Workshop: Littlewood and Delaney

In the late 1950s, the Royal Court was not a platform for proletarian solidarity but 'a theatre of middle-class transition',[27] often expressed in imagery
of combat (the gladiatorial appetite for hostility expressed in Osborne and
Creighton's *Epitaph for George Dillon*, the gatling gun levelled at the audience
in Arden's *Serjeant Musgrave's Dance*) and through plays depicting characters
'dislocated from their origins, either removed by their education from the class
into which they were born (largely represented, in the theatre at least, as the
family), or in conflict with it'.[28]

In contrast to the Court, Theatre Workshop was a worker's theatre project
initiated between the wars by Joan Littlewood and Ewan MacColl, which had
moved to London in 1953, and gained some acclaim through transfers of its
radical productions of classic texts. Theatre Workshop defined themselves
in terms of actor-based, improvisationally-developed, working-class-oriented
*theatre* whilst the Court defined themselves in terms of text-based, author-
centred, middle-class-oriented *drama*. Theatre Workshop did not secure Arts
Council funding until 1957 (the Arts Council praising the company's success in
their 1956 annual report while refusing to fund them; they were subsequently
awarded £1,000 dependent on matching funding by the Local Authority).

Sixteen days after the premiere of *LBIA*, Theatre Workshop premiered
Brendan Behan's *The Quare Fellow*, gaining critical acclaim and a West End
transfer, and followed it up two years later in 1958 with Behan's *The Hostage*.
Behan's plays centralised underclass characters conventionally relegated to
the margins of social and theatrical visibility, and Littlewood animated their
broad canvasses of characters with ensemble and experimental detail. Under
Littlewood's stylistic management, Behan's plays became both realistic (representative but also consciously politically interpretative) and chaotically
disruptive of conventional stylistic unities, in an attitude of irreverence informed
by popular and musical theatre.

Theatre Workshop's next major success and transfer was provided by
Littlewood's production of Shelagh Delaney's *A Taste of Honey* (1958), a
script written by its teenage author as a deliberate riposte to the sheltered,
comfortable compartmentalizations of Rattigan's lesser drama. Littlewood's
production process involved actor improvisation around the text to inform

rewritings by the author (or others; whilst there have been doubts raised about the extent and terms of collaboration in Littlewood's methodology, Delaney, like Behan, seemed generally happy to accept her influence). The premiere production incorporated not only characters' direct address to the audience but also individual signature tunes to be played by the band as characters entered or left the stage; however, the text can also be played more realistically. Delaney's sympathetic presentation of a young, independent, unmarried, pregnant Salford teenager, her defiance of her itinerant mother, and her friendships with her black boyfriend and her homosexual flatmate, were new to popular mainstream drama of the time. Lacey notes how the allusive formal qualities of the play distinguish it from the work of Osborne and Wesker: 'There is no attempt to connect the play to a wider social world, by "argument" (characters do not debate the issues between themselves); nor does the play articulate a position on that world (there is no obvious authorial "point of view" on display) . . . rather the issues are visible in the texture of the personal relationships themselves'.[29] Interestingly, Leeming contextualises its spirit of pragmatic persistence, despite experiences of disconnection and reduction of choice, as being reflective of general public consciousness of the escalating arms race and imminent potential for widespread destruction.[30]

This mood resurfaces for different treatment in the 1963 Theatre Workshop show *Oh! What a Lovely War*, a non-naturalistic blackly satirical revue ostensibly based on the First World War, but more memorable for its presentation of contradictory images of national service, trench warfare and obedient patriotism than for its historical analysis. *Oh! What a Lovely War* harks back to the note of *ironic deference* found in elements of the English music hall: for example, the apochryphal positioning of the singer of the sentimental ballad 'My Old Dutch' (with its lyric proclaiming several decades' marital devotion to a wife) against the painted backdrop of a workhouse (which practised the segregation of inmates by gender, and the forcible sundering of married couples). *Lovely War*'s irreverence also reflects the effect of National Service in inspiring, not patriotism, but increasing youthful discontent at enforced regimentation in publicly-funded futile procedure, and protest against authoritarian social construction (evident in Wesker's *Chips* and Henry Livings's *Nil Carborundum*, 1962). The cancellation of National Service ironically coincided with an increased awareness of the possibility of multilateral 'passive' destruction through nuclear warfare. *Lovely War* juxtaposes the forced gaiety and artificial frivolity of the consciously outdated pierrot show format with archival slides of soldiers killed and wounded in trench warfare to expose satirically the discrepancy between the spirit of hearty participation invoked, and the human consequences demanded, by twentieth-century warfare. One scene involves a participant in a bayonet drill running amok towards a female member of the audience until he is restrained by the sergeant, who apologises for the indiscriminacy in expressing the aggression he has demanded; this leads into the song of a prostitute, who promises to 'make a man' of new recruits, who have been exhorted to demonstrate their masculinity by reference to propaganda posters which are slide-projected behind her. A parade of wounded soldiers is similarly counterpointed with the paternalistic promises of popular consumer medicines ('*IF YOU ARE RUN DOWN, TAKE BEECHAM'S PILLS*'). Questions of social authority, discipline and control are lightly but provocatively raised by the soldiers' question amidst the forced cheer, 'How shall we spend the money we earn?', given an average life expectancy in battle of four minutes, and an officer's threat concerning a messenger 'if he's been shot, I'll kill him'. The survivors are themselves indicted for preserving the heroic myths in which lives, faculties and resources have been 'invested': 'And when they ask us, how dangerous it was, / Oh we'll never tell them, no, we'll never tell them'; the facts of blindly obedient sacrifice to a tangle of blundering misinformation would be too humiliating: 'There was a front, but damned if we knew where.' More generally, the production satirises the apparent British appetite for social regimentation still expressed in the 1950s and early 1960s through the crowded, celebratory unison associated with popular leisure occasions and amenities (the 1951 Festival of Britain, Bank Holiday trips on overpopulated trains to similar seaside resorts to watch pier-head shows or stay in the manufactured solidarity of the holiday camp). Thus, whilst *Lovely War* is predicated on the events of World War One, its attack on invocations of 'national spirit' and the exploitative nature of social conformity and notional participation reflect a spirit of transition to a less deferential age.

## Ann Jellicoe's *The Sport of My Mad Mother*

Whilst Littlewood and Delaney's initiatives represent a step away from an exclusively male-defined drama and theatrical aesthetic, the most startlingly innovative 1950s play by a female dramatist is Ann Jellicoe's *The Sport of My Mad Mother* (1958). This premiered at the Royal Court – oddly, for a theatre associating itself with social realism, but perhaps reflecting the (increasingly) subordinate strand of that theatre's interest in experimental European theatre styles such as absurdism – until cancellation after 14 performances. Not that *Sport* can be readily subsumed into an absurdist tradition, or any other; if anything, it anticipates British assimilations of Artaudian precepts (most obviously manifested in the Peter Brook/RSC forays into aspects of Theatre of Cruelty in the early 1960s). However, stylistically it represents 'the first really experimental play at the Court'.[31] Jellicoe's Preface describes it as 'an anti-intellect play not only because it is about irrational forces and urges but because one hopes it will reach the audience directly through rhythm, noise and music and their reaction to basic stimuli'. This is manifestly different to the principally argumentative plays offered by Osborne and Wesker at the time. Indeed, Jellicoe continues: 'the play is based upon myth and uses ritual. Myth is the bodying forth in images and stories of our deepest fears and conflicts. *The Sport of My Mad Mother* is concerned with fear and rage at being rejected from the womb or tribe. It uses a very old myth in which a man, rejected by his mother, castrates himself with a stone knife'. However, Jellicoe's play does not follow or enact this myth literally, but responds to it in an improvisatory and associative *theatrically poetic* way that demonstrates knowledge of how poetry is not just baroque verbal imagery, and how theatre is not just the drama text. Tynan wrote of it as a *'tour de force* that belongs in no known category of drama. It stands in the same relationship to conventional play-making as jazz does to conventional music'.[32]

The title springs from a Hindu hymn which provides the epigraph 'All creation is the sport of my mad mother Kali', and the play indeed explores and demonstrates a chaotic creativity which is ultimately resistant to rationalising control; this, and its unclassifiability, prompted hostility from critics and audiences who resented the alternately strenuous and playful demands for instinctive and associative responses. A percussionist, Steve, eases the audience into the action with his detached, slightly comic and patronising 'layman's' approach to the theatre, which (unlike mathematical figures in accounts) isn't 'real', but which allows him to observe, relax and play along. Dean, an American dressed in a style of *'expensive relaxation'*, describes scenes of working-class London with a mixture of tourist's fascination and Kafkaesque bemusement: this establishes a sense that the ostensibly familiar may turn mysterious, nightmarish and threatening, particularly against outsiders. Three London teenagers, Fak, Cone and Patty, erupt onto the stage with sparringly energetic doggerel tales and exclamations, establishing a background of petty theft, gang warfare and awed respect for the as yet unseen Greta, tribal leader and elemental force ('Everyone's got something inside and she makes it grow and grow and come bursting out'). Dean makes *'a great effort to collect himself and dominate them'* from a rationalist viewpoint that interprets their *self-expression* as failed *communication* ('What are you trying to do?'). The teenagers knock him out: Cone coaxes Fak through guilt to *'a state of euphoria or post ecstasy, their minds and nervous systems unslung'*, suggested by the percussive backdrop which also accompanies Dean's partial stepping out of the situation. He voices possible audience disorientation ('I don't get it . . . I like to understand things and I don't understand this') but also determination to explore the terms of a 'nasty joke' which suggests a danger to be confronted. Dodo, a very young or very old inarticulate character, is startled by the theatre audience and tries to amuse them through physical clowning. Dean is made into a human totem pole for Dodo by the others, but he breaks the frantic activity by insisting on a minute's silence, *'including the audience'*, like a beleaguered teacher. Steve expresses sympathy for Dodo at the first interval: 'you let them push you around so much in the play'; like Dean, his detachment is giving way to involvement. In Act II, Dean is joining in the gang's games and trying to lead them, expressing distaste at reports of the violence towards police and rival gangs which their adventures supposedly often involve. The mischievous, shadowy matriarch Greta materialises to tease Dean and mete out her justice: *'GRETA beats CONE up in an easy, lazy, rather splendid manner. He gives himself up in a sort of ecstasy. When she has done he lies relaxed and peaceful'*; Dean is *'sickened'* by this and expresses puzzlement at Greta's suddenly apparent pregnancy. Act III opens with *'STEVE playing a terrible noise*', suggesting a gang fight during which Cone terrorises Dodo; Dean professes his paternalistic concern and protectiveness over her huddled shape, in the manner of an imperial power ('I understand, I understand your fear. . . . Every privilege of my strength I share with you') and also his determination to 'master and control' the 'mess', 'waste' and 'violence' he considers to be generated by the 'loose, vicious, destructive' Greta. Ascribing a moral mandate to Dodo's cowering, he builds himself up into a confrontation with Greta, mythologising himself into a triumph of enlightened liberal technocracy ('I watch so much television I flicker') as she mythologises herself into kinship with the animal, primeval and pagan. Cone tries to persuade Fak into a murderous coup against Greta,[33] but Patty pulls him away into a life of conventional conformity ('You're getting a job, steady'). Cone rages against the sleeping Greta, then *realizes she is pregnant. A very long pause. If possible play without words otherwise add in* CONE: You won't want me anymore'. Greta faces a final confrontation with Dean – underworld 'chaos' versus 'Mr Big Business' – in which he does his best to demonise her ('Man/woman, cruel! Unstable! Frigid!') until she overpowers him and seems to induce a sense of suicidal despair in Dean; however, it is Cone who literally commits suicide offstage, denying even that gesture to Dean, who skulks off. Greta births a baby, delivered by Fak and Patty with Steve in nominal and deliberately unconvincing role as 'father': Greta's power and *'lively interest'* in her baby are ultimately triumphant, as she exults: 'Rails, rules, laws, guides, promises, terms, guarantees, conventions, traditions: into the pot with the whole bloody lot. Birth! Birth! That's the thing!'. However, this should not be taken as a simplistically romantic affirmation of the maternal and matriarchal, given Greta's earlier boast that she bathes 'In babies' blood', as an ingredient in her splendid irresponsibility.

Thus, *Sport* shares with *A Taste of Honey* an insistence on a specifically female right to ungovernable self-determination, but does not play this out in realistic or domestic terms. Rather it pits them against the significantly American representative of crucially incorporated technocracy and imperialism masquerading as 'enlightened rational liberalism', and locates the duel in an urban-primeval London of strange dark childishness. It nevertheless does not regard teenage rebellion with moral panic (rather, Fak and Patty's frightened recoil into conformity seems an index to their imaginative limitations). Formally, *Sport* anticipates Heathcote Williams's *AC/DC* (1970) in its depiction of Anglo-American contemptuous fascination, rivalry for the favours of a mysterious central figure whose appearance is delayed, the characters' tactics in generating an irreducible argot, or 'psychic static', which demands they be taken on their own (technological–cosmological) terms; and the self-mythologizing 'rap' duel through verbal incantation. Moreover, it appears as theatrically innovative, verbally exciting and purposefully challenging for the twenty-first century as it did in 1958.

Jellicoe's *The Rising Generation* (1969) was commissioned by the Girl Guides Association for possible performance in Wembley Empire Pool stadium with a cast of 800 girls and 100 boys. It was rejected and subsequently produced at the Court with a full cast of merely 150. *The Rising Generation* provides an antithesis to *The Sport* in depicting a mother-spirit turned malign and sexually (feministically) Manichean and supremacist, triggering a nuclear explosion from which the survivors attempt to escape to start anew in outer space. Since the mid-1970s, Jellicoe has concentrated on community drama, with her theories and experiences being documented in her book *Community Plays: How to Put Them On* (1987). This movement into 'large-scale productions in non-theatre settings which dissolve the usual boundaries between audience and performers' indeed seems 'a logical continuation of her interests',[34] but should not be regarded as a summary of her importance.

# Notes

1. Lacey, *British Realist Theatre* (1995), p. 42.
2. Banham, *John Osborne* (Edinburgh, 1969), p. 10. Banham later refers to Porter as 'a misfit whose experiences could be widely shared', p. 16.
3. Morgan, op. cit., p. 189. See also Hoggart, *The Uses of Literacy* (1957), on the 'shining barbarism' of the 1950s.
4. Lacey, ibid., p. 14.
5. Foreword to Browne's *Playwrights' Theatre* (1975), p. iv.
6. Rebellato, op. cit., p. 66.
7. Fourth draft of the Court policy, quoted by Roberts, *The Royal Court Theatre and the Modern Stage* (Cambridge, 1999), p. 9.
8. Quoted in Browne, op. cit., p. 12.
9. Rebellato, pp. 10–36; Lacey, pp. 32–9.
10. See Barber and Worsley, quoted by Lacey, op. cit., pp. 18–19.
11. Tynan, *A View of the English Stage* (1975, 1984), p. 178.
12. M. Hallifax, quoted in Doty and Harbin, *Inside the Royal Court, 1956–81* (Baton Rouge, 1990), p. 38.
13. Quoted by Banham, op. cit., p. 90.
14. Sinfield (ed.), *Society and Literature 1945–1970* (1983), p. 70.
15. Posthumous suggestions that Osborne may have been bisexual indicate perhaps that the dramatist was not only resentfully incarcerated within the form of the well-made naturalistic play, but also restless within a sexual closet which in 1956 still recently carried the fear of criminalisation.
16. Kennedy, *Six Dramatists in Search of a Language* (Cambridge, 1975), p. 205.
17. Sinfield (1999) notes how 'the declining years of the Macmillan–Home Conservative governments had been marked by sex-and-spy scandals, at least one of which (the John Vassall case) involved the blackmailing of a homosexual', p. 262.
18. Osborne, *Almost a Gentleman* (1992), p. 43.
19. Wilcher notes how *Chips, Golden City* and *The Friends*, can be read respectively as 'a prologue, an allegorical counterpart, and an epilogue to that endeavour'; *Understanding Arnold Wesker* (South Carolina, 1991), p. 55.
20. Ibid., p. 17.
21. Ibid., pp. 40–1.

22. Wesker, Author's Note to *The Wesker Trilogy* (1979).

23. Hinchcliffe, *British Theatre 1950–70* (1974), p. 104.

24. Wilcher, op. cit., p. 103.

25. Wesker, *Contemporary Writers: Arnold Wesker* (1988 Book Trust/British Council pamphlet).

26. Wesker, letter to the author, 10/12/89.

27. Hirst, *Edward Bond* (1985), p. 26.

28. Lacey, op. cit., p. 79.

29. Lacey, op. cit., pp. 94–5.

30. Leeming, Introduction to Methuen Student edition of the play (1982), p. xxvii.

31. Roberts, op. cit., p. 63.

32. Tynan, review quoted on the inner leaf of Ann Jellicoe's *The Sport of My Mad Mother* (1964, 1968).

33. The play contains a number of theatrical motifs which repeatedly remind me of an updated, feminised version of *The Tempest*: this abortive, semi-comic uprising against the mage, but also the huddling beneath rags and newspapers for shelter, the percussive suggestions of how 'the isle is full of noises' and storms, and the poetic-fantastic reflections on power: territorial, imperial, magical, generative.

34. Graham-White, 'Ann Jellicoe' in *International Dictionary of Theatre – 2: Playwrights*, ed. M. Hawkins-Dady (1994), pp. 521–3 (523).

# Chapter 3

# Beckett and Pinter: Terminal Contractions of (In)Consequence

Religious essentialism and social determinism were challenged increasingly in the late 1950s by the philosophy of existentialism: this locates a transcendent, significant potential in the self, which defines itself most conspicuously through choices under extreme circumstances. Traditional chains of consequence are questioned; meaning and significance are, liberatingly and/or dauntingly, matters of active human fabrication. The first (but, importantly, not last or only) influential theatrical manifestations of existentialism occur in the (reductively) so-called Absurdist work of Ionesco, Beckett and Pinter, in which certainty in the supposed social and dramatic 'givens' of circumstance, personality and language are undermined. Sinfield identifies this drama as being particularly responsive to the problematisation of absolutes represented by the Cold War: 'These plays challenged establishment complacency by declaring to a world under threat of extinction that life is more complicated and dangerous than is dreamt of in the philosophy of boulevard theatre'.[1] However, he claims that the work of Beckett 'does not . . . celebrate the liberation of language from a referenced reality but rather despairs at the lack of such a consequential solidity'.[2] He suggests that such drama posits practical action to be futile, and that the overall drift of the plays is towards passive complicity with existing society. These deductions become more evidently questionable when placed against Beckett's and Pinter's late-century work.

## Samuel Beckett: burning to be gone

> First I was the prisoner of others. So I left them. Then I was the prisoner of myself. Which was worse. So I left myself.
>
> (Beckett, *Eleuthéria*[3])

Beckett's early work might be more critically socially realistic than is usually considered, if one locates the landscape of his writing within a rural Irish rather than urban English context. DeValera's theocratic Ireland insisted on a sense of its own apostolic mission through a demanding and vengeful Jansenist Catholicism which gripped a writhingly bewildered and traumatised post-famine dereliction; however, Beckett's imagery of impotence, sterility and involution (such as an overgrown 'Boy' in his 40s, led about in a halter, self-conscious autocrats presiding over wastelands, accidental or enigmatic infanticide) repeatedly suggests a moribundity in what presented itself as the surrounding civilization and culture. Though Beckett's work intrinsically resists any single, authoritative or literal interpretation, it is within a landscape recognisable as an expressionistic vision of these conditions that Beckett depicts the Artaudian process of the destruction of defence mechanisms of egos conditioned to repression, of 'precipitating a crisis of social dissolution so that the warring forces of the psyche can surface'.[4] Often, conventional perceptual strategies are involved in confrontations which provoke or accelerate processes of radical separation, be they externally entropic, internally frenzied or both. From one perspective, Beckett has been associated with a development of the Chekhovian form which has dominated English dramatic realism from the Thirties to the present; specifically, its elegiac and *nostalgic* 'demonstration of how commonplace detail can be used to bring out the complexity and pathos of ordinary lives' and 'the almost unbearable sadness of time's effects upon them'.[5] However, this essentially *consistent* worldview distorts Beckett's persistently *(self-)contradictory* vision, which is more deeply Irish in its compulsive problematisation of binary oppositions, sense of infinite reversibility and tendency to glimpse life as a mysterious farce, with an eye 'at once wistful and wiry'.[6] Hinchcliffe proposes 'Beckett portrays not nihilism but the inability to be nihilist which frustrates man'[7] (and English critics in particular). Rather, his radical distillations of theatrical imagery activate an oscillation between the equally terrifying and ludicrous possibilities of determinism and nihilism, between the frenetic certainty of comedy and the isolating finitude of tragedy, silence as void and silence as plenitude, so that definition and separation are continually calling themselves into question.

Kalb observes:

> Beckett's theatre does not represent scenes from another time – or rather it does not only do so. It creates scenes whose subject matter is their duration in present time. His dramas are not *about* experiences; *they are those experiences themselves.* This heightened authenticity in Beckett . . . is similar in many ways to the ethic of 'immediacy' that pervades much contemporary performance art and avant-garde theatre.[8]

Krapp's self-description as 'Drowned in dreams and burning to be gone' reflects the state of many Beckett characters: subjected to projections of (external?) expectations and (internal?) memories, they re-view their social and personal restrictions with imaginative hyperactivity, in longing for ultimately elusive closure. Whilst Beckett's themes are thus focused on the compulsive self-dramatisations of the human consciousness, and its displacements of pain through compensatory but fictional shadowplays, his theatre is paradoxically 'intensely physical', sculptures of space, light and sound minutely designed to draw the audience into a 'disturbing and releasing experience of inwardness and heightened perception'.[9]

In *Waiting for Godot* (1953), two tramps, Estragon and Vladimir, find their expectations of a meeting confounded, and their sense of certainty in their environment disconcertingly undermined. The circular structure of the play permits minor variations on their situation in Act II, whilst Estragon and

Vladimir attempt to fill the silence and either to energise or leave their minimal set (a bare tree, which nevertheless leafs in the second act). A second pair offer some diversion: Pozzo intends to sell his roped slave Lucky, a prodigiously relentless articulator of thought, at a fair. However, when they return in the second act, Pozzo has gone 'blind as Fortune' and is led and steered by Lucky (now dumb): their positions are reversed, in a striking image of the reversibility of power which nevertheless also suggests residual interdependence. Memory, identity, consequence and change are all drained of reliability.

The experience of indefiniteness, both depicted and offered, provokes a troubled and uncertain laughter because the play refutes any consistent allegorical interpretation. Kalb notes the implicating reflexivity of the theatre experience: 'One's thoughts quickly finish with local questions – Who is Godot and why doesn't he arrive? Why do Didi and Gogo stay together and keep returning? – moving presently, almost automatically, on to more comprehensive ones: for whom is any performance given and with what expectations? Why am I in the theatre, and what am I waiting for?'.[10] Iser claims that both the play and the laughter it provokes ('not contagious or communal'[11]) are appropriate expressions of the human condition, which reveals itself only through the demonstrative insufficiency of any interpretative frameworks that it provokes and generates, and which 'are moulded, not by reality, but by man's need to explain reality'.[12] Perhaps the most artful description is provided by States, who defines *Godot* in terms applicable to other Beckett plays, as 'not a created object but a creative one . . . a concatenation of possibilities, limited by nothing but the mind's capacity to endow shape with meaning', so that 'there is a freedom of inference, passed over to the reader [or audience member]' who 'must "finish" the text on his own'; 'the play derives a mythic tension from the constant "oscillation" . . . a coming in and out of focus of what are often contradictory loadings of the same shape'.[13]

Like *Godot*, *Endgame* (RC, 1957) has a basic narrative striving for closure. *Endgame* depicts the tensions between hesitation and severance, retention and relinquishment of control by the self-consciously histrionic monarch of a wasteland ambivalently approaching a ritual of renunciation. The action, speeches and apocalyptic wasteland setting generate many suggestive allusions outwards (particularly to religious imagery and in this case also to chess and to classical and Shakespearian tragedy) which point towards, yet refuse to cohere into, allegory. Worton suggests 'These various references fragment the surface message of the text by sending the reader [and audience] off on a series of speculations', operating for the audience as 'an opening-up of the text' which 'counterbalances the progressive closure of entropy experienced by the characters'.[14] Pauses operate similarly, inviting the spectator 'to explore the blank spaces between the words and thus to intervene creatively – and individually – in the establishment of the play's meaning'.[15] *Happy Days* (1961) is another ironic view on the individual drive to define and control, as the protagonist Winnie is embedded in, and progressively swallowed by, the earth. Like many Beckett characters, she busies herself 'making up tales that seem somehow connected to . . . survival while also functioning as pastimes'.[16]

*Krapp's Last Tape* (1958) initiates a series of plays which examine the landscape of memory, depicting an individual's bid to impose selective meaning on his life, in this case through Krapp's annual ritual of reviewing and augmenting his collection of his own tape-recorded reflections. His determination to shape a life defined in terms of isolated pursuit of vision and literary achievement is mocked by his final preference for an account of the physical intimacy he felt it necessary to reject. His ironic jeer at his twilight self, 'Once wasn't enough for you', is itself ironically undercut by his decision to terminate his current bitter reverie for a repeated play of an imperfectly idyllic occasion of contact, irrevocably lost to everything but memory of touch and sight. Krapp's realisation demonstrates that time does not necessarily heal or dignify, and that reopening wounds can be preferable to the sour restrictions of diminishing returns.

Beckett's staging of the reflexes of identity as a robotically spasmodic spectacle extends into the purgatorial interrogation of *Play* (1963), in which a questioning force (represented by a beam of theatre light) compels repetition in the unresolved search for meaning, identity, closure, and cessation. This extends to the even more remorseless *Not I* (1972): again the audience is subjected to an experience of extreme concentration upon a consciousness suffering from extreme concentration. An old woman, speechless until the age of seventy, abruptly finds herself possessed and overwhelmed by her own garrulous Mouth, simultaneously overturning a lifetime of self-repression and refusing to speak in first person and admit the years of loss. Her consciousness has become both uncontrollable and self-divisive in its refusal to acknowledge its own suffering, even as her ability to express attempts some form of expiation through incessant narrative speech. With bleak irony, 'Her attempted private evasion of self turns into a cruel public self-exhibition'.[17] Meanwhile, in performance, analogously obsessive concentration on the stationary Mouth is likely to make the theatre audience question the obedience of their own perceptual senses, as the orifice may appear to move, enlarge, or transform.

*That Time* (1976) pursues more fractal, dialogic manifestations of consciousness and memory, as three voices replay past occasions for a prone (perhaps ill or dying) Listener. The situation recalls Krapp, with tapes bypassed, but ends with a smile of pleasure and acceptance rather than undercut renunciation and irrevocable loss. This may suggest an appreciation of the paradoxical faculty of imaginative recall, even of non-idyllic immediacies, of how 'Every object, every space, every memory exists in time: you are different but you are the same'.[18] Even after Listener accuses himself of Mouth-like evasion ('did you ever say I to yourself in your life'), his final expression may suggest a self-acceptance, in the conscious persistence of narrative arrangement, and sense that it is never too late for admission. *That Time* may thus constitute Beckett's most (guarded yet deliberately surprising) optimistic vision. If *That Time* reverses the conclusion of *Krapp*, *Footfalls* (1976) can be read as an interrogation of the ironic perspective on self-deception in *Happy Days*. Whereas Winnie was presented as grotesque and ludicrous in her persistently Panglossian delusions, May's self-displacing fictionalising is presented more sympathetically and compassionately, as she bids to transcend the terminal contraction of caring for her bedridden mother well into her own old age. The measured pace of her restless but restricted pacing is recalled in *Rockaby* (1981), in which a woman seeks, not to escape an oppressive but loyal and dutiful connection to her mother, but to enfold her own life and death into those of her mother, through a transformative analogy, physically represented by the activity of rocking in a chair. As in *That Time*, the acceptance of death holds surprising reconciliations in its will to confront the supposedly unmanageable; the artifice of imaginative structure renders the apparently impossible thinkable and doable (as in theatre).

*Catastrophe* (1982) is dedicated to Vaclav Havel, imprisoned for subversion at its time of writing and performance, and ironically presents the processes of theatrical rehearsal as an analogue for political repression and its play of power. The Protagonist of the play is in fact fixed in a tableau of subjugation by a Director and his Assistant, to be presented as a startling image of power's inscription upon the human body for the consumption of an audience seeking sensationalism. Brater suggests that the Director is aiming for 'a catastrophe of the old comedy', 'Edmund's description of his brother Edgar in *King Lear*', but another meaning of the term – a sudden reversal – prevails so that 'The image of depersonalization has been made personal in an ironic reversal of previous events'.[19] The stage directions specify: 'Distant storm of applause. Praises his head, fixes the audience. The applause falters, dies. Long pause. Fade-out of light on face'; an effect reverberatively described by McMullan: 'the actor . . . stills the audience's applause, overpowering their gaze by his own powerless one. In the end therefore, he asserts his subjectivity and his very powerlessness is seen as the source of his power – an authority of a different order from that of the Director'.[20] The image in performance acquires an unforeseen self-contradictory power (which might perhaps constitute its breakthrough to Art), reversing the certainty of the Director and his presumption of imaginative closure through the presentation of power, and demonstrating the instability of order.

In considering Beckett's theatricality, it is important not to lose sight of his affection and respect for traditions and routines of clowning, as manifested in cinema (Keaton, Chaplin, Laurel and Hardy) and the music hall and variety show. The sensibility and experience of the comedian Max Wall gave him a notable skill as a Beckett performer (in *Waiting for Godot* and *Krapp's Last Tape*) with regard to thoughtful and instinctive timing, linguistic relish, and stoically intent explorations of detail and attempts at dignity. His performances consequently achieved a sense of the simultaneously sad and comical which resisted self-pitying generalisation in ways that many so-called classical actors do not, in playing Beckett.[21] The precise performance of severely challenged but indomitable persistence in the face of repeatedly disappointing and undercutting experience is crucial to and in the Beckett ethos, best summarized by the maxim in *Worstward Ho*, 'failed again no matter try again fail better'. Consequence may be uncertain or minute, but no central action in Beckett's drama – even that of cessation – is despairing.

# Harold Pinter: the enemy within

Language is actually used to keep thought at bay.

(Pinter[22])

Whilst Beckett elaborates minutely on the cost and obligation of dogged persistence, Pinter is a poet of anxiety for whom the apparent dissolution of certainties represents opportunities for the emergence of a vague but terrible force of consequence, inimical to the individual perspective. In 1948, at the age of eighteen, Pinter registered as a conscientious objector as a protest against the escalations of the Cold War. He has stated that he would have fought in the Second World War to oppose fascism, but saw America's dropping of the atom bomb on Japan as being a warning and provocation to Russia, effectively preparing for the 'Cold' war before the 'hot' one had finished. He subsequently worked as a professional actor, touring Ireland and playing in several English repertory companies. Thompson has identified the similarities in premise between some Pinter plays and popular 1950s repertory middlebrow dramas (the investigative interrogations of the detective thriller, the politely concealed rivalries and strategies of cocktail comedies and eternal triangles).[23] This use of theatrically familiar situations and apparently inconsequential colloquial speech contributes towards an initial recognisability, and recognisable Englishness, for the theatre audience, especially when compared to Beckett's abstracted theatrical extremities. However, both inconsequentiality and recognisability are *initial* impressions, only, as Pinter's situations and characters resist rationalisation. Kennedy notes 'Not only is the dialogue "idiomatic", it is saturated with idioms "played" to show up their idiocy'.[24] Hence, verbal gestures of ostensible accessibility become, in dramatic usage, ironic indications and reiterations of the persistent separateness of individual perspectives and interests. The resulting atmosphere, here succinctly characterized by Cahn in terms of a 'condition of incertitude regarding society and self', is thus particularly resonant – often initially comic, then troublingly immediate – for an English middle class audience in particular:

> Pinter's characters live in perpetual suspicion, regarding both familiar figures and strangers with trepidation. His characters are also protective of what they see as their own, objects and territory over which they can assert sovereignty. . . . Such holdings are the most defined entities in Pinter's dramatic universe and a source of stability for men and women baffled by so much else. As a result of this state of mind, his characters are forever on guard against invasion, both physical and psychological. They are always nervous that whatever few rights and possessions they claim may be snatched away, leaving them even more alienated.[25]

It is precisely this location of regressiveness, manifested at national and class level, within the individual psyche, which established Pinter's immediacy and pre-eminence as an English dramatist. The parallel with Chekhov is more pertinent to Pinter than Beckett. The Irish dramatist is, significantly, anti-systematic and anti-deterministic, however bleak the surrounding contractions of possibility. In his earliest (and also in his most recent) work, Pinter presents essentially consistent demonstrations of a deterministic process; his characters' 'linguistic battles are not the product of an arbitrary desire for dominance but crucial battles for control of the means by which personality is created in the social systems to which they belong',[26] and the frequent result is the disintegration under pressure of an already flawed masculinity. If Pinter's sense of gamesmanship recalls that of Coward – characterised by Worth in terms of 'pauses, sudden silences, snatches of half-heard dialogue and crossed conversational lines to suggest that the characters aren't even trying to talk meaningfully to each other but are involved in some esoteric ritual where each has his appointed role to fulfil'[27] – Pinter's deterministic investigations and exposures of individual inadequacy may also recall Priestley, Eliot and Greene. His emphasis is not on existential *defiance* (demonstrating the human capacity to redefine and renew one's self on one's own terms) but on existential *nausea* (demonstrating the often fatal vulnerability of the individual's own terms under pressure of repression from without and regression from within).

*The Birthday Party* (1958) throws into relief how its characters' speech – and by implication many social bids for linguistic communion – seek not *dialogue* but *confirmation*. Unlike Petey, Stanley does not semi-automatically confirm Meg's impressions and insistences regarding cornflakes and the world. She regards him as a naughty boy who is nevertheless endearingly subject to part-maternal part-sexual reconciliation and control: she reminds him of her 'lovely afternoons' in his room, and his flirtatious teasing turns into a recoil of disgust (perhaps not least at his own complicity). His bid to scare her, with the simultaneously ludicrous and Kafkaesque fantasy of pursuers, slides out of his control with the sound of a knock at the door; the new arrivals, Goldberg and McCann, do not bring a 'wheelbarrow' as Stanley wilfully imagines, but they resist rational comprehension even as they suggest references to rationalizations so various as to be mutually exclusive: McCann alleges Stanley's disloyalty to one sort of conformist idealism (a vague paramilitarism vengefully focused on betrayal of land and 'movement'), Goldberg invokes sentimental Jewish stereotypes of the family and success and fulfilment through hard work. Even then, the fragility of their performed masculinity is apparent: McCann will be discomforted by the extent of Stanley's disintegration under their interrogation; Goldberg's romanticization of early rising only just keeps at bay his Websterian sense of the body as 'a corpse waiting to be washed', and his own proud sense of certainty and purpose finally falters (into his inability to complete the utterance 'BECAUSE I BELIEVE THAT THE WORLD . . .'). The strange incompleteness of these would-be Eumenides makes them more, rather than less, unsettling (as when Goldberg is finally shown to be dependent on McCann blowing in his mouth). There are further instances of nightmarish disorientations in Pinter's memorable curtain scenes: a toy drum is turned from an instrument of infantilising control (Meg's intention) into one of savage possession (Stanley's response); and the central birthday party becomes a torchlit ritual of isolation and violence, regression and rape, when Stanley attacks the sexually provocative Lulu as if in anger at the ambivalent challenges to individuation which are thrown at him by Meg and the mysterious duo who ominously enclose him. Goldberg and McCann claim to provide 'the answer' to Stanley's adolescent withdrawal. Their platitudinous promises of integration ('We'll make a man of you/And a woman/You'll be re-orientated/You'll be rich/You'll be adjusted/You'll be our pride and joy/You'll be a mensch/You'll be a success') seem bids to reassure themselves more than Stanley, particularly when faced with his appalling breakdown into incoherence. Petey's ineffectual challenge to the process subsides into reconfirmation of Meg's blithe self-assurances.

*A Slight Ache* (1959) and *The Room* (1960) also depict masculinity thrown into fatal consternation by the incursion of a rival into the home space. Violent male repressions of female fantasies of renewal presage the disintegration of male and female respectively. These plays demonstrate how the separateness of gender terms can render male and female interests, in terms of power and security, inimical. The women are not traditionally submissive, but as hungry for control as the essentially fearful male characters. The male mixture of impotence, frustration and violence before female sexual and maternal challenge at this stage of Pinter's drama is pithily crystallized in *A Night Out* (1960), which might be Stanley's fantasy of self-assertion in the face of the Megs and Lulus who represent both provocation and control.

Other plays of the period show Pinter's interest in the desperate shifting of alliances under the pressure of social control and/or exclusion. *The Dumb Waiter* (1960) depicts the fatal breakdown in the relationship between two professional killers, whose instincts for obedience are manipulated by an unseen force sending increasingly outlandish requests down to their hiding place, the basement of an apparently disused restaurant. Rather than resist or question, their limited intelligences drive them to attempt to placate the demands by offering their food; their bids to ingratiate demonstrate their own dependence and plasticity in the presence of higher status. One protests that they have nothing left: ultimately, his more subservient partner is directed to kill him. The semi-comic working relationship, or 'double act', becomes increasingly strained as the duo find it more difficult to confirm each other's terms, or the terms of their surroundings, ending in an extreme demonstration of their ultimate instrumentality. *The Hothouse* (written 1958, staged 1980) shows the workings of an institution housing inmates who are not criminals but who need to have instilled a renewed 'confidence in . . . the world'; the Ministry in charge of the institution shows itself prepared to sacrifice both staff members and inmates in order to vindicate its practices. *The Caretaker* (1960) depicts a tramp's bids to ingratiate himself with two brothers alternately, only for them to unite against him; thus, in a contracted but strategic landscape in which the terrain of advantage is constantly shifting, he is involved in a collision with 'the limits of his verbal resources'.[28] However, Pinter maintained at this time 'I'm not committed as a writer, in the usual sense of the term, either religiously or politically. And I'm not conscious of any particular social function'.[29]

This first phase of Pinter's dramas of displacement gives way to a second phase, more oblique and less systematic, often pivoting on antithetical propositions of memory and definition. This is not the same as the *self-contradictory* oscillating poise between nihilism and existential dignity that I have noted in Beckett's drama. Pinter's plays are usually more linear, even fatalistic, in their depiction of a single, apparently inexorable process. Their structural entity is essentially consistent, though it may contain or even be comprised of antithetical propositions. *The Homecoming* (1965) is perhaps Pinter's finest technical example of this. Kennedy notes how the central event, a black family ritual for the ambivalent initiation of a new female member, is principally invoked by ritualised language 'arranged in broadly juxtaposed patterns of ceremony and its violation', best exemplified by the patriarch Max and his 'schizoid-seeming shifts from the language of celebration to verbal defecation (and the other way around)'.[30] The conspicuous glimpses and bursts of neoromantic aggression between baroque lattices of decorum is recognizable as a development of Goldberg's idiom (it also recalls the work of Jacobean dramatist John Webster, for whom Pinter has acknowledged an enthusiasm[31]). As in earlier Pinter work, the location of a family home 'calls attention to the dual nature of a family home as both physical and psychological common ground' and 'physical and psychological battleground',[32] and the battle centres on Teddy's introduction of his new wife Ruth to his savage London under-world family. As the wife of an American-based academic, one might expect Ruth to be nonplussed by the family's extreme yet co-existent tendencies to sentimentalise and to debase physicality, but instead she finds it a surprisingly conducive environment (she divulges the possibility – or fantasy? – of her previous professional life as a nude model) which she decides to preside over as a matriarch combining totemic aspects of mother and whore, discarding her more traditional husband and children. Lenny, the most cocksure and independent son (and professional pimp), parodies social and dramatic decorum by offering Ruth a drink of water as if it were alcohol ('I bet you could do with this'), then outlines his violent treatment of upper-class women whom he decides to be 'diseased'; however, Ruth denies that she has taken 'quite enough' water to drink and moreover insists on her ability to 'take' Lenny in a ritual of erotic subordination. The father Max initially vilifies Ruth as a 'stinking pox-ridden slut', then accepts her on learning that she is a mother; accordingly, he can describe his own late wife Jessie as 'the backbone to this family' with a 'will of iron, a heart of gold' then condemn her as a 'slutbitch'. As a former butcher (and perhaps petty gangster), Max is a trader in flesh like Lenny, and even more extreme in his alternating veneration and vilification of its properties. However, Ruth proves mesmeric in her sense of how physicality can command and captivate:

> Don't be too sure. You've forgotten something. Look at me. I . . . move my leg. That's all it is. But I wear . . . underwear . . . which moves with me . . . it . . . captures your attention. Perhaps you misinterpret. The action is simple. It's a leg . . . moving. My lips move. Why don't you restrict . . . your observations to that? Perhaps the fact that they move is more significant . . . than the words which come through them. You must bear that . . . possibility . . . in mind.
>
> (Act II)

Ruth permits a powerfully limited sexual acquiescence to the youngest son, whilst Teddy looks on, maintaining his own 'intellectual equilibrium' which permits him to write academic criticism, regard his family as 'objects' and not 'get lost' in physicality himself. She agrees to and pragmatically negotiates terms to bring in income as a prostitute, and displaces Max from the centre of the family, to his mingled resentment and admiration. Quigley notes that the 'certain kind of freedom' Ruth has won is also 'a certain kind of captivity', with 'a final irony in the repeated suggestion of cycles in this play, for if the London family is confronted once more by the power of a Jessie-figure, so, too, is that Jessie-figure confronted once more by the power of the London family'.[33] However, the play suggests that all freedoms might be alternately viewed as captivities, and vice versa, and charges the tension with particular erotic dynamism, suggesting that the avoidance of such tensions constitutes a comparatively arid abstraction.

Quigley rightly notes how 'in Pinter's work, development on one level leads only to awareness of circularity on another'; the basic movement of many of his plays 'is one of expansion and contraction of vision set against a temporal process which reminds the audience repeatedly that while, from one point of view, everything changes, from another, everything remains the same'.[34] This objectification of manners against a sense of human entropy is what links his work to that of Chekhov, and even to that of Eliot; and similarly his work can thus embody a bleakly ironic consistency which is almost reassuring, in flattering an audience's sense of inevitable contraction. *The Homecoming* is unusual in being too fiercely visceral and sexually volatile to support senses of consistency, inevitability or contraction such as Teddy represents: his expulsion represents not an acceleration of entropy, but an intensified delimitation, paving the way for active excavations of physical, and psychic depths conventionally designated as taboo, and testifying to their strange compulsions. Thus, whilst *The Homecoming* is an identifiable development of Pinter's own style, it is also his own least anxious and most Artaudian play.

*Landscape* (1968) counterpoints the antithetical monologues of Beth and Duff in order to throw into question Duff's assertion, 'We're together. That's what matters'. Rather this couple, like the matter and manner of their speech, seem *adjacent*, but separate, essentially divergent in their selective definitions of any experience they may have shared: he is brusque, carnal, bewildered; she elaborates and poeticises in (attempted?) romantic serenity. The arrangement has the arrested grace of perfected stasis and convivial involution. *Old Times* (1971) depicts Kate's visit to her old friend Anna and her husband, Deeley. Both Kate and Deeley seek to make their rival claims of primacy in Anna's life and affections through invocation of memories which both contrast and conflict, as when they both maintain they took Anna to see the same film. Deeley's initial interest in Kate's effect on Anna ('I'll be watching you. . . . To see if she's the same person') turns to defensive attempts at control through initiating the shared completion of popular song lyrics (specifically, of inventory ballads such as 'These Foolish Things' and 'They Can't Take That Away From Me'), and seeking similar confirmation of memories, which may be fantasies.

Kate's reverie of Anna dead and besmirched seems to locate the battleground of the play in dreams or fantasies which may nevertheless be more exposing, liberating, significant or catalytic than literal, supposedly realistic detail – with the suggestion that Kate *can* Take That (the significance of detail) Away from Deeley. Kate's narrative of discovered independence represents a triumph over Anna and Deeley; thus *Old Times* inverts *The Caretaker*, to show the incomer victorious over the couple, and male anxiety fatally and inexorably backfires, as in *The Room* and *A Slight Ache*. There are further echoes of *The Caretaker* in *No Man's Land* (1975): two old men meet on the renowned gay cruising site of Hampstead Heath. Spooner, an itinerant 'man of letters', professes relief that Hirst, a once successful author, is not sexually interested in him, but is voyeuristically intrigued by his situation and reminiscences. Hirst's two servants – who frequently resemble dominators – thwart Spooner's attempted ingratiation, so that he remains homeless, in contrast to Hirst who is effectively the prisoner in his home. Both nevertheless occupy a 'no man's land', separated from conventional supposed consolations of age. *Betrayal* (1978) is an apparently casual, wry comedy of manners which plays scenes from an adultery in reverse chronological order. The premise is not innovative – Priestley's *Time and the Conways* (1937) uses temporal disjunction to demonstrate the poignancies and ironies of disappointed hopes – but the play is elegant, cruel and unusually accessible in its identifications of the vulnerabilities exposed by passion: the bids for confirmation of memory; the bitter significances of discrepant awareness when one partner knows of the other's infidelity; the brief elevation of the commonplace (such as a park in mist) into a shared myth; and the reckless excitement and mutual challenge of adoration (the word 'adore' effectively carries an explosive force amidst the resolutely controlled language of the participants) as opposed to the consistent securities and congruent familiarities associated with love. This vein and style of Pinter's writing is further mined by Patrick Marber's *Closer* (1997).

The third distinct phase of Pinter's writing is heralded by *One for the Road* (1984: the title is an echo of Goldberg's line, when he momentarily falters after the breaking of Stanley, and requests McCann's supportive inspiration). This play initiates a series of dramatic presentations of the repressive processes of authoritarian political regimes. This transition by Pinter to a self-consciously and self-proclaimed explicitly political dramatist seems partly prompted by his mid-eighties investigation of Turkish restrictions of Kurdish human rights for the international writers' pressure group, PEN. However, Pinter took care to emphasise that the events in *One for the Road*, *Mountain Language* (1988) and *Party Time* (1991) were not solely about the plight of Kurds, but also about other repressed and dispossessed races – Irish, Welsh, Basque, Estonian, Urdu – and that the plays reflected what was happening in 1980s Britain under the Conservative Thatcher government: specifically, insidious but purposeful anti-democratic increases in state power and allied assertions of police power to pressurise any dissenting voice. Indeed, though the settings of the plays are non-specific, most of the names and colloquialisms featured are unapologetically British. In a BBCTV *Omnibus* documentary transmitted to coincide with the premiere of *Mountain Language,* Pinter identified symptoms of authoritarianism in 1980s Britain: restrictions on, and implicit threats to, freedom of speech in the media and in university teaching and funding; increased police powers to oppose the early 80s miners' strike; and Clause 28, forbidding the 'promotion of homosexuality' in education and art: all of which designated any alternative or questioning voice as alien, and therefore to be legally and systematically rejected and repressed. Pinter also took the opportunity to revoke his 1961 disclaimer, which denied any political commitment or function to his drama, for using 'politics' in a limiting way. Indeed, he recharacterised *The Birthday Party* and *The Dumb Waiter* as metaphorical but nonetheless critical depictions of authoritarian postures, in which power was used to crush the asocial or questioning voice (and emphasized *The Hothouse*'s early account of political dissidents kept in a psychiatric hospital). Pinter's explicit dramatic target was henceforth active or passive complicity in such postures and regimes: not just the torturer, but the successful law-abiding citizen sucked into a political structure that was essentially if complacently debilitating; not just the Turkish, but American foreign policy; not just America but implicitly all American allies such as Britain who countenance America giving military assistance to repressive factions and regimes in Nicaragua, El Salvador, Guatamala and Chile. Pinter's principal dramatic theme was now the political fact of how language covered up hideous truths in a brutalising world:

> When the Czech police use their truncheons in Wenceslas Square, we describe that as an act of brutal repression consistent with the practices of a totalitarian regime. When the English police charge students on horseback on Westminster Bridge we describe this as a maintenance of law and order and are advised that it is a containment of essentially subversive forces. . . . Do the structures of language and the structures of reality (by which I mean what actually *happens*) move along parallel lines? Does reality essentially remain outside language, separate, obdurate, alien, not susceptible to description? Is an accurate and vital correspondence between what *is* and our perception of it impossible? Or is it that we are obliged to use language only in order to obscure and distort reality – to distort what *is*, to distort what *happens* – because we fear it?[35]

Initially, Pinter's new-found purposeful impatience with language as moral subterfuge pushes him towards – uncharacteristically – theatrically *presentational* and *demonstrative* work, revealing the political fact of how decorous procedural or sentimental language covers up hideous truths, but in a way which documents rather than imaginatively challenges bleak consequences. *One for the Road* critically depicts the appalling degree of power represented by authoritarian coercion, but is a formally coercive play: the dramatic and imaginative experience it offers is that of association with Nicholas's authorised sadism or with his victims' fearful impotence in the face of violation.[36] *Mountain Language* apparently gives the audience access to an imaginatively separate space (such as is crucially denied to the interrogatees and audience of *One for the Road*) by permitting them to understand both languages spoken in the play (as in Friel's *Translations*): the language represented by the military, and the rural language it attempts to outlaw as part of an ethnic repression. When the Prisoner and the Elderly Woman are forbidden to speak the mountain language, a dialogue continues through voice-overs: this may either represent what they would wish to say, or else reflect their assumptions of what the other is likely to want to say. Finally, when given the chance to speak her language, the Elderly Woman either does not trust the edict or is traumatised into catatonia by the entire experience, and her withdrawal compounds the suffering (and perhaps disintegration) of her son. Whilst more formally complex than *One for the Road*, *Mountain Language* similarly remains a demonstration of a Catch-22 situation in which the oppressors have a right to do anything that their victims cannot stop them from doing, and in which love of others constitutes a fatal vulnerability which can and will be exploited appallingly. As political drama goes, this is harrowing and bleakly consistent; but it is also fatalistic, imaginatively paralysed like natural prey by the power of a mesmeric predator, lacking precisely the self-contradictory perspective on nihilism and hopelessness which makes Beckett's dramatic moribundities paradoxically vivifying. Fortunately, *Party Time* breaks out of this imaginative *impasse* through a formal affinity with Beckett's *Catastrophe*. Whilst the respectable citizens of a totalitarian society discuss their lives, with only brief conversational intimations of the ongoing military clampdown which permits their lives to run on 'normal, secure and legitimate paths', Pinter interposes glimpses of a detainee, Jimmy, the brother of one party guest. This effectively makes the stage a reversible double image, with one imaginative space simultaneously inlaid within the other. Like the intermittent light from the door which indicates Jimmy's marginal but intense space, glimpses of accommodated brutality shine through the party banter which consciously evokes the comedy of manners cocktail party. Sentimentality and romanticism are the guests' imaginative strategies to cosmeticise complicity in brutalising repression. Though isolated, Jimmy is unbroken, insisting: 'I sit sucking the dark. . . . It's the only thing I have. It's mine. It's my own. I suck it'. To adapt Brater's comment on *Catastrophe*, the activity of military depersonalisation is 'made personal in an ironic reversal of previous events. We move from observation to participation'.[37] Jimmy's confrontation with, and acceptance of, his situation contrasts with the practised but imperfect aversions of the guests. Unlike their attempted but strained objectifications, Jimmy's assertion of his own subjectivity intensifies under pressure, in an image of imaginative defiance which can demonstrate the reversibility of power. This repudiation of the inevitability of victimisation makes *Party Time* the strongest of Pinter's political plays.

*Ashes to Ashes* (1996) depicts further accommodation of brutalisation. Rebecca seems to have eroticised postures of repression, whilst her interrogator or colleague Devlin sees no contradiction in his professional requirements to be 'A man who doesn't give a shit. A man with a rigid sense of duty'. As in the preceding three plays, deliberate imaginative self-amputation permits the dehumanisation of opponents through the strategic dehumanisation of the self. Rebecca insists that the performance of submission (or even disintegration) becomes itself a resurrectory art: 'You can end once and then you end again'.

An echo suggests the reverberations of a trauma (or fantasy?) of the snatching of her baby, as part of a systematic ethnic assault, and her assimilation of this,[38] even as she develops the eroticism of the subjugation of her will to another.

The literalism and conservatism of critics in their responses to Pinter's political plays is aptly represented by Esslin's objections to *Party Time*:

> If the play was meant to be set in an English, or British, milieu, it would be politically unconvincing. No such round-ups, disappearances or tortures and quick deaths are likely in this milieu and to suggest anything like it would amount to a case of paranoia. Are the British conditions and linguistic quirks thus meant to suggest another country? In that case the location is left too vague, and the English idioms and party manners become very much out of place.[39]

Rather, Pinter deserves respect, not only for his scrupulously self-refining writing, but for his use of his literary acceptance to become a public spokesman against the self-congratulatory complacency whereby people allow themselves to become part of a hegemonic structure which is imaginatively limiting and politically debilitating. Characteristically, he has challenged the implicit assumptions and alliances of Blairism[40] as he did the ostentatious repressions of Thatcherism. Pinter's summary of his writing life in terms of 'relish, challenge and excitement'[41] may be somewhat surprising, given his characteristic dramatisations of anxiety, vulnerability, regression and subordination. But his sense of responsibility as an artist, involving the compulsive problematisation of imaginative evasions and political accommodations, demonstrates an appetite and capacity for challenge which his characters often fail to discover or achieve.

# Notes

1. Sinfield (1983), p. 184.
2. Ibid., p. 243.
3. *Eleuthéria* (1947), quoted by Fletcher and Spurling, in *Beckett: A Study of His Plays* (1972, 1978), p. 50.
4. J. Goodall, 'The Plague in Artaudian Theatre', in *Modern Drama*, 33, 4, Dec. 1990, pp. 529–42 (541).
5. Worth, op. cit., pp. 7–8.
6. Ricks, *Beckett's Dying Words* (Oxford, 1993), p. 1.
7. Hinchcliffe, op. cit., p. 119.
8. Kalb, *Beckett in Performance* (Cambridge, 1989), pp. 3–4.
9. Worth, in *Beckett the Shapechanger*, ed. K. Worth (1975), p. 185.
10. Kalb, op. cit., p. 35.
11. Iser, in Connor (ed.), *New Casebooks: Waiting for Godot and Endgame* (Basingstoke, 1992), p. 64.
12. Iser, ibid., p. 67.
13. States, *The Shape of Paradox* (Berkeley, 1978), pp. 6, 25, 29.
14. Worton, in *The Cambridge Companion to Beckett*, ed. J. Pilling (Cambridge, 1994), p. 69.

15. Ibid., p. 75.

16. Kalb, op. cit., p. 10.

17. Elam, in Pilling, op. cit., p. 152.

18. Brater, *Beyond Minimalism* (Oxford, 1987), p. 49.

19. Brater, op. cit., pp. 145–6.

20. McMullan, in Pilling, op. cit., p. 205.

21. Wall's other legitimate theatre performances included Archie in Osborne's 1974 production of *The Entertainer* at the Greenwich Theatre, and Manny in Wesker's *The Old Ones* and Old Gocher in Barker's *Fair Slaughter* (1977) at the Royal Court.

22. Pinter, *Various Voices* (1998), p. 197.

23. See Thompson, *Pinter: The Player's Playwright* (Basingstoke, 1985), especially pp. 38, 54, 81, 61.

24. Kennedy, op. cit., p. 167.

25. Cahn, *Gender and Power in the Plays of Harold Pinter* (Basingstoke, 1994), p. 2.

26. Quigley, *The Pinter Problem* (Princeton, 1975), p. 276.

27. Worth, op. cit., p. 16.

28. Quigley, op. cit., p. 170.

29. Pinter, 'Writing for Myself', 1961, reprinted as Introduction to *Plays: Two* (1991), p. x.

30. Kennedy, op. cit., p. 185.

31. Pinter, Introduction to *Plays: Four* (1998), pp. x–xi.

32. Quigley, op. cit., p. 176.

33. Quigley, op. cit., p. 225.

34. Ibid., p. 272.

35. Pinter, *Various Voices*, pp. 173, 182.

36. See Rabey, 'Violation and Implication', in *Themes in Drama 13: Violence in Drama*, ed. Redmond (Cambridge 1991), pp. 261–8.

37. Brater, op. cit., p. 146.

38. The echo is a further suggestion of Pinter's affection for Webster, particularly *The Duchess of Malfi* (1613), in which the torture of an ultimately defiant woman reflects a sense of shame into at least one of her persecutors, and a providential echo unsuccessfully prompts resistance to a tragic fate. Rebecca in *Ashes to Ashes* further reminds me of the character in Sylvia Plath's poem, 'Lady Lazarus'.

39. Esslin, *Pinter the Playwright* (1992), p. 213.

40. See Pinter, *Various Voices*, pp. 201–2.

41. Pinter, Introduction to *Plays: Four* (1998), p. xii.

# Chapter 4

# Out of the 1960s and 1970s: *Whose* Is the Kingdom?

As the 1950s turned into the 1960s, Britain's political fabric seemed to foreshadow (not for the last time) the apocalyptic lines from Yeats's poem, 'The Second Coming': '*The centre cannot hold . . .*'.

In 1957, Anthony Eden resigned as Prime Minister in response to the Suez crisis: an independent military initiative which had left the country isolated and condemned by international law, including Commonwealth and American allies. Britain was forced to accept that its days as a freebooting major imperial power were gone. Eden's successor, fellow Tory Macmillan, was left to pick up the pieces, and set about a discrete dismantling of the trappings of the British Empire, particularly in Africa. He also prioritised the development of Britain's nuclear capability (a supposed defence against potential Russian invasion of Western Europe) at the expense of the conventional forces which might have been associated with previous imperial ambitions and their embarrassments. The next crisis for the British Left came in 1959, when Khrushchev began the traumatic process of educating Russia away from Stalinism, and thus subverting the Western 'Fellow-Traveller' mythology of ideological comradeship.

The dissatisfaction of Osborne and the Socialist impatience of Wesker anticipated and partly heralded a new national self-consciousness at the turn into the 1960s: a less secure, deferential age in which traditional underpinnings were to be questioned and actively loosened. This spirit was taken up by the first generations to be empowered by the 1944 Butler Education Act (the egalitarianism of which governments since the 1970s would systematically and progressively undo). Harold Wilson's Labour government (1964–70) attempted to identify itself with technocratic industrial progress whilst moving into the political middle ground with a strategic mixture of municipal utilitarian rhetoric and opportunism. It even attempted belated self-associations with emergent youth culture (the creation of Radio One in response to pirate radio, recommendations of MBEs for The Beatles). This new tide of popular culture tended rather 'to override, or at least mask, long-standing social distinctions', 'setting styles which marked off generations rather than classes';[1] but it often sought to enfold the youth 'market' in the self-absorption and pseudo-accessibility of consumer capitalism, rather than involve it in an informed political critique of existing structures (and this has subsequently increasingly been the case).

Nevertheless, less manageable foreign developments informed new self-identifications and assertions of personal and civil rights: Women's Liberation, racial equality, sexual re-evaluation (represented principally by the widespread availability of the contraceptive pill, promising a voluntary sterility on terms then considered biologically harmless, and the legalisation of homosexual acts between private consenting adults in 1967). *A United Kingdom* was an increasingly problematic concept in its possibility, or even desirability. By the late 1960s, Wilson's rhetoric was increasingly exposed as specious, as when he publicly conceded a case for trades union reform, but lacked the unions agreement or Commons majority to implement it. His 'commonsense' posturings and populist invocations held limited appeal for an increasingly volatile and educated population, who were aware – whether fearfully or sympathetically – of informed political defiance by students and others in France, America and elsewhere.

The early 1960s saw London become the base of two major national subsidised theatre companies: under Peter Hall, the newly named Royal Shakespeare Company established its London base at the Aldwych Theatre; and the National Theatre, with the decisive support of Laurence Olivier, at the Old Vic. Less centrifugally, many regional theatres operated repertory companies, offering regular theatregoers the chance to see a recognisable pool of resident performers who were, at best, challenged and extended by the demands of different fortnightly productions, reflecting popular successes from the previous ten years of London theatre.[2] Nottingham Playhouse established a strong reputation for premiering new writing (*The Ruling Class*, *Comedians*, *The Churchill Play*, *Brassneck*) alongside fresh views of classical drama (Ken Campbell in Jonson's *The Alchemist*, 1978) through the 1960s and 1970s. Peter Cheeseman's work at Stoke-on-Trent's Victoria Theatre provided a good example of specifically regional theatre, addressing local history and issues. The BBC's 1966 broadcast of Jeremy Sandford's neo-documentary drama about contemporary homelessness, *Cathy Come Home*, directed by Ken Loach, indicated the potential immediacy of television drama in informing national consciousness.

The 1970 General Election replaced Wilson's tenancy with Edward Heath's more interventionist and confrontational Conservative government. Many plays of the time reflect 'the collision between the exuberant excesses and personal explorations of the Sixties and the inherited power of established institutions – apparently obsolescent, but soon to reassert their power in a society rapidly polarising'.[3] This polarisation was manifest in spirals of unemployment, inflation, trades union disputes, the reinflammation of Ulster and the institutionalisation of a British military presence there. Remaining vestiges of postwar consensus were engulfed by a wider sense of disintegration. Significantly, the Heath government went into a 1974 general election on the theme of 'Who Governs Britain?', but were brought down partly by a concurrent miners' strike, having misjudged their own rhetorical ability to unify the country. The Labour Party under Wilson was returned to office, and based itself upon a strategy 'directed towards self-preservation rather than innovation',[4] doing little to arrest the national mood drift towards a depressive, even vicious, sense of impotence. In seeking different forms of galvanisation for the future, in the context of perceived and sensed national discouragement, many Labour voices increasingly inclined towards the left, and many Conservatives toward the right.

# Arden and D'Arcy: anarchy *v.* closure

Whilst Arden's first plays appeared at the Royal Court soon after Osborne's and Wesker's, they were less immediately successful. Devine's maintained belief in Arden's drama, expressed through his defence of an artist's 'right to fail' commercially, may constitute his principal achievement in terms of a public commitment to principles which have been subsequently and ubiquitously dismantled (Roberts: 'If Osborne had opened up the possibilities for the Court, Arden had stated unequivocally what the Court was for'[5]). Critics accustomed to having judgments made for them objected that they found Arden's style incomprehensible. Gray points out how *Look Back* can be discussed using the same vocabulary as one might about Rattigan or William Douglas-Home;[6] and Hunt notes how 'The question of identification is central to a theatre of illusion', which is 'essentially a theatre of acceptance', as when at the end of *Roots* the audience are led to identify with Beatie's excitement to the point of ignoring that *what* she says is, as before, a repetition of her boyfriend's ideas.[7] In contrast, Hunt aligns Arden – and D'Arcy – with popular, Shakespearian and Brechtian traditions of drama, sceptically questioning appearances rather than seeking to persuade through the intrinsic simplification of appeals to common sentiment and to rational organization. Hunt: 'in a naturalist play, the prime demand is for "consistency", a consistency that allows us to pin a character down in rational terms'; thus the ideological effect of the theatre of illusion is 'the narrowing down of social processes' to a re-presentation of an ultimately conventional image of 'real life'.[8] Arden and D'Arcy prefer to highlight the *provisionality* of any social solution, and the contradictions at work in characters. Significantly, a 1963 *Peace News* interview with Arden is titled 'A theatre of sexuality and poetry', but critical commentary (often itself a business of rational simplification) tends to ignore the keen poetic awareness of the specifically sexual allure of the contradictory and dark 'nightenglish' in his and their works.[9] Arden has identified the English ballad tradition as a bassline of violent, amorous ungovernability in the land's poetic-historical imagination.[10] D'Arcy, as an Irishwoman in England, observes how 'To the superficial glance of an urban dweller the only rural culture [at the turn into the 1960s] was county/Tory anglicanism; however, with a bit of scratching-around, the underside was revealed, the ancient folklores, the old mother-goddess still breathing her message of randomness, chaos, anarchy, anathema to the military–industrial complex'.[11] The couple's subsequent relocation to Western Ireland has reflected further conscious alignment with the margins of the metropolitan and imperial, where their 'scratching-around' has striven to extend the range of drama outside the conventional terms of theatre and national identity.

Arden's *The Waters of Babylon* (1957) is a characteristically problematising story of an immigrant landlord attempting to outdo native English corruption and create his own little 'empire' in exile; the play questions moral absolutes in a deliberately artificial style which recalls Shakespeare, pantomime and music-hall, as when characters speak verse at moments of contradictory tension or excitement. Arden's masterpiece, *Serjeant Musgrave's Dance* (1959), extends this heightened self-consciousness into the ballad form and character-isation of the play itself. Like the poetry of Ted Hughes and Geoffrey Hill, nearly every line of this 'Un-Historical Parable' generates *resonances*, often with myth or folklore, whilst simultaneously defying single reductive *inter-pretations*. Such resonances also arise from a tense, suspenseful story in a manner which is both organic and mysterious, set in a world which is both naturally and artificially isolated and pressurised ('wintered up' by bad weather, selected for the representative status which Musgrave seeks to establish), peopled by characters who suggest social types yet remain capable of crucial surprise. The combined effect is to charge the play with a ritual momentum, most clearly manifested in Musgrave's religious sense of his mission (a self-dramatisation ironically parodied by the Bargee), but compounded by the mounting tension and climax associated with a cinematic Western (by which the play was partly inspired). Nothing is completely foreknowable: four de-serters guard the corpse of their colleague, but their grim humour does not assuage an uneasy sense of supernatural intimation; Musgrave plans an anti-war demonstration, but no one knows its form, and even he is surprised by fetching up at the former home town of the dead soldier; the local authorities and miners see the soldiers as explicit or implicit strike-breakers, but Musgrave's compulsive enfusal of military determination with Old Testament judgement strategically permits his apparently conservative rhetoric to be associated by the Mayor and Constable with their own repressive jingoism, whilst simul-taneously amplifying the audience's sense of his darker subversive purpose. Musgrave's plan is not pacifist: the ethics of war, colonial or otherwise, are 'generalities', 'not material': 'this is particular – one night's work in the streets of one city, and it damned all four of us and the war it was part of. . . . We've come to this town to work that guilt back to where it began' (Act I). Their mission embodies both the thrill and the horror of answering absolutism with absolutism, both abjectly vengeful ('We're wild-wood mad and raging. We caught it overseas and now we've got to run around the English street biting every leg to give it to *them*') and implacably superhuman ('Let the word dance . . . God's dance on this earth: and all that we are is His four strong legs to dance it'). Musgrave's demonstration goes beyond mere verbal protest, into a revelation of Artaudian possession that is his 'Dance' beneath the skeleton of his comrade. When the colliers' leader maintains 'we're not bloody inter-ested' by violent poetry, Musgrave moves to the poetic violence of simultan-eously located but random slaughter, in which the theatre audience stand in for the hitherto sceptical or indifferent proletariat. Only the dead man's lover can link the colonial war with the miners' riot, as 'the same corruption', but in terms the others cannot: 'A bayonet is a raven's beak. This tunic's a collier's jacket. That scarecrow's a birdcage. What more do you want!'. The towns-people are saved from slaughter by the cavalry, who represent however the interests of the Mayor and Constable to the exclusion of those of any other characters. It is the status quo that is 'Saved'. If the play's story demonstrates the inefficacy of ending war by its own rules, it also offers a disturbing glimpse of the irrational drive to do so, and shows how the 'rationality' of the collier

Walsh leads him to cynical enclosure. *Musgrave* represents and remains (distinctly and unusually) English theatre at its most profoundly radical: it cuts all ways, and through physical, linguistic and spatial poetry, rather than by striving to privilege a single argument in the standard patterns of identification and acceptance. And its fictitious location continues to reflect the foreign and domestic political consequences of all defences of imperial 'outposts', before and since the play's premiere.

Arden's subsequent collaborations with D'Arcy are experiments with ideas and purposes of 'play' which subvert the self-perpetuating consistencies of theatrical and social convention. *The Business of Good Government* (1960) is a characteristic response to the earlier tradition of church drama, a nativity play which estranges familiar characters to question the conventional deductions. *The Royal Pardon* (1966) is a rambling tale of a deserting soldier who joins a theatre troupe and is pursued by a constable, who is finally turned to stone by a humble girl in a gorgon mask: an appropriate image of self-conscious carnivalesque reversal for Arden and D'Arcy's work as a whole, ending a play which suggests *A Penny for a Song* rewritten by Augusto Boal. *The Hero Rises Up* (1968) alternately celebrates Admiral Nelson as a man of unruly appetite and impulse, and questions the nature of the 'freedom' allowed by the governors for whom he was an imperfectly controllable ideological instrument. *The Non-Stop Connolly Show* (1975), *The Little Gray Home in the West* and *Vandaleur's Folly* (1978) animate characters from the margins of official Anglo-Irish history in increasingly satirical and melodramatic terms. The essentially fixed moral perspectives of satire and melodrama carry predictabilities, consistencies and sentimental pieties of their own. Arden's plays often revolve around the scapegoating of unrepentant anarchists by the forces of decorous corruption which claim the privileges of social control – in *Musgrave*, *The Workhouse Donkey* (1963), *Armstrong's Last Goodnight* (1964), *Pearl* (1978). They might be regarded as more variously engaging developments of Whiting's austere and stoical *Coriolanus* processes. In the later collaborations with D'Arcy, characters are victimised, and retaliation is morally legitimised – generating a simpler and, literally, melodramatic appeal.

One of their most artistically striking and ambitious collaborations, *The Island of the Mighty*, was ill served by a 1972 RSC production which conflated a trilogy into a single evening and insisted on treating the subject matter – events in and beyond the rule of King Arthur – in a heroic rather than sceptical manner. This proved a significant clash with the normal range and tone of established British theatre, with which Arden and D'Arcy have never subsequently re-engaged.[12] The trilogy's objective, to reconsider English national foundation myths within a context of Irish, Welsh and Scottish ones, is radically powerful, if purposefully uncomfortable for traditional heroic complacencies in its presentational emphases and deductions. Their Arthur attempts to associate himself with the heyday and methodology of the Roman Empire, in paternalistic response to challenges from within and without. Uninformed self-definition has fratricidal consequences for Balin and Balan, the former defending empire, the latter 'going native' amongst the Picts in a literally intoxicated way. Nations, genders and individual characters are all shown to suffer from (self-)deceptive pride (like Arthur and Gwenhwyvar dancing in demonic masks at their marriage) in a bid to *dramatise themselves more powerfully*. Whilst *The Island of the Mighty* creates many opportunities for bold and striking stage imagery through costume, battle, verse and dance, it is important that the production exposes and undercuts the self-aggrandising posturings at the heart of many characters' tactics and decisions. Whilst Arthur directly invokes the audience's responsibility for the 'continued religion and civilization of Britain', other characters make similarly urgent appeals, and invoke national myths differently. Familiar motifs from Arthurian legend and literature – such as Arthur's sword being thrown into the lake – are de-familiarised for surprising effect, and frequently for exposure as a strategic political fabrication. This Merlin is not viciously debilitated, but suffers a breakdown akin to Bond's Lear in his failure to formulate an appropriate response to his responsibilities as a poet: to articulate culture in an age of self-deception. English myths are shown to have repercussions into others (such as the Welsh myth of Blodeuwydd), subverting the traditionally exclusive perspectives of both by this startling recontextualisation. The deformations of retentive power only serve to amplify a rising tide of counter-pressure, which transforms people into vengeful living corpses, 'So hideous and bloody greedy / We take hold of the whole world!'.

Arden and D'Arcy's series of radio plays, *Whose Is the Kingdom?* (1988), examines another creation myth in a purposefully deglamourising way, detailing the Roman Empire's adoption of Christianity – originally perhaps a revolutionary movement for political deliverance – as an officially enshrined form of authority and integration, demonstrating again that no 'traditional' motif can or should be separated from the political purposes of those who invoke it. However, these plays lack the subversive immediacy of *The Island of the Mighty*. Wike comments on the fiction on which Arden has subsequently concentrated: 'Instead of a Brechtian conception of the dramatic moment, in which the audience is carried forward toward an understanding of emergent historical possibilities, Arden's view is primarily retrospective. History is seen as a process of suppression in which potentialities are closed off, not opened up . . . the status quo cunningly preserves itself, emerging in new guise despite superficial movement.'[13] This is, however, also true of *all* of his work with and without D'Arcy since the 1960s.

## Mercer: where the difference begins

'I believe in crossing lines not drawing them' says the title character of David Mercer's *Flint* (1970). Thus he embodies one dynamic of Mercer's drama, exuberant social impropriety inspired by desire, a defiance of the constraints of social normality and their constructions of maturity and sanity. Morgan, in the television play *A Suitable Case for Treatment* (BBC, 1962, filmed as *Morgan*, 1966), is a similar character, particularly in his repudiation of the assurance that violence will get him nowhere: 'Where has gentleness got me? Where has love got me? Violence has a kind of dignity in a baffled man. The rich have the law, the poor a simple choice between docility and brutality. I am full of love. I shall punch you with love. Will you have love between the eyes or in the teeth?'.

However, Mercer's drama *as a whole* depicts the drawing, more often than the crossing, of lines: delineations of disappointment between generations, genders, classes, nationalities, ultimately sundered by historical circumstance. The television play *Where the Difference Begins* (BBC, 1961) begins a dramatic enquiry into the relationship between personal freedom and deracination. Two sons – one conventionally successful, the other a jaded, drifting former idealist – both prove sympathetically unrecognizable to their working-class father. The disillusioned son observes how his dad cannot 'get the hang of the changes', but himself admits that increased prosperity is not everything: 'where do we go when the cities aren't fit to live in, when we have everything to live with and nothing to live *for*?'. *After Haggerty* (RSC, 1970) reprises the generational confrontation with different emphasis. This stage play depicts the individuation of two characters: theatre critic and lecturer Bernard, from his working-class reactionary father; and single mother Claire from the oppressive casualness of her child's father, Haggerty. To Bernard's friends, his father *'represents a world stubbornly impervious to their experience'*; Chris, who is gay, is the first to challenge the security of the old man's moral presumptions. Then Bernard rejects him personally and precisely: the father refuses to strike him, maintaining 'I'll not touch thee'; Bernard negates his superiority, replying 'You *never have* touched me', placing a funeral wreath around his father's neck in irrevocable dismissal. Thus *After Haggerty* challenges the impulse to enshrine working-class experience and presumption with persistent moral authority. Bernard nevertheless lacks a sense of personal alternative possibility, as shown by the self-loathing in his mechanical reviewing of 'crap' plays and his tired peddling of critical clichés about Fry, Whiting and Osborne to Eastern European audiences who are experiencing more profound social change. If Claire is freed from her former sexual subordination to Haggerty by the news of his death, the empty coffin which accompanies the news mockingly manifests what the deliberately separate man, Haggerty, was and remains: an emotional void, ultimately untouchable. Bernard and Claire will evidently continue to be thrown painfully back upon their own resources in developing their processes of self-liberation.

Mercer's work shows a restlessness with the Chekhovian form of naturalistically depicted decline to which he brought a specifically English and politically informed edge. *The Governor's Lady* (1965) shows the nominal head of a colonial outpost regressing into animalistic abandon. *Duck Song* (RSC, 1974) develops this sense of character disintegration into the breakdown of conventional form. Laing notes how its production in the year of the three-day week, the miners' strike and the last days of the Heath government caught a national mood of 'crisis and dissolution' in its initially conventional analogy of middle-class family home and nation; the characters' 'dialogue and situation become more fragmented and bizarre'[14] as they are required to deal with absurdist changes of costume and removal of furniture from around them, and with the appearance of a Native American visitor who begins a purposeful regression to the primal state of a hunting brave. The besieged middle-class sensibility, *in extremis* in some way it cannot define or admit, is increasingly bewildered and forsaken, in a way that recalls the generalised meandering into oblivion of later Osborne.

Mercer's last wave of writing is more incisive in its purposefully articulate reanimation of the heightened naturalist form and representative social grouping. *Cousin Vladimir* (RSC, 1978) and *The Monster of Karlovy Vary* (RC, 1979) are his most acutely painful comedies, and the most striking flourishings of his abiding preoccupation and concern with parochial English responses to the problematic interrogations posed by Eastern European politics, and their possible indications for the viability of state socialism. 'Cousin Vladimir' is a wily, cynical refugee, briefly transplanted by his cousin Katya's marriage of convenience to Austin, leader of an English drinking circle called the Hard Core, who (comically and painfully) epitomise a latter-day Chekhovian cycle of disappointment, deferral, trivialisation and infantilism. Their moral superiority towards Russia and Vladimir's Schweykian postures provoke his observation: 'I sometimes think this loud moral crusade . . . is also welcome diversion from your terrible apathy towards your own predicament. Your own society.' The English have taken the problems and failures of Eastern Bloc communism as a vindication of the complacent political generalisations which perpetuate their own childish inertia, compounded by alcohol, dulled wits, apathy and self-pity. Even Austin recognizes how English law, civilised traditions and an abhorrence of dogma are 'stretched out tight like the skin on a boil':

> Beneath that skin there's a meanness, a rancour, a mindless violence brewing . . . which for the first time in three hundred years we can neither take to war nor export to some remote colony, dressed up as civilisation, honest commerce, religion or any other kind of mumbo-jumbo . . . I doubt you'll ever again find so much impotent fury draining like pus into the glum business of daily existence. Or else into macabre fantasies of where to point the finger and who to smash, who to blame, how to legitimise a new order of hatred on the grounds that the old one's succumbing to violence and anarchy.
>
> (I.5.)

However, he uses this observation to license his own dipsomaniac withdrawal. Katya concludes 'I would rather fight on my knees, in Russia – than one day to die in your kind of freedom . . . Heartbroken', and Vladimir adds 'your freedom is something you do not know what to do with'. Thus Mercer's finest play invokes the associations of Chekhovian form – the observation, but also the humanist forgiveness, of dissipation and paralysis in response to ostensible, but self-perpetuating, 'inevitabilities' – in order to identify and reject the 'taint' of Western moral approval, as Vladimir discovers an excoriating eloquence amidst the surrounding drive to generalisation and inarticulacy. In withdrawing the traditional liberal compensations from the Chekhovian form of identification, Mercer's initiative is fiercely original and astringent. *The Monster* reverses its predecessor's premise by placing an English 'worried armchair revolutionary' in Prague; his blackly farcical odyssey through convolutions of corruption and identity undermine all of his familiar moral and ideological self-assurances, but his final foolhardy action in the name of 'Resistance' inspires a formerly cynical film director towards a demonstrative and expressive art (which Bernard in *After Haggerty* would hastily dismiss). *Then and Now* (1979) returns Mercer to observation of historical disappointment, as the optimism of a wartime couple is also shown 24 years on. Barriers of class, age and gender generate envious fetishisations of sexual cruelty which end in recrimination, shame and self-loathing.

## Nichols and Wood: smile, boys, smile

Peter Nichols turned from writing the 'keyhole naturalism in monochrome' which then constituted almost all television drama, to seeking a more active role for spectators in the theatre, challenging 'the game of illusion by understood rules'.[15] *A Day in the Death of Joe Egg* (1967) demonstrates how the father of a handicapped child finds '*Clowning may give way to ineffectual hectoring and then self-piteous gloom*', and thus recalls the flagging ironies of *The Entertainer*, particularly Archie's ostentatious but strained repudiations of emotional commitment. However, Nichols locates entropy in (self-)oppressive performances of the familial and the masculine, rather than in national disintegration, which would seem to be the theme of *The National Health*, staged in 1969 by the National Theatre as if to substantiate the claims of that establishment. This microcosmic portrait of a hospital ward self-consciously lurches into parodic romance in a bid to counterpoint (rather than arrest) patients' irreversible decline. The ward includes reactionary and patriotic patients seeking displacements for their fears, whilst 'the ship of state' that is the hospital drifts on, trusting 'her coolies in the engine room'. Nichols's ironic presentation suggests and satirically reflects a national heartlessness, but in a laconically fatalistic way. Nichols's most incisive play, *Poppy* (1982), follows the lead of Auden and Isherwood's *The Dog Beneath the Skin* (1935) in subverting 'the one indigenous British theatre form', the pantomime: a nineteenth-century invention to help theatres balance their annual budgets, 'an expansionist imperial spectacle that matched the Victorian mood of fantasy, trans-sexuality, opulence and jingoism'[16] (by further irony, it became the first new play presented by the RSC at their expansionist new home, the Barbican Centre, in Margaret Thatcher's New Victorian age[17]). *Poppy* also refers playfully to Brecht's *The Good Person of Setzuan* in its depiction of China as '*a place where gods and emperors can meet*' and its diagnoses of addictive economic double-binds. The traditional British pantomime protagonists – Idle Jack, heroine Sally, principal boy Dick – struggle to acclimatise to a 'New England' of instinctive emotion sublimated into imperial expansion and mercantile competition. 'Poppy', as well as being slang for money, signifies

Chinese opium, rendered 'a nice little earner' in the respectable form of laudanum, 'the oil that keeps the wheels of industry turning' by stupefying infants while their mothers work 12-hour factory shifts. This becomes a suitable focus for English buccanneering, developing from the heroes' success in foisting a profitable blend of Christianity, commercial subservience and displaced sexual oppression upon India ('For years we'll find The White Man's Burden crippling/Until it's clothed in words by Rudyard Kipling'). The officially, commercially sanctified release offered by 'poppy' is a significantly circumscribed relaxation of restraint. This occurs in a national climate which is becoming more hierarchically polarised and predatory: Dick marginalises and disenfranchises Jack, and leads the attack against China (where he ensures that 'All the villages from Canton to the sea Are . . . Burning to be free!'); Sally's self-repression implodes into opium addiction; and a final admission that 'Happy Ever After' can only be 'for some' leads into a reprise of the song and dance number 'Civilisation, Commerce and Christianity'. *Poppy* is Nichols's most searching exploration of content through form, effectively subverting the pantomime's theatrical familiarities in order to challenge the national assumptions they reflect, and the imperialistic consequences which these assumptions demand.

Nichols's sense of national life – and its displaced eruption, war – as sinister farce can be compared to that of Charles Wood, whose play *Dingo* was written in 1961 but not staged until 1967 at Bristol Arts Centre and the Royal Court (and revived by the RSC in 1976); though Wood notes it is 'best done in warehouses, drill/church halls, small ramshackle theatres that are simple performing spaces'.[18] Its subtitle, 'A Camp Concert', suggests affinities with other plays of performative nationality, *Oh! What a Lovely War* and Nichols's romantic melodrama *Privates on Parade* (RSC, 1977), but *Dingo* is leaner and more savage than either. Indeed, Wood's harrowingly humorous play is unusually relentless and remorseless in the non-linear experience it creates for the audience (significantly, Wood is one of the few visible and acknowledged British influences on Howard Barker, whose plays *No End of Blame* and *The Power of the Dog* in particular share some affinities of style and impulse with *Dingo*).

Dingo and Mogg are disenchanted British squaddies in the Western Desert in 1942: '*burned bloated splashed with gentian violet*', eloquently nihilistic and masturbating listlessly. Their naïvely idealistic colleague Tanky is traumatised by the death of his comrade Chalky, but tries to render this manageable by clowning with the charred-black corpse as if it were a ventiloquist's dummy. An officially sanctioned Comic appears in a mobile theatre designed to maintain morale with jokes and striptease, on an increasingly darkening stage; Dingo lacks Mogg's gullible interest. A Navigating Officer blunders around the camp lost, insisting that places are where he says they are, because he is the Navigating Officer. Characters who are effectively from a parallel reality – the 'Hero Colonel' and 'Hero Sikh' – stride on to strike valiant postures, and the lower ranks are blown to bits. As the Comic cracks jokes, a '*HERO SCOT laughs, coughs blood and dies*'.

Act II finds Dingo and Tanky in a boxing ring representing a German prison camp. Dingo opposes Tanky's frantic cheerfulness, by vowing 'I'll not dig my own grave . . . dig his first . . . I'll make sure I do my ghosting in the sand table rooms of Sandhurst . . . I'll be there. Whenever there's a Tactical Exercise Without Troops – I'll stand in for the blood and snot. I'll be there – twirling in the air behind them'. Mogg, however, has been mesmerised and schooled in obedience by the Comic, and is now *'dressed as a Sergeant Major and a Hero'*, and therefore capable of an alarmingly casual violence towards Tanky in the name of restoring morale. An escape bid, under cover of a drag show, results in Tanky's death at the hands of a guard, though this is treated immediately (even by Tanky) as theatrical slapstick. Dingo untangles Tanky from the ropes, tells him 'you're a hero, having died' and suggests he say goodbye to the theatre audience, particularly the mothers, to whom he always appeals. Tanky asserts 'They should be home burning their kids' toys', but Dingo tries to quieten him in acceptance: 'No no – look at them, we're all going home . . . and you'll be left as a cross, so have a good look . . .'. Dingo goes home determined to vote in such a way as to wipe 'the childish grin of satisfaction' from the face of Churchill, rather than be 'pissed on twice'. Tanky repeatedly calls out at Mogg 'He killed me' as all other cast strike a tableau and the curtain falls.

*Dingo* is an infinitely unforgiving play, as fiercely memorable as laughing up blood. The camp concert, boxing ring, portable theatre and whitewash merge to form a highly original and appropriate expressionistic performance space on which to parade and explode military posturings, the docility of humility, and politicians' vanity. Even further than in *Lovely War* or *Poppy*, the British *susceptibility to forms of populist theatricality*, in political rhetoric as in entertainment, is identified; and integration through military heroism is critically depicted in terms of the ultimate visceral consequences of 'blood and snot' on which it tacitly insists and depends. Wood's scenic and linguistic invention repudiate the ironic displacements associated with conventional British models of theatrical 'play', by depicting the absolute collapse of all categories save that of privileged power; this is itself exposed as a joke devoid of imagination, through the simple savagery of the repeated identification of a naked act: 'He killed me'.

Wood's *'H': or Monologues at Front of Burning Cities* (NT, 1969) is another anatomisation of the business of soldiering, with different emphases. Unlike the brusquely rough *Dingo*, *'H'* is made up of scenes and tableaux played out in front of painted cloths and drops in a way which draws attention to issues of artificiality and perspective in its account of the British response to the Indian Mutiny of 1857. The play recalls both Shakespeare's *Henry V* (in depicting alternately both the heroism demonstrated by many soldiers and the anti-heroic aspects and consequences of their actions), and Arden's cool epics: Brigadier Havelock ('H') is a national maverick, like Nelson, who has Musgrave's grim sense of religious approbation. Wood's antithetical technique is crystallised by Havelock's lines on the death of a soldier: 'His was a Happy Death my Lambs, he died in the Service of his Country. (*Softly*) Some of him is on my boot!'. Surgeon Sooter, phlegmatic when not drunk from exhaustion, provides recurrent pragmatic commentary on stoically received amputation and disfigurement. Straight lines of national meaning are tangled from the opening line, by a Bengali Bombardier: 'Has you never seen a black Irish?'. His sense of proud but marginalised lineage proves decisive ('It is not the English hold India, / it is the Irish and the Jocks, / and they do it through their / pricks. Which gives you the strange / condition of the black Irish, the / Kilkenny Kaffir'). This mixed-race mutineer Bombardier is an Irish Catholic, when he turns mutineer, he is not constrained by the Hindu Indians' ultimate tabu on rape: Mrs Jones-Parry, formerly haughtily dismissive of reminders of victimisation, is fetishised (crowned as Queen) then ravaged and impregnated by the Bombardier. Before he is caught and killed, her husband visits reprisals on other Indians through the ultimate offence of sewing them in pigskins. Wood is merciless in showing the co-existence and mutual dependence of sentimentality and atrocity, depicting the way that stirring courage is never far away from moments where *'we see the greasepaint for a moment'*. The Epilogue shows Captain Jones Parry inducting a *'very brown'* child into the sacred heritage of English aristocracy as represented by imperialism. Mrs Jones Parry counterpoints his two-page eulogy with the line, 'here is where your father was shot and died in agony'. 'H' makes large demands on resources and cast – Wood's introduction to the play suggests 'It ought to be an opera' – but necessarily, in order to provide audiences with an experience of profound and complex counterpoint.

# Performing possession/possessing performance

A number of stage plays of this period respond to a sense of generational schism, whilst also reflecting dramatically the increasing contemporary prioritisation of the theatrical 'event' through performance art, 'happenings' and Artaud's ideas filtering from abroad into British theatrical discourse. Jean Genet's *The Balcony* had arrived in London theatre in the late 1950s; however, Peter Brook's and Charles Marowitz's late 1960s and early 1970s experiments constituted the first British high-profile entertainments of Artaud's impulses towards a Theatre of Cruelty. Artaud aimed to provide the audience 'truthful distillations of dreams where its taste for crime, its erotic obsessions, its savageness, its fantasies, its utopian sense of life and objects, even its cannibalism' gush out not 'on an illusory make-believe, but on an inner level'.[19] Brook's experiments included Peter Weiss's *Marat/Sade*, paradoxically but strikingly a scripted Brechtian 'framing' of neo-Artaudian turbulence. In 1974, the RSC mounted a revival of David Rudkin's *Afore Night Come* (written 1960, first staged by the RSC in 1962). Rudkin's first stage play (written with no foreknowledge of Artaud's theories) suggests destructive and darkly creative cosmologies lurking beneath the superficial civilisation of the English Black Country, in a tale of repression and sacrificial ritual which notably locates English regional drama's promise and potential beyond the superficialities of the English domestic interior and the limitation of the individual to inarticulate repression, polished rhetoric and/or banal witticisms. In some ways an imaginative projection out of the 1935 popular melodramatic thriller, Emlyn Williams's *Night Must Fall* (both in title and in the detail of a severed head), Rudkin's play brings an Artaudian vein of savagery and ritual to the English stage. In an orchard, the equipment for a ritual sacrificial murder is assembled in a casual and realistic way, unlikely to strike the audience as odd or meaningful, but the scapegoating of an Irish outsider suddenly reilluminates all preceding events and details as leading inexorably towards a process of separation and elimination. This implicates all denizens of an English rural landscape which resounds in a new, harrowingly apocalyptic way (as in Whiting's *Saint's Day*). There is also a sense that the process climaxing in the murder of the Irish tramp is only narrowly averted from being trained upon the audience representative, a young student who discovers his own sexual complexity amidst the vicious upsurge of marginalisation and vengeful sterility.

No other British dramatic texts of the period glimpse the possibilities of an indigenous ritualistic 'total theatre' as originally, organically and seriously as Rudkin's, until Barnes's work in the early 1970s. Peter Shaffer's *The Royal Hunt of the Sun* (NT, 1964) takes a theme proposed by Artaud: the conquest of Mexico, and that nation's sense of the immediacy of the occult, by Spanish rationalist imperialism and Catholicism. The author's notes to the play hope for a 'total' theatre, 'involving not only words but rites, mimes, masks and magic' to suggest the power of belief which is supplanted by reason. However, whilst the play incorporates stylised design and ritualised physicality, this serves to decorate a fatalistic demonstration of the coloniser's power; theatrically, Shaffer invokes the trappings of Artaudian theatre in order for the conventional narrative to subsume them. *Equus* (NT, 1973) combines the traditional family drama of thwarted individuation from Shaffer's *Five Finger Exercise* (1958) with the magical primitivism indicated by *Hunt*, via the detective thriller. The 'voice-over' introduction and commentary provided by psychiatrist Dysart evoke *film noir*, its sense of a mystery to be solved which will also evacuate conventional moral stabilities. As the story of his patient Alan unfolds, there is a sense that the boy is less in the dock than Dysart – secular priest to the creed of Normality – and the social reintegration he promises. In its own way, *Equus* strives to confront – from one remove – the envied passion of youthful abnormality compared to the drabness of conventional routine and commonplace trivia, though this wilful abnormality is not centrally articulated as in *Look Back in Anger*, or presented without commentary as in Pinter's *The Lover*. Dysart's perspective on Alan is self-consciously *voyeuristic*, drawing back from commitment to sensual primitivism yet acknowledging its appeal, and the form of Shaffer's play replicates this theatrically by inserting neo-Artaudian sequences into the familiar fundamentals of English family melodrama. Shaffer's *Amadeus* (1980) repeats the voyeuristic perspective by centralising the envious composer Salieri, who observes the precocious Mozart (whose erotic babytalk might be a parody of Jimmy Porter's) with sexual distaste and grudging admiration for the magic of his music. Salieri dramatises himself as satanically excluded and therefore compelled to visit his destructive envy upon Mozart: 'We are both poisoned, Amadeus. I with you: you with me'. This unbearable recognition is implicitly *parental* (Salieri complains 'I must survive to see myself become extinct!'). Salieri justifies his persecution of Mozart as an absolution of 'Mediocrities everywhere – now and to come'; his ironic self-canonisation both criticises and enshrines vengeful parental resentment, foregrounding him by association with his more talented (and less orthodox) victim. The popular success of Shaffer's drama lies in the similar ways that it permits an older audience to glimpse, acknowledge yet ultimately *define itself through separation from* youthful discovery, suggesting a tragic dignity in the acceptance (choice?) of self-repression.

David Storey's *Life Class* (RC, 1974) similarly bids to incorporate and comment on facets of *contemporary performance* within the boundaries of text-based *naturalistic drama*. The abolition of theatre censorship in 1968 had permitted total nudity on the theatre stage, not only in performance art but also in London shows such as *Hair* (one of 'several commercial productions which seemed to be cashing in on the underground theatre genre', a commercial counterfeiting of dissent Elsom identifies as 'Modcom'[20]) and erotic revues from Kenneth Tynan's *Oh! Calcutta!* (1969) to the Raymond Revuebar. *Life Class* uses this newly increased freedom, and also narratively refers to 'invisible theatre' represented by 'the happening': performance which purposefully disrupts civic decorum through its apparent realism or unpredictable immediacy.

*Life Class* centres on an art teacher leading an evening class in life drawing. The formal barrier between the model, Stella, and the pupils remains intact, though flirtatiously questioned by banter from both sides, until the penultimate scene in which the teacher Allott presides over an 'invisible event', the performance by two class members of an apparent rape of the model (who is reduced by the rhetoric of the occasion to the pronoun 'it'). Allott reflects to Stella after the event on the importance of this, his 'personal statement' against impassivity: 'Violation, they tell me, is a prerequisite of art' for 'disruption of prevailing values'. However, Stella's complicity in the event remains vague, unspecified, even (im)passive. The performance of the rape of a naked woman by the forcible endeavours of two clothed men problematises the issues of contact and rationale for all involved, until it becomes manifest that the apparent rapist has – both within and without the fiction – never removed his penis from his trousers. The terms of import for this 'invisible theatre' are primarily (if perfunctorily) explored in relation to the characters in the dramatic fiction. The secondary audience, in the theatre, remain just that: probably shocked by the enactment (which the script paces with realistic gruelling awkwardness) but finally returned to a sense of their own gullibility in relation to fictional dramatic action, which is characterised as the realm of inconsequential make-believe. The play's primary admonishment of the characters' passivity implicitly licenses that of the audience (who are fictional 'observers' only). Allott, a professional artistic mediator in his late 30s imaginatively alienated from both his juvenile students and his conformist institutional superiors, briefly articulates his own lack of significant expression ('How does one live as a revolutionary . . . when no one admits there's a revolution there?'), and may be propelled into unforeseen volatility by marital crisis. Ultimately, Storey's drama subordinates the performer's experience to the fictional meaning of the text, and reinforces the *status quo* of conventional text-based drama, and conventional response. Contrastingly, subsequent textual drama fictions by Morrison, Nigel Williams, Barker[21] and Kane will demand that the performer *dis-close* themselves through staged nudity that interrogates conventional terms of closure associated with representative impersonation, thus problematising the categories and definitions of fiction, artifice, natural-ness and performance.

Trevor Griffiths's *Comedians* (1975) is another socially realist play focused on a night class, but the middle act, in which a group of aspirant comedians present their performances for reaction and assessment, involves the audience in disturbing roleplay which constitutes a development from that in *The Entertainer* or even in *Serjeant Musgrave's Dance*. Griffiths's opposition of experienced comic tutor Waters and his most promising yet unpredictable student Price also presents an image of generational schism, both politically and theatrically. Price departs from Waters's traditional but reformist guide-lines to veer into shockingly direct performance art through which to express his own political dispossession and anger. Waters steers his pupils away from predetermined gratifications, 'entertainment' and slick success, towards what the audience 'fear to express': 'a true joke, a comedian's joke, has to do more than release tension, it has to *liberate* the will and desire, it has to *change the situation*'. Nevertheless, Price insists on his own difference, from not only his fellow pupils, but from his tutor. The stakes of the first performance in a working men's club are raised by the presence of an adjudicator and booking agent who is a longterm adversary of Waters, and who advocates performance which offers the audience 'escape'. With great delicacy of characterisation, Griffiths suggests how the characters' performances reflect their hopes, fears, disappointments and individuality. One Irishman endeavours to follow Waters's educative liberal-humanist precepts with an artful subversion of national prejudice: 'I never knew we wuz troublemakers until I got to England. You don't, you know . . . I mean, what are you lot, eh, do you know? . . . You'd have to go to India or . . . Africa . . . or Ireland to find out. Mmmm?' The other performances manifest tensions of objectives and a readiness to ditch principles for self-interest and commercial success. Price delivers an initially Grock-influenced act which takes his stylized self-transformation into *'half clown, half this year's version of bovver boy'* to its grim conclusion with an attack on two dummies representing *'well dressed beautiful people . . . perhaps waiting for a cab to show after the theatre'*. The theatre audience who have enjoyed the imaginative mobility of playing the working men's club audience, probably laughing with a mixture of irony and surprising directness at the preceding jokes, now find themselves backed into an imaginative corner, stereo-typed as aloof, arrogant and insulting by their very presence. Price's character tells the dummies 'There's people'd call this *envy*, you know, it's not, it's hate'; then, having wreaked his bloody mischief, tells the audience 'We're coming up *there* where we can gerrat you'. The performance is too extreme to invite or permit· any sense of solidarity: class, national or even liberal-sympathetic.[22] The adjudicator predictably rewards the most cynically conventional and cheaply integrationist acts, maintaining that 'people don't learn, they don't want to, and if they did, they won't look to the likes of us to teach 'em' and that 'you're there on *their* terms, not your own'. Waters offers sympathy (but not understanding) to Price: 'You've always been a bit wild, it's why I liked you, reminded me of me at twenty-five'. However, Price insists 'I can't paint *your* pictures'; 'love, care, concern' were not discarded, but 'never there' in his 'brilliant' performance, which Waters nevertheless rejects as 'ugly . . . drowning in hate. You can't change today into tomorrow on that basis. You forget a thing called . . . the truth'. Price counters 'You think the truth is *beautiful?* You've forgotten what it's *like*' and insists on his own right to 'stand upright', perform on his own terms and 'bang [his] head on the ceiling' of convention. Stung by Price's accusation, 'Maybe you lost your hate', Waters confesses a memory of a Nazi extinction camp, 'the logic of our world . . . extended', which nevertheless stirred him in a way he finds unacceptable. Thus his determination 'We've gotta get deeper than hate' seems a fearfully willed recoil away from unacknowledged complexity and guilty imaginative complicity. Price, contrastingly, places his faith in the 'ice' of hatred and disobedience expressed: 'I stand in no line. I refuse my consent'. Their finely-drawn opposition makes *Comedians* one of the most resonant British plays of its era. Whilst Price's act is nominally enfolded by a naturalistic setting, the character's deliberately anti-realistic choices in performance offer the audience a discomfortingly immediate theatrical experience which highlights the flimsiness of the insulating fantasy of naturalism (with its implicit propositions of the audience's superior awareness and intangibility). The icy blood-flourish expressed by the chilling young maverick Price, without irony or distancing mitigation by Griffiths, represents the start of a movement in British drama towards admitting more immediate, amoral and threatening perspectives in the late 1970s and early 1980s: not looking back in anger, like the writers of the previous generation, but refusing consent, and looking forward with grim fascination to occasions when 'anarchy is loosed upon the world'.

# Notes

1. Clarke, op. cit., p. 292.

2. For example, my own programme collection confirms Birmingham Alexandra Theatre's repertory company presented plays by W. Somerset Maugham, Daphne du Maurier, Emlyn Williams, Waterhouse and Hall's *Billy Liar* and Shaffer's *Five Finger Exercise* (1970); Rattigan's *French Without Tears* (1971); Patrick Hamilton's *Gaslight* (1972). By 1976, the Alexandra was hosting visiting companies, presenting Ayckbourn's *Absurd Person Singular* and Willy Russell's *John, Paul, George, Ringo and Bert*.

3. Laing, Introduction to *Mercer: Plays : Two* (1994), p. x.

4. Morgan, op. cit., p. 361.

5. Roberts, op. cit., p. 73.

6. Gray, *John Arden* (Basingstoke, 1982), p. 3.

7. Hunt, *Arden: A Study of his Plays* (1974), p. 24.

8. Ibid., pp. 30–1.

9. Unusually, Lacey observes how Arden characteristically 'both challenges certain stereo-types about the "Englishness" of contemporary social life, and relates to a tradition of dissent and exclusion', op. cit., p. 132.

10. Quoted in *Arden and D'Arcy: A Casebook*, ed. Wike (New York, 1995), p. 57.

11. D'Arcy's Introduction to *Arden/D'Arcy: Plays: One* (London: 1991), p. ix.

12. See Hunt on the vicissitudes of the production, and also on the inappropriateness of Brook's approach to *Musgrave*, op. cit., pp. 157–67.

13. Wike, op. cit., p. 236.

14. Laing, op. cit., pp. xiii–xiv.

15. Nichols, Introduction to *Plays: One* (1991), p. xiii.

16. Nichols, *Plays: Two* (1991), p. 407.

17. Nichols records his preference for a subsequent rougher version at the Half Moon Theatre to the RSC's embarrassingly 'opulent' production, ibid., p. 408.

18. Wood, Introduction to *Plays: Two* (1999), p. 7.

19. Artaud, *Artaud on Theatre*, ed. Schumacher (1989), p. 101.

20. Elsom, *Erotic Theatre* (1973), p. 204.

21. In Barker's *No End of Blame* (1981), a life class model discovers an unruly expressiveness. Her name, 'Stella', offers a mischievous riposte to Storey's play.

22. Reinelt proposes an aspect of the performance's divisiveness that is dramatically unac-knowledged: 'the violence perpetrated against the female dummy tends to reinscribe the female as object', *After Brecht* (Ann Arbor, 1994), p. 160.

# Chapter 5

# Bond: Blind Power

Since the 1960s and into the next century, Edward Bond seeks to illuminate and resolve situations of cyclical social aggression, proceeding from his belief that 'the idea that human beings are necessarily violent is a political device, the modern equivalent of the doctrine of original sin'.[1] Bond illustrates the madly systematic (self-)destructive compulsions which a distorting society has inscribed into the national unconscious, its instinctive 'nightenglish'. He attempts to enlighten the reactionary reflexes of this benighted 'nightenglish' through reference to a politically rationalised 'dayenglish' of analytic explanation. Sometimes his own terms of explanation appear prescriptive and systematic in their rationalism. At best, they are shockingly incisive regarding national patterns of ignorance and instrumentality.

*The Pope's Wedding* (RC, 1962) exemplifies how Bond's drama draws from the confluence of naturalistic determinism and the Brechtian epic, and their common materialist precept that characters are primarily defined (and limited) by a systematic social degradation, which deliberately denies them the expressive and analytical tools – language and imagination – to recognise or change the terms of their existence. Scopey is the first in a line of Bond characters 'who are searching for something, and who themselves become lost'.[2] His resentment of another's mystery makes him seek to possess it through violence, but this leads to Scopey being marginalised and demonised rather than centralised. *Saved* (RC, 1965) begins with scenes of contemporary working-class romance between Pam and Len. His enthusiasm despite their constrictions ('This is the life') suggests his ability to enjoy basic simplicities. Other characters tend to compound their own *reductions* to *mean* simplicities: exemplified by the domestic routine of Pam's parents, who never mention each other ('E puts 'er money over the fire every Friday, an' thass all there is'); and the gang of local lads who bid to outdo each other's bravado in the tale of running over a child, and then in the action of killing Pam's baby.

The Royal Court had to assume club status in order to by-pass the licensing control of the Lord Chamberlain, and permit a performance of *Saved*. The groundswell of support which mobilised behind the defence of theatre and play was a major force in the abolition (in 1968) of the requirement of the Lord Chamberlain's licensing of plays for production. Most of the controversy centred upon a scene which illustrated deliberately and critically the consequences of social degradation: the youths reduce an unseen baby to a sub-human thing, an intrinsically contemptible 'yeller-nigger' or 'yid' with 'no feelin's', to license their own violence. This sequence is, however, importantly contextualised by other examples of reduction: Pam regularly drugs the child into a stupor, and Bond adds a bleak irony after the fatal stoning by showing her pushing the pram off without a glance inside; and Len refuses to intervene in the murderous taunting, and is therefore complicit. His tendency to locate the idyllic in the simple (as when he watches Fred fishing) may be another facet of an irresponsible capacity for escapism and self-effacement, which effectively merges him into his degrading surroundings. The prevalent limitations of choice, particularly regarding self-definition and gratification through consumerism and sentimentality, are succinctly highlighted by Pam's feeding the baby aspirin to ensure peace during her own 'treat' of feeding herself chocolates, and the contending options of jukebox songs, 'I Broke my Heart' or 'My Heart is Broken'. Whilst Bond suggests that Len's final mending of a chair reflects his resilience,[3] his engagement with the material object may be so searching as to suggest a near-merging with it (particularly in his odd final position of rest).

Len is also the name of a character in *Early Morning* (RC, 1968) who represents the working-class male mesmerised into unsuspecting, disposable subservience by his would-be superiors. *Early Morning* breaks with social realism to adopt the style of a Lewis Carroll odyssey turned nightmarish black farce, in which characters like Queen Victoria, Gladstone, Disraeli and Florence Nightingale become gargantuan monsters of appetite and duplicity dominating the currency of nightenglish, the dream of an English political subconscious, which reflects and shapes its present (the distorted reanimation of historical detail aptly anticipates Margaret Thatcher's bid to remanifest 'Victorian values' in 80s Britain). Stylistically innovative, *Early Morning* is also more optimistic than Bond's previous plays, in that (like *Mankind* and *Heartbreak House*) it depicts a protagonist's dream of individuation, which passes through identification with a necrophilous pessimism towards a transfiguration which ultimately (and here literally) raises the protagonist above the confinement of their social circumstances and definitions. Arthur's regressive Siamese twin George represents a socialised self which chafes Arthur until he sheds its residual fearful reflexes in order to stand apart from accordance in what he sees. Working-class terms of existence are stipulated by an oppressively inclusive afterlife, in which all engage in a cyclical, futile round of gratification through mutual consumption (the deferential populace blithely cannibalise queue-jumpers as they await films of populist sensationalism). Len's line – 'I'd be rollin' in clover – if me internal 'aemorragin' 'olds out' – is perhaps the quintessential remark of the misplaced optimism by which a proletariat reconciles itself to the predatory directives of authoritarian control: a fatal ingratiation repeatedly demonstrated in Bond's drama. It is perhaps unfortunate that this style of savagely comic but unpredictable political expressionism goes undeveloped in his subsequent work. It shares some points of contact with Peter Barnes's blackly farcical depictions of a nation hypnotised and petrified into predatory reflexes by the 'basilisk' of Authority.

Hirst notes how 'by juxtaposing images from different periods and contexts', Bond 'forces us to appreciate a dislocation between what we observe and what we are taught to believe'.[4] This has conscious affinities with Brecht's

*Verfremdungseffekt*, and the influence is made more manifest in the Eastern parable style of *Narrow Road to the Deep North* (1968). A poet, Basho, introduces himself in a conventionally sympathetic manner, but proceeds to act with a pseudo-artistic, self-important aloofness, claiming authoritative insight in a way which recalls Merlin in *The Island of the Mighty* and has similar damaging social consequences. Shogo forms an extreme counterpoint in his readiness for ruthless action, 'the lesser of two evils' which claims to 'prevent suffering' through imprisonment and killing. He forms an uneasy alliance with the English evangelist Georgina, who cultivates moral control through her doctrine of original sin by which people are 'born evil' and redeemed by external regulation. However, both are ultimately engulfed by the social pathologies they invoke.

This effect is also evident in Bond's *Lear* (RC, 1971), which subverts Shakespeare's tragedy and updates its historical eclecticism. The dramatic metaphor of the Wall becomes a simultaneous symbol of defence and entrapment, as Lear and his daughters successively perpetuate violent social restriction in such a way as to fuel an ultimately uncontrollable cycle of aggression. Again, fear and belief in natural evil lead to their own confirmation and the justification of repressive social institutions; the meekest law-abiding citizen implicitly helps to maintain a rule of terror through the acceptance of its supposed social 'necessity'. *Lear* also contains memorable stage images laced with savage black humour which recall and often surpass those of *Early Morning*: notably the daughters' withering asides on their husbands, and their enjoyment of torture (one soldier turns aside from his victim to protest ''Oo's killin' 'im, me or you?') Bond's principal subversion centres on his refusal of notions of reconciliation and atonement which popular assumption seeks to locate (misguidedly) in Shakespeare's play. Bond's Cordelia is not Lear's natural daughter, but a Stalinist revolutionary from whom Lear is increasingly estranged when, like his daughters, she finds herself, in turn, enslaved by the violence enshrined by the Wall. She strenuously attempts to justify her political means, contradicting her initial assertion that 'When we have power these things won't be necessary'. Lear is tempted by the intimations of ghosts – of the Gravedigger's Boy, of the daughters before their actual death – which resemble the residual characters of *Early Morning*, spectres of nostalgia and withdrawal. His achievement of a belated calm appreciation of the beauty of the viscera of his (literally) anatomised daughter is shattered by his blinding. This is conducted – shockingly – by a fellow prisoner who opportunistically seeks to 'bring [him]self to notice' by this exercise in human vivisection, which he narrates with the chillingly ironic professional politeness of a dentist. Like the protagonist of *Oedipus at Colonus*, Lear becomes fearless in his lack of things to lose, and confronts Cordelia with the tyrannous manifestations of her supposed resistance to tyranny: 'A revolution must at least reform'; 'your morality is a form of violence'; 'you decent, honest men devour the earth!'. Here as elsewhere Bond attacks the valorisation of social order by the poor, who seek and claim to hold on to their minimal security in fear of losing everything. The Wall serves as a resonant metaphor for the arms race and many other forms of political 'foreign policy', as well as for their domestic consequences. Lear's final individual bid to unbrick its repressive determinism is a heroic, unsupported existential act, futile in isolation but necessary as example. ⚔

*The Sea* (RC, 1973) is a black comedy of smalltown manners, in which Mrs Rafi and Hatch dominate groups with their hubristic personal visions, in a social world which the hermit Evens says permits neither tragedy nor laughter, 'only discipline and madness'. Bullied by Mrs Rafi, Hatch bullies others with his xenophobic fantasies of alien invasions, which lead him to fear both the living and the dead, as offered up by the sea. Bond challenges the conventional liberal sympathies which the audience might grant to Hatch and Mrs Rafi for their Chekhovian and comic aspects – the younger Rose reminds sea-survivor Willy (and the audience) that 'The town's full of [Mrs Rafi's] cripples', who seek to cripple others.

Bond's next plays deal specifically with 'this problem of culture, with the problem of the burden of the past which makes change so difficult'.[5] Mangan notes how, in *Bingo* (1973), Bond avoids conventionally obvious moral directives within the play; rather, 'the aim is to engage the audience as meaning-makers, and the strategy is to construct a play in terms of a series of discrete but thematically linked scenes, to which meaning is given by their juxtaposition and ordering'.[6] Thus the audience are invited to define and extend their social and political self-consciousness through imaginative activity which may lead them beyond 'the socially prescribed response'.[7] *Bingo*'s choice of Shakespeare as a protagonist challenges (as did *Lear*) conventional associations of poetic abstraction, isolated divinity and serene humanism which might surround the national dramatist's work. Every scene of *Bingo* hinges on an issue of money and property. Bond's Shakespeare, who has avoided involvement in issues of peasant revolt in the name of 'protecting [his] interests', is confronted at every turn by the cost of staying alive in a repressive social world maintained by his inactive compromise. He realises that his bids for economic security depend on and exacerbate the hardship of others. *The Fool* (RC, 1975) is a companion play based on the life of poet John Clare. Clare seeks literary fame away from his rural background, but a genteel conversation around a prizefight in Hyde Park ultimately puts Clare in his social place: 'Who controls the brute in man? Polite society. Well, your verse undermines its authority. There'd be chaos. The poor would be the first to suffer'. The irony of the scenic image is not lost on Clare, who reflects on how the boxers 'git paid for bein' knocked about. I git knock about. Why on't I paid for it?'. Clare disintegrates mentally, victim of a social climate that denies him 'a proper life': a situation which, even when accepted as necessity (as by his wife), defies restitution.

Those who (however well-meaningly) inure themselves to complicity in tyranny through wilful imaginative mutilation, akin to a sort of self-blinding, are increasingly opposed, in Bond's work, by characters who can develop a purposeful myopia towards the liberal humanist sympathies which would ultimately divert them into completely blind instrumentality or paralysis. Having identified 'problems', Bond now seeks to discover 'answers' in plays suggesting that, in this kingdom of the blind, the one-eyed man may be the only effective revolutionary. This is best dramatised in *The Bundle* (1978), a conscious reworking of *Narrow Road* to propose that events might have more than one possible outcome. The 'Shogo' character – now named Wang – grows up to be a liberationist guerrilla rather than an imperial tyrant. Wang identifies the holes in the logic of his adoptive father, the Ferryman, who seeks to placate the landlord of the river and earn his protection: 'We steal the fish to stay alive to pay taxes so that there'll be no more stealing'. Basho turns away from 'those so poor they can only seek self' – that is, survival. In fact, it is he who is too self-absorbed to extend help to a deserted baby; the Ferryman is too empathetic to do anything but help the child, notwithstanding his own poverty; but Wang is too focused on tackling the root causes of such poverty to be distracted by the child. The audience, like the Ferryman, may be reluctant to acknowledge Wang's equation of 'food and clothes and knowledge' with rifles. Wang identifies such hesitation as potentially fatal, even treacherous: 'You saints who crucify the world so that you can be good! You keep us in dirt and ignorance! Force us into the mud with your dirty morality!'. Later he observes 'Today we should look on kindness with suspicion. Here only the evil can afford to do good'. Wang's ethical interrogation redesignates conventional 'evil' as occasionally necessary action, without which there is no chance of change. Belatedly but decisively, the Ferryman discovers in himself a similar resolve: 'shouldn't we change our lives so that we don't suffer? Or at least suffer only in changing them?'.

*The Bundle* shrewdly and surprisingly suggests that puritan ruthlessness can have a place and time in the world of practical action. However, Bond's next 'answer plays' suffer (like *The Fool*) from containing an obviously *authorially* prescribed response to events: the audience are less engaged as meaning-makers (what is termed educationally an 'expressive', or evocative, objective), more subjected to the pedagogical authority of Bond's analysis (what is termed educationally an 'instructional', or prescriptive, objective[8]). *The Woman* (NT, 1978) is a sceptical demythologisation of the Trojan War, which nevertheless becomes more programmatic than, say, *The Island of the Mighty*, by being essentially (even melodramatically) presentational of what Bond himself identified as 'a socialist rhapsody'[9] of political heroism. *The Worlds* (1979) examines the control orientation of conventional moral language in its references to terrorism, in the story of a kidnapped businessman. One worker arrives at dislocating moral deductions like the Ferryman in *The Bundle*, but the activists tend to substitute a worker-based authoritarian ideology for a management one, adopting rather than dismantling the machinery of power (like Cordelia in *Lear*). *Restoration* (RC, 1981) subverts the form of Restoration Comedy to show a working-class mesmerised into fatal inertia by duplicitous upper-class invocations of moral decorum. The characters break out of role – and the imaginative blinkers imposed upon them – to present acerbic musical commentaries on the situations depicted, but only Rose (whose name and colour seem to unite the hopeful associations of characters in *The Sea*, *The Fool* and *The Woman*) deduces from experience in time to realise her potential for survival, learning and action. *Restoration* derives satirical humour from the energy of Lord Are, but the working-class characters ultimately play out their supporting parts in demonstration of a favourite Bond theme: complicity in, and internalisation of, oppression. The play was given an added edge by textual amendments for the RSC 1988 production, which included references to the Falklands War: specifically, to working-class Tory support for a politically opportunistic war in which their representatives would serve as cannon fodder, to re-float Thatcher's Prime Ministerial career on a cynically manipulated tide of jingoist populism.

Bond's appetite for morally paradoxical dynamics – whereby the surprising, conventionally 'wrong' action throws into relief the ultimately worse evil of the generally accepted social 'order' around it – is continued in the trilogy *The War Plays* (1985). Bond directed this for the RSC in his final major collaboration with the large subsidized producers; he expressed growing dissatisfaction at an institutionalised (and ultimately reactionary) aesthetic which he perceived to be fostered by such contexts. *The War Plays* are set in the aftermath of a nuclear holocaust, tracing the subsequent actions of survivor communities. They offer moments of startling and memorable poetic imagery (such as the detail of victims flayed by the explosion 'waving their wounds' like huge sea anemones) but are (perhaps inevitably?) dramatically presentational of response and moral outrage in the face of the central imposed event. However, each play pivots on one moment of severely limited choice, focused on response to a relatively helpless person. *Red, Black and Ignorant* responds to the ultimate determinism of a future consisting of 'Two fists of ash' ('Where is the freedom in that?'), the destruction of future generations in the name of tortuous claims for nuclear 'protection' and 'survival'. A charred Monster-child plays out and comments on 'scenes from the life [he] did not live', including the internalisation and socially ratified projections of fearful violence. *The Tin Can People* shows a community given apparent 'labourless luxury outside financial time'[10] by discovery of an abandoned warehouse full of tinned food. However, their consumerist bliss contains the seeds of violence in their fearful reflex to preserve it at the expense of outsiders. They progress to abandoning their passive dependency on the tin cans and working actively to creating their own, more truly human, social world of informed effort. The third play, ironically titled *Great Peace*, shows a subsequent social world of 'discipline and madness' in which a notional order is again founded on human sacrifice to military ideology and its 'logically' condoned random slaughter. A woman loses her child and invests a bundle of rags with human personality in her bid to make meaning in her survival. Others try to build a post-military community, but she is too psychologically dislocated to work for incorporation into this. Her psychological ventriloquism recalls Beckett's images of hair-splitting survival, and her small-scale courage in enduring through defining herself by the circumstances which damaged her life recalls Brecht's *Mother Courage*. But there is a danger here that Bond proposes a future too recognisable, both in its fatalism (its military reflexes) and its utopianism (its corrective worker-hero idealism). The plays are more *demonstrative* than dramatic.

Parent-child relationships are also central to the television plays *Tuesday* and *Olly's Prison* (both BBC, 1993) and the Theatre-in-Education play *At the Inland Sea* (1995). Again, well-meaning but fearfully insecure parents attempt to provide and maintain order and discipline; this degenerates into a distortion of vision, insisting on further violence rather than acknowledge the mutilatory consequences of repressive objectification. In *Olly's Prison*, Mike's maintaining a principle of obedience drives him to strangle his daughter. He is 'barricaded' into the sense of his child as an investment which refuses to mature in social terms of validity. When Mike is released from prison, the police officer Frank (a representative of 'madness and discipline') seeks to profit further at Mike's expense by compounding his stigmatisation: he beats up Olly, already blind in one eye, to blame it on Frank. Olly agrees to this for the promise of financial compensation, but Frank's hateful enthusiasm blinds Olly completely. This may be Bond's most striking dramatisation of the willing social pawn, whose politically unimaginative complicity earns them unforeseen victimisation: Frank hammers Olly in the face, shouting 'I give you money . . . Love it! Scum! It's good for you', until Olly can only reply to Frank's mixture of shock, exhilaration and rationalisation with the starkly simple reiteration of consequence: 'I can't see'. Money cannot buy sight. As a social invention and index, it may be infectiously damaging to sight's reach.

*Coffee* (published 1995, staged 1997) represents a new dynamism in Bond's work. Rather than present an allegory or thesis in fundamentally consistent terms which imply a correct explanation, *Coffee* provides an expressionistic dreamworld odyssey of dislocating experience and discovery, like *Early Morning*. Indeed, *Coffee* recapitulates many Bond motifs, but yokes them with startling sharpness of focus. Nold is a secure and tidy individual whose curiosity nevertheless makes him don a jacket and follow the stranger Gregory through a door, thus becoming another Bond variant on Lewis Carroll's Alice. He finds himself in a nightmare landscape of twentieth century European war, encountering a woman who is tyrannised by her daughter and the doll she compulsively, vengefully animates (like a malignly inverted version of the Woman in *Great Peace*) to play out vicious scenarios of rejection and consumption. Gregory reappears twenty years younger as a sergeant in charge of a laconically murderous group of soldiers at The Big Ditch, an execution site for civilians. In the play's dreamlike condensation of time and effect, Nold has joined the soldiers, but finds he cannot ultimately submit to Gregory's 'order' to kill the Woman and Daughter; he turns his gun on his fellow soldiers instead. Back in his room, now shared with another refugee and a child, Nold replies to the question 'What did yer do?' with the assertion 'I survived': not only in terms of his endurance, but in terms of moral imagination, through his existential choice to stand against systematic programmes of dehumanisation. *Coffee* represents a surprising and valuable development in Bond's exploration of his assertion that 'We define ourselves by the things we allow to make us angry';[11] it suggests that we do so, moreover, by the *unpredictable* terms of our responses.

# Notes

1. 'Author's Note' in Bond, *Plays: One* (1977), p. 10.
2. Mangan, *Edward Bond* (Plymouth, 1998), p. 10.
3. Appendix, *Plays: One*, p. 309.
4. Op. cit., p. 108.
5. Bond, in Hay and Roberts, *Bond: A Study of his Plays* (1980), p. 266.
6. Mangan, op. cit., p. 35.
7. Bond, 'Note on Dramatic Method' in *The Bundle* (1978), p. xiii.
8. Eisner's terms, quoted by Robinson, in *Learning Through Theatre*, ed. T. Jackson (2nd edition, 1993), p. 256.
9. Bond, *Plays: Three* (1987), pp. 269–70.
10. Bond, commentary, *Plays: Six*, p. 345.
11. Bond, *Red, Black and Ignorant*, in *Plays: Six* (1998), p. 16.

# Chapter 6

# Subversion and Conciliation: Comedy from the 1960s to the 1990s

Comedy can be seen alternately as a subversive defiance of contingency (a meta/physical disobedience) or a palliative distraction which seeks to reconcile the audience with the imposition of (ostensible) inevitabilities. Leggatt goes so far as to claim 'There is no such thing as comedy', only 'comedies', an accumulated 'set of expectations within which writers and audiences operate',[1] usually focusing on a problem-solving story. Even dramatists who play against conventions of ordered resolution (frequently symbolised by marriage) 'invoke the expectation by denying it'.[2] He also notes 'comedy concerns itself with the way people live in spaces',[3] how they respond to constrictive definition and to expansive relief.

Several plays considered so far have self-consciously highlighted the process of comedy as a metaphor for larger processes of social life: specifically through comedy's preservation of, or challenge to, definition: the way it reinforces or problematises conventional patterns of inclusion and exclusion, as may be represented by the reciprocated or flagging energy between comedian and audience. Osborne's *The Entertainer* depicts the comedian dislocated by a shrinking and unresponsive audience with whom his rapport breaks down, in a shared failure of energy. As Osborne's audience, we have witnessed the domestic, financial and political pressures that Archie's act can no longer keep at bay. In Nichols's *The National Health*, the comedian Barnet becomes maliciously reductive towards outsiders, whilst insisting on his own indestructibility (like *Musgrave*'s Bargee); *Poppy* and Wood's *Dingo* expose the human costs which fuel such palliative reflexes. Griffiths's *Comedians* depicts several options (including Waters's proposition of comedy as 'medicine') but climactically presents the comedian as outsider, exposing and expressing social antagonism and hate in a revolutionary unsettling of his audience's attempted self-defences, deliberately dividing and complicating their responses in political terms. Thus comic drama can reinscribe and reinforce social space, or problematise or explode it, and resolve a problem in a way which may be neither ordered nor conventional. It may ridicule evasion, with a detachment which is discomforting.

## From Cooper to Orton: curious rooms

Orton's anarchic appetite for disclosure creates a distinctively 1960s comedy of stylish exuberance and cynical buoyancy which unsettlingly reilluminates the domestic interior, the detective thriller, the comedy of manners, and farce. His distorting perspectives on domestic and professional interiors suggest how 'the ease with which that room becomes odd, simply by a trick of the light' – or of the word – 'embodies another comic anxiety: how close the normal lies to something quite other' (Leggatt[4]). In Kennelly's terms from my Introduction, they suggest the spatial proximity of the sphere of nightenglish to that of dayenglish, even the inevitability of their constant co-existence.

Precursors of Orton might be located in earlier parodies of conformity. N. F. Simpson's *One Way Pendulum* (1959) subverts Kafka's *The Trial*: a black-clad introvert, more at home with his collection of speak-your-weight machines than with people, is tried as a serial killer but discharged in deference to his potential for worse crime; the machines celebrate and mock the representatives of stereotypical domesticity. Giles Cooper's *Everything in the Garden* (1962) is a comedy of manners set in a suburban household predicated on the docile consumerism and leisured lassitude offered by the 1950s. The couple's materialist ambitions and the wife's subordination – which, she protests, renders her less a person than a belonging whose initiatives are received with ridicule – are harnessed by a Polish refugee, who escaped from a wartime camp which taught her 'Nothing is disgusting, unless you are disgusted'. As in earlier plays (*Absolute Hell, Saint's Day, A Penny for a Song, The Waters of Babylon*), a figure from wartorn Europe exposes the puerility and escapism of English bourgeois pseudo-respectability. Cooper's reinventive outsider suggests 'What you do is up to you' and offers the wife a successful career in prostitution. Several wives of the neighbourhood rapidly agree to co-operate in this convenient generation of a second income, with the full blessing of their husbands, whose qualms are dispelled by material gain. A second outsider, an 'artist' who senses himself outside their 'club', guesses the truth and is killed and buried in a garden, sacrificed like the outsider in Rudkin's *Afore Night Come* to preserve the apparent inviolability of the group; although in Cooper's play the murder results from the accidental cruelty of unthinking carelessness (such as Ayckbourn will later expose), rather than the darkly regular and determined ritual of Rudkin's community. Cooper shows the impulse to preserve the conformist appearance of the suburban house, lest people think 'something wrong in' it, to be a demanding addiction – 'Ours must look like all the others' – which may even be financed by prostitution and murder. The preservation of the terms of the English space are paramount, and reinforced by practices which decorate the abandon of nightenglish with dayenglish's appeals to rational necessity (in ways which, the Pole admits, have shocked Nazis).

Osborne's *Under Plain Cover* (1963) and Pinter's *The Lover* (1963) and *The Homecoming* (1965) also parody domestic sexual conformity, but the most bracingly nihilistic comic attacks on sexual and legal decorum are presented by Joe Orton. Lacey goes so far as to link Orton's 'savage, Dionysiac comedies' with Brook's early 60s RSC experiments with Artaudian theatre: both were concerned 'not so much with representation as with confrontation'.[5] Indeed, foreshadowing the drama of Brenton and Barker, Orton's plays discover a vivacity in shamelessly articulate unpunished criminality, and identifying the duplicities of pseudo-respectability and authority. Most of Orton's writing was completed and staged before either the 1967 decriminalisation of private homosexual acts between consenting adults or the 1968 abolition of theatrical censorship, and the tension of his humour principally derives from a knowing implication of the audience in the pushing of these boundaries, and in entertaining possibilities of the dissolution of further boundaries. One character in *Funeral Games* (1968) remarks: 'All classes are criminal today. We live in an age of equality', capturing the sense of seductively articulate abandon with which many Orton characters smartly and surprisingly expose and embrace the irrationality of British life. Indeed, in Orton's drama, all classes and characters are artificially articulate; Orton characteristically foregrounds and valorises deliberate artifice, and refutes the implicit authoritarianisms of realism and normality. In the realm of nightenglish, everyone is potentially eloquent.

*The Ruffian on the Stair* and *Entertaining Mr Sloane* (both 1964) show the influence of Pinter's *The Room* (1957), *A Slight Ache* (1959), and *The Birthday Party* (1958); but it may be noted that the fastidious and sentimental couple in *Ruffian* are a thug and an ex-prostitute with designs on the suburban respectability of Cooper's characters; their sense of an idealised norm is nevertheless unbalanced by the frank admissions of an incestuous homosexual. *Sloane* subverts the thwarted regression of *The Birthday Party* when bisexual lodger Sloane kicks Kemp (the male stereotype of domestic ineffectuality corresponding to Pinter's Petey) to death, whilst maintaining an archly decorous innocence which makes him the sexual goal of both infantilising matriarch and upwardly mobile gangster. Their *ménage à trois* is an unconventionally harmonious resolution. Orton extrapolates the traditional terms of consensual normality into the zealous monomania of moral panic (one reported character in *Ruffian* so reveres the British Legion that he ritualistically eats poppies for the week before Armistice Day) whilst suggesting that the inexhaustibility of possibility – particularly sexual – offers a wellspring of unpredictability and glee.

One of Orton's most artful subversions of the comic space and the social boundary occurs in *Loot* (1965), in which the crooked policeman Truscott reminds all involved that 'What has taken place is perfectly scandalous and had better go no farther than these three walls'; as Leggatt observes, despite the attempted cover-up, 'the missing fourth wall makes the audiences witnesses and their silence makes them accomplices'.[6] The law-abiding McLeavy, who has maintained that the police are 'a fine body of men' deserving wider powers rather than being hamstrung by red tape, is finally arrested for summary execution, caught between the heartlessly resilient energy of his son Hal, his male lover and an accomplice in robbery (a nurse who specialises in opportunistic euthanasia), and the 'open-minded' – that is, blithely corrupt – Truscott. Hal uses his mother's corpse and coffin with the disquieting detachment of a social performer so skilfully unhesitant that he reduces the human to the material commodity, and from there to the stage 'prop' that is basis for comic improvisation. Truscott justifies and extends his official social licence through wilfully presumed guilt ('If I ever hear you accuse the police of using violence on a prisoner in custody again, I'll take you down the station and beat the eyes from your head'). All agree to sacrifice McLeavy and thereby 'keep up appearances', in shared knowledge that everything has a price. Their style of operating is breathtakingly deft, thorough and deliberate, crucially unlike Cooper's fumbling, inadvertently murderous herd.

*What the Butler Saw* (1969) also suggests that guardians of ostensible 'normality' are the most circuitous and hypocritical in the face of the disarmingly forthright anarchy of human appetites. *Butler* uses the farcical mechanism of the escalation of increasingly baroque and incriminating façade, generated by an initial strategic lie. Orton's wild(e)ly paradoxical and epigrammatic style reaches its apogee in a frenetic Dionysian demonstration that daylit exclusive social categories of sanity, legality and sexuality are essentially authoritarian determinism, the inventions of monomaniacs clinging desperately to their own theoretical status. When the psychiatrist Prentice tries to disguise his sexual pursuit of his secretary, Geraldine, he triggers a comedy of errors which calls into question all manner of social compartmentalisation. Rance, the investigative superior psychiatrist and government representative, seeks to fathom and classify events and characters, and determines to certify the hapless Geraldine insane; when she protests her sanity, Rance replies 'Why have you been certified if you're sane? Even for a madwoman you're unusually dense'. As appointed representative of lucrative dayenglish, Rance explains without reference to personal evidence and experience ('Civilizations have been founded and maintained on theories which refused to obey facts'), and protest only confirms his assurance ('No madman ever accepts madness. Only the sane do that').

*Butler* is Dionysian in its propulsion of its representatives of dayenglish – psychiatrists and police – into embroilment in increasingly outlandish postures involving transvestism, violation, traumatisation, drugtaking, blackmail, voyeurism and violence. In accordance with traditional farce, the initially stereotypical characters act like cartoons on elastic; unusually, several end up shot and bleeding, whilst two increasingly frantic rival psychiatrists attempt to certify each other with the aid of syringe or pistol. In a brilliant spatial redesignation, the alarm circuitry imprisons the characters within the asylum, and the audience with them. This stand-off provides space for discovery of incest and premarital rape which parodically instigates the neo-classical formation of a new family unit, as Prentice and his wife learn that the objects of their sexual voraciousness are their long-lost children, and even Rance rejoices: 'Double-incest is even more likely to produce a best-seller than murder – and this is as it should be for love *must* bring greater joy than violence'. The play concludes in further classical parody, concerning the inspirational potential of a homicidal phallic section from a statue of Winston Churchill, and the characters' '*weary, bleeding, drunk and drugged*' ascent into heaven, leaving the audience in the artificially lit space, from which they may be returned to reality with the final injunction 'Let us put our clothes on and face the world': a world in which, it is suggested, everything can be similarly suddenly redesignated, with immediate consequences for constriction and freedom.

# Gray, Frayn, Leigh, Stoppard: irony in the soul

This is simultaneously bland and acid, is it English?

*(The Common Pursuit,* I.2)

Rather than develop Orton's piratical anarchy, mainstream British comic drama from the 1970s to the 1990s – with some notable exceptions, to be discussed subsequently – tended to centralise the besieged individual, who is aware of the breakdown of their systems of perception, in a form of Chekhovian ambivalent sympathy which increasingly accorded with new terms of social and political retrenchment.

Simon Gray's drama characteristically foregrounds an individual who is 'uncompromisingly himself and cannot be otherwise',[7] conscious yet defiant of the bathos wrought by time and the revisionism represented by forces of attempted change. As Bull observes, such characters invoke a tradition of Englishness (centred in London and the Home Counties) to 'define their own sense of discomfort or despair with the contemporary'; their articulacy 'extends to an understanding of the irredeemably past nature of that tradition', even as (unlike that of Orton's characters) it maintains and 'embraces the social divisiveness fostered by the tradition'.[8] *Butley* (1971) depicts a lecturer's laconic avoidance of complexity in favour of 'friendship' of the type generated by public schools: 'Abuse, jokes, games' . . . 'It's only a language, as good as any other and better than some, for affection'. The question might be, affection for whom or what, and on whose terms? The answer seems to be for the freedom to be either dismissive or predatory. Simon in *Otherwise Engaged* (1975) resembles a comic version of Maitland in Osborne's *Inadmissible Evidence*, struggling to maintain his splendid isolation by shunning all claims upon him. *Quartermaine's Terms* (1981) and *The Common Pursuit* (1984) record a disappointment at the failure of Britain to sustain the coherence of mid-century academic promises of emotional immunity and detachment from the problems of others. *The Rear Column* (1978) is an historical excursion in which the characters' actions ultimately defy comic reclaimability. In a Victorian outpost of the empire in the Belgian Congo, five officers' maintenance of traditional decency collapses. However, the play frequently claims a comically sympathetic intimacy with this breakdown of convention, even though this involves a trade in local native flesh. Colleran's thoughtful analysis identifies how this ambivalently treated degeneration shows the men to be 'victims as well as victimisers' but thus 'diverts attention from the play's – and history's – more profound victims', the repressed natives who 'remain on the drama's periphery' through Gray's marginalisation of them, if 'not ideologically' then 'dramatically'.[9] This re-enactment of the dynamic of selective detachment, which permits the 'good' to repress others, thus forms an antithesis to the political critiques of Taylor's *Good* (1981) and Edgar's *Albert Speer* (2000).

Michael Frayn's *Make and Break* (1980) depicts an English building sales team at a trade fair. They fear but also respect and admire the commercial energy of their managing director, Garrard, a Thatcherite figure who relieves them of imaginative choice and autonomy by dismissing all forms of activity, thought and feeling which are not justifiable in commercial terms. His energy makes him attractive to the subservient secretary, Mrs Rogers, perhaps because he represents a release from the spiritual complexity she is uncertainly investigating through Buddhism. Garrard's exclusive valorisation of the work ethic as life's purpose is challenged by his apparent heart attack after sex with Mrs Rogers. He is reduced to tearful terror at the prospect of uncertainty and 'Nothing more ever', apparently glimpsing the futility of his evasion of mortality. However, Garrard's problem turns out to be a mere slipped disc; it is another member of the sales force who dies suddenly. Garrard is irritated by the consequent delay and obstacles to efficiency; the surrounding characters are '*chilled and uneasy*' at Garrard's refusal to learn from experience and his callous dismissiveness of his late colleague. Bull rightly notes how Garrard turns the play 'from a gentle comedy into a savage if ambivalent celebration of the world of trade'.[10] This 'ambivalence' is explained by Frayn: 'Is Garrard more monstrous than the rest of us? If he seems so, isn't it because he lacks our saving hypocrisy – because he fails to dissemble the appetites that we all have, that we all *must* have if we are to survive'; Frayn insists that walls and doors are necessary, and is concerned simply to show 'what they cost'.[11] Like Gray, Frayn presumes hypocrisy in any suggestion that survival might not necessitate reductive exploitation of others. Garrard's evasion of mortality and emotion stands in for comic irrepressibility and imaginative will when it is a deathly robotic parody of both, resembling Orton's character who ate poppies for a week to demonstrate patriotic zeal. But whereas Orton implies the character is deluded, panicked and ridiculous, Frayn – like the salesmen – can imagine no energy equivalent or opposed to Garrard, who is permitted (perhaps even pitied from the ultimately paralytic moral height of liberal humanist sympathy) because of his materialistic efficiency; this is presumed to atone for any lack of imagination associated with his pursuit of selective detachment. The scenography of the play frequently suggests the collapsibility of walls; the narrative insists that this be fearfully ignored, lest one discover the irreconcilability of 'Nothing' which, like Garrard, it glimpses and recoils from, seeking refuge in the energy of displacement.

Mike Leigh's *Abigail's Party* (1977) also raises issues of masculine avoidance of mortality as it pushes the careless banality and implicit territorialism of conversational banter, identified by Pinter, into grotesque caricature. The precisely suburban milieu of Leigh's play permits conservative audiences and critics such as John Peter a further ironic detachment from, and assumed superiority to, what he terms 'the chromium-plated, leather-upholstered nastiness of the *nouveau riche*'.[12] Leigh's distorting-mirror gallery of social options is fiercely bleak: workaholic Laurence glibly accepts that his high chance of an early death 'can't be helped' whilst his unfulfilled wife Beverley works and talks energetically to foster a sentimental sense of friendship with her neighbour Angela and her husband Tony. The women are cheerful but insensitive towards another neighbour, the divorcee Sue, whose withdrawal and self-effacement is symbolised by her vacating her house while her teenage daughter, Abigail, holds a party. The adults' sense of a 'party' transpires to be even more awkward, clichéd and ultimately hurtful than the teenage gathering which they view with a sense of uneasy separation. The mounting tension of the characters' aimless enclosure with each other almost erupts when Laurence points a knife at Beverley after she goads him about his lack of virility, and he waspishly remarks to newcomer Tony how the 'tone of the area' has gone down with the 'class of people' moving in. A bid to subdue the characters' increasingly frictional monomanias through a dance only leads to a heightening of sexual tension and resentment, which climaxes in Laurence having a heart attack. Angela's bid to resuscitate Laurence is undercut by her contracting cramp in one leg, and Susan calls her daughter's name into an unresponsive phone to complete the sense of desolation. Whilst *Abigail's Party* presents a savage critique of suburban sentimentalities, it also permits ironically superior audiences to conclude that 'the tone of the area' has 'gone down' because of the 'class of people' represented by all the self-deluding characters. Contrastingly, Leigh's subsequent film, *Secrets and Lies* (1997), is less ironic in its bleak awareness not only of empty convention and lost opportunity, but also of the resurgent need for the immediacy of unconventionally direct human contact. It indicts English inhibition, insensitivity and aloofness rather than present them as comically awful inevitabilities.

Tom Stoppard, the most frankly right-wing dramatist of this period, attacks Leftist totalitarianism and, increasingly, discredits opposition to the new right-wing materialism of the Thatcherite conservative resurgence. *Every Good Boy Deserves Favour*, the television play *Professional Foul* (both 1977), and *Cahoot's Macbeth* (1979) identify and locate authoritarian repression in representative communist states, and the individual's recourse to imaginative subversion, couched in terms of musical or linguistic style, that may briefly but tellingly subvert an uneducated literalism. Stoppard's concern for Soviet and Czechoslovakian dissidents is just and serious, but his exclusive identification of repression with social alternatives to Western capitalism implicitly affirms the British status quo against alternatives, in contrast to Mercer's equally witty but ubiquitously challenging analyses of East–West relations.

*The Real Thing* (1982) constitutes an attempted self-defence by right-wing comedy against the potential claims of (then recently resurgent) left-wing drama of political commitment. The play opens with a typical scene of comically stylish adulterous manners; this transpires to be a scene from a play by dramatist Henry, who will begin an affair with the actress, Annie. Henry satirises Annie's campaigning on behalf of a soldier, Brodie, who has committed an act of pacifist civil disobedience. Henry maintains that all 'Public postures have the configuration of private derangement': the ultimate motivation of all social action is the presentation of self in a way calculated to impress or ingratiate. The surrounding characters disagree, but cannot defeat Henry's argument in comparably articulate terms: one huffs, 'You may have all the answers, but having all the answers is not what life's about' – except, one might add, in comedies of manners.

Brodie also turns out to be an aspirant dramatist, and is dismissed by Henry: 'he can't write', in terms of traditionally endorsed style. Annie counters 'You're jealous of the idea of the writer. You want to keep it sacred, special, not something anybody can do'. Henry locates an objective quality in traditionally designed material objects, such as a cricket bat: 'This isn't better because someone says it's better, or because there's a conspiracy by the MCC to keep cudgels out of Lords. It's better because it's better'. Words are the same in their neutrality and quality, he suggests, whereas abstract values such as 'politics, justice, patriotism – they aren't even like coffee mugs. There's nothing real there separate from our perception of them'. Henry maintains Brodie's definitions are inevitably politically twisted. However, Annie's persistent support for Brodie leads Henry to explode resentfully, 'Do you fancy him or what?' – a suggestion which both immediately consider insultingly reductive. Nevertheless, Stoppard promptly shows Annie's head turned by an actor with whom she works on Brodie's play. Henry satirises the suggestion that Brodie's work may be institutionally marginalised because of its politics, and thereby suggests that institutional and traditional terms of success and style are inevitably, neutrally and 'objectively' correct. Annie responds by characterising Brodie's civil disobedience as a bid to impress her, and her championing of him as the response of her gratified vanity: Brodie is dismissed in comic slapstick terms.

Stoppard pre-emptively incorporates attacks on Henry's apparent omniscience: his first wife's complaint that his female characters function as mere 'feeds' to illuminate superior wit, and Annie's insistence 'You say things better so you sound right. But I'm right about things which you can't say'. However, in the terms and genre of the play, he who can 'say clever things' will always be right. Henry's 'moral system' is expressed elsewhere as part of a disingenuous expression of dependent affection for Annie: 'what you think is right is right. What you do is right. What you want is right'. This vindication of what might be most charitably described as enlightened self-interest – and most critically be described as the pseudo-objectivity of authoritarian vanity – represents another side of words, their powers of strategic concealment, elsewhere acknowledged by Henry: 'Sophistry in a phrase so neat you can't see the loose end that would unravel it. . . . You can do that with words, bless 'em'. Stoppard's play works to reassure its audience in their accordance with Henry that what they *think, do and want is inevitably* and *intrinsically* right, so that it is difficult to see the loose end which unravels the pseudo-neutrality of its elevation of language and traditional institutionally-approved style above other alternative values or claims of politics, justice or relevance; difficult, but not impossible.

# Ayckbourn and Bennett: blood and chocolate

At the start of the twenty-first century, Alan Ayckbourn and Alan Bennett have emerged (steadily rather than suddenly) as Britain's most popular comic dramatists. However, the comic reliability and familiarity which they represent is, in their best plays, offset by their problematisations of conventional comic resolution, in ways which can suggest more imaginative and formal energy than the rearguard actions against social change and ultimately deterministic conclusions offered by Gray, Frayn and Stoppard. Ayckbourn's apprenticeship in seaside theatre, in Scarborough, manifestly developed his instinct for comedy of social recognisability, and both dramatists are favourite choices of amateur theatre groups. But whilst their presentation of myopic and monomaniac social postures is often immediately gratifyingly familiar – as is the traditional and socially ritualised appeal of the packaging of a well-established selection box of chocolates – their deliberate refusal of traditional reconciliation can be as surprising as a familiar soft centre which suddenly divulges the flavour of blood.

Ayckbourn writes exclusively for the theatre, attributable to his fascination for 'how it presents time, and how its space can be changed, and the peculiarity which it possesses that, when you warp time on stage, you're warping time for an audience as well as for the actors – you're doing it positively, in front of people's eyes', with more immediacy than filmic and televisual convention permit.[13] His *forte* is the primarily comic development of the absurdists' play on discrepancy of perspective and unforeseeable consequence (tragicomic in the plays of Beckett, menacing in the plays of Pinter). Ayckbourn's first experience of theatre in the round (a form to which he is necessarily committed at Scarborough's Stephen Joseph Theatre) was a production of Sartre's *Huis Clos*, in which a trio of dead people find themselves in a thoughtfully upholstered version of hell; their punishment transpires to be the constant mockery of their misplaced idealism and their persistent laceration of each other's feelings. Characteristically, *Absurd Person Singular* (1972) exposes social and personal disintegration occurring despite – or because of – conventional rituals of social integration: in this instance, a three-year succession of Christmas parties between three couples who imperfectly identify themselves as 'friends'. In fact, the characters only ever interact incompletely and, as White observes, read into situations only that which fits their own manic point of interest, such as household cleanliness or handyman abilities: 'myopic endeavours as substitutes for real human concerns'[14] or communication. The farcical emphasis on the irrepressible recurrence of the social *faux pas* steadily darkens to include hilariously botched (and misconstrued) suicide attempts, English bewilderment in the face of emotional need, pseudo-utilitarian interpretation of human complexity in terms of material order (in Act III, one character remarks of his two wives 'they've given me a great deal of pleasure over the years but, by God, they've cost me a fortune in fixtures and fittings'), and the rise of a financial meritocracy: a new-made tycoon finally instructs the less fortunate characters in a grotesque dance of forfeits.

Ayckbourn's exploration of the consequences of banal preoccupations and minor disturbances is humorous, but ultimately neither minimal nor entirely hilarious; it shows how a slow trickle of ridiculous banality can build up to a merciless devastation. *Absent Friends* (1974) satirises the destructive inadequacy of social convention in the face of death; *Just Between Ourselves* (1978) and *Woman in Mind* (1985) depict the progress of uncomprehending destructiveness. Billington identifies the recurrent theme of 'what Terence Rattigan once called the real *vice Anglais*: fear of expressing emotion'.[15] *Just Between Ourselves* shows how 'emotional urgency on one side is met by a non-comprehending perplexity on the other'[16] until a female character is literally rendered catatonic. Both she and her husband are comically but sympathetically depicted as victims of pressures towards the conventional postures of suburban adulthood, which in fact only compound isolation, division and resentment. *Woman in Mind* enters the perspective of the emotionally neglected wife and implicates the audience in her point of view through idiosyncratic reception of language, sound and stage lighting. This renders Susan's subjective reactions theatrically objective for the audience, but not for the other characters. Her daydreams of an idealised fictional family slide out of control, generating a dawning suspicion that 'There's something wrong with me'. The 'place [she] wouldn't choose to live in, not even in [her] wildest nightmares' turns out to be the comic but degrading stage world in which she is trapped – rather as if a fully imaginative woman found herself caught in an Ayckbourn play, surrounded by a characteristic gallery of grisly, careless obsessives. Dislocated from her former certainty in roles of 'wife and mother', and denied any response by her husband to the 'really joyous part of us' that is sexuality, her fantasy world becomes enticingly preferable, yet increasingly uncontrollable: a personal defence mechanism which becomes potentially destructive to others, and addictive but unbalancing to the subject. Ayckbourn's dramatisation of Susan's awareness that she is losing control over the products of her own imagination is one of the most harrowing sequences and endings in comic drama, principally in its insistence that the audience share the perspective of a character isolated and illuminated by a flashing blue light, desperately speaking a restricted code which is becoming increasingly incomprehensible even to the speaker. The terrifying experience of loss of control over one's own physical and mental resources, which constitutes psychological breakdown and illness, is presented in such a way that neither character nor audience can distance themselves from it. Ayckbourn shows how failed attempts to accommodate oneself to the interlocking self-amputations of conventional social, marital and familial intercourse can lead an unusually searching imagination to calamitous isolation, and estrangement to oneself. *Woman in Mind* is the most innovative and haunting of Ayckbourn's developments of comedy.

*Henceforward* . . . (1987) represents Ayckbourn's (sub?)version of Gray's usual premise: an articulate but aloof man, attempting to dissociate himself through technology from the pressing challenges of social upheaval, particularly as represented by femininity and youth. Ayckbourn previously depicted the male reflex towards evasive technical specificity in the face of complex emotional demand: the bungling Dennis in *Just Between Ourselves*. Jerome in *Henceforward . . .* is more intelligent and technically proficient but develops this male preference to relate to technological objects which promise to be more logical and reliable than people.[17] Set in a dystopian future, the play charts Jerome's bid to adapt a robot child-minder to impersonate his wife, a farcical but also sad bid to reanimate memories for purposes of social acceptability. As his scheme collapses, Jerome becomes increasingly dismissive of humans for their unpredictability; however, a recording of his ex-wife's cry of the word 'Love' provides him with the missing ingredient for his 'perfect', individually-assembled technological aural composition. He rejects all human contact to immerse himself in sonic abstraction, like a comic version of Beckett's Krapp; his one poignant moment of self-awareness comes in a Krapp-like realisation that this may not be enough, in his isolation (which is, unknown to him, about to be broken by a vengeful neo-feminist). The increasingly linear British masculine self-definition through reference to technocratic consumer objects, in both professional and private life, has made *Henceforward . . .* a more satirically pertinent caricature of the national masculine siege mentality since its premiere.

Alan Bennett's *Forty Years On* (1968) depicts a public schoolboys' entertainment devised by the prospective headmaster, Franklin, for the last term of his incumbent superior. The setting – 'Albion House' – is thus microcosmic and pivotal, just as the date of the play's premiere suggests a watershed of generational order. Significantly the traditional school song emphasises the inevitability of decline, decrepitude and mortality as the binding inheritance of its young pupils. However, Franklin has interpolated satirical material into the school play without the Headmaster's knowledge or approval, and the boys are exuberantly, irrepressibly subversive of both teachers' directives. By contrast, a brief image of their obedience – in the wake of a eulogy to privileged, leisured England, the boys are revealed in uniform amongst rumbling guns, as *'the doomed youth of the 1914–18 War'* – suggests conformity in expendability, as did *Oh! What a Lovely War*. Franklin's play increasingly offends the Headmaster's comic prurience. If the school is in a rut, the Headmaster maintains that the advantage of ruts is that 'when one is in them one knows exactly where one is'; and 'I'm all in favour of free expression, provided it's kept rigidly under control'. Moreover, he suggests that Franklin's artistic irreverence is rebellion rather than revolution: 'once you're at the helm the impetus will pass. Authority is a leaden cope. You will be left behind, however daring and outspoken you are . . . just as I have been left behind'. Franklin, and the play, finally fall in with this emphasis on Britain's diminished fading into a 'sergeant's world': consumerist distractions, civic order and the desolate fade into death:

HEADMASTER: Once we had a romantic and old-fashioned conception of honour, of patriotism, chivalry and duty. But it was a duty which didn't have much to do with justice, with social justice anyway. And in default of that justice and in pursuit of it, that was how the great words came to be cancelled out. The crowd has found the door into the secret garden. Now they will tear up the flowers by the roots, strip the borders and strew them with paper and broken bottles. (Act II)

This conclusion is satirised, but gently and affectionately, and strikes a very different note to Orton's suggestions that the 'great words' exist to be redeployed wittily, and that the library books of a culture are more enjoyably and effectively subverted than burnt. Bull notes how the 1984–85 revival of *Forty Years On* re-presented the play as 'a comically sympathetic enactment of nostalgia'[18] ultimately in accordance with Thatcherite invocations of Imperial mythology: the Headmaster, rather than Franklin, became the sympathetic focus of the play.

The comic exuberance of Bennett's characters in *Forty Years On* and *Habeas Corpus* (1973) made these plays, like Ayckbourn's, popular and enjoyable choices for amateur actors. *Habeas Corpus* is a farce in which characters fumble towards an embrace of the new sexual licence they associate with the 'permissive society' ambivalently identified by the popular press of the late 1960s/early 1970s. Bennett enacts and celebrates the dependable familiarities of stock farcical types and situations as often as he satirises (rather than subverts) them. Nevertheless, *Habeas Corpus* contains a persistent awareness of mortality which is unusual in farce. This is immediately established by the protagonist doctor targeting an audience member in order to parody conventional hopes surrounding his own diagnoses: 'He wants me to tell him he's not going to die. You're not going to die. He is going to die. Not now, of course, but some time'. Conventional monogamous normality is mere avoidance and pretence, 'Sentence suspended'. The final emphasis is on a *carpe diem* philosophy, simultaneously poignant and subversive. With startling directness, the audience is asked to review their own erotic actions, fantasies and memories, to seek reconciliation with their own sexuality in order to furnish a riposte fit for death's door: the closing moment when they think, not of things done, but chances missed, 'The word not spoken, the cheek not kissed':

> Lust was it or love? Was it false or true?
> Who cares now?
> Dying you'll grieve for what you didn't do.
> The young are not the innocent, the old are not the wise,
> Unless you've proved it for yourselves,
> Morality is lies.
> So this is my prescription: grab any chance you get
> Because if you take it or you leave it,
> You end up with regret . . .
> Whatever right or wrong is
> He whose lust lasts, lasts longest.
> *(He dances alone in the spotlight until he can dance no more.)*
> CURTAIN                                                          (Act II)

Bennett admits the ostentatiously comic title of his next play, *Enjoy* (1980), may have been a mistake: '*Endure* would probably have been better, though hardly a crowd-puller'.[19] He also acknowledges the influence of Peter Gill's 1970s Royal Court season of D. H. Lawrence plays[20] on what begins as an apparent N. F. Simpson-style absurdist skewing of stereotypical domesticity, but turns into an acidic consignment to history of an older generation, more reminiscent of a savagely comic *After Haggerty*. Dad and Mam represent a *reductio ad absurdum* of conventional matrimony, as hellishly bound as a Beckett duo:

> DAD: And everything you've said, you've said before. Sixteen times. Every question you ask, you've asked before. Every remark you make, I've heard. I've heard it nineteen times over. Day after day after day.
> MAM: We're married.
> *(Long pause.)* (Act I)

However, this glumly British Chekhovian comedy is fractured when Dad hits Mam, to the alarm of the hitherto impassive Social Services observer, who turns out to be their disowned son in drag. Unusually, *Enjoy* shows Bennett purposefully extirpating potential sympathy for and amongst his characters: the daughter dismisses the claims of her parents ('I don't want love. I want consumer goods'; 'I hate my loved ones. Folks do these days') and embarks on a career in prostitution, towards which her parents are initially comically, determinedly oblivious, then Ortonianly encouraging. Dad's bids to involve himself in literally overseeing his daughter's new career is particularly challenging to any residual nostalgic affection the audience may harbour for the character. The bewildered older generation become subjected to increasingly distancing analysis, as when their son itemises their habitually hoarded 'relics of the recent past and a testimonial to the faith that one day the world will come back into its own'. He finally literally consigns them and their home to a museum. Dad protests against this, 'Given the proper environment, I'd be a different person', but Son repudiates this flatly: 'No'. Dad then pleads for Son to kill him, but is terrified when, instead, Son offers a kiss: 'I'd rather you killed me than kissed me ... Men don't kiss'. Son grimly replies 'I'm not a man', and apparently kills his father with an embrace. However, Dad recovers, to take his place in a hospital: Son reflects on this preferable arrangement, 'they wheel him out onto the balcony and we talk'. The characters are finally compartmentalised and isolated, with a mixture of desolation and relief. *Enjoy* pursues its unforgiving anatomy of the English nuclear family with an unusually discomforting insistence.

Bennett's most popular success and association was with his series of monologues for television, *Talking Heads*, in the late 1980s and 1990s. These generally showcase Bennett's writing at its most Chekhovian, with wryly comic emphases on lost opportunities, routine banality, frayed apology and empty lives. His work widely identified with this resigned impotence and reconciliation with unfulfilment, Bennett settles further into this niche with his stage play for the National Theatre, *The Madness of King George* (1991), later adapted to film. This play depicts the court of the supposedly mad English king George III, whose eccentricities under pressure are fastened upon by his opportunistic followers, who bid to 'cure' him, or adapt him to their ends. The King is a figure of pathos, 'fashioned' to the 'ordinary passion' as a matter of particularly English 'convenience'. However, the play never suggests his potential for radical action or reform which this might thwart, preferring to emphasise the crucifixion of a liberally sympathetic figure by political careerists, in a costume drama setting. Bennett's decision to play to his most obvious point of appeal produces a vacuous play, which might be radically contrasted with Barnes's dramatisations of royalty, authority, madness and sentiment.

## Peter Barnes *v*. the basilisk of authority

Barnes memorably defines his own project thus: 'I wanted to write a roller-coaster drama of hairpin bends; a drama of expertise and ecstasy balanced on a tight-rope between the comic and the tragic', in a language so exact and high-powered as to 'have a direct impact upon reality' by making the 'surreal real', going 'to the limit and then further'; 'a drama glorifying differences, condemning hierarchies, that would rouse the dead to fight'.[21]

He also remains committed to the comic form, even as he self-consciously tests it to breaking point. Barnes shows how humour can reconcile people to the essential injustice of authority, even whilst he depicts the true courage of the human spirit in terms of irreverent subversion, beleaguered yet compulsive resilience, and joyously anarchic performance. In the process he has forged a distinctive dramatic style which draws upon apparent disparates – Brechtian/Artaudian, literary/popular, historical/contemporary, sympathy/cruelty – in unique fusions which demonstrate exclusive dichotomies to be further means of repression and exclusion. He demands huger feats of imaginative visual staging than any dramatist so far considered, and both linguistic and physical athleticism in the performer. The frequent journalistic criticism of his work as 'excessive' misses the point: Barnes's theatre is deliberately unEnglish in its *purposefully* excessive assault upon conventional cultural and aesthetic norms, yet – unusually but bravely – strives to redefine a human, and English, spirit in truly Shakespearean (and Jonsonian) terms, of exuberant inclusiveness, irreverence, generosity and enquiry. However, despite critical acclaim for his major plays of the 1970s (*The Ruling Class, The Bewitched*) and 1980s (*Red Noses*), Barnes has been unfortunately uninfluential on mainstream British drama. It must be acknowledged that his lesser work can be reiterative of his major plays, and that, as Weeks comments, 'his theatrical style has not evolved significantly – that is to say, unexpectedly – since *The Bewitched* . . . the solidification of a "Barnesian" style combined with the infrequency of production has contributed to a certain stalemate in the critical debate',[22] but this is in itself culturally indicting.

*The Ruling Class* (1968) opens with a view of an England and empire 'Ruled not by superior force or skill/But by sheer presence', expressed in terms of privilege and ritual to 'beat back the turbulent sea of foreign anarchy'. Thus the thirteenth Earl of Gurney proposes a toast to the sway of his fellow aristocracy, before engaging in a ludicrous auto-erotic ritual which proves surprisingly fatal. His successor proves a particularly disquieting representative of a younger generation, embracing and exhorting transcendental benevolence and free love whilst identifying himself with deity incarnate. His elder family members are appalled less by his hippie-style blissful eccentricity than by his literally counter-cultural proclamations of destroying property and proclaiming equality: 'My God, he's not only *mad*, he's *Bolshie*!' Barnes's characteristically rich and large gallery of supporting roles includes the servant and would-be communist agent Tucker, whose gleefully incongrous performance of delight at being bequeathed a fortune fades to a reacceptance of servility out of ingrained habit – 'Family of servants. From a nation of servants. Very first thing an Englishman does, straight from his mother's womb, is touch his forelock. That's how they can tell the wrinkled little bastard's English'. After various farcical bids to incorporate Jack, the fourteenth earl, into familial conformity, his relatives call upon McKyle, a vengeful Scottish technological presbyter who proclaims himself 'High Voltage Messiah' and 'AC/DC God'.[23] McKyle's self-identification with the 'holy terror' which makes the world 'the bloody mess it's in' challenges Jack's pantheist optimism, and causes a monstrous bestial spirit to possess Jack, who from then begins to answer to his name. Jack's promising development into proper Englishness, which is monitored by a 'Master of Lunacy' named Truscott (an echo of Orton's *Loot* two years earlier), is indicated by his traditionally Conservative agitation that 'The barbarians are waiting outside with their chaos, anarchy, homosexuality and worse!'. He effects a transition from identification with God of Love to that of God of Judgement, through possession by the guilt-scourging-and-compounding spectre of lethal English sexual distortion, Jack *the Ripper*.

This transformation exemplifies how Barnes's characters do not 'develop' conventionally. They demand psychophysiological location rather than explication ('The meaning is in the lines, not between them'[24]) and require performers to throw themselves into the characters' *intensifications* (which are frequently monstrous, animalistic and sado-masochistic), with unEnglish Artaudian insistence. Significantly, this new murderous version of Jack is confidently accepted by the grotesque encrustation of authority which is The House of Lords, comprised (as Orton suggested in *Butler*) of corpses and madmen. His opportunistic consort maintains her association with his 'manly grace' up to the point that the lights fade just before her '*single scream of fear and agony*'. Barnes's transition from satirical comedy to excavation of psycho-political consequences proves truly subversive of conventional sympathy and ironic distance.

*The Bewitched* (RSC, 1974) both wildly satirises and politically develops Whiting's *The Devils* into a grotesque anatomy of authoritarianism which shows up Bennett's *George III* as an instance of comparatively flaccid self-limiting English liberalism. *The Bewitched* takes deformed King Carlos II's reign in seventeenth-century Spain as an example of the self-destructive idiocies of both authority and obedience, and contains Barnes's most extravagant and harrowing stage imagery. Like Jonson's characters, Barnes's royalty constantly tremble on the edge of reversion to the predatory animal and viciously mechanical, infecting others with their degradation. They become literally possessed by vengeful spirits from a clenched past, in a grotesque carnival which exteriorises the fears which make men lick the boots of death. Importantly, Carlos is shown as both victim and victimiser: bewildered, pathetic, childlike instrument of the socially controlling machinations around him, he can only express his pain and anger through wilful elaborations of pandeterministic repression. The extent of experience which the audience negotiate from Carlos's perspective commands sympathy, even as his actions challenge it: as when the jester Raphael, with whom Carlos has enjoyed his only moments of sympathetic laughter and playful abandon, is heard honking with laughter but tortured to death, whilst the hymn 'Praise My Soul the King of Heaven' accompanies Carlos's descent into uncontrollable sadistic monstrosity. *Gormenghast*, vaudeville, *The Crucible*, slapstick and *Psycho* occasionally bob to the surface in the surrounding panorama of gothic characters, capable of hideously comic fixation and even stranger poignancy in disappointment. Barnes's actors are required to physicalise the monstrous shadows of nightenglish which are thrown by the political rationales of dayenglish. Again, the characters do not complicate so much as intensify, in alternately comic and appalling manifestations of physical and linguistic expressionism.[25] After successive, frenetically sacrifical attempts to secure progeny, Carlos reaches a post-epileptic epiphany:

> Now I see Authority's a poor provider.
> No blessings come from't
> No man born should ha' 't, wield 't.
> Authority's the Basilisk, the crowned dragon . . .
> 'Twill make a desert o' this world
> Whilst there's still one man left t' gi' commands
> And another who'll obey 'em.

Carlos attempts to dismantle the surrounding mechanism of power with his fading strength, realising the universe 'contains no reasons, patterns, explanations. They're words to soothe a soul's terror o' our impotence. My reign's a glorious monument to futility'. But his revelations are unforgivable: he dies isolated by the guardians of the social mechanism, who appoint an even more freakish idiot in his place, ending the frenzied black circus of the play in the orderly desolation of power maintained. Despite its apparently distant historical and geographical setting, *The Bewitched* surpasses even *The Ruling Class* in its theatrical size, range and ambition, and its excoriation of the sexual psychology of power.

*Laughter!* (RC, 1978) considers the function and efficacy of humour as a response to injustice in Barnes's bleakest terms: the concluding image of comedians singing and dancing as they succumb to Auschwitz gas suggests the limitations of comedy's indefatigability (and may recall Griffiths's *Comedians*, and its question, if anything goes deeper than hate). *Red Noses* (RSC, 1985) seems to be Barnes's own antithetical suggestion of an optimistic response, though Barnes notes in introduction that the play was written in 1978, and the intervening years had given fewer grounds for optimism. One darkening social factor was the interim spread and diagnosis of the AIDS virus, which gave a new poignancy to the play's setting of the Black Death ('There's no pity, faith or love left when the breath, touch or look of a loved one's pestilential'). The jeopardisation of human erotic contact, and authority's bid to manipulate fears into profitably restrictive social cohesion, thus acquired a resonance beyond fourteenth-century France.[26] The hero of *Red Noses* is Flote, a bereaved convulsive monk who determines to move wild laughter in the face of death, if only by bad old jokes, in situations most demanding to charitable companionship: 'it's easy finding someone who'll share your life, but who'll share your death?'. His mission distinguishes him from the pre-Marxist guerrillas, the Black Ravens, who seek to infect the rich and so 'turn the world underside up'; Flote acknowledges, but does not share, their hatred. He also opposes the conventional piety proposing 'God wants to be feared not loved'; Flote asserts both man and God deserve more, to be 'moved by joy as well as tears'. He attracts and assembles a troupe of appallingly inept and handicapped performers, whose endeavours demonstrate the Christian spirit of hope over experience, and who are dubbed the 'Red Noses'. Their popular appeal with 'those who aren't lucky, rich or clever enough' draws the suspicion of Pope Clement, a lycanthropic figure of social control determined to 'remove the terrible necessity of free choice from mankind'. Alternately characterised as lubricant and irritant, Flote soldiers on despite death and treachery within his ranks, demonstrating the belief: 'Don't do Death's job for him. Don't start dying before you die, already half dead. Don't go easy . . . fight dirty'.

When the plague passes, the social order of the church is more threatened. Clement decrees: 'The remedy of disorder is terror; / Go break the spine of the world. / The plague was a time of tearful innocence, / Now a greater darkness falls / For we return to normal'. When the Black Ravens are executed alongside the radically puritan flagellants, Flote leads the Red Noses into more subversive and agitational depictions of power, inevitably dismissed as 'not funny', but more suited, not only to Clement's France, but to Thatcher's Britain, and extension of power at the expense of life: 'It isn't funny when they feed us lies, crush the light, sweep the stars from the heavens. Isn't funny now inequality's in, naming rich and poor, mine and thine. Isn't funny when power rules and men manifest all their deeds in oppression. Isn't funny till we throw out the old rubbish, and gold and silver rust. Then it'll be funny'. Executed as unforgivably subversive, the Noses stand and die together, but a coda suggests their continuance of mutual support, questioning ('God's up for judgement') and hope that they go to a less authoritarian place.

*Dreaming* (1999) recalls *Red Noses* in following the odyssey of an outlaw troupe, but returns the setting to England in the aftermath of the War of the Roses, and opens new areas of enquiry: principally, what might constitute 'home'? For Bess, it is slaughter, for the younger Davy it is money; for the war hero, Mallory, dislocated from the power he was trained to serve, it is a dream. Mallory's flash of uncontrolled class anger at the vauntings of an aristocrat seems less possible at Richard of Gloucester himself, a 'pragmatic' authoritarian (like Clement) who insists there is 'no such place' as home (and exhorts 'take what's real', whilst rehearsing his own historical mythologisation). Barnes upends Shakespearean history into Mallory's pilgrimage: part pantomime, part *Peer Gynt*. Mallory condemns the reverence of the oppressed; if God forbids their resistance, 'God is their oppressor', 'Nothing's sacred or powerful unless you make it so'. But though Mallory briefly blows a priest into the grave, the peasants (and corpses) resume their postures of obedient cowering in fright. A tavern conversation suggests 'Roots can pull a person down', age them from the attitude 'Why not?' to that of 'Why bother?'. A slapstick interlude between the typically Barnesian, compulsively performative supporting characters yields an idyllic moment of accepting personal difference. However, Mallory leaves for an antithetical encounter with a blackly comic family who sell 'trash goods on a darklin' plane, midwinter', and whose retentive profiteering strategies prove fatal. Mallory has rejected love for war and death, because 'love makes a man vulnerable, opening paths to the heart'. As if in response, his dream of his family is exposed as merely that: he finds his house derelict and his family dead. Nevertheless, his wartime cronies have followed him, to form a new social unit, one which – like the rehearsals and performances of the Red Noses (and all theatre groups) – respects alterity whilst allowing for serious interaction. Mallory has discovered that 'home is no longer a place', but his companions suggest, more existentially, that it might prove a journey, race or dance.

Gloucester argues that 'Choice is why men like me rule. We take the burden of choice from your shoulders'; but Mallory cannot accept this infantilising control as a worthwhile promise of home, or an England worth fighting for. Instead, he mistakes a distraught fugitive, Susan, for his dead wife Sarah; his determination to see her only 'by inward optics' is both humorous and poignant. Again, Barnes excels at mobilising audience affection for a supporting gallery of comic types: Bess, who (like various Barnesian messengers) insists she is not a minor character, 'I'm too full of piss and ginger, I've got size!'; Davy, who helps, to find out why he's helping, beyond profit; and another renegade priest, Kell, who acknowledges that all of them are only 'part of Mallory's dream' (and Barnes's), but discovers a joy and release in 'playing roles to the hilt', as when the group complicate the marriage of Mallory and Susan. She too has agreed to 'dream his dream' but hates her need of Mallory, who in a characteristically Barnesian stroke of playful theatricality, commands the others to 'speak out of character' as an exercise, as befits the play's emphasis on the promise and pain of self-authorisation. As the scene and social climate darken, Mallory is told that his dream killed Davy and will kill them all; Kell blames it for sucking in and costing him Bess, but nevertheless dies for his friends.

Cornered by the forces of repression, Susan claims Mallory gave them 'something else', beyond the bureaucratic fundamentalism of disciplined death; Mallory protests that he was never sure what it was, but Susan counters 'you believed it, that's enough'. Like a dramatist or director generating theatre, Mallory finds his self-doubts ('I failed') poised against others' discoveries:

'No, you let us glimpse another world'. The couple achieve an *Antony and Cleopatra*-like monumentalisation in isolated death on a Welsh mountain, which draws Gloucester's contemptuous dismissal ('This is what comes of dreaming') yet also refutes his terms of incorporation. *Dreaming* gives dramatic resolution to the recurrent Barnes problem of *faith*: the conviction that the invisible and imaginary may be significant, possible and attainable. It insists that when England appears unrecognisably unkind and irrevocably necrophilous, it may yet be imagined, and therefore made, anew; and that the microcosmic demonstration of this can effect the social macrocosm. It is profoundly comic.

# Notes

1. Leggatt, *English Stage Comedy 1490–1990* (1998), p. 1.
2. Ibid., p. 3.
3. Ibid., p. 9.
4. Leggatt, op. cit., p. 93.
5. Lacey, op. cit., p. 191.
6. Ibid., p. 11.
7. Stafford, in Demastes, op. cit., p. 178.
8. Bull, *Stage Right* (1994), p. 124.
9. Colleran, in *Simon Gray: A Casebook*, ed. Burkman, (1992), p. 132.
10. Op. cit., p. 170.
11. Frayn, Introduction to *Plays: One* (1985), p. xiii.
12. John Peter in *The Spectator*, quoted on the back of Leigh's *Abigail's Party/Goose-pimples* (1983).
13. Ayckbourn, in Watson's *Conversations with Ayckbourn* (1988), p. 70.
14. White, *Alan Ayckbourn* (Boston 1984), p. 53.
15. Billington, *Alan Ayckbourn* (1990), p. 111.
16. Ibid., p. 117.
17. Ayckbourn: 'Computers are, on the one hand, quite reassuringly constant', but 'dangerous because you don't in the end, get anything back from them. No conflict and no criticism'; in Watson, op. cit., p. 147.
18. Bull, op. cit., p. 12.
19. Bennett, Introduction to *Forty Years On and Other Plays* (1991), p. 19.
20. Ibid., p. 20.
21. Barnes, Introduction to *Plays: One* (1996), p. viii.
22. S. Weeks, 'Peter Barnes', in Demastes, op. cit., p. 45.
23. An idiosyncratic self-mythologisation through technology's terms of notional access, in ways which anticipate Heathcote Williams's 1970 play *AC/DC*.
24. Barnes, op. cit., p. 123.
25. My own imaginary structures for performing the role of Carlos in the 1987 Lurking Truth production of *The Bewitched* included the images of a three-legged tiger and a child increasingly, wilfully, smearing self and others with his own infectious excrement.

26. *Red Noses* was chosen for performance by the RSC in preference to a commission from David Rudkin: *John Piper in the House of Death*, a black city comedy freely based on Defoe's *A Journal of the Plague Year*. The similarity of the two themes was deemed to exclude Rudkin's play, though this (regrettably unpublished) work contains more contemporary references to the AIDS crisis. For details, see Rabey, *David Rudkin: Sacred Disobedience* (1997).

# Chapter 7

# Out of the 1970s and 1980s:
# Rage at a Blocked Age: Four Odysseys

The political polarisation of Britain intensified in the late 1970s and early 1980s. Entry into the EEC in 1973 did not change the suspicious insularity of national culture. In 1968, Conservative MP Enoch Powell had made apocalyptic and inflammatory speeches on immigration, fuelling an English racism (defining nationality in terms of blood and race) which would smoulder and flare throughout the period, finding neo-political form in the National Front Party, who threatened to make racial conflict more conspicuous than class conflict.

Issues of national identity and civil disobedience were also reinflamed in Ireland. In 1972, a clash between British troops and civil rights marchers led to the death of thirteen unarmed Catholics: an incident ('Bloody Sunday') which, like the introduction of internment without trial, did little to convince Catholics of the supposed 'impartiality' of the British military presence and government. This generated increased support for the IRA, who extended their campaign to bomb attacks on English military and civilian targets throughout the period (see Chapter 9 for further consideration of recent Irish events). In 1979, higher levels of industrial unrest were recorded than at any time since the 1926 General Strike, and the intensification of tension appeared to confirm the Marxist terms for a more potentially revolutionary situation. The various strikes were not co-ordinated as in 1926, but class as well as race divides, and Scottish and Welsh separatism, all contributed to a public mood and sense of confrontation.

But a refusal of confrontation can maintain injustice and cowardice. There were also victories for egalitarianism, independence and the dismantling of many repressive clichés of social relationships, particularly sexual and (inter)cultural. Youth culture was variously, conspicuously and even provocatively tribal, rather than unified: punks and skinheads opposed the legacy of the long-haired 'peace and love' previous generation with stylistic references to 'hate and war'. For the musically and sartorially brusquely inventive punks, these were usually ironically pacifistic; in the case of the frequently right-wing extremist skins, they often sought literal aggravation; mods and teds also reappeared alongside rockers and rude boys. Punk rock and new wave countered mainstream rock's tendencies to abstraction and indulgence, and made Britain a stylistic epicentre for music that could be calculatedly nihilistic (The Sex Pistols) but also politically aware and passionate (The Clash, The Jam), mischievously theatrical (Ian Dury, Siouxsie and the Banshees), even eloquent on the relationships between sexuality and power (Elvis Costello, Tom Robinson). In a period of increasing nuclear brinkmanship by the super-powers (particularly Ronald Reagan's hawkishly Republican American presidency), the Campaign for Nuclear Disarmament was renewed, and British youth counter-culture in the late 1970s and early 1980s was more politically literate than before (or since). The term 'anarchy' was identified not merely with destructive anathema, but with challenge, excitement, experimentation and release. The general mood of Britain seemed, ubiquitously, less disappointed; more combative.

However the social climate had proved all too volatile for avuncular James Callaghan, who had succeeded the increasingly furtive Wilson as Labour Prime Minister. In the 1979 'winter of discontent' widespread industrial action successfully challenged government incomes policies, and changed many elder voters' impressions of which political party was best equipped to deal with unions. Traditional working-class loyalty to the Labour Party was also disintegrating, with a third of trades unionists voting Conservative in the 1979 election which brought Margaret Thatcher to power. Her government had no more success with the economy than Callaghan's, and the 1981 urban riots in Toxteth, Brixton and Moss Side suggested further problems of civil unrest, particularly in areas where economic recession and marginalisation were felt with particular intensity by black youth. The subsequent Scarman Report indicated that insensitivity and provocation by police were also factors.

In opposition, the Labour Party swung to the left (more through the influence of Tony Benn than Michael Foot's leadership) and bravely responded to the escalation in global arms tension by establishing a unilateralist defence policy. However, Thatcher was primed for a second election success by the Falklands War. She established and manipulated a widespread mood of jingoism which suggested by analogy that other political problems could be solved by similar unquestioning belligerence. Indeed, any questioning of her policy – by church, university or media – drew her wrath, often expressed through legislative pressure restricting traditional rights. She vengefully dismantled previous liberalising reform, her philosophy centrally promoting and sanctioning acquisition (rather than nourishing production or creativity); this propagated a pseudo-American so-called 'enterprise and business culture' expressed through Thatcher's philistine assurance that there was 'no such thing as society',[1] only the ostensibly natural single-minded self-interest of individuals and families to which she appealed, through a highly idiosyncratic invocation of 'Victorian values' in support of monetarism. Generally supported by a partisan national press, during the 1984–85 Miners' Strike she forced the police into the position of specially empowered co-ordinated action against the so-called 'enemy within' (dissenting union and community representatives) in ways which decisively and manifestly identified the police with government and management interest, resulting in skirmishes startlingly close to blatant class war. As the 1980s went on, Britain was increasingly, disquietingly sewn up and ugly, with opposition to her beliefs systematically and cynically discredited. As Falklands casualties, miners, the growing numbers of poor and unemployed, nurses, teachers, lecturers and whole communities could testify, 'Thatcher achieved her victories at a terrible cost, usually borne by others'.[2]

This chapter considers the work of four dramatists who came to prominence in the 1970s; who initially shared some concerns and methods, but diverged in their responses to the new demands of social change in successive decades.

## Howard Brenton: perverse freedoms

Brenton was the first graduate from the fringe theatre movement of the late 1960s and early 1970s (with the Portable Theatre company) to the major subsidised national companies, via Richard Eyre's artistic directorship of the Nottingham Playhouse. Brenton's early *Plays for the Poor Theatre* (1969–75) are, theatrically and politically, deliberately rough, provocative, and inconclusive, inverting conventional moral and stylistic stabilities. *Revenge* (1969) opposes a criminal offering 'spectacle and danger' and a policeman who bypasses standard police procedure for 'diabolical' means to arrest him. Both characters, played by the same actor, discover that the criminal's dream of a society founded upon profitable wrongdoing comes true in a future 1980s ('The whole country on the fiddle, the gamble, the open snatch, the bit on the side'). The effect is to undermine the moral polarities of their mock-heroic opposition. *Christie in Love* (1969) shows two policemen bewildered by the savage humour of popular sexually vicious limericks, confounded by the insufficiently diabolical aspect of mass-murderer J. R. H. Christie, who is invoked and sacrificed to safeguard their own kitsch definitions of love: 'you have got to keep love in bounds. Else it gets criminal'.

A kindred neoromantic spirit to Brenton at this stage of his writing is David Halliwell, artistic director of Quipu, an experimental London theatre company who initiated lunchtime performances. His *Little Malcolm and His Struggles Against the Eunuchs* (1965) is an ambivalent view of the self-dramatising male ego, also foreshadowing Berkoff's impulses. The fascistic fantasies of Malcolm – who resembles an amalgam of Jimmy Porter, Just William, Billy Liar and Oswald Mosley – are brought into crucial conflict with the challenge posed by female sexuality. Halliwell's *K. D. Dufford* (1969) is more discomforting and anticipatory of Brenton's *Christie*: a grotesquely disturbing series of perspectives on a child murderer deconstructs the media melodramatisation and demonisation of the 'monstrous' offender by ostensibly 'normal' society members. Halliwell also directed Poliakoff's first major play in 1971.

*Magnificence* (RC, 1973) begins Brenton's series of epic plays, aimed 'not to convert but simply to agitate, to strike out against complacency, acceptance and decay',[3] investigating revolutionary impulses with unconventionally sympathetic violence. *Magnificence* opposes its guerrilla hero Jed ('Stripped down. Pure. Angry') against a 'peculiarly English kind of fascist' Tory MP (a decadent conciliator nicknamed Alice, contrasted to Jed's straightforward uncompromising virility). Jed provocatively relishes the opportunity to desecrate the idyllic 'English garden with its Englishman', and Alice's English mind:

> with the picture of English Life in its pink, rotten meat. In your head. And the nasty tubes to your eyes that drip Englishness over everything you see. The cool, glycerine humantity of your tears that smarms our ANGER. I am deeply in contempt of your FUCKING HUMANITY. The goo, the sticky mess of your English humanity that gums up our ears to your lies, our eyes to your crimes . . .

> (Sc. 8)

The speech chokes into inarticulacy, as if reflecting a loss of faith in the English language itself. The play dissolves in a conflagration which envelops both modern malcontent and target, and concludes with palpably unsatisfactory liberal moralising, in a self-consciously 'New Jacobean' style. Nevertheless this speech – virtual *raison d'être* of the play – is a prime example of Brenton's characteristic liberal-baiting.

*The Churchill Play* (1974, RSC, 1978 and 1988) is a dystopic vision of a 1984 fascist Britain. Brenton envisages a state of martial law, in which the army have gone from patrolling Ulster streets to breaking miners' strikes in Wales, and interning political dissenters. The prisoners of 'Camp Churchill' rehearse a play about the eponymous Prime Minister as a subterfuge for an escape bid. Brenton's play is sharpest in its transfixion of the liberal sensibility: a female hostage protests at the prisoners' sneering at domestic ideals: 'Not wrong to want that . . . the lawn, the plants, the children playing'; one prisoner completes the description: 'with a garden . . . and barbed wire round it t'stop dirty animals like me getting in?'; he insists 'I'm coming out the dark' to 'Redecorate your living room with you, nailed to the ceiling'. When she protests innocence, he maintains 'You put me in 'ere, lady', by her self-interested complicity in the country's political drift (Act IV). Her husband appears ready to defect to the prisoners' cause, but the ending suggests it is already too late. The internees' 'Churchill Play' also crucially redesignates the Second World War as a continuing and obscured class war, in which the people have to 'take' a beating but vow to 'give it back' to their own leaders one day.

*Sore Throats* (RSC, 1979) is an underrated excavation of the intersection of sex and money. When a policeman leaves his wife, she begins 'an experiment in living' with a female prospective lodger. Despite the social realist setting, the imagistic dialogue discovers and pursues a liberating nightenglish of cruel and transformative fantasies, as the two women deliberately embrace social abjection whilst the man remains in the world of fetish, of which the ultimate example is money.

*The Romans in Britain* (NT, 1980) demonstrates Brenton's desire to write a huge anti-imperialist epic deploying the full resources of the National Theatre. However, the attempted prosecution of the play's director (for 'procuring an act of gross indecency' by directing an emblematic scene of homosexual rape) overshadowed the play's argument, which parallels the contemporary English military presence in Northern Ireland with Roman and Saxon invasions of Britain. Legal and critical controversies have prevented further productions

of the play, and the National Theatre have not since attempted such culturally interrogatory drama. Rather than lurid, the play is cool and ironic, a
demythologising of national origins which recalls the ambition of *The Island
of the Mighty* whilst more prosaically emphasising political instrumentality
and casually lethal dismissiveness. An English agent undercover in Ireland
realises that the original Britons were, in fact, the Celts, and the invading
Romans the forebears of the English race, with disorientating repercussions
for national mythology: 'King Arthur! Celtic warlord. Who fought twelve
great battles against the Anglo-Saxons. That is, us. . . . If King Arthur walked
out of those trees, now – know what he'd look like to us? One more fucking
mick'. The increasingly hallucinatory dream-logic of the play brings the agent
to the recognition that he is 'the great wrong in Ireland', the latest representative of 'The weapons of Rome, invaders, Empire', but he achieves romantic
insight too late. A parallel Saxon episode shows young Celts and English
renouncing their allegiance to traditional hostilities, allying to construct their
own experiment in living, a pragmatic romanticism.

Dreams offer educative release in several Brenton plays. In *Thirteenth Night*
('the play for when the celebrations have to stop';[4] RSC, 1981) they permit
Beaty, a Labour Party supporter resigned to opposition, the prospect of pursuing socialist ideas in a future British government. The principal of several
Shakespearian parallels is with *Macbeth*: Beaty is interrogated and ultimately
defeated by three anarchists who proclaim the distance of governors from
governed. The play debates who shows more (ir)responsibility: Beaty, who
sanctions murder, 'embraces the butcher', to change his country's position in
the world; or the anarchists who suggest that Beaty could, like Bond's Cordelia,
become the sort of authoritarian he sought to destroy.

*The Genius* (RC, 1983) draws upon Brenton's experience of adapting Brecht's
*Galileo* for the National Theatre (1980) to inform a parallel drama for the
contemporary Cold War and sense of imminent nuclear danger. American
mathematician Leo is exiled to an English Midlands university, where he discovers a prodigious student, Gilly. She arrives independently at the same theories of nuclear physics that he has failed to prevent falling into the hands of
American weapons developers. This brings them to question the efficacy and
role of a university in a climate of prospective nuclear destruction, leak their
discoveries to the 'enemy' and finally join other female characters in a protest
at an arms base, similar to that actually begun at Greenham Common two
years earlier. Their final embrace is arguably sentimental, but their actions and
consequences demonstrate decisively that 'From private love / Can grow / Public
opposition',[5] and that the only country they claim is the people they love.

Brenton's writing thereafter moves away from epic theatre to satire and
fantasy. *Pravda* (in collaboration with David Hare, NT, 1985) satirises Fleet
Street corruption through the rise of Le Roux, a right-wing monster of
Jonsonian acquisitiveness, free of compunction and self-doubt. Like Caryl
Churchill's *Serious Money* (RC, 1987), *Pravda* runs the risk of celebrating the
frank energy of what it purports to expose critically (I recall leaving a 1987
workshop at the Royal Court's Theatre Upstairs to find coachloads of stock

market financiers, the ostensible satirical target of Churchill's play, arriving outside the main house to enjoy a reflection of their own predatory amorality, and ensuring the Court's highest box-office returns of that year). Wilcher argues that Le Roux is not an object of satirical exposure, as 'what he stands for makes little attempt to disguise itself'; rather, 'he is the satiric instrument by means of which the audience's gaze is directed back upon itself',[6] and upon its own mesmerised helplessness before questions of will and opposition which it will not answer. *Greenland* (1988) is a satirical view of a future Utopia, with an unsurprising lack of substantial dramatic conflict. *Berlin Bertie* (1992) returns to a contemporary domestic setting, representatives of dysfunctional London meeting refugees from East Berlin and attempting a personal 'reconstruction'. Brenton claimed the play to be an unusually complex, character-driven rebellion against the political clichés and stylistic orthodoxy of ' "British epic" theatre with its "issue plays"'.[7] The play's incorporation of poetic asides, in which the characters voice desire for change, in fact develops from *Sore Throats*, which similarly shows characters embracing disintegration to discover opportunities for redefinition. *Berlin Bertie* contains one soliloquy of heretical eroticism which is a promising departure for Brenton, but the play finally invokes the idyllic release of *Greenland*. Brenton's production diary acknowledges his difficulties in writing *Berlin Bertie*, along with his determination to avoid satire;[8] disappointingly, his subsequent output has restricted itself to occasional party-political satires written in collaboration with Tariq Ali (former civil rights activist, turned television producer).

Brenton has always preferred immediacy of effect to considerations of literary longevity, and he is the British dramatist whose work most directly reflects the political preoccupations of its immediate era. The confrontations of the late 1970s and early 1980s provided him with the era of his most fertile difficulty, in which he could testify to the wilful estrangement of the known, and suggest that hate might be the natural condition and expression of oppositional love.[9]

## David Hare: tragedies of manners

Like Brenton, Hare writes about perverse saints. But whilst Brenton's protagonists are usually consciously marginal and briefly incandescent, Hare prefers to examine middle-class characters whose ideals burn and smoulder over a longer period, tracing the consequences of English social history where 'corruption and disillusionment offer only the choice between madness and complicity'.[10] The repeated collision of individual idealism with public political cynicism impacts social entropy into a sense of personal deadlock or disintegration for these characters.

*Knuckle* (1974) is, however, a visible emergence from the Portable Theatre era in its opposition of criminal and power broker, and its epigraph which fantasises about the city coming alive like the Bride of Frankenstein, destructively but alluringly. *Knuckle* locates a pulp fiction narrative in Guildford and

Eastbourne to probe 'moral gumrot, internal decay', where 'There are no excuses left . . . Men are bad because they want to be'. The amoral gunrunner Curly strikes a posture of loud disgust with the hypocritical morality of his father, an investment banker. When investigating the disappearance of his sister Sarah, Curly's pseudo-American hard-boiled *film noir* narrative strikes a crucially different note to that of the traditional detective and stage thriller narratives (even familiar subversions like *An Inspector Calls*) by not enforcing an established morality or achieving a manifest resolution. Sarah has feigned her murder or suicide to extract guilt from her father. She has deliberately withdrawn from complicity in English society in this bid to 'Keep the wound fresh'; however, her father is more resigned than wounded. *Knuckle* offers blackly humorous reflections on the custom and cost of collusion. The absent Sarah is the first instance of a recurrent Hare character, a woman whose integrity leads her to isolation: Maggie in *Teeth'n'Smiles* (Royal Court, 1975) performs a similar limited rebellion, which is absorbed by the forces of social stasis and control around her, yet nevertheless she insists on the relative cleanliness of personal martyrdom.

Hare's erotic pity for 'people who have no apparent place in the much touted modern Western ethos, and who will never know any of its equally touted rewards'[11] is best dramatised in *Plenty* (NT, 1978). Hare describes *Plenty* as a play about 'the cost of spending your own adult life in dissent';[12] and as Dean observes, the protagonist's disillusionment becomes emblematic of her own postwar-and-Suez era but also of Hare's post-1968 generation.[13] The deterioration of national ideals is reflected in the experiences and dislocation of Susan, whose former sense of active possibility was engendered by her work as a resistance courier in wartime France. Dramatically, *Plenty* is laudably demonstrative: the play avoids conventional exposition, and the essence of characters is expressed through action rather than proclamation,[14] even as it shows Susan's nervous energy and appetite for existential danger floundering in the restitution and maintenance of the formalised distance and static artifice represented by English manners. The 'peace and plenty' supposedly offered by post-war Britain actually affords her only the conventionally deferential pursuit of self-interest through commercial consumerism (symbolised by her job in advertising). In her husband's world of professional English diplomacy, 'Behaviour is all' – but Hare's play distinguishes *behaviour* from *action*. Like manners, behaviour in this context involves the preservation of distance from consequential effects. Its prime example in the play is the political complicity surrounding the Suez Crisis, a demonstration of the cynical expediency in both right- and left-wing elements of the post-war national establishment. Susan's husband Brock and his professional superior acknowledge a contradiction between public roles and private convictions ('Mostly we do what we think people expect of us. Mostly it's wrong'), but only she assaults the tactful frivolities of a foreign office dinner party with her characteristically wilful indiscretion. Brock aptly protests that Susan claims 'to be protecting some personal ideal, always at a cost of almost infinite pain to everyone around', and that she takes this as a license to be 'selfish, brutal, unkind'. But his condition for progress – that Susan admit she has 'failed in the very, very heart of her life' – would involve capitulation to lobotomised passivity. She leaves him, and briefly contacts a wartime comrade: whilst she has to believe that there's 'Somebody else who's been living like me', he has opted for a conformist life very different to her compulsive self-isolation and loss of control. Their snatched evening of doped sex is ironically contrasted with a flashback to the optimistic certainty and companionship of her wartime experiences. The historical events of the play offer no consolation. It is the performance of Susan's experiences which offers the audience a (fictional) testimony for moral judgement, inviting them to discover a different history, a kindness of feeling which might reach out to (if not embrace) the heroine, in a way which received fact and national manners do not admit.

Hare's film *Wetherby* (1985) effectively continues his aim of 'contrasting the ordinariness of people's lives with the operatic passion of their unspoken feelings'.[15] A man commits suicide because he can find no admission that anyone else is living like him; that is, struggling to defend primary emotions and make contact in a politically Conservative decade which separates and isolates people. The premise of Hare's writing is manifestly edging further towards that of Chekhov, though Hare's characters are enabled to articulate his primary theme – the 'extraordinary intensity of people's personal despair'[16] – in relation to a specific political climate which confronts those who seek radical change with 'an overwhelming sense of their own powerlessness'.[17] *The Secret Rapture* (NT, 1988) presents the collision of two sisters: Isobel, who lives her life by a simple altruism and honesty; and Marion, a Conservative junior minister who sees her sister, and everyone else, as competition to be overcome. Marion and her husband intervene in Isobel's design firm with the effect of polarising Isobel and her business and domestic partner, Irwin. The play shows the difficulties of surviving with integrity in a climate of values devoted to the 'sanctification of greed'. Isobel's adherence to her anti-materialistic values becomes increasingly provocative to Irwin and her family. Irwin blames Isobel for his sense of emptiness without her love and moral approval, and shoots her for her continuing passive defiance. Marion decries the 'obscurity' of what people want, which she finds frightening ('people's passions seem so out of control'), and continues to blame Isobel, even in death, for persisting in a wilful perversity: 'Isobel, why don't you come home?'.

*The Secret Rapture* pushes Hare's drama further towards the presentational and melodramatic (the appearance of the revolver becoming increasingly predictable in his work). Donesky notes how Hare simplifies politics to a 'clash of sensibilities', based on 'the consoling fantasy of the weak and alienated, found in all sentimental literature, that flatters their sense of goodness and at the same time justifies their inability to act upon such goodness'.[18] Indeed it seems that Hare's admiration for Chekhov leads him to a corresponding deterministic fatalism, in which passionate emotion must always be disappointed or thwarted. This trope recurs in Hare's trilogy on British institutions for the National Theatre: *Racing Demon* (1990), *Murmuring Judges* (1991) and *The Absence of War* (1993). *Racing Demon* depicts the incursion of marketplace competition into the formerly comfortingly intuitive world of the Church of England. *Murmuring Judges* recalls John Galsworthy's 1910 play *Justice* in dramatic method, revealing to the audience the legal process and social sanctions they tacitly support, where the veneer of legal professionalism mitigates against decisive emotion: 'All this behaviour, the honours, the huge sums of money, the buildings, the absurd dressing up. . . . It's anaesthetic. It's to render you incapable of imagining life the other way round'. The 'justice system' permits only superficial ethical debate, and the police force has no inbuilt provision for appeal to 'alternative' viewpoints (this issue gained currency in the 1980s, in the wake of several proven miscarriages of justice in Britain with reference to Irish suspects, and the increasing deployment of police as instruments of government power). *The Absence of War* depicts an unsuccessful Labour Party campaign for a General Election (based on Hare's observations of the 1992 election which Neil Kinnock lost to John Major). Labour leader Jones is a formerly passionate and intuitive speaker who never 'comes across' in modern media terms. His election team struggle to sell him in generally palatable neo-conservative terms and thereby muffle his characteristically central invocation of 'justice'. This drive, to make the Party 'respectable' (rather than 'dangerous'), involves a suppression of dissent, such as one activist too briefly expresses: seeking to 'out-Tory the Tories' is a 'game they can't win', because '[They're] not bloody Tories'. Hare's opposition to Conservatism increasingly leads him to defending the ideals and instincts formerly supposed to be the heart of traditional institutions. He admits Thatcher 'made conservatives of us all. We all found ourselves defending institutions which previously we would have had no time for, because these institutions were better than barbarism'.[19]

Donesky suggests that Hare is trying to reanimate a national moral consensus to replace that lost in the Suez Crisis, but runs the risk of offering 'revenge fantasies of the alienated . . . in which the spiritually and emotionally unenlightened gang up on saints',[20] whose passive emotion and moral authority are unforgivably provocative and fatally isolated. Indeed, *The Secret Rapture* might mistake the political climate of the 80s in presuming that Thatcherism was so concerned to obtain a consensual moral authority as a means to exercise or maintain power. As Hare acknowledges (in *Via Dolorosa*, 1998), his subject is, increasingly, faith: which might be defined here as a conviction that the invisible and unarticulated might nonetheless be morally significant: a difficult premise for a predominantly social realist dramatist. Hare's drama accordingly becomes less demonstrative (than, say, *Plenty*), and more presentational of a rapidly manifest moral opposition. *Skylight* (NT, 1995) reanimates the Isobel–Irwin polarity of *The Secret Rapture* as that of Kyra, a schoolteacher, and her materially successful ex-lover, Edward, now estranged from her, his son and himself. *Skylight* vindicates Kyra's insistence on personal targets and values even (or particularly) amidst material deprivation, and the suggestion of Edward's son that 'For everything you repress there's a price to be paid'. Ironically, the polarisation is finally briefly dissolved by the ritualised adoption of formalised table manners. *Amy's View* (NT, 1997) counterpoints the eponymous heroine's boyfriend and mother, film critic Dominic and West End actress Esme respectively. Amy represents a spirit of charitable love (like Isobel and Kyra). She is (surprisingly) attracted to Dominic (who claims to represent 'the future'), and frightened of Esme ('the past'). Unsurprisingly, Dominic and Esme clash repeatedly: Dominic resents the 'snobbery' with which Esme regards populist culture. In the mid-1980s, Esme attempts ingratiation with television soap opera; but after Amy's death, she returns doggedly to the theatre; and a form of courteous reconciliation is achieved with Dominic. As will be apparent, characterisation is schematic and Hare is sentimentally vindicating an institution – West End theatre – that he once opposed.

It is logical that Hare's movement towards presentational moral statement and faith in individual testimony, 'speaking from the heart', should lead him to performing his own pre-written monologue. *Via Dolorosa* (1998) involves no overt theatricalisation; it presents Hare in his own person, the 'Writer' of his plays, presenting his experience of moral confusion and testifying to his concern regarding Israeli–Palestine relations, edging him closer to the status of social commentator akin to J. B. Priestley. His movement from political analysis to almost metaphysical statements of moral authority, his bid to enfuse British institutions with Lib–Lab social compassion, and his inclusive but generalised appeals to values as evangelical as they are imprecise, have made him the dramatist who embodies the appeal, postures and contradictions of Blair's twenty-first century New Labour most conspicuously. His next logical step might be a first-person move into the political arena, on this very platform.

# David Edgar: through a glass darkly

Edgar's proposition – 'The universe is complex and comprehensible. It is the writer's duty to comprehend it'[21] – reflects his attitude, as the most directly and precisely analytical political dramatist of his generation. In his manner of writing plays in order to address specific contemporary issues, he is closer to the intellectual enquiry of Shaw than to the instinctive revolt of Brenton; like Shaw, Edgar presents compulsive discussion as deliberate challenges to assumptions of audience members, involving surprising transfers of sympathy and emotion, evocations and then denials of theatrical expectations. His characters demonstrate an *active reflectiveness* – inviting that of the audience – concerning their beliefs, their historical context and their contribution to a creative evolution of political awareness. His drama might be termed that of a *dynamic dayenglish*: like Wesker and Hare, Edgar frequently depicts idealism embattled, even swamped by despair, but in order to present resurgence, reconnection and compulsive resistance by characters who appeal articulately, rationally and even philosophically to an ideal of enlightened human reason and holisticity, to be manifested in pragmatic action. Edgar characteristically deploys a working knowledge of Shakespearian form and echo, and a sense of

Biblical allusion, to subversive effects (the best dramatic use of such analogues). The active reflectiveness of his social realist drama aims to re-examine recent history, but in a way which restores the political dimensions to apparently private interests, and identifies the distortions of human experience by those who would therein identify a historical fatalism or determinism.

*O Fair Jerusalem* (1975) introduces a key theme in his writing: the way characters representing a broad spectrum of society – who would convention-ally be separated from each other as 'strangers' – can work together, drawing on subjective experiences to inform collective expression, in this case through rehearsal. *Ball Boys* (1976) is a fine (perhaps the best) example of the articu-late anarchy of 1970s Arts Lab theatre: a marginalised duo make a defiant intervention in a society of commodified hierarchy, here expressed in terms of the supposed determinism which divides people into the active/beautiful and the passive/ugly. This dramatisation of vengeful uprising against voyeur-istic culture echoes Williams's *AC/DC* and early Brenton, but is more deft in exposition.

*Destiny* (1976) manifested Edgar's own chosen form of strategic interven-tion. Whilst Griffiths claimed that television offered the dramatist the widest national audience, and John McGrath held fast to a Marxist model of political theatre which assumed the working-class to be the potentially progressive force for change, Edgar refuted the indiscriminacy of the first approach and the potentially generalised populism of the second to write an anti-fascist play specifically aimed at middle-class audiences such as frequented the RSC, who first staged it. *Destiny* shows Turner, an extreme-right-wing by-election candi-date, trying to unite his disparate potential constituents through appealing to their sense of dispossession, which his party analyses in racist terms. However, Turner discovers that he himself was dispossessed of his self-employed liveli-hood by the corporate business whose interests he now represents; this demon-strates how right-wing parties ultimately support the large commercial forces they claim to oppose in the name of libertarian individualism. Edgar presents the decisive insecurities of all characters in terms of readily identifiable emo-tion, demonstrating how 'People looking for an identity' can embrace a fascist dogma and consequently be imprisoned, transformed and made 'more animal' by it.[22] One particularly resonant scene shows two former friends imprisoned together after a picket line skirmish: one claims history to be the struggle of classes, the other the struggle of races; tellingly, it is the first who is concerned about the second, but reconciliation is impossible: 'it was like looking in a mirror . . . The bleeding wrong way round' (III.3). Edgar will return to fur-ther negative images of emotion inverted, averted and distorted, rather than reflected in sympathy or reciprocity.

*The Jail Diary of Albie Sachs* (RSC, 1978) dramatises the protagonist's unnatural deprivation of the possibilities for human interaction when he is held in solitary confinement in South Africa for his vocal opposition to apart-heid. Albie derives some initial support from the audible whistling of a fellow prisoner, who thus turns 'me into we'; thereafter, the audience share in (and thus to some extent, as witnesses, imaginatively mitigate) his experience

117

of self-conscious isolation. Edgar's presentation of sensory deprivation and heightened perception, and the mutual interrogation of rational motivation and physical contingency, recalls Beckett's theatrical tactics in *Waiting for Godot*. However, the void around Albie, which the audience is invited to enter and fill, is, crucially, political rather than metaphysical. Albie has to make his isolation, not a punishing disintegration, but a road to freedom, a willed fashioning of existentially political meaning which discovers sense in distance (from his captors and even the audience). Furthermore, Albie's imprisonment distances him from his former comrades, but one insists that it has generated an inspirational historical figure, a publicly-forged 'Albie Sachs', who takes precedence over the private individual in its demonstrative authenticity. Edgar emphasises the importantly human derivation of political consequence from the Beckettian experience of inconsequence.

*Mary Barnes* (1978) – like *Albie Sachs*, a free adaptation of a recent histor-ical biography – consciously attempts a corrective to Mercer's depictions of individual disintegration under social pressure and so-called psychiatric 'care',[23] by presenting a more positive view of progressive psychiatric practice in the context of 1960s counter-culture. Like many Hare heroines, Mary is driven to breakdown by internalisation of public irrationality (feeling 'the bomb's inside her'); Angie suffers from the more usual, but powerful, sense of contradiction between her parents' values and her boyfriend's. In reaching out to help Angie, Mary re-individualises herself. The consequences are not utopian – Angie ultimately opts for electric shock treatment which fogs her memory of Mary – but a member of the experimental psychiatric commune which accepts Mary deduces, 'We didn't build the future. But we are no longer, other, to ourselves'. Thus Edgar prompts a re-evaluation of a conventionally demonised period of social re-evaluation.

Edgar's skill at counterpointing action and narration reached its zenith in the 1980 collaboration with a particularly strong and searching ensemble of RSC actors, to generate the adaptation from Dickens, *The Life and Adven-tures of Nicholas Nickleby* (1980), in which 39 actors played 123 speaking roles over 8½ hours of performance. Layers of (self-)consciousness and collec-tive scrutiny were manifested by actors commenting in third person on their character's thoughts, feelings and actions, whilst non-speaking actors watched: techniques familiar from 1960s and 70s Theatre-in-Education and devised and fringe theatre, but never before trained so precisely on the reperception of a classic English non-dramatic text. The result was unusual, and unusually successful, for an English theatre which would prove further accommodated to self-restriction and neo-Chekhovian fatalism. *Nickleby* activated the cel-ebration of *largesse* associated with melodrama, but avoided melodrama's celebration of conventional sentiment in favour of proposing a romantic radicalism. Nicholas was frequently violent in his moral interventions into an ultimately unsupportable monetarist ethos, in ways which audiences found a justifiable and thrilling release of tension. Whereas Nicholas's arch-capitalist uncle Ralph refused to see his own reflection in his abandoned, crippled son, Smike, Nicholas maintained and urged sympathetic companionship to

Smike and comparable figures, even at the cost of breaking the novel's final picture-frame ending of retreat into domestic bliss: Edgar's Nicholas steps out to hold out an abandoned child to the audience, re-emphasising the persistence of cruelty and despair and the need to take action against them. As Painter comments, this ending warns the audience against 'the Thatcherite emphasis on families and individuals and suggests that there is (and must be) such a thing as "society" and collective values'.[24] Edgar saw the production's huge success as partly attributable to the historical moment, 'a year into Thatcher, our audiences wanted to be assured that there was more to life than money' and join in assertion that 'material self-interest is neither the first nor the most effective motor of human behaviour'.[25] *Nickleby* activated instead an appeal to less frequently cited national values of fair play and inclusiveness. The international success of *Nickleby* prompted the RSC and other theatres to attempt other forms of large-scale 'theatre events' (most conspicuously, *Les Misérables*) which always lacked *Nickleby*'s radicalism and detailed ensemble teamwork. Along with their productions of Barker's *The Castle* (1985) and *The Bite of the Night* (1988), *Nickleby* represented the highest achievement of the 1980s for the RSC – and for British theatre.

*Maydays* (RSC, 1983) addressed the difficult task of following *Nickleby*, involving playwright and company in an almost Dickensian narrative of interweaving chronological and international settings since the mid-1940s, tracing the refracting hopes and supposed failures of – and disillusioned defections from – the political Left. This was a provocative project for a major subsidised production, and manifested Edgar's determination to use all the practical resources at the RSC's disposal (as had Brenton's *Romans* at the NT) on a consciously 'British epic' production. *Maydays* follows the fortunes of four central characters: Crowther and Glass, left-wingers who defect to the right; Lermontov and Amanda, who hold faith with 'something in the nature of our species which resents, rejects and ultimately will resist a world which is demonstrably . . . wrong and mad and unjust and unfair'. The significantly-named Glass can find in himself no recognition of Amanda and her convictions, when he finally confronts her at Greenham Common, in presentation of confrontation between feminism and the formerly traditional left (to be contrasted to Brenton's more romantic *The Genius* and Barker's more metaphorical and sexually excavatory *The Castle*). Despite strong scenes such as Lermontov's verbal mutiny at a dinner-party, inciting those around him (including the audience) to reconsider their relationship with those who 'resist', *Maydays* tends towards characterisation through the verbally presentational, suggesting the constraints of social realism. This effect is at its most schematic in Edgar's *That Summer* (1987), about an academic couple who host the children of Welsh miners – 'two perfect strangers' – during the 1984–85 strike. Fortunately, *Entertaining Strangers* (a community play for Dorchester in 1985, revised for the NT in 1987) is more dramaturgically fluid and evocative in its address to similar themes. The conflict between the rigorous pieties of the Rev. Moule and the unapologetic practicality of brewer Sarah is enveloped by the cholera outbreak of 1854 and its repercussions throughout the community (with resonances of the 1980s 'plague' hysteria surrounding AIDS). Crisis calls forth unexpected reserves of effort and teamwork capable of negating reductive prescriptions of human potential, teaching Moule the essentially hopeful possibility of Hebrews 13: 'Be not forgetful to entertain strangers: for thereby some have entertained angels unawares'. As Edgar's drama testifies elsewhere, the only 'Jerusalem' worthy of the name is shown to be an ideal discovered and developed by the co-operative interaction of the many, not the discriminatory, repressive impositions of a divisive authoritarian self-styled 'elect'. However, the play works through mysterious revelation and cumulative allusion to suggest resurgence and renewal, rather than restrict itself to the verbal presentations of the self-consciously theoretically articulate (but sterile).

The problems of dramatising ideas, and people who deal in ideas, arguably for an upper-middle class audience who *correspondingly* deal in ideas, recur through Edgar's drama, in which characters often principally define themselves through self-conscious verbal performance, and passion is matter for rational expression. *The Shape of the Table* (NT, 1990) examines the strategic verbal fencing and ideological distinctions involved in the transference of power in Eastern Europe. But practical manifestations of issues and consequences of actions are kept at bay by the committee room setting. This is partly Edgar's point: mirrors are banished from the room, lest they show people transforming into what they would replace. But the dramatic reflection of procedure runs the risk of being *theatrically* restrictive, even as it ostensibly identifies the restrictiveness of abstraction, distinction and ideological theory. Edgar's chosen form of social realism admits no imaginary space or theatrical 'world elsewhere', which may even suggest a pessimistic fatalism about processes of transfer of power, principally their possible susceptibility to accompanying (male) self-delusion. *Pentecost* (RSC, 1994) depicts two art historians – Oliver (British) and Leo (American) – who are taken hostage during the renovation of a painting in a south-eastern European country, a former 'Illyria' whose upheavals contain much to confound British insularity and American careerism. A central anecdote of erased history ('we must not eat our names. Otherwise, like Trostky, we end up with our jailor's') reverberates through events, whether focusing on the function of classical art ('all the time they are reminding you of dreadful precedent, how everything goes wrong before') or generated by the incursion of guerrillas who take the historians hostage and change clothes with them. The outer reflection of inward loyalty is problematised by this transformation, to the extent that Oliver is shot dead by 'rescuing' forces,[26] suggesting the importance of the choice or imposition of national costume. Leo's neo-colonial air of professional commodification is, like Oliver's, crucially complicated by his experiences. The events also pose the question as to what role is possible for foreigners in relation to such national upheavals: is one possible, beyond those of passive spectator, or crossfire victim? *Pentecost* apparently criticises but ultimately reinscribes as inevitable the tragically paralytic posture of the Western liberal humanist: the social realist form, predicated upon presentation of the *symptomatic* rather than the *transformational*, demands as much, and edges Edgar back to the melancholy conclusions of Wesker.

*Albert Speer* (NT, 2000) investigates the eponymous character's bid to avoid the permanent weight of complicity in Nazi crimes. The final re-entrance of Hitler recalls the ending of *Destiny*, but casts Speer's relationship with his leader in Faustian shape, with Hitler finally claiming Speer's soul. The theme of the play recalls Taylor's *Good* (1980), but the flashbacks from Speer's viewpoint resemble the narrative method of Shaffer's *Amadeus*: the disingenuous murderer seeks absolution by appeal to contemporary imaginative mediocrity. Speer the character claims the possibility of change, as the performer of Speer changes himself to impersonate Speer at different ages, raising the question as to whether the audience are witnessing (analogous) transformation or (superficial) impersonation. Characters ask whether Speer sacrificed his soul to save his life, or blotted out memories of concentration camp conditions because his sanity could not accommodate them, in a state ethos ostensibly founded on the will of the single individual but actually insisting on the Procrustean deformation of the moral imagination: 'Everyone was told: you need only be concerned with your domain'. The parallels with Thatcherism, and more immediate bids for political rehabilitation, are apparent. Hitler finally denies Speer's claim to be a character in a liberal tragedy and insists on his ultimate instrumentality: 'You did what I required of you. You realised my vision. And if you are in a hall of faces then the face is mine'. Thus the play attempts to subvert its own form, though its reflective method again displaces action and consequence from its centre or indictment from its conclusion, and thus mitigates its own power (the ending compares poorly with *Destiny*'s forceful conclusion). Peter Flannery's *Singer* (1989, considered in Chapter 10) remains the most powerful recent dramatic address to, and deduction from, German Nazism and analogies for British national self-perception.

Edgar's *The Prisoner's Dilemma* (RSC, 2001) returns to the theme of Eastern European negotiations, and avoids some of the sterility and fatalism implicit in *Table* and *Pentecost*. The heroine, a conflict resolution expert, reminds negotiators and the audience that, however much working for the refinement of a treaty may seem an arid hair-splitting exercise in abstraction, the alternative to agreement 'is yet more sons and husbands dying pointlessly, and yet more wives and daughters too'. The dominant superpower rhetoric, of 'each trying to persuade the other that they might be insane enough to stick to their position even if it ends with blowing up the world', is contrasted to the surprisingly hopeful possibility: 'Somone did the opposite of what you might expect of them. Did something better than you might expect of them. Someone faced with a hard choice who made a brave one'. Like *Entertaining Strangers, The Prisoner's Dilemma* suggests the revolutionary power of the unpredictable and unexpected, and concludes with a witty reference to Augusto Boal's forum theatre, briefly casting the audience in the role of participants in a less passive and logocentric theatrical situation: an indication and reminder, at least, that what we value is determined by how much we will risk for it, and that revolution involves running the same risks as the people at its sharpest end.

# Stephen Poliakoff: beneath a rubber moon

Poliakoff is superficially a social realist like Edgar; frequently concerned with disappointment's consequences like Hare; ambivalently repulsed by, and drawn to, the barely glimpsable subterranean agendas of dark freedoms in disintegrating cities which block and parody intimacy, like Brenton. But dwelling on his similarities with these dramatists may obscure his distinctive originalities. He presents unsettling fables of the uneasy relationships between impulses of order and compulsions to chaos, repeatedly emphasising the sudden reversibility of power through characterisation which defies predictability, shot through with a poetic sensitivity to imagery of decaying artifice ('Look there is a little rubber moon here, comes away in your hand', *Sienna Red*, II.1). His drama presents a political archaeology of the ever-present parallel world that is nocturnal English cityscape. Bull aptly notes 'the pervading sense of isolation in supposedly crowded locations that gives his plays their peculiar clarity. . . . The absence of characters who must be understood to be present in night spots such as discos and casinos intensifies the way in which Poliakoff's characters see themselves as part of, yet separate from, the contemporary world'.[27] Demastes suggests he activates the atmosphere of Pinteresque absurdism (or perhaps disconnection?) in plays which 'invite social commentary' whilst 'inviting us to move beyond the linearity of plausible narrative to probe other regions of human activity' which influence material reality.[28] Poliakoff himself has remarked how the landscapes of his plays 'are never passive or literal as they would be on film, but part of the characters' internal world too, their state of mind . . . the settings in the plays are always attempting to be both specific and general at the same time'; the everyday is experienced and mediated with an intensity that entwines 'character and outer world so that they are practically inseparable'.[29] The situations (rather than the language) of dayenglish constantly threaten to warp and slide into exposing a subtext of actions from a predatory nightenglish.

*Strawberry Fields* (NT, 1977) is a fine early example of Poliakoff's neon-carved political impressionism, which had already generated several plays about 'a personal reaction to violence and the ugly mood of the mid-seventies, about people growing inward and private and lonely, after the noise and frivolity of the sixties'.[30] Nick hitches a lift with Kevin and Charlotte, who transpire to be members of an extreme right-wing splinter group. When they shoot a policeman, Nick's sense of plausibility is overturned. Like an audience member or theatre critic, he seeks to dismiss the odd couple as eccentric cranks (notwithstanding their occasionally surprisingly vivid pronunciations), yet finds himself inescapably drawn into their journey; his dismissive moral, imaginative and sexual superiority is, itself, purposefully dismissed when Charlotte turns on and shoots him. But the basic plot, with its thriller twist, is less notable than the texture and atmosphere of the play, in which the certainties of the English landscape seem to melt and distort as if to generate some monstrous progeny from Kevin's tacky sci-fi rhapsodies, a political rough beast slouching through bubbling motorway tar towards English hillside battlefields and henges to be born. Kevin testifies to the sense of being a human 'soft machine', overloaded recipient of cheap(ening) media imagery, like the characters of Williams's *AC/DC*; Charlotte seeks to flush the cistern on supposed leftist disruption and reanimate a mythical tidier world; Nick imagines the apparent familiarity of the modern English hamburger bar mutating into something which serves grenades.

Kevin's memory of a small boy onstage at Glastonbury Festival, a smiling embodiment of the future, informs *The Summer Party* (1980). A similar child, Mr David, is headlining a festival; he is scheduled to climax its ostensible, vaguely counter-cultural celebration by the apparently magical telekinetic breaking of assorted consumer objects. However, his act is fraudulent, and his true child's petulance is a partial reflection of the childish egocentricity of his surrounding elders. The police representative, Kramer, takes the stage to prevent a riot when David's act falters; Kramer orchestrates the crowd's attention towards an enjoyment of the sunrise. The audience also may well have found Kramer a more sympathetic, realistic and naturally authoritative character than the gratification merchants who surround him. Kramer then suddenly reveals his own shocking enjoyment of his power to manipulate and intimidate: 'I have this power . . . to make people feel less. . . . They want a few certainties again, to feel safe. . . . To be told things won't change anymore, to be able to believe there's a God in heaven again. To be protected. . . . It doesn't have to be real. It's the way its's done. . . . The right tone of voice. They all want to be reassured now'. This throws into relief the way that the theatre audience may have correspondingly been taken in and willed Kramer into his ultimate authority. *The Summer Party* thus provides a brilliant image of how authoritarianism garners appeal through repressive tolerance of, and political intervention in, populist 'glittering occasions' (which people buy into and attend 'to prove themselves alive'), both at the dawn of the 1980s (Kramer's appeal to order is an appealing mediation of contemporary Conservative promise) and subsequently.

*Favourite Nights* (1981) explores seductive artificiality as offered by a language school for foreign businessmen that doubles as an escort agency by night, and the casinos, monitored by closed circuit cameras, which provide arenas for night-time entertainment. Catherine, who works in both milieux, explains to her sister Sarah how the mannered calm of casinos barely masks the 'sweaty smell of anxiety' which neurologically wires the clients together; 'the more uncertain things become, the more allergic people are to failure'. Here money is more alluring and shocking 'than people making love or knifing each other', and Catherine herself is addicted to 'night adrenalin', gambling to 'skim across depression'. Sarah observes how the depression is born of disappointment; Catherine worked hard to earn academic qualifications, but finds herself unable to use them to 'contribute anything' in a country dominated by inherited wealth and financial speculation: 'everything is luck now'. So Sarah rolls dice to win money from Catherine, to stop her losing it and 'to give me something to start off with, in this big city'. The play is not reducible to its plot, nor satirical, nor overtly moralising. Rather it imagistically generates an enclosed world with wider resonances for early 1980s (and 1990s) Britain: alluring but costly erotic composure, the fetish of sleek surfaces, the promise of speculation and the damage of displacement. Moreover, it never unfolds predictably; each level broached illuminates the characters differently.

The theme of displacement is pursued more overtly in *Breaking the Silence* (RSC, 1984) and *Coming in to Land* (NT, 1986). *Silence* is set in the Russian Revolution: an inventor faces upheaval from his research into film technology when arbitrarily appointed telephone examiner of the Northern Railway; his wife, son and servant also attempt to adjust to the transitions involved. On appearance, *Silence* was more widely acclaimed than Poliakoff's previous drama, perhaps because of its resemblances to Chekhov's *The Cherry Orchard* (the classical normative template for dramatic excellence for most British reviewers in the 1980s and 1990s). *Silence* also foregrounds the roles of the wife and the female servant for more development than is usual in Chekhovian drama; their influence is pivotal to the drama. Nevertheless, Poliakoff's distinctive talent is in identifying the *contemporary* dissolution of stable reference points – 'eviction from certainty' as Neville in *Coming in to Land* puts it – whereas *Silence* may flatter an audience's sense of historical hindsight and superior awareness. In the later play, Neville is caught between the machinations of a Polish refugee and those of the Immigration Services considering her bid for asylum, and finds his own previously unassailable senses of national identity and personal 'necessity' interrogated.

Like *Favourite Nights*, *Sienna Red* (1992) interrogates the tensions and forces beneath smooth English surfaces, the unpredictable *frissons* of sexual chemistry which make for an intriguing tension with their uncertain containment by an enclosed world: this time of interior decoration. The refined wife of a store manager has an affair with a bisexual designer who is distinguished and imaginatively empowered by being 'unafraid', not least in his suggestion that people will find 'the mysterious and inexplicable' more enjoyably stimulating than the ordered familiar.[31] His lack of fear of exposure gives him a freedom from control. Against all her ingrained instincts and beliefs, she responds to his demonstration of the beauty of a present moment, jettisons her conventional life and resolves to dog him, in an infatuation which is not reciprocated and may even prove mutually destructive. This adumbrates the premise of *Sweet Panic* (1996), in which a child psychiatrist finds herself stalked by the mother of one of her clients. The intensifying duel of the all-too-human authority figure and the vengeful supplicant who demands release from contradiction, absolution and confirmation echoes David Mamet's *Oleanna* (1993). Having initially attempted to dispel her stalker's regressive nostalgia for a supposedly more secure past, the psychiatrist is brought to acknowledgement of panic as the natural and intelligent response to the demands of contemporary life.

A sub-series of Poliakoff plays considers the problematic national status of the researcher/inventor in a culture of myopic inertia, consumerist dependency and supposed 'information' which barely conceals a politically significant amnesia. *Playing with Trains* (RSC, 1989) focuses on the family tensions of one such inventor. *Blinded by the Sun* (NT, 1996) traces the effects of commercial management paradigms invading and determining the field of academic research. When the market-driven social ethos is centrally and commercially *reductive*, genuinely exploratory work, procedure and employees (such as the 'long-distance creator') are redesignated 'outmoded': 'mystery is expensive, infuriating, and uneconomic'. *Remember This* (NT, 1999) centres on the discovery that videotapes of the last twenty years are gradually but irrevocably deteriorating, a commercial ploy to keep consumers upgrading their possessions. But the discoverer, Rick, finds out inadvertently and ambivalently; he experiences a furtive 'freedom' at the loss of the image of his father (and memory of his values), which might leave him free to 'exploit the future'. He is briefly but significantly troubled when his son extends the principle of built-in obsolescence to his own academic work. Rick concludes that 'muddle and contradiction' (rather than commercially viable market prediction) may be all he can offer. In these plays, the social climate determining science also appraises art, and the analogy with the theatre can be readily drawn. However, they progress through jumps in time, and are not so firmly located in a definite but surprising location as is Poliakoff's best work; the resultant tendency towards verbal abstraction reflects the characters' predicament but makes the plays theatrically rarefied.

His best excavation of this theme – the irrevocable loss resulting from the philistine functionalism of the commercial emphasis on immediacy – is the television drama *Shooting the Past* (BBC, 1998), which has the characteristically definite, yet labyrinthine and surprising, setting of a photographic archive threatened with dispersal. Indeed, Poliakoff's best recent work has been that as a writer–director of television films and series. His foregrounding of scrutinised detail and sense of the lingering power of image makes for unusually precise television drama, which slowly and engagingly unfolds into unforeseen consequences and deeper implications. *The Tribe* (BBC, 1998) depicts the charisma and social irritation generated by a self-consciously artificial and strategically contradictory community: an *asocial* group in Eugenio Barba's sense[32] (like an effectively radical theatre company), manifesting an alternative to the conventional but tawdry 'sociality' of the dominant London rapaciousness. *Perfect Strangers* (BBC, 2001) unravels the mysterious stories concealed within the history and present of a large family, and discovers surprising estrangements and compulsions between relatives who might formerly have considered each other familiar and unremarkable. The protagonist reflects on how the surprising natures of his relatives make his own nature, by implication, similarly unknown (and perhaps unknowable) to himself. *Shooting the Past, The Tribe* and *Perfect Strangers* are strikingly well written, directed and photographed dramas which suggest that Poliakoff has (like Barker in the theatre) emerged as the best director of his own television writing, and perhaps the best writer–director currently operating in this medium; and that television and film, rather than theatre, may constitute his principal avenue of future expression.

Poliakoff's dramatic approaches to his identifiably recurrent themes are variably successful, but this is true of all dramatists. His characteristic foregrounding of a character who turns out to be unreliable or unforeseeably complex often makes for an initially disorientating dramatic experience, in which the narrative direction is obscure; however, this permits late-stage reversals and surprises which accrue when foregoing events and characters are reilluminated from an unsettling new angle, and makes him one of the more creatively unpredictable dramatic storytellers of his era. His vivid responsiveness to the anxiety of detail (occasionally recalling that of a feverish or enervated hypersensitivity) and to the compulsions which resound beneath the rationalising *maquillage* of social surface, along with his interrogation of the spiritual consequences of a culture of commodification and disposability, distinguish him as an unacknowledged forerunner to works by Clare McIntyre, Joe Penhall, David Greig, Patrick Marber and Mark Ravenhill in the 1990s. Thus, his work may have transpired to be more conspicuously influential on immediately subsequent dramatists than that of Brenton, Hare or Edgar.

# Notes

1. Quoted in Morgan, op. cit., p. 438.
2. Clarke, op. cit., p. 400.
3. O'Connor, in Demastes, op. cit., p. 100.
4. Brenton, Preface to *Plays: Two* (1996), p. xi.
5. Brenton, 'Sonnets of Love and Opposition', no. 50; published with *Sore Throats* (1979), p. 43.
6. R. Wilcher, '*Pravda*: A Morality Play for the 1980s', *Modern Drama* 33, 1 (1990), pp. 42–56 (54–5).
7. Brenton, 'Poetic Passport to a New Era', *Guardian*, 7 April 1992.
8. Brenton, *Hot Irons* (1995), pp. 245ff.
9. Terms drawn from 'Sonnets of Love and Opposition', no. 74.
10. Dean, *David Hare* (Boston, 1990), p. 9.
11. Hare, *Writing Left-Handed*, p. xiv.
12. Ibid., p. 79.
13. Dean, op. cit., p. 57.
14. Hare observes this in a 1993 interview quoted by Donesky, op. cit., p. 63.
15. Hare, op. cit., p. 130.
16. Ibid., p. 33.
17. Ibid., p. 11.
18. Donesky, op. cit., p. 114.
19. Hare, *Asking Around* (1993), p. 94.
20. Donesky, op. cit., p. 155.
21. Edgar, quoted in Painter, *Edgar the Playwright* (1996), p. 52.
22. Ian McDiarmid, who played Turner, quoted in Painter, op. cit., p. 44.
23. See Rabey, *British and Irish Political Drama in the Twentieth Century* (1986), 180ff.
24. Painter, op. cit., p. 73.

25. Edgar, quoted in ibid., p. 74.

26. The shocking execution of the crusty but sympathetic representative of audience national identification recalls that in Christopher Hampton's *Savages* (1973).

27. J. Bull, 'Stephen Poliakoff', in *International Dictionary of Theatre – 2: Playwrights*, ed. M. Hawkins-Dady (1994), pp. 767–8.

28. Demastes, op. cit., p. 332.

29. Poliakoff, Introduction to *Plays: One* (1989), pp. x, xii.

30. Ibid., p. xi.

31. The closeted homosexual central character of Poliakoff's *Talk of the City* (RSC, 1998) moves more gradually to being decisively 'unafraid'.

32. See Barba, *Beyond the Floating Islands* (New York, 1986), pp. 210–12.

## Chapter 8

# Melting the Boundaries:
# New Expressionism from the 1970s
# to the 1990s

This chapter focuses on selected dramatic works which chronologically parallel but stylistically diverge from the predominantly social realist work considered in the last chapter. My title partly invokes the theatrical precedent of early twentieth century German Expressionism, which sought to valorise dramatic performance as a uniquely immediate form of explosive sensory experience for performers and audiences alike. Edschmid's 1917 proclamation remains a useful foundation: 'The Expressionist does not see, he beholds. He does not describe, he experiences. He does not reproduce, he creates. He does not accept, he seeks'.[1] In terms of our central polarity, Expressionism centrally and insistently explores nightenglish as the principal means to experience a properly radical critical perspective upon dayenglish; Expressionism is 'concerned with the expression of the inner self, the subconscious and its tension with surface reality'.[2] According to Eugene O'Neill, Expressionism offers an 'intensity of vision which tries to catch the throb of life, necessarily doing violence to external facts to lay bare internal facts'.[3] Expressionism refuses the constraints of mimetic realism in order to present a more extravagant image of the subjective world: the tension between the supposedly 'objective' (and perhaps literally objectifying) social pressures it undergoes, and the explosive defiance it can express. This involves a consciously heightened form of presentation which is unapologetic about its anti-conventional strangeness, in which often 'exterior facts are continually being transformed into interior elements and psychic events are exteriorised',[4] in a passionate expression of, and search for, individual regeneration. This form of renewal is prioritised as preliminary to epic theatre's foregrounding of social relations to address the political collective. Nevertheless, Expressionism is a response to social and political forces, but poetic rather than literal, metaphorical rather than realistic, and thus exposing and challenging the implicit political agendas of the 'literal' and 'realistic': the explanatory rationalisations of a fundamentally reactionary dayenglish. Unlike Absurdism, which may reflect a loss of faith in language, reference, action and consequence, Expressionism recreates an unconventional faith in consequence: the power of individual defiance to trigger wider seismic upheavals of power, countering 'information' and passivity with a demonstrative capacity for active *transformation*. By implication, it involves a style of presentation and performance which provides a precisely externalised exposure of conventionally internalised processes, visually vocally and physically orchestrated, countering traditional English preferences for evasive irony as emotional insulation of theatre and life. The dramatists considered here frequently stage explicit and violent scenes as a deliberate challenge to artistic and social terms of control; seize the challenge of dramatising the non-rational; use deliberate reference to earlier theatrical forms, and subvert conventional notions of theatricality; and deploy stylised language and challenging stage directions to create a visceral modern poetics of intensely visual stage performance and *mise-en-scène*.

## *AC/DC*: dismantle thyself

The cover blurb descriptions of Heathcote Williams's *AC/DC* (RC, 1970) describe the play as 'likely to be seminal to the 70s', 'the first play of the twenty-first century' and 'the kind of work that may save the theatre from being abandoned by the young'. Drama criticism of the 1970s acclaimed the play surprisingly widely;[5] even conservative critics[6] afforded grudging respect, often by highlighting its Artaudian properties rather than its political reverberations. However, the play remains a uniquely uncompromising proposition; hence, its influence is not seminal or formal, but obliquely reverberative (in Snoo Wilson's *The Glad Hand*,[7] 1978, Edgar's *Ball Boys* and Poliakoff's *Strawberry Fields*) in a predominantly neo-Chekhovian social realist English theatre. Notwithstanding its 1970s cultural and media references – and Williams does specify that the text be 'convertible at all points to the frequencies of the actors and the director' and their own analogous references – *AC/DC* retains a power to shock and challenge modern audiences and students.

The play opens with three characters – Melody, Gary and Sadie – experimenting with 'ego loss', but their liberal configuration is rapidly challenged by Sadie's impulse to individuation, to 'go solo'. On colliding with the gay couple Maurice and Perowne, Sadie joins their attempt at psychic jiu-jitsu to counter 'media overload', a shamanistic generation of the 'DETAILS OMITTED' by 'newsbugs'. Melody and Gary recoil with unease at Sadie becoming 'really Evil'; she dismisses them as fundamentally passive and conventional 'TV sets', 'pair-binding property pigs'. The action transfers to Perowne's room; he is in a state of *ennui*, with Maurice desperate (but failing) to amuse. The central premise of Sadie's incursion into this neo-domestic grudging stability recalls earlier dramas of sexual territorialism and exclusion (Pinter, Osborne's *Look Back*) with the unconventional differences that the outsider is an ultimately victorious sexually self-confident woman and the 'prize' of the psychic duel is a (potentially) bisexual man. Sadie and Perowne are mutually intrigued; he challenges her to 'prove her vibrations', the practical efficacy of her deductions from media bombardment and her voodoo counterblasts; she challenges him to change his 'ground crew', break from infatuation with 'precious Maurice'.

Perowne's recall of an attack upon a (real) media figure contextualises and develops the central event of Williams's earlier play *The Local Stigmatic* (1966) and locates Williams in a vein of counter-cultural iconoclasm which includes not only Orton, but also American novelist William Burroughs and British novelist J. G. Ballard (particularly his 1973 novel *Crash*): artistry of creative defacement, which demonstrates the reversibility of received cultural discourse, technology and media, in order to melt the (perceptual and political) structures in which we find ourselves trapped.

Sadie seems to be gaining ground until a TV set triggers Perowne's epilepsy. This turns out to be a deliberately induced form of auto-eroticism: Perowne and Maurice have attained a mutually dependent equilibrium of 'fits and shocks'. They threaten to close ranks against Sadie, but she fights back with a ritual masturbation using a roll of film, releasing an energy which overcomes their defences. Maurice leaves, admitting that he was not 'demagnetising' Perowne but 'radiating' him, compounding his tendencies to make him more dependent. Sadie now proposes Perowne undergo amateur surgical trepanning designed to expose the Third Eye, reassuring him that she has also 'done it' (how else could she survive their joint psychic attack?). He gives himself to what is a surgical-sexual rite of either initiation or contamination, depending on the veracity of Sadie's claims. The ending may suggest a withdrawal into the private pursuit of the potentially lethal 'high'; but it may also suggest, even manifest, a form of transcendence: Sadie is finally intimate, demanding, concerned, impatient, jointly searching; Perowne conquers his fear, goes beyond conventional language, to where expression is more important than comprehensibility, and eludes the otherwise ubiquitous political commodification of predetermined media imagery.

*AC/DC* is best experienced in theatre-performance-time, not reading-time (with breaks). The overall experience offered by the play should not and cannot be reduced to the rational comprehensibility of any argument advanced by one or more characters. The text alternately withholds directive to specific choreography and lays down startling challenges to performer and audience alike (particularly the scenes of masturbation and trepanning). No British play of the period is so extreme in its creation of a vocabulary which demands of its audience an alternative perception of the theatrical event: the audience is gradually but inexorably stripped of the ability to take refuge in confirmation of 'normal' structures of certainty, in which lives are lived but limited; by the end of the play, language itself is dismantled, in suggestion that power is not only something given, but is also there to be taken. More recent developments – virtual reality, cyberpunk, recycled Britpop, the Internet, conspiracy theories and increasing media overload – make the 'deep landscape' of the play even more immediate, particularly if freed by production from its 1970s celebrity references to more contemporary updates. Its power, intransigence and relative neglect might be partly accounted for by the way that it cannot be 'bought into' through fetishistic consumerist paraphernalia and laddish mimicry, like more commercially foregrounded mediations of revolt, such as the various formulations of Irvine Welsh's *Trainspotting*. *AC/DC* is ultimately resistant to this, like the most thorough examples of revolutionary literature.

# David Rudkin: twilight of the gods

As noted, Rudkin pushes the apparently naturalistic form (and audience) of *Afore Night Come* (1960) into an eruption of ritual violence which is nevertheless a disturbingly 'natural' development of the play's cumulative imagery. *The Sons of Light* (1976, RSC, 1977) goes further and deeper; though its initial setting of a remote Scottish island may, like *Afore*, recall Irish dramatic images of cultural periphery, myth, crisis and continuity. Increasingly, it develops a recurrent story-pattern in Rudkin's work: a process whereby characters find their apparatus of identity is 'article by article broken away; characters learn that what makes them true and what they are is not as they thought the tokens by which they belong', but 'precisely those attributes that make strangers, exiles and transgressors of them, so that at the end of the drama they are left naked and alone and at a beginning: an issue fairly central to existence, and one which digs deeper into the fibre of being than law, religion or the pantomime of politics'.[8]

In Part One, called 'The Division of the Kingdom' (consciously echoing *King Lear*), Pastor Bengry arrives at the desolate island with his three sons. The vengefully insecure islanders try to direct and limit his attentions, but cannot prevent his enquiries about the mysterious local 'benefactor' Bain, the marginalised homosexual Yescanab and the vagrant Child Manatond, who is an extreme psychotic embodiment of primal repression. Yescanab and Bengry's twins stumble across disorientating depths in the island (and play): its unusual but apparently consistent Syngian setting is revealed as the mere surface of an interpenetrating gothic underworld, burgeoning with imagery associated with German Expressionist film, Jean Genet, science fiction thrillers and graphic novels: frightening but tempting. Part Two, 'The Pit', serves as exposition of the underlying Platonic propositions being worked out through islanders and subterranean workers alike. The presiding technocrats, Nebewohl and Wemwood, monitor experiments in the deconstruction of the human personality and its reassembly around an (externally defined) ethic of self-transcendence through productivity. Yescanab tries to liberate one of the robotically diligent workers, Gower, but he is reclaimed and – like the twins – destroyed by the monstrous *polis* of the island, both purportedly benign and savagely murderous. In Part Three, 'Surrection', Bengry's remaining son John emerges as a mercurial figure, involving Yescanab and Child Manatond in his hi-jacking of the island's control imagery. He tells the subterranean workers a parable which opposes the promise of self-transcendence with the troubling freedom of self-confrontation, and opposes the deferral of an externally granted future with the individual possibilities of immediacy. Child Manatond's father is exposed as the monstrous figurehead of the island's repressive collective dreamscape, in ways which painfully unlock aspects of her own schizophrenic self-division. John bids farewell to her, Yescanab and Bengry, before triggering a decisive cataclysm and upheaval in the Pit, in a Promethean self-sacrifice.[9] Child Manatond resolves into an admission of female form, embodying the play's insistence on present becomings, rather than deferral and displacement.

131

This plot summary can only hint at the play's extent of transformative experience. Numerous potential closures are subverted to invite persistent conjecture, not least about the political agenda informing the construction of modern identity in terms of cultural and religious approbation of the work ethic. *The Sons of Light* presents a compelling and ultimately irreducible dramatic world[10] which plays out and demonstrates the individual transcendence of myth and ritual, and the creation of new ones, as decisive political subversion. Its astonishingly stratified but interpenetrating battleground can be read as an image of the individual psyche, of Platonic social engineering, of imperial boundaries, or as a combination of these: any purposefully compartmentalised and hierarchic power structure which operates to discourage holistic (and therefore subversive) knowledge. Its tightly coiled narrative and wealth of mythically evocative yet ultimately mysterious detail makes it a masterpiece of existential and expressionist drama.

Rudkin's heroes are often Promethean figures, inly compelled to oppose homogenising orthodoxies, determined to break interpretative restrictions, and accepting the excommunication and isolation which their bid for radical transformation may involve. His bleakest work, *The Triumph of Death* (1981), significantly foreshadows the neo-rationalist philistinism, conservative populism and internalisation of reactionary priorities which would hold sway for the next two decades. The play is a 'triumph' in the original sense of a pageant or series of tableaux which interpret the present through reference to the past; but also in the sense that it warningly depicts the victory of the negative force embodied in Mother Manus. She is an agent of deathly order, attending and guiding a monstrous religious figurehead, Papatrix, instilling and imposing obedience through fatal self-estrangements. The first such is war, as exemplified by the Children's Crusade, from which three survivors escape to establish a forest commune. The procession of the play then leaps to the Inquisition, in which Papatrix demonises not a foreign infidel but an enemy within. Mother Manus tricks Enester, in whose estate the forest tribe dwell, into leading him to their matriarch, whom she kills. Enester is central participant in ecstatic pansexual ritual festivity with the forest dwellers; however, this is demonised as a 'witches' Sabbath' and brutally quashed by the agents of the Inquisition. Wilcher notes how the play observes a number of 'temporal disjunctions and mergings' through which the 'struggle is fought over and over again in different terms between Mother Manus and the Jesus/Lord/Enester figure who invites succeeding generations . . . to the anarchic exercise of a love that resists the socially, psychologically, and politically repressive systems created by the rational imperative for order'.[11] Rudkin's characterisation technique involves a core of performers bodying the evolution of one character into another, whilst retaining and manifesting vestigial reflections and reflexes. The potential new matriarch, Jehan, is persecuted as Joan of Arc, with the complicity of a version of her brother (who seems '*a lifetime self-repressed*') and Enester, who buries his ritual Pan costume in the earth, reflecting on the hunted criminality of love. Jehan's other brother has transformed into a bestialised outcast who seeks apotheosis through desecration, a lycanthropic Gilles de

Rais figure who nevertheless recoils from his own crimes. Luther – depicted as daughter of Joan and Gilles – reflects on the development of Protestant mythic self-consciousness: from toiling to live, to living to toil; from proud self-elevation to shameful disavowal of his physical dimensions: 'Shame to guilt. Guilt into debt. Debt to mortgage. Ever, ever to be "redeemed": Ever, ever and never, to be "worked off"'. Against this culture of deferral, Luther claims 'The Resurrection of the Body is in this life': in present activity, ease and welcome. But she too is criminalised, as Mother Manus enters as twentieth-century psychiatrist and supposed 'enlightened humanist' to dismiss Luther's identification of 'our compulsion to death' as an offensive, unbalanced obsession. Luther is left in a reflex of retentive fear, of which 'Capital is the sublime conclusion'. Mother Manus seems triumphant in her discrediting of opposition to her order; for the moment. The play thus extends its catechism, to enquire of its present-day audience how much they feed their own compulsion to death, pursuing self-transcendence through amputation and mutilation of the self; and demonstrates the purposeful criminalisation of any self-authenticatingly alternative way of being. Moreover, it creates a uniquely compacting and resonant theatrical language of characterisation and consequence to do so: as Rudkin observes, 'I turn myself inside out on the stage and require of actors that they do the same';[12] a process which is also crucial to the narrative and exploratory thrust of his enquiry:

> It's not granted to each of us to be a hero or a martyr. But in our culture, with its benign appearance of satisfying our primary needs, and its increasingly sophisticated techniques of diverting and exhausting our essential energies, it is more and more a struggle for us, this continual process of *re-authoring* ourselves. If I insist on the vital necessity of this 'self re-authoring', it's because the impulse of political institutions is always reductive: to limit us to identities that can be mechanically satisfied, thereby 'managed' – i.e. controlled; to reduce us to identities that are predictable. I see it as our human duty to resist that reductive pressure; as our existential duty, to subvert it at every turn. I won't describe this as moral. It's a matter of survival really.[13]

Rudkin's major dramas are, in content and form, amongst the most profoundly existentially challenging, anarchic and darkly romantic of our period. His further meditations, on national determinism and identity, will be considered in the next chapter.

## Steven Berkoff: dance of the screamers

The central relationship of Berkoff's sketch *Dog* (1993) – between a 'repulsively attractive' man and his pet, 'amplification of his own insane and undirected energy' – provides a kernel image for Berkoff's bold if repetitious extravagances. At best, Berkoff demonstrates a belief in the power of both language (an amalgam of high and low references alternating between heroic, mock-heroic and bathetic) and a distinctively unEnglish choreographed physicality (developed from European mime training, Artaudian impulse, and a lionisation of English working-class physical 'attitude'); he aims to 'curse and purge' 'undirected passion and frustration', through a series of expressive exorcistic rituals in 'compounded argot' conducted 'as if the ordinary language of polite conversation was as dead as the people who uttered it'.[14] At worst, Berkoff's ambivalent elegies parade ironised attitudes of superficially 'outrageous' but fundamentally conventional characters, more aptly designated populist types, as if the celebration of energy were in itself radical (when it is at least as likely to be reactionary).

In his determinedly idiosyncratic way, Berkoff attempts to expand the conventionally English narrow vocabulary of being. Like Barnes and Rudkin, he insists on the vitality of the socially marginalised, the archaic, the unregenerate when opposed to the deathly control at the root of modern notional 'progress'. Like them, Berkoff suggests that a national disposition towards fearfulness and obedience leads to a soporific death-in-life. Unlike them, he maintains an insistent faith in a form of 'popular baroque' language of expressive being to combat this paralysis, self-consciously combining references to Shakespearean and Anglo-Saxon epics with street slang and strangely fluid references to popular culture (which span and amalgamate the 1950s and the 1980s, thus reflecting the nostalgic and regressive rhythms of cultural stagnation). His scenes and characters cannot always support the weight of such references. *East* and *West* successfully capture the swashbuckling gusto of adolescent self-mythologisation, and a wiry bathetic humour (as when heroic vaunts are capped with anti-climactic phrases, 'Well, wrap up warm, it's bitter out' and 'maybe I'll go dancing after all to keep my mind off it'; and when an inventive, poetically various hymn of praise to 'cunt' is anti-climactically end-stopped by a symptomatically English timidly euphemistic, regressively self-limiting reference to 'crumpet'). Elsewhere, Berkoff's *diminuendos* suggest a sudden loss of invention and self-inventiveness, as characters who 'defend themselves within their shells of self-delusion' are returned to their 'awful sadness as they try to claw happiness out of their day'.[15]

*East* (1975) is a series of sketches which establishes the landscape for Berkoff's best play, *West* (1983): a world of swaggering hooligan male pride, bound with a homoeroticism which claims bastard descent from Shakespeare's Rome, and expressed through frankly Oedipal revolt (the central theme of *Greek*, 1980). *West* adds a plot: the clash of enemies whose opposition is mythically magnified through references to Shakespearean histories, *Hamlet*, *Beowulf* and *High Noon*. The hero, Mike, thus dissociates himself from dutiful repetition and passive consumerism ('Why should I yoke myself to nine to five . . . I'd rather be a toad and live in the corner of a dungeon for other's uses'), and the Chorus asks the audience to reflect on the value of their daily self-repressive tolerance: 'How many times did you want to lash out? / Give vent to what you felt? / The bile that's choked within. / Instead ate humble pie. . . . And swallowed some offence. / A mouthful of slagging vile. / And wished next day / When safe at home that you had taken chances'. Mike's uneasy victory is essentially a triumph of performance ('like an actor on the stage / scared shitless in the wings but once he's on then he's the king') which nevertheless leaves him isolated with his ultimately conformist dreams: 'I conquered my own doubts when sick inside / that's great / so tell me where to go and what to do / and what's the trick that makes for happy days and nights'. He turns on the audience, resolving 'to be the beast you fear', but his rebellion smacks more of envy than of the hate Gethin Price performs in Griffiths's *Comedians*. Price expresses himself and accepts the consequences, whereas Berkoff's cockney Coriolanus nevertheless hankers after the dubious integration offered by consumerism.

*Greek* envisions the curse of Thebes in modern terms of a 'British plague' associated with a short-changing, isolated sterility: 'the country's awash in spunk not threshing and sweetening the wombs of lovers but crushed in Kleenex and dead in cubicles with red lights'. This seems a starting point for *Massage* (published 1993). Its plot essentially a more sexually explicit version of Pinter's *The Lover*, *Massage* wittily exposes the dominant English view of the male orgasm as 'relief' – dissipation of unhelpful energy in order to facilitate proper tidiness and focus in pursuing industrial, commercial and financial forms of self-validation. In its depiction of poetic effusiveness and final recoil into euphemistic profitable containability, *Massage* identifies expressive fixations of the English money–sex–power nexus in broadly comic terms, with its plot twist updating the suggestion of Cooper's *Everything in the Garden*: that money represents the pre-eminent English aphrodisiac and fetish. For all of Berkoff's hymn and pursuit of expressive energy, his characters effect transformation only fleetingly, before succumbing to an almost (stereotypically English) postcoital melancholy. His dramatic *oeuvre* increasingly tends towards the monotonous; but his theatrical identifications of the relationships between language, the body and the self are informative about English constructions of masculinity.

## Caryl Churchill: reshaping reality

Churchill conducts a broader and subtler examination of constructions of gender and power relations, through the questioning, and brief but significant dissolution, of imposed structures and dichotomies: such as subjective/objective, past/present and masculine/feminine. Characteristically, *Cloud Nine* (RC, 1979) examines the fierce distinction between being *in power* and being *empowered* through a farcical lampooning of imperial and sexual oppression in a Victorian British outpost in Africa; the second half moves to 1970s London, but with a time passage of only twenty-five years for the characters. Cross-gendered casting is incorporated to suggest characters uneasily accommodated within, or struggling to escape, externally imposed restrictions. The conventional hierarchic compartmentalisation of power oppresses all characters, who nevertheless struggle to maintain appearances of conventional 'order'. The second half depicts the abandonment of some of this pretence; characters achieve a new directness, but still encounter manipulation through the expectations of others. The play ends with an image of hard-won reconciliation between past and future. *Top Girls* (RC, 1982) depicts an unsettling correspondence between past and future by dissolving briefly the temporal barriers between Marlene, a modern executive career-woman, and her historical forebears, but, as Kritzer notes, the initial mood of self-congratulation and achievement gives way to a sense of sacrifice and loss. Marlene's Thatcherite attitude to her sister and fostered child again suggests that competitive power and reciprocal empowerment occupy politically separated worlds.

Churchill's collaboration with David Lan, *A Mouthful of Birds* (RC, 1986), examines 'possession, violence and other states where people felt beside themselves',[16] through a series of scenes which suggest how marginalised people are particularly open to Dionysian experiences and transformations which further manifest a natural disunity. Kritzer's valuable observations have resonances for other plays considered in this chapter:

> As part of their assertion of natural duality and multiplicity, rather than division and opposition, Churchill and Lan challenge the opposition between rational and irrational. In particular, they offer a view of irrationality that connects it to political resistance . . . using epic theatre structure, which Brecht insistently identified with rationality, to overturn the validity of any view of art or politics that excludes the irrational. The episodic structure of *A Mouthful of Birds* is clearly Brechtian in origin, but the content and overall effect are anti-Brechtian. The play explores the irrational and asserts the value of what cannot be understood or accomplished through intellect alone. The turning point for each of the episodes is emotional rather than logical, and results in each of the characters temporarily abandoning conscious choice and self-control. The interludes, rather than promoting thought, undermine the attempt to create a rational narrative of what is being presented. The play, in fact, is premised on the idea that possession, dream, obsession and other states brought on by abandonment of reason may provide a means of political change.[17]

However, *A Mouthful of Birds* does not romanticise irrationality. If, as a result of their experiences, some characters are no longer other to themselves, they and their fellow Dionysians may also experience an isolation and dislocation which leaves them awaiting future opportunities for expression (like the characters at the end of Churchill's 1976 play about social revolution, *Light Shining in Buckinghamshire*).

Churchill's *The Skriker* (NT, 1994) is a further, bolder exploration of interpenetrating (subjective/objective, magical/real) worlds dramatising discoveries at the limits of rationality, which may include (mutual) dependency, addiction, pandeterminism, irrevocable solipsism and concomitant associations of the nightmare or 'bad trip', in which the imagination loses control over its ostensible products. The Skriker is a damaged spirit (from 'before England was an idea . . . and people knew we mattered') whose very speech emotively relates the conventionally discrepant, and vengefully mingles traditional separations. Perhaps herself the former victim of infanticide, this Rumpelstiltskin-like shapeshifter lures women into appeasing her with further sacrifices. She finds Lily, who is pregnant, and Josie, who has killed her baby, perhaps through postnatal depression; hunting a child to possess. The Skriker shapeshifts to be wherever they turn. Lily and Josie have the kind of possessive, but occasionally simultaneously jealous, close female friendship which hovers on but never crosses into lesbianism. Drawn to human desperation, the Skriker needs to be 'used' to feel warm and healthy; she and the constantly surrounding spirit presences specified by the script represent a supernatural world bordering on, and intervening in, human affairs out of a sense of duty, compulsion and its own crotchety appetites (recalling the characters of Neil Gaiman's *Sandman* graphic novels and Angela Carter's reanimations of fairytales). At one point the Skriker becomes a sinister demanding child who expresses her cuckoo impulses to gain a mother by displacing Lily's baby. Josie's suspicion of the child – 'She's horrible. There's something wrong with her' – seems mad, but detects the Skriker's invasiveness. In a Faustian pact, the Skriker transports Josie to the Underworld, until Josie breaks a rule and returns to Earth Time. Josie finds she misses the vampiric, mutually addictive Underworld (a possible drug metaphor in a city play which works particularly well if the women have regional accents, activating the mythic promise of the city 'paved with gold' which turns out to have its own surprising demonologies). As if acting for the Skriker, Josie tries to convince Lily that her baby is a changeling and to put it in the fire. Lily wishes Josie free of possession, but opens herself to the danger with which Josie seems intimate: 'Have you been wishing? . . . She'll get you now'. As if in parallel to the human world, the seasons seem ecologically out of kilter, but Lily's male suitor expresses an excitement at death and disaster, and is attacked by Josie as the Skriker in disguise. When the Skriker reappears as a young woman, Lily rejects her, but Josie 'feeds' the Skriker with murders to keep her alive. Finally, Lily goes to the Underworld, to keep the Skriker alive, out of pity at her apparent helplessness; however, Lily is transported into the future, an apocalyptic world of ecological disaster and nuclear winter. Confronted by her own descendants, she is hated as someone from the 'distant past', who drifted into complicity with disaster through greed, vanity, apathy, obedience and death-fixation; when she accepts food, she is lost in the Underworld/future forever.

The central narrative of *The Skriker* is bordered by mysterious activities of other spirits, who might surround and examine the playing space of the human world (as in the Cottesloe premiere production), or even border and subsume the audience's space to associate their viewpoint more closely with that of Lily and Josie. The spirit world has the same mixture of allure and menace as the media bombardment in *AC/DC*: an alternately bewitching and vampiric source of energy which problematises (or manufactures?) 'reality' whilst suggesting that the magical and miraculous have corresponding and opposing (re)sources in ourselves. *The Skriker* is the most ambitious and originally realised of Churchill's demonstrations of 'the literally or realistically impossible' onstage, which Kritzer identifies as her significant power: 'By presenting her critique of contemporary life in a theatrical context that vaults over the realistic constraints of necessity, practicality and compromise, Churchill produces plays that, instead of imitating life, challenge audiences to reshape reality using their moral vision and their example of daring experiment and creative play'.[18]

# Timberlake Wertenbaker: persistent questioning

Wertenbaker's drama often ranges from the domestic to the mythic within each play, identifying social situations which depend upon dispossession and restriction of human potential. Moreover, she demonstrates how these effects are the deliberate and intrinsic effects of language systems and terms of response which define the rights of the individual in exclusively patriarchal and imperial terms. This authoritarianism is specifically paternalistic in nature; that is, it pretends fostering care whilst simultaneously eroding systematically any belief in a possible separateness and difference of individual interests. The ultimate threat of this governing system is to deprive the individual of speech, and of the right of expression of selfhood; but hope persists, in the defiant reactions of her marginalised protagonists. She also pursues her enquiries with a destabilising humour, and characteristically ends her plays with 'inconclusions' which may seem to offer a still point of reflection, but extend the process of questioning beyond the story and death of individual characters.

*The Grace of Mary Traverse* (RC, 1985) self-consciously makes stylistic references to earlier drama. Set in the Eighteenth Century, the play reflects an age at the crossroads between aristocratic privilege and industrialisation, and highlights the gender roles which both demand. The characters' names – Lord Exrake, Mr Manners, Mrs Temptwell – suggest their functions, as in a Restoration comedy; and indeed the characters initially seem to have consciously chosen to adopt the postures suggested, apparently colluding in making themselves typical and functional. However, these characters' conscious limitations of themselves emerges in the play as something harmful, suggesting that their dealings with others will tend to deny imagination and choice in others, to limit the capacities of others through manipulation (like Iago in *Othello*). Moreover, these characters refuse to be contained completely by the masks they have strategically adopted: they retain the ability to surprise others, as when Gordon, a ludicrous fop disarmingly aware of his own ineffectuality, sadistically rapes Sophie to hear his name spoken in fear. Mr Manners similarly appears a one-dimensional character, who pronounces 'Imagination is one of my best discards', luring the audience into a superior, dismissive attitude, until it emerges that he is the dismissive one – it is the imagination of *other people*, rather than his own, which he discards, to stand in control as a presiding genius of his society, ensuring that 'nothing must change' in its fundamental structures, prepared to sacrifice countless individuals to his god of Order: 'There is nothing so cleansing as massive death. People return with such relief to their private little sufferings and stop barking at the future'. However much industrialists like Giles or rebels like Mary and Jack may think they are acting independently, Manners runs the show, giving them as much rope as they need to fulfil his overall purposes, then hanging them when they threaten to challenge his terms too far. His innocuous appearance is a strategic weapon in maintaining control.

Mary Traverse, as her name suggests, is something of an Everywoman figure who crosses class and gender boundaries in her search for knowledge and grace. Mrs Temptwell's name recalls the medieval Vice, and Mephistophilis in Marlowe's *Dr Faustus*, playing a larger game at the expense of the tempted who will buy their pleasure dearly. Mary rebels against her father's restriction of her experience and expression, beginning an excursion beyond the walls of the patriarchal home by inventive reference to his wants: 'It'll only improve my conversation and Papa will admire me'. In a neo-Jacobean *coup de théâtre* of vengeful cruelty, she plays on words and finds a black ironic justice in her revelation of herself as her father's whore, exposing and dismissing the structures of assumption in Giles's terms of language and status. Their relationship has changed since the arresting first image of them together with an empty chair, a scene which highlights how Mary has been trained to avoid asking direct questions, even as it provokes audience curiosity as to what is going on in this odd physical–spatial arrangement. Questioning is an important and natural human activity in Wertenbaker's drama: asking questions and gaining first-hand experience are the ways in which people break through into knowledge for themselves. Whilst Manners is superficially victorious at the end, the other characters have learnt from personal knowledge 'Not to take orders. Not to give them. Not to want to give them'.[19]

*The Love of the Nightingale* (RSC, 1988) also begins arrestingly, with the physical activity of warfare, whilst highlighting the ways that 'man' and 'woman' can both be used as terms of abuse, and how war involves silencing someone whose viewpoint is consigned to irrelevance: 'corpse'. Against this background of sacrifice, two sisters, Philomel and Procne, ask questions. *Nightingale* is a modern retelling of the myth upon which Shakespeare drew for *Titus Andronicus*, in which another woman is raped and silenced. As Philomel and her brother-in-law Tereus watch the play of *Hippolytus*, she observes 'When you love you want to imprison the one you love in your words, in your tenderness'; thus she identifies the jealousy and possession involved in the sort of 'love' which is hostile to difference rather than according it respect (it might more properly be termed an admiration which depends upon an essential control). But the sisters submit to the determinism of their society, just as the players conclude their tragedy with the motto: 'Fate is irresistible. . . . And there is no escape'. Athens is a male society dominated by *logos*, what is deemed factually true and provable by experience; Thrace a female society associated with *mythos*, revelation and unprovable assumption; but as Elsom notes, 'Myths may not be provable, they may be provably false, but this does not stop them from being useful . . . aids to perception embedded in language'.[20] The Manichean male tendency of seeing things in terms of polar opposites or antitheses comfortably provides stable definitions and reassuring moral purpose, but depends on stifling the impulse to enquiry, so that individuals smother their difference out of unease and become a mute wall of political complicity. However, Wertenbaker's male characters introduce scenes they 'did not see', either literally, or preferred not to acknowledge. Philomel's playing out of her story demonstrates the power of theatre to cut through condescension and control. The Female Chorus attacks the future as incarnated in Tereus's son, identifying their violence as the inevitable consequence of the dispossession of their rights to question and express. Tereus characteristically tries to blame his own lack of imagination on others. He has pushed the women to the point where they have nothing to lose, and thus they experience an awful freedom. Even when the principal characters are transformed into birds, Philomel sets in motion the process of questioning restrictive terms of existence, in a process of recreation: of enquiry through linguistic and imaginative interaction, in order to revalue the conditions and terms of life. Transformation seems the only way to stop the violence, the forsaking of (notionally or intrinsically?) human determinism in cyclical aggression.

Wertenbaker's drama offers two principal challenges. The first is practical; the way she combines poetic language with cues for actions of extreme violence and intimacy; however, her stage directions are spare, when they appear at all. In productions of *Grace* and *Nightingale*, costume is useful in establishing the traditional theatrical contexts (post-Restoration comedy or Greek tragedy) which Wertenbaker's words and actions subvert through their added dimension of explicit enquiry. However, there are few intrinsic demands for set or props. Language establishes scene and atmosphere succinctly, throwing emphasis on the (often shocking) interaction of characters. The spatial relationships between the bodies onstage provide the challenges for audiences, directors and performers alike. The practitioners have to devise ways of staging each particular theatrical crux of the plays (in *Grace*, the spatial arrangement of the first scene, Mary's encounter with Hardlong, Gordon's rape, the cockfight, the cunnilingus, the masturbation and the riots; in *Nightingale*, the mutilation of Philomel, the performance with dolls and the transformation into birds). Again, Wertenbaker is insisting that practitioners exercise imagination, in ways which correspondingly invite the audience to exercise theirs.

The second challenge is to do with expectations associated with dramatic form and genre. *Grace* suggests comedy of manners and melodrama, but refuses the tidy resolutions associated with both; *Nightingale* suggests classical tragedy but avoids the determinism of an irresistible fate which this dramatic convention reflects and supports. Wertenbaker purposefully and explicitly stages the actions which these forms conventionally preclude. Defying her resigned nurse, Philomel refuses to avoid or forget pain; and so do Procne, Mary and Sophie, who resolve rather to look, speak, question and act, and thus demonstrate the only forms of grace, knowledge and love which are worthy of the names.

Wertenbaker's *Our Country's Good* (1988) celebrates the discovery of resources through language and of subversive strategy through theatre, and this liberal element of celebration is arguably a principal reason for its popular acclaim and success for Max Stafford-Clark's regime at the Royal Court. Her subsequent plays consider 'the ability of art to transform life',[21] less forcefully until *Dianeira* (BBC Radio 3, 1999): a return to the mythic style of *Nightingale*, examining the self-begetting power of anger, as compounded by obedience.

# The imagined place: recent Welsh drama

the imagined place is what politics is all about

(Seamus Heaney[22])

Wertenbaker's *Nightingale* contains a pertinently resonant image: that of the nurse, representative of a small country repressed and silenced by its larger neighbour, now colluding in self-repression out of fatalism. Recent Welsh and Wales-based dramatists seem naturally compelled towards bids to identify and break cycles of self-repression, and correspondingly often prefer a New Expressionist dramatic style in order to interrogate or repudiate the implicit causality of a language of notional, often televisually imported, 'naturalism' or 'realism'.

Edward (usually 'Ed') Thomas is the major Welsh dramatist to emerge from the last quarter of the Twentieth Century, bringing an almost Mediterranean sense of volatile passion and sly reinventive magic to bear upon traditional and modern Welsh pitfalls of entropic closure. Thomas is repeatedly drawn to the problems of self-authorisation, in which people attempt to be the readers and writers of their own lives, often through discovering memories or creating new ones in a rootless society, chasing the dragon of their own subjective associative energy (like Cartwright's compulsively poeticising characters) in the hope that it will lead them to find or make 'somewhere good'. *House of America* (1988) shows the lure and addiction of imaginative imperialism, through the desperate and deliberately artificial illumination provided by the American cultural references which three young people paste onto the material constrictions of their home life in the South Welsh valleys. *On the Road*, Jack Kerouac's novel of 'sex, jazz and freedom', is embraced as a new bible by brother and sister Sid and Gwenny, with an addictive dependency. This permits them brief transcendence of their domestic routine, which imitates the inconsequentiality of Welsh television soap operas. However, the downside of their addiction involves the gradual mutation of this falsely cheerful inconsequentiality into an appalling sequence of evasions and disclosures reminiscent of Eugene O'Neill's drama. Their mother insanely and vengefully wears a traditional-parodic Welsh hat and daffodil to reveal that she killed their father (supposedly an emigrant to the freedom of America) because 'he didn't want to belong any more . . . at least my kids know who they are'. However, Gwenny and Sid have found the scenarios of Kerouac's novel more tenable than their own lives, and the compulsively performative characters find their own 'acts' and 'scenes' sliding beyond their control, into incest and fratricide. This is characteristic of the way in which Thomas's characters initially relate naturally and engagingly to each other and to the audience, but increasingly open up unusual structures and surreal scenarios which course beneath conventional understandability.

*Flowers of the Dead Red Sea* (1991) takes further the dramatisation of both the attraction and the fear of freedom, blending the argumentative conceptual drive of Barker with the verbal pugilism of Sam Shepard, and transmuting

141

Beckett's sense of entropic shrinkage into a wasteland symptomatic of contemporary economic and materialistic brutalism. The play opens with two slaughtermen, Mock and Joe, counting the audience and casting them as beasts to be slaughtered ('not a bone of revolt in their bodies'). Mock insists he is a craftsman who will not 'work in a bloodbath of shame', rejecting complicity in the falling standards decreed by the 'power and anger' of slaughterhouse owner, Cragg. Joe subverts Mock's self-confidence with tales of Mock's sleep-walking admissions of shame; as if in response, useless consumer objects drop from the sky, and dark water encroaches around a shrinking playing space. Joe puts his faith in a crash helmet, supposedly to protect him from 'the ravages of progress and the general good', but in which Mock suggests he has effectively left his memories and brains. Mock's father is unknown, and there is a suggestion that the duo may be brothers, which compounds their dependence and aggression. Remembering a female artist's insistence that 'art can save culture', Mock struggles to repudiate the populist materialism embraced by Joe, who is compelled to insist viciously that Mock acknowledge himself 'THE SAME AS EVERYONE ELSE': defeated by paternalist (or, under Thatcherite terms, maternalist) authoritarianism. The ending poses the question as to whether Mock is irrevocably sold up and hung up like a carcass, or 'still here'.[23]

*East from the Gantry* (1992) is, contrastingly, expansive: a literally fantastic extrapolation of domestic involution, in which a mysterious stranger becomes a projection of desire, fear and nostalgia for the central couple. The stranger eloquently confesses his own sense of lost chance and deracination, before all three join in hope of personal reinvention, and of thereby making of a 'good place' to entertain others properly.[24] *Song from a Forgotten* City (1995) is set in a dystopic metropolis of the mind, an hallucinatory trawl through the suicidal sterility of masculine disappointment, in which the searches for new personal and national mythologies crash. *Gas Station Angel* (RC, 1998) is Thomas's best play since *Flowers* and his imaginatively furthest ranging, initially set in two Welsh 'white trash' households which border simultaneously on supermarket check-outs, cynical fun-pubs, the raging 'tantrum sea' and an underworld of angels and succubae. The hope for the imminence of the *magical* behind the *quotidian* is dramatised throughout the community, but with more of a sense of contemporary difficulty and complexity than *Under Milk Wood* sought to provide. *Angel* locates capacity for transformation in redemptive eroticism and imagination, as attained by two members of rival families. This permits them to recognise the fairies, angels and spectres of their parents' generation as distorted reflections of lost brothers and sons 'gone mad', and to attempt more liberating self-mythologisations and self-exposures. As in all his plays, Ed Thomas's improvisatory humour and surreal invention co-exist with the most profound articulations of pain, anger, bewilderment and disappointment. The characters' slippery eloquence is shown to be both imperfectly self-defensive and resiliently hopeful, as they desperately and literally play for time. He thus articulates the range and contradictions of Welsh hopes and experiences with a unique, tenacious precision. Thomas is also exemplary within British theatre in his formation and leadership of an independent company (Y Cwmni, formed 1988, retitled Fiction Factory in 1997) to perform his own work as a dramatist/director (one of only two long-lasting British companies formed to present the work of a single dramatist[25]). Thomas's company has proven it possible to start from slender resources yet operate on one's own terms, and nevertheless and thereby to attract the support and commission of major metropolitan British theatres such as the Royal Court and Glasgow Tramway, and to develop an international reputation which exceeds the grudging parochialism of London-based journalism.

Another Welsh writer, Dic Edwards, is one of the two subsequent dramatists most visibly inspired and respected by Edward Bond[26] (the other being Sarah Kane). *Looking for the World* (1986) is perhaps his most Bondian play, showing how the British abroad – even a Welshman who proclaims himself a democratic socialist – can be complicit in imperialistic-industrial assumptions (based on heroic masculinity[27]) which logically conclude in murder. *Wittgenstein's Daughter* (1993) is closer to Barker's *Victory* and Wertenbaker's *Mary Traverse* in its structure: the odyssey of a young woman, Alma, struggling to make new sense out of her literal and imaginative heritage, which has been shrouded in a phantasmagoria of shame: her husband is a fascist who has taken the name Céline (from the French author); the dismissive ghost of her father Wittgenstein is bandaged and presented by a decrepit boxer, mischievously named Beckett, who impregnated Alma's mother on Wittgenstein's behalf. However, Beckett's youthful transgressive homosexual self prompts his older self to discover pity for Alma, to desecrate Wittgenstein's grave in order to 'reconstruct' his bones and re-evaluate his values in a way she may find meaningful. Alma takes the skeleton to be that of her deceived mother, and vows to reclaim language, ideas and meaning for her child from the centralised, deceptively respectable, professionally nihilistic centres of English theoretical meaning, as represented by Cambridge. As in Bond's *Lear*, the ghost represents fearfulness, expressed as reactionary regression.

Edwards's *Utah Blue* (1995) also depicts the persistence of a spectre: that of the executed American murderer Gary Gilmore, who haunts his brother Mikal, as a 'posthumous presence' who repeats and projects 'the patterns of his own upbringing'.[28] Edwards dramatises how fatalistic social malaise – a culture which elevates murder and denies the value of art – informs a similarly fatalistic sense of sexual failure for the disempowered. Mikal has to transcend Gary's deliberately, socially theatricalised self-damning in order to begin to make meaning for himself. In *Over Milk Wood* (1999), Edwards shows Dylan Thomas's character Huw Pugh trying to escape from the associations of the 1954 play, and from a culture which exploits itself by eulogising resignation, failure and mediocrity[29](just as Barker stages the revolt of Chekhov's character against mutually compounding social and theatrical determinism in *(Uncle) Vanya*, 1993). Huw travels to America, where an Irish woman similarly tired of her country 'choking on its past' tries to help him overcome his persistent regressive nostalgia. Dylan Thomas's ghost also materialises to mourn the fetishistic but profitable re-presentation of cowardice which has not only dogged Huw and the future Welsh but also evicted Dylan from association with his own better work. Here as elsewhere, Edwards characteristically makes his characters initially give Brechtian self-presentational addresses, encouraging the audience to achieve 'a critical scepticism towards all versions of the story, including the "official" one'; then foregrounds the naïvety, contradictory emotions and self-interpretations which these characters express, 'challenging and subverting . . . clichés of "understanding a character"', demanding that the audience 'read the characters existentially, much as they do themselves'.[30]

Wales-based dramatist Greg Cullen's play *Frida and Diego* (1989) depicts the stormy relationship and artistic careers of the revolutionary Mexican painters Frida Kahlo and Diego Rivera and, like the characters, seeks an appropriate style, in which 'a moment is not an instant, isolated, lost, without cousins / But a prism through which all history can be focused and cast onto a surface'. The play visually evokes dialectical iconography from the original Aztec culture of Mexico, which informed both artists' work: not only in dividing the stage space between the rival claims of characters and events, but in the constant onstage presence of *Calaveras*, animated skeletons who playfully counterpoint human actions as reminders of death, both as a limitation to the power of human systems and as the source from which life springs anew. Kahlo and Rivera's paintings, which self-mythologisingly image the history of their nation, are enacted and animated by characters and Calaveras. This reflects their work's testimony to how a sense of spiritual values has to augment that of social process in any secular belief that might seek to displace Catholicism. Kahlo develops Rivera's confidence to locate himself in his own murals, as she illustrates the history of her nation through the kaleidoscope of her own experiences. The Aztec base of Mexican culture directly informs both the dialectical materialism of the couple's Marxist principles and Kahlo's expressionist images. *Frida and Diego* is a social dreamplay, asking, like Rivera's murals, that the audience look not at one thing in isolation, but at the relationship between several (Cullen's Notes on the Play note how 'Duality makes things whole rather than singular and isolated as in our dominant perception'), even as the central relationship repeatedly involves the admission of contraries, and highlights the process between the socially *informative* and the imaginatively *transformative* (Frida emphasises the importance of the artist's pride in and use of subjectivity: 'An artist never draws an object, they draw their feelings for it. In this way we make a strong relationship with the world'). Rivera concludes their story, itself an illustration of the entwined activities of love and sociality, by offering his paintbrush to the audience (a concluding image similar to that of Barker's *No End of Blame*), inviting them to further scenes of (self-)overcoming through discovering their own forms and responsibilitites of expression. *Frida and Diego* is a good example of Cullen's artful subversive fables which are always grounded in the visceral realities of political repression, but insist on the possibility of some radically chaotic 'rough magic', which is both pragmatic and unrationalisable in effect, and opposed to entropic conservatism and deadening social orthodoxy.

*Frida and Diego* is also a significant example of how dramatists in Wales often strategically and expressionistically reanimate existing works of art, and the notional rules of their landscapes, to dislocate the associations of inherited or imposed culture from a single monolithic authoritative perspective. Rather, they demonstrate the possibility of absolute play, with analogous resonances for the reperception of the possibilities of social life and the active reinvention of the mythologies which inform it (other examples might be Lucy Gough's *Our Lady of Shadows*, BBC Radio 3, 1994, which releases Tennyson's Lady of Shalott from her tower; and my play *The Back of Beyond*, 1996, which takes the apparent closures of *King Lear* as a springboard for further speculation). Social realism (a more popular and implicitly normative medium for Scottish and English drama), with its (even critical) re-presentation of rationalised necessity, is often bypassed in favour of a more dualistic and admissive vocabulary of possibility (which is not escapist, but engaged in a politics of the spirit).[31] Ed Thomas is the most voluble, artful and persuasive Welsh dramatic spokesman for this essential hope of imaginative redefinition.

The dramatist who has created the largest and most persistently, deeply radical body of New Expressionist English drama is, however, Howard Barker (the frequent cross-references to him in this chapter also suggest he may be one of the more influential of living English dramatists, without being one of the most imitated).

His work is considered in its own right, and distinctive terms, in Chapter 11.

# Notes

1. Quoted by M. Patterson, *The Revolution in German Theatre, 1900–1933* (1981), p. 51.

2. A. Bogart, *A Director Prepares* (2001), p. 33.

3. Quoted in Bogart, op. cit., p. 34.

4. L. H. Eisner, *The Haunted Screen* (1969), p. 15.

5. See Taylor (1971), Worth (1972), Cohn (1991).

6. Hayman (1979).

7. Wilson, like Williams, develops Burroughs's concept of the 'reality film': the exposure of 'reality' as a predetermined, prerecorded control factor, which may nevertheless be subverted by the introduction of the unforeseeable. The characters in *The Glad Hand* are involved in the manufacture of competing political versions, in the knowledge that 'Between you and your perceptions is the mirror which you think reflects reality. But you can reach out and point it in any direction you like. The world is convertible. By *belief*'. However, Wilson's play emphasises absolute playfulness through the trappings of science fiction comedy, compared to *AC/DC*'s acute senses of bombardment and breakthrough.

8. Rudkin, interviewed for 'Postscript: Outriders', BBC Radio 3, 4/2/99.

9. Rudkin also notes that, complementary to the severe theme of deconstruction of identity in his work, and 'plaited to it like a rope', is the theme of the 'protagonist who follows one note he knows to be true, or is guided by one point of inner flame', who may sacrifice his life as 'gift to humankind and enrichment of the earth'; ibid.

10. For a detailed analysis, see Rabey, *David Rudkin: Sacred Disobedience* (Amsterdam, 1997), pp. 75–92.

11. Wilcher, 'The Communal Dream of Myth: David Rudkin's *The Triumph of Death*', *Modern Drama*, 35 (1992), 571–84 [576]. See also Rabey (1997), 93–103.

12. Rudkin, 'Postscript: Outriders'.

13. Rudkin, from 'A Politics of Body and Speech': lecture given at The University of Wales, Aberystwyth, 30/3/2001.

14. Berkoff, Introduction to *Collected Plays 1* (1994), p. 3.

15. Berkoff, *Collected Plays 2* (1994), p. 148.

16. Churchill, Introduction to *Plays: Three* (1998), p. vii.

17. Kritzer, *The Plays of Caryl Churchill* (Basingstoke 1991), pp. 179–80.

18. Kritzer, op. cit., pp. 197–8.

19. Giles's lines in the final scene of the first version of the text (1985); compared to which I find the final scene of the second version (1989) sometimes over-condensed.

20. J. Elsom, *Cold War Theatre* (1992), pp. 176–7.

21. McDonagh, in Demastes, op. cit., p. 407.

22. Heaney, in a 1984 lecture, quoted in Pine, *Brian Friel and Ireland's Drama* (1990), p. 190.

23. For Welsh-speaking audience members, Mock's last line, 'I am still here', will carry echoes of Dafydd Iwan's political song 'I Ni Yma o Hyd' – literally, 'We are still here' – which asserts the persistence of a political independence and the Welsh language.

24. The first version of *Gantry*, published in *Frontline Intelligence 1*, ed. P. Edwardes (1993), contains the suggestion that the wife and stranger might be older versions of Gwenny and Boyo from *House*; and other details which make the second version in Thomas's *Three Plays* (1994) an over-condensation, to my mind.

25. The other being Howard Barker's company, The Wrestling School.

26. Bond provides an Introduction to Edwards's *Three Plays* (1992), and a selection of their correspondence is printed in *State of Play*, ed. H. Walford Davies (Llandysul, 1998).

27. An observation made by A.-M. Taylor in *State of Play*, p. 76.

28. Savill, in *State of Play*, p. 67.

29. See Edwards's Introduction to *Americana* (2000) for this provocative link, and others, between *Utah Blue* and *Over Milk Wood*.

30. Savill in *State of Play*, pp. 65, 67.

31. Perhaps significantly, one recent native expressionist play which received a major production – *The Body* (RSC, 1983) – is by a Cornish dramatist, Nick Darke. With particular affinities with Dic Edwards's work, Darke's comedy disinters secrets from a rural landscape in which an American airbase has effectively evicted local farmers from their traditional if complacent relationship with the land, and animates dead bodies to comment ironically on the (self-)destructive complicity of the living. Darke's play is, however, focused on one specific political issue, of national instrumentality in American imperialism.

# Chapter 9

# Irish Drama: Twilights and Tigers

A necessarily brief analysis of contemporary Irish drama such as this chapter will inevitably be highly selective and somewhat reductive. Entire critical books are available on the topic,[1] and a parallel volume in this series considers *Irish Literature Since 1800*.[2] However, I would argue that it is unsatisfactory to ignore the interrelationship of English and Irish terms of cultural and dramatic definition, particularly during this period, when understanding one culture frequently involves considering the impacting margin of the other. I have written elsewhere how:

> Both sides feel compelled to strike grotesquely self-parodic postures in relation to each other; this compulsion is rooted in a hysteria which derives from an unacknowledged shame. This inadmissible shame refers to the possibility that each has betrayed what is best in the other, and what is best in his self, and that these processes are a consequence of each other.[3]

This observation links with Pine's, that 'We live in a constant state of mutual embarrassment because of our failure to reconcile myth with logic, past with future'.[4] Pine refers to the dispossessed characters of Friel and Murphy, but his description of those characters' imperfect conceits of indifference towards, along with their inability to keep silence about, their neighbours, resonates beyond a single incompletely individuated culture. And, if the English imperial myth has formerly licensed a self-assurance at the literal expense of its marginalised territories (by equating a selectively expansive modernity with an ancestral heritage), Pine's remarks on the cultural effects of social division in Ireland also find resonances in 'the mythologies of fantasy and hope and self-deception'[5] of Scotland and Wales:

> It has led to a mutation of the *aisling* (dream, vision) culture of loss and poverty of the Gaelic seventeenth-century kingdoms into a Chekhovian dream of national hope focused on tomorrow, an introspection on the part of the dispossessed, a second-class citizenry, on the glory and wealth of that which they once held, and which they dream of regaining: language, identity, self-respect. That such a demeanour should be servile, and yet eloquent, is a characteristic of depression.[6]

Hence, 'Magnificence has always seemed in Ireland to reside in pathos', though 'Irish writers have traditionally sought their salvation in ecstasy' in an attempt to transcend the brutalizing violence and 'spastic paralysis' of Irish institutions and culture.[7] Many English, Welsh and Scottish will accord with the longing expressed by an Irish character in Bernard Shaw's *John Bull's Other Island* (1904): 'I wish I could find a country to live in where the facts were not brutal and the dreams not unreal'. But even Irish plays in which the

Ireland/England intersection is not the key issue frequently refer to an indigenous form of determinism – a depressive location of magnificence in pathos – and the problematising forms of 'ecstasy' which might promise 'salvation'.

## The lie of the land

The Irish relationship with *land* has always been existentially crucial, and compounded and often cruelly dramatised by immigrants, emigrants and neighbours. The potato famine of the mid-nineteenth century is a resonating crisis of alienation of people from their nature and ecosphere, and the exacerbation of the sense of national *failure* in primal or traditional self-definition may be identified as 'an effect integral to the capitalist process' until 'a race of dispossessed people effectively becomes part of the landscape'.[8] Tom Murphy's documentary drama *Famine* (1968) dramatises the bleak pragmatism of this precise historical crisis, depicting the shrinkage of choice for famine victims, the division of families into squabbles for bread, and the discovery of a shocking dignity in a maddened father's decision to kill his wife and children at least by his own hand.

However, the Irish cultural valorisation of expressive articulacy represents, at best, an opposition to a spirit of fatalism. Hugh in Friel's *Translations* identifies and represents the eloquence of a conscious and resigned impotence, where poeticisation attempts a magnificently pathetic response to externally imposed 'inevitabilities'. However, Irish discourse (literary, theatrical and otherwise) exhibits – fortunately – at least as often a bid to demonstrate the *reversibility* of all things, literally attempting to talk things into their opposites: the transfiguration of content by form, the displacement of habitual power. Murray notes how in the land of the 'grotesque, unbelievable, bizarre and unprecedented', 'the Irish imagination is very much at home. Freud is reported to have said that the Irish are the only race that cannot be psychoanalysed since they are too ready to invent dreams or invent lies more interesting than the truth'.[9] At worst, this issues in a culture self-benighted by whimsy, however disingenuously attractive: a community predicated on defensive *anecdote* rather than admission of feeling or acknowledgment of lost opportunity. Conor McPherson's *The Weir* (1997) depicts this syndrome with some ambivalence, but the play's commercial success and palatability in London and further abroad reinforces this cultural association.

As noted in Chapter 3, the sense of terrible inconsequence in Beckett's drama can be traced as an imaginative projection out of post-famine social dereliction, in which the warring forces of the psyche surface to defy repressive consistency. Though O'Casey is significantly better known for the tragic pathos associated with his naturalistic Dublin Trilogy, his later work in the 1940s and 1950s questions the nature, demands and effects of 'realism' (or imposed causality) through spatially and socially transformative elements and effects. Even the carnivalesque social anatomies offered by Behan, *The Quare Fellow* (1954) and *The Hostage* (1958), paradoxically work to emphasise choice rather than fatalistic inevitability, even as they end in death: the first suggests that 'If [the public] don't like [capital punishment], they needn't have it'; the second shows a young English soldier reduced to the associations of his uniform, but is mindful of his choice of that uniform, in reaction to social pressures, and suggests that racial, political and even sexual identities are matters of continual (re)construction, with inescapable consequences. Death is the ultimate leveller even as Behan celebrates human vitality in variety. Perhaps the most wilful bid to refute 'realistic' determinism is the impulse which drives Bernard Shaw's frankly utopian *Back to Methuselah* (1921); Shaw proposes creative evolution as a transcendence of the very terms of human mortality, through an appeal to imaginative and intellectual curiosity.

M. J. Molloy's *The Wood of the Whispering* (1953) is a blackly comic riposte to literary lionisation of picturesque peasants. Murray notes its Beckettian reversal of 'de Valera's idealisation of the pastoral life', showing 'the misery of making do'[10] in a spirit of grotesquely cheerful resignation (as when the protagonist observes 'We won't always be miserable. . . . We'll die at last'). The literally maddening effects of poverty and emigration are also apparent in John B. Keane's *The Field* (1965), which dramatises the power of the Irish reflex: 'Land is all that matters. Own your own land'. However, the consequences of desperate retentiveness are barrenness and fatal distortion. The Bull McCabe has invested his hopes – and the manure of his cows – in a field where they have been permitted to graze. When the field goes up for sale, Bull attempts to sway the deal by tribal pressure, threatening to organise his relatives into a boycott of the auctioneer's shop if he is not granted purchase. However, a rival bidder – an outsider from England – disrupts the plan. Bull's rhetoric of investment ('A total stranger has come and he wants to bury my sweat and blood in concrete') has demanded that his relationship with the field take priority over that with his wife as definition of his masculinity; this sense of purpose and licence impels him and his son into murdering the rival. The community closes ranks against investigations by police and church, though the policeman wonders if the public ever 'really get what they want'. Bull's answer is brutally simple, 'if there's no grass, there's the end of me and mine', in a brutalising situation: 'there's no law' to protect their survival. Bull is unrepentant, though, as the community *turn their faces from him*', he is isolated in his culpability, which he knows to be inescapable. He accepts his role as the unforgivable embarrassment, monumentalising himself with a vengeance which preserves the space around him, and his distance from all others, forevermore.

Keane's indication of the problematised entwinement of land and identity establishes the territory for Brian Friel's *Translations* (1980). However, it is pertinent to summarise the considerable change in Irish social landscape and relations between Keane's play and Friel's. Since the partition of 1920, much of Ulster had been governed and controlled by a Protestant ascendancy, particularly in matters of allocation of jobs, housing and education. 1967 saw the creation of a Catholic civil rights movement. In 1968–9, there was frequent sectarian confrontation fuelled by extremist Protestants (frequently invoking the suppression of Catholics in the 1690s by William III, 'King Billy') and extremist Catholics (who shunned the constitutional reforms promised by the new Social Democratic Labour Party in favour of the literally incendiary tactics of the Provisional IRA). In 1969, the British Army was sent in as a 'peace-keeping force' between sides, but their presence exacerbated resentments. The 1971 introduction of internment without trial contributed to the impression of an army of occupation (or even invasion) protecting English vested economic and political interests in a divided Ireland; so did the role of British troops in the death of thirteen Catholic civilians in the events of 'Bloody Sunday' (30 January 1972; Friel's 1973 play *The Freedom of the City* presents a view of the various claims made on and for this loss of life) and the 1972 suspension of the Northern Irish government at Stormont, returning the province to direct rule from Westminster. The alienation of both Catholics and Protestants led to an escalation of violence and terrorism, which, as noted earlier, manifested itself upon 'mainland' Britain (specifically, England), and contributed to British and Irish senses of disintegration, ubiquitous retrenchment, deterministic racism and embittered cynicism.

## Celtic twilights

Friel's *Translations* addresses Anglo-Irish relations through a historical parallel with 1833, when members of the British Army conducting an Ordnance Survey arrive at an Irish-speaking community in Donegal. Friel grants the Irish-speaking characters an artificial understandability to English-speaking audiences (but not characters), thus manifesting the ironies and suppressions of nuance involved in the army's task of 'standardising' (or translating) Irish place names; and in the negotiations undertaken by the prodigal Irish son, Owen, on behalf of his British paymasters. *Translations* satirises the condescension of the paternalistic British army officer, who addresses the Latin-speaking pupils in a community hedge-school as if they were children; the audience's access to the pupils' enthusiasm, seriousness and humour renders his belief in his innate superiority ridiculous. Nuances of meaning are not simply 'eroded' – as even a young British soldier, Yolland, comes to suspect – but distorted, when Owen obscures the importance of cartography to new British initiatives in taxation. In an ironic but romantic comic interlude, Yolland tries to communicate with a local girl, Maire; their mutual attraction intensifies resentments, which spawn violence: first, the 'disappearance' of Yolland, and then the army reprisal which proposes to level all dwellings in the community. Owen chooses to mediate this final threat with the direct brutality which its official jargon conceals and purports to rationalise. Friel's portrait of the motives and effects of crossing borders resonantly identifies ironies, romanticisms, insensitivities and resentments (the basic plot of the play, and Yolland, might be relocated to Bombay). However, the rural idyll of the hedge-school houses various Irish theatrical stereotypes: the drunken patriarch and his drinking crony (the end of *Translations* directly echoes that of O'Casey's *Juno and the Paycock*), the son who has stayed and the son who has emigrated, the romantic female flirt. As with *The Field*, the challenge for a production is to suggest how the characters and their circumstances have combined to intensify, consciously and deliberately, their own typicality (or desperate mechanicality) for purposes of mutual ingratiation. If not sensitively directed and played, a production can present a sentimentalised vision of a bygone age, yielding opportunities for generalised romantic, comic and melodramatic acting of a particularly familiar and easy Irish type. The drunken schoolmaster's final classical parallel might also suggest a romanticised inexorability about the persecution of the Irish, and seem to vindicate that character's refuge in the pseudo-spirituality of linguistic fantasy as 'our only method of replying to . . . inevitabilities'. Friel's 1990 play, *Dancing at Lughnasa*, is a picturesque celebration of rural female (but domesticated and inarticulate) ecstasy, where unspoken (indeed, pre-verbal) communication becomes associated with a lost sense of belonging. *Lughnasa* has proved significantly popular in Ireland, England and Wales for its nostalgic portrayal of what the Welsh term '*gwerin*': a folk community, resistant to wider socialisation, sentimentalised in its irrevocable unrevivability. Friel's elegiac tendency seems increasingly equated, by the dramatist and by some of his audiences, with Chekhovian classicism.[11]

Tom Murphy's *A Whistle in the Dark* (1961) investigates the compulsions of national–familial determinism and Irish masculine self-definition in a dramatic situation strikingly similar to that of Pinter's *The Homecoming* (1965; O'Toole goes so far as to claim Pinter 'used [Murphy's play] as a direct model'[12]). *Whistle* depicts the reunion of an Irish family, the Carneys, in Coventry. The youngest son, Michael, has married an Englishwoman, Betty, and seeks to 'fit into' his new life and adopted country. However, his father and four brothers are determined to live up to their family reputation as fighting 'hard men' and their national pride in playing out associations of the 'paddy': proclaiming that if that is what the 'British boys know' they are, 'we can't disappoint them'. The patriarch, Dada, incites their clannish brawling, heroising the fighting posture of 'back to the wall. . . . And keep swinging' for self-protection and attrition of the enemy, the ultimate independence. Michael argues that 'A fine man isn't a thug', but Dada counters 'Any man can't fight isn't worth his salt'; and later Michael shamefully confesses to Betty how his brothers came to his aid when he himself was the victim of a recent racist attack. Even she suggests he 'Fight! Do something! Fight anything!' to prove his courage and recover his self-esteem, and Michael goes off to show himself 'Carney too, another Carney'. However, in a moment of drunken rambling, Dada admits to Betty that the source of his aggressive anger is not pride but shame: he 'hate[s] the world', for his sense of exclusion from its centre. The physical closeness of the family has been built on his wrestling and fighting with them: a contact of sorts. Betty becomes disgusted by their baiting of Michael, and issues the ultimatum 'Are you coming with me or staying with them?'; they exhort 'Don't leave us . . . Hit her'. Responding to provocation, Michael plays out the role of Carney to the hilt, appallingly: he kills one brother by smashing a bottle on his head. Dada refuses blame for events, but '*is isolated in a corner of the stage*' by his sons, much like the Bull McCabe by his fellow villagers: he is left unrepentant and ingratiating, but unforgivable and isolated. In *The Homecoming*, Pinter shows how the female outsider can assume the role of tribal matriarch through a sexuality which renders the men dependent. However, Murphy's Betty can find no way into the exclusively male-defined freedom-and-captivity of the Carney tribe. Rather, Murphy dramatises the terrible, near-inevitable release in Michael's reversion to type, whilst suggesting that the shameful arid jealousy of an older generation has its consequences in the alienated, externally-directed aggression and inclusive but distorting tribalism of the younger.

Murphy's *The Gigli Concert* (1983, revised 1991) counterpoints and entangles two quests for a transcendent ecstasy. JPW is a dissolute Dublin-based English quack psychologist claiming to help people reach their potential; he is consulted by an Irish Man, whose sense of domestic enclosure has been resulting in turbulent aggression towards others, including his wife. The Irish Man asks to be helped to sing like the Italian tenor, Beniamino Gigli. JPW's self-preoccupation frequently precludes meaningful interaction with the Irish Man; the impulse behind his original professional psychological 'mission' is long lost; he has slid into a casual and mutually short-changing affair with an Irish woman, and capitulates regularly and readily to the Dublin habit of alcohol as simultaneous social lubricant and crippling dependency, compounding an innate solipsistic fecklessness. But like the psychiatrist in Shaffer's *Equus*, JPW is troubled by his client and comes to envy his idiosyncratic bid to transcend a hollow materiality. Their consultations become more spiralling and freewheeling, given JPW's insomnia and the increasing reliance of both on vodka, and drift into rambles, wryly characterised by JPW as a game called Slobs, in which 'The winner proves himself to be the most sentimental player'. Finally, the Irish Man spontaneously recovers from his depression, which he claims to be regularly sporadic; JPW, however, resolves to complete the quest himself and '*sings*' with '*Gigli's voice*' at the climax of a personal ritual of 'magic'. JPW's performance of breakthrough is just that: a performance, witnessed by none but the theatre audience; technically, the JPW actor is absolved from singing by the playing of a recording of Gigli, to which he mimes; and the 'Trump card' of JPW the character in attaining his sense of breakthrough is a cocktail of vodka and Mandrax. Nevertheless, JPW reads out of this artificial epiphany a 'Rebirth of ideals, return of self-esteem, future known'. An intrinsically rambling play, *The Gigli Concert* raises some questions about Anglo-Irish relations, specifically about English fetishisation of Irish quasi-spirituality and the unreciprocating self-obsession of both masculine cultures. Its ending appears to substantiate and celebrate JPW's subjective rhapsodic fantasy, rather than interrogate JPW's self-aggrandising charlatanism by asking what precisely might be the difference between creative self-mythologisation and neo-adolescent self-deception. Subsequent Murphy dramas of disorientation give further examples of 'games of Slobs', in which characters stumble rhetorically towards submission and release, a 'letting go' of a vexatious self-consciousness and relief from the demands of others, as licensed and justified by a compulsion to generalised confessional expression. The viscerality with which *Whistle* and *Famine* show the proximity of the troublingly appealing and the violently appalling is no longer characteristic of his work.

The (arguably retrograde) Syngian themes of smalltown social enclosure, vicarious mythologising and missed opportunity are adeptly handled by Billy Roche's determinedly naturalistic *The Wexford Trilogy* (1988–91), with its engagingly familiar deployment of stock types. There is, however, a tendency for (particularly Irish) dramatists to garner plaudits from (particularly English) critics in direct proportion to their ability to remind critics of earlier writers and styles (the fly-leaf of Roche's *Trilogy* exhibits quotations comparing him approvingly to O'Casey, Chekhov, 1950s American movie-makers, Joyce, Friel and Chekhov again). Thus, Irish dramatists are particularly palatable to and welcomed by the English theatrical establishment if they work within genres rather than fracture or develop them, and identify Ireland as the spiritual home of pathos, inertia and depressive impotence – haunted spiritual atrophy, depletion of energy and fatalistic acquiescence (as in plays by Roche, Martin McDonagh and Sebastian Barry, and McPherson's *The Weir*) – rather than explosive confrontational potential for self-repossession or transformation. Contrastingly, other compulsively unassimilable dramatists present ubiquitously uncomfortable discoveries, writing as if life – rather than romantic death – depended on it.

## Paradoxical significance

Murray has noted the persistence of 'the O'Casey model'[13] in drama about Northern Ireland (perhaps more precisely identifiable as the *early* O'Casey model[14]): combinations of tragedy, comedy, and melodrama, 'colourful' socially representative characters speaking a heightened speech based on local usage, debunking militancy for its cost to ordinary citizens. Recent examples of such drama include plays by Graham Reid, Christina Reid and Anne Devlin. However, in this section, I will examine the work (performed initially and principally in England) of three dramatists (one of mixed Anglo-Irish race, and two Irish emigrants) who range, in form and content, beyond the limits and predictabilities of this model.

Whilst David Rudkin's work has already been mentioned in Chapters 4 and 8, his dramatisations of Anglo-Irish relations are too searching and innovative to be neglected here. In *Cries from Casement as his Bones are Brought to Dublin* (BBC Radio 3 and RSC, 1974), Rudkin foregrounds the very issues of perspective and style involved in historical and dramatic narrative presentation. The numerous voices which play across the central historical figure of Roger Casement, seeking to establish and invest meaning in historical 'fact', are audibly apparent throughout as Irish or English or, as in the cases of the Author and Casement, modulations between the two. For Casement, the words '*Sinn Féin*' have a resonance beyond Republicanism, relating to himself as 'Three times an exile. Irishman in England. Ulsterman in Ireland. Queer in the world';[15] he struggles to use the Copula, the Irish verb To Be which is proclamatory rather than descriptive, to 'Say of me something I inly, by my own definition, am . . .'. Casement defies assimilation, but insists on political and sexual self-definition (as a homosexual Protestant seeking an independent united Ireland); yet he finds 'me in my life a symbol of Ireland's seceding, a token of her fracture in my death: an exile even in my grave. Am I to have no rest from paradoxical significance?'. Subjected to displacement even beyond death, Casement nevertheless speaks to future generations of an inheritance of dissent which may yet transform the 'old bitch Erin . . . to be the land you live from, not your incubus and your curse'. Rudkin's *Ashes* (1974) addresses the parabolic dimension of a couple struggling to conceive a child; its initial naturalistic determinism opens out into images of blank effacement. The attempted father questions whether he seeks fatherhood, or 'the myth of "manliness"' expressed through incorporation into and extension of tribal lineage. When he is finally marginalised at a family funeral, tribal 'patriarchal logic has collapsed'.[16] This leaves the couple in an existentially indefinite space, with a sense of dispossession shared. *The Saxon Shore* (1986) constitutes Rudkin's most far-reaching and resonant alienation of audience security regarding the apparatus of identity: this gothic narrative is set in 410, in a community of 'Roman British Saxons' shadowed by Hadrian's Wall, a marginalised and uprooted social group who form a fragile bulwark for the Roman Empire against the native Celtic Britons. Tribal determinism here issues in the symptomatic communal psychosis of lycanthropy; the protagonist Athdark both resists and capitulates to the pressure of his community to join them in raids as a murderous werewolf. Simplistic means of association – such as provided by journalistic constitutions of 'realism' and melodramatic naturalistic acting – are insistently problematised by the play, which estranges the facile equations of contemporary national creation myths and also offers a dramatic critique of the mutually uncomprehending romanticism at the centre of Friel's *Translations*:[17] the apparent Romeo and Juliet motif is shockingly inverted when the romance between two representatives of warring tribes climaxes fatally in the stage direction '*He sinks his teeth into her throat*'. Rudkin's play explodes national security in definition, all comfortable presumptions of what it may mean to be 'Celtic', 'British', 'Welsh' or 'Saxon'; it subverts the terms both of cultural identities and of literary moralities, refusing dispossessive reconciliations in a sublimely monstrous expression of the cost and release of self-authorisation. *The Saxon Shore* exposes the instrumentality of the plantationer community for the Roman Empire, with implicit parallels for Ulster Protestants, simultaneously left vulnerable and exhorted to defend a nominal 'heritage' by a colonial squirearchy wilfully oblivious to their own inflammatory effect. Athdark acknowledges his 'fiend'-like deeds but puts aside his residual reflexes into wolf; he chooses to stand his ground alone, with a spade to tend it, anticipating Welsh raiders but awaiting the passage of the night as '*the beginnings of a man*'. His isolation is compounded, like that of the couple in *Ashes*; however, like Casement, he finds dignity in the discovery, choice and articulation of new terms of being. The performer, required to demonstrate how these 'human characters *experience*' and believe 'themselves as wolves' ('An Acting Note' to the Methuen text), faces an analogous challenge, to transcend English and Irish limitations of performance to conventional comfortable order.

Like Rudkin's, Bill Morrison's Ulster plays show many characters' choices to be externally imposed; their free will is limited, yet their act of choice is *integral*, and again analogously demonstrated by the physical commitment demanded of the performer. *Flying Blind* (1977) shows the tribal lines of antagonism in 1970s Belfast both manifested and complicated by physicality. The sexually cowed tranquilliser salesman Dan is entertaining an old friend, university lecturer Michael, who now teaches sociology in London. The morning after a heavy drinking session, Dan attempts to dress alone and uninterrupted, but finally proceeds with scant regard for visiting gasmen or neighbour Boyd, who comments to Michael on the spectacle:

> BOYD: . . . If we were evolving properly, he would be bullet-proof. But we're not. If you want evidence that we don't adapt to our environment and that evolution is a cruel accident, look at him. It's just not up to the job. Look at the skin. What a pathetic envelope.
> DAN: It is waterproof.
> BOYD: You're not likely to get licked to death. (Act I)

The wry marginalisation of the erotic which is implicit in this joke seems accurate, in the world of the play: anxiety and lost chances are frequently cited as the predominant experiences and prospects for the characters. However, when events turn to black farce – Dan is interrupted in his bid to piss when he is taken hostage by prurient paramilitaries – the essential unruliness of physicality disrupts attempts to impose power. Dan demonstrates his unstoppable right to piss in a waste bin in his own lounge if needs be; he and a neighbour, Bertha, confound the gunpoint menace of the IRA by undressing, intending to make love as their last act alive; they even invite the appalled IRA members to join in, identifying their refusal to do so as fear of eroticism. Even Michael tries to exercise his primarily financial power over the student Carol, promising her an escape to London in exchange for sexual favours, but he is thwarted by the self-compounding cycle of desperation and impotence. Dan manages to laugh at the discovery of his own wife's infidelity with Boyd, acknowledging the unnecessary polarizations and double binds that the dominant culture of fear has instilled in them all. Boyd is shot by the IRA in a way that emphasises bathetic fragility and physical waste: 'BOYD, *the gown open and flapping round him, exposing his vulnerability, runs out of the kitchen. There is a shot behind him and he is flung forward*'. The paramilitaries are eventually routed, principally by their own fear, shown to be needless given Boyd's pistol – his own acknowledged source of any sense of power ('It's like having a permanent erection') – being unloaded, re-emphasising the poignant discrepancy between Boyd's bid for control of self and others, and his manner of death. The last gunman is doused with the bucket of Dan's piss, a farcical expression of physical contempt. The responses to the challenges of events seem to clear the way for a reconciliation and mutual acceptance between Dan and his wife, in classic farcical mode, but the presence of corpses adds shade and desperation. Morrison locates hope for vitality in the irrepressibility of the body to seek a *carpe diem* eroticism which overturns fear and power, opposing both the tranquillised order by which Dan's customers suppress their neuro-physical responses to habitual horror and the puritan ideological linearity of the paramilitaries. When Dan and Bertha issue the erotic challenge of their naked bodies to their armed captors (Dan proclaims 'if I may die for no reason then I will live the way I please'), it is as if the characters are trying to shed tribal identity and antagonism along with their clothes, and to demonstrate the possibility of confusing fusion (Dan even offers to 'love' Una, the leading IRA Volunteer). Though the actors remain in character, it is as if their preparedness for play and playfulness might momentarily call into question notions of the essential and so deconstruct paramilitary logic. However, the murder of Boyd prevents an easy celebration of such idealism: the actor playing Boyd is clothed up until the very moment that his *'vulnerability is exposed'* and the character is shot dead: this suggests that nakedness may not elude recrimination, rather its vulnerability might be seen to invite desecratory exercise of power. If the nudity of Dan and Bertha bids to divert the play from tragedy to farce, the final nakedness of Boyd is associated with a refusal of reconciliation. This leaves the closing embrace of Dan by his wife seeming blatantly artificial (Dan is, in any case, not focused on her, but repeating Charlie Parker's legendary, insistent but ultimately bereft, call to his former sideman, Bud Powell. The final effect is closer to Feste's conclusion of *Twelfth Night* than to the Dionysian resolve of *What the Butler Saw*). Morrison's 1988 comment encapsulates the difficulty and achievement of the play: 'I try to make sense of what I feel and see around me, and mostly fail – which is why I write comedy and farce. The story of my time is the story of murder exposed as farce'.[18]

However, Morrison's *A Love Song for Ulster* (1993) is an ambitious development beyond comedy and farce, a trilogy of plays spanning events from the 1920s to the 1990s. The parabolic story of an arranged marriage between Catholic and Protestant, forced to share the same house and withstand the pressures of their in-laws, initially uses representative character types, then accumulates vitality as the very determinism associated with these social and dramatic types is questioned. *Love Song* is a fine example of Theatre-in-Education for adults, informing and questioning, and then pivoting forcefully into encouraging new perspectives on established associations. McFerran's complaint that by the last play of the trilogy the 'characters are weighted down with too much metaphorical baggage'[19] misses the point; rather, Morrison increasingly and significantly stretches the boundaries of social realism to produce a state-of-the-nation anatomy theatrically akin to Shaw's *Heartbreak House*, Hugh Leonard's *Kill* (1982) and Thomas's *House of America*. Whilst the chronology accompanying the text of the script (and, perhaps, a programme accompanying performance) invites the reader to make links between historical events and emblematic theatricalisation of them, Morrison's characters are not merely functional; they prove always capable of enlivening surprise.

Willie and Mick (like Conlag and Daui in Brenton's *Romans*) provide a comic introduction to the play, and to the recurrent motif of Abraham and Isaac, questioning the value of 'blind obedience' to a specifically patriarchal authority as a way of keeping the faith to ensure 'all turns out right in the end'. Female complicity in sacrifice is also indicated by Mary's withdrawal from her Catholic daughter Kate, bartered in marriage to a Protestant, John. The emblematic assembly of John's costume – first as Orangeman, then as B Special volunteer – shows him willingly accepting the reduction of uniform, and the blood on his hand and face after first coupling with Kate emphasises the emblematic dimension of events. Kate's brother Gabriel asks her for a loan; a realistically convincing brother–sister action which also works as a metaphor for Northern political funding of Southern Republican activity. She finds contraception, as a means to 'be in charge of [her] own life', outlawed by the Catholic church. When John is killed by Gabriel, John's fiercer brother Victor takes his place with Kate, and their son – called both Boyd and Patrick by his different parents – struggles to make sense of his inheritance. Kate claims that in schooling him to blind obedience, Victor poisons his own seed but when Boyd finds and points a real gun, Kate's complicity in John's murder is revealed. Victor's attempted acceptance of blame ('Maybe we both helped to kill him') and Boyd ('Tell him he's our son'). The first play ends in an eating scene, to be held '*as long as possible*'; the most naturalistic detail now becomes freighted with wider resonance.

The second play emphasises how elements of both factions engage in profiteering activities, and have vested interests in maintaining violence and the rhetoric of partition. Boyd kills Gabriel; blaming the 'Indians' (a term Boyd has been taught to associate with the 'heathen savages' who do not know what to do with land) for various problems helps Boyd's conservative friends make more money. The Catholic Mick initially offers to help to heal old divisions, but the Protestant Willie becomes Mick's rival for the hand of Kate's daughter Anne. Willie tells Mick that Boyd killed his father, and the fragile trust between Mick and Boyd is broken by the discovery of planted dynamite.

Mick is forgiven for Anne's sake, but even he wonders if the only way to make change is to 'blast it out of' his enemies, who kill his child. Victor asks for help from British troops, to support 'law and order' and 'the interests of the Alliance'; Mick will not accept their authority, and indeed denies it; he is subjected to humiliating internment. For every injunction to break step ('Be yourself. Not your history. Not a father living up to a father'), there is a reaction against upsetting the 'applecart' of profit ('we have invented an economy where there wasn't one') and sacrificing the ram of pride ('For love of land . . . makes us do terrible things'). Whereas Anne claims 'I don't want your history. I want my own', the situation seems more entrenched for the male characters: Willie's lack of hope ('For the rest of my life I am the sacrificial bloody lamb') provides his justification for destruction; Boyd goes to his death glad he did not have a son, 'He'd only have got his throat cut'. The conclusion offers fragile hope through the possibility of 'undreaming a dream', changing the patterns of life by accepting the imaginative responsibility to do so; Anne's more utopian insistence that the meek 'inherit the earth' does not seem borne out by the events of the play, even though repeated challenges to optimism should not deny its possibility.

Willie and Mick's roles as friendly choric ghosts, when they are not actively incarnated in antagonism, suggests that they might be friends anywhere except in such social conditions. Morrison's historical perspective contextualises the 1990s without making light of present or future problems, raising then frustratingly dashing hopes in and for the characters (the female characters frequently voice and represent the choice not opted for). The Trilogy's dramatic irony makes the audience privy to more possibilities than any of the characters, who are restrictive towards others because themselves restricted; in such a climate, no character is judged on her/his own merits for long. *Love Song* also emphasises the *triangular* nature of the conflict, in which the so-called pacifiers widen the divide. Principally, from first to last, Morrison deconstructs the concept of sacrifice, which is undercut as a positive ideal; the events of the play suggest that individuals (capable of humour, love and tolerance in ways social and religious institutions are not) bear the full brunt and consequences of the sacrifices nominally undertaken by groups. Unique in its powerful depictions of historical range and nuance, the Trilogy might fruitfully be expanded by Morrison into a Quartet, to take account of events since 1993.

Terrorism is itself a paratheatrical form, with an involuntary audience. In Ron Hutchinson's *Rat in the Skull* (RC, 1984, 1995), the '*measured, sly, almost humorous*' commentary of Republican bomber Roche sets the blackly comic tone for the most searching theatrical exploration of the vocabulary and grammar of sectarian hate. More so than any of the plays considered in this chapter, *Rat* is (like its characters) direct, hard-hitting, surgically violent, abrupt and claustrophobic: attention is focused (by scenography, lighting and an intensifying lack of variety of things to look at) on the language of seductive aggression. Roche defensively plays 'Mick the Lip' when faced with Nelson, an RUC officer, being imported into his London cell to lead cross-questioning: 'I says the only way I want to see a member of Her Imperial Majesty's Royal Orange Constabulary is down the hairs of an Armalite cross-sight. I says the only way I'm going to talk with one is through a medium'. In fact, Roche and Nelson achieve communication through and because of the tribal barriers between them. Their interpretation of 'historical fact' differs, crucially, but Nelson aptly identifies and understands the idiom of Roche's self-performance, insisting 'I will get inside you'. Nelson is Roche's performative equal: a fiercely intelligent, deliberately unstable specialist with a skill for penetrating and parodying the mindset of his suspects, to provoke them into surprising admission; who is even willing to use his own variance from (familial and marital) normality to express a surprising empathy. In comparison, the attendant London policeman Naylor has no feel for the 'particular conjugation in the grammar of hate' which unites Roche and Nelson in opposition, and separates them contemptuously from the English, 'a nameless people going nowhere' with 'no past that echoes, no future that haunts you . . . whose past stops at last week's football results, whose myths are American imports on the telly, and whose nearest thing to poetry is the bingo-caller's patter'. But, like *Love Song, Rat* demonstrates the triangularity of the relationship. Naylor (like any English member of the audience) *is* implicated, however much he may wish to 'tow that entire fucking wet island and its incomprehensible bleeding tribes into the Atlantic, pull the plug and give us all some fucking peace and quiet'; his superior, Harris, ironically notes that, however much Naylor has 'thought this out in the political as well as the civil engineering detail', disingenuous self-separation is impossible; so 'some of us have to try'. It is Naylor's *passionless* mediation of Roche's Republican rhetoric which dramatises the importance of *ways of speaking* as expressions of purpose and belonging. Nelson knowledgably parodies Catholic, then Protestant, upbringings, assumes the insulting stereotype of the Orangeman and plays it to the hilt, professing to be motivated by 'sheer blind sectarian hate'[20] and planting the 'rat' in Roche's 'skull' by inflaming a possible disjunction between motivation and tactics: 'if it hadn't been for the likes of you, the eejits with the shooters, England would have dumped the Protestant Embarrassment years back'. However, Nelson is also destabilised beyond his apparent performance of volatility: his wife has defected to the enemy (a Catholic who resembles Roche) and his father's death has indicated his own place in the 'line of grim men who all add up to me'. Nelson and Roche effectively tribalise themselves within the London police station, and share meaning – the request for the 'cup of tay' that will release them into the roles of 'two fellas in a ditch, clubbing each other till the one dropped dead'. Their shared vocabulary of hatred transcends immediate location, and exposes Naylor's lack of sense of context even within his own notional 'patch', releasing a linguistic world of nightmarish imagery that lies beyond British containment. Harris claims that the aggressive empathy Nelson discovers with Roche is 'Turning on your own' (the police), but Nelson insists 'He is my own' (Irish); with Naylor, Harris suggests some protection of Nelson ('He's one of ours and we have to know our loyalties, don't we?') but ultimately dismisses all 'Paddies': 'Animals they are'. Roche and Nelson fulfil a wryly humorous agreement to meet and stand their own ground 'When the Brits pull out. When the gloves come off'; the final suggestion of *'all hate gone, all anger spent'*, in *'having come to this place'* which permits a *'reminder of the beauty at the heart of both men's obsession'*, even suggests a melancholy eroticism at the heart of this psychic space and potentially fatal juncture: the passionate eloquence of a truly terrible beauty. Hutchinson's exploration of the importance and consequence of language – not just as communication but as expression and self-discovery – makes the minimal action of *Rat* charged with a paradoxical electricity and tensile theatricality. It demonstrates the performative power of language to *transform* the speaker and audience, with visceral consequences (artfully, the play continually anticipates and charges the prospect of physical contact between Roche and Nelson, yet continually withholds and defers that contact). Lawlor aptly notes how *Rat* 'enriches that most vital tradition of Irish drama – its concern with the nature and power of rhetoric'.[21] It offers no resolution, but an ambivalent release.[22] If *The Saxon Shore*'s werewolf motif dramatises the ease with which an identification of sub-humanity (of others, in self) can provide a release into war, then *Rat* suggests, not how we may all *shed* the werewolf, but how we may all *become* the werewolf.

Hutchinson's *Pygmies in the Ruins* (1991) anatomises the inheritance of a Belfast police photographer, Washburn, a self-consciously anthropomorphised ('I'm Scene of Crime') figure in a landscape whose 'barrenness' is an 'act of will', of political disfigurement and covert profiteering. The premise of the play suggests a murder mystery, but leads to the recognition that 'Every death matters. . . . There's a line between them all'. Washburn confronts benign and malign ghosts from a former Belfast, leading him to the question 'is this done to us or do we do it to ourselves'; which is unresolved, but which brings him to the conviction that 'it should not be done'. Washburn decides 'I have a right to say I am an emigrant . . . I am of me before I am of Ireland, North or South. I claim a greater inheritance than this'. As I have noted before, *Pygmies* 'is probably part dramatised justification of Hutchinson's own decision to emigrate to America, but the play is a poetic amplification of self-interrogation and decision which argues for the possibility of transmuting betrayal (of inheritance, and its terms) into release'.[23]

# Dancing in the ruins?

In 1993, negotiations between British and Irish Prime Ministers John Major and Albert Reynolds and Sinn Féin representatives led to a rhetoric of concession, and an IRA cease-fire, which lasted two years, then floundered on conditions regarding the 'decommissioning' of IRA weapons, and gave way to bomb attacks in Manchester and London. On Good Friday 1998 all factions involved declared a further agreement on a plan for an elected assembly for Ulster, and the Irish Republic's undertaking to remove territorial claim to the North from its constitution. This agreement reflected constitutional moves towards devolution for Scotland and Wales under the aegis of Tony Blair's New Labour government. However, the terms of the agreement were deemed untenable by hardliners on both Loyalist and Nationalist sides, and the initiative faltered in 2000. The injection of EEC subsidies into the Irish Republic assisted a heady economic confidence in the South: rapid growth and electronic globalisation proposed an essentially materialistic solution to the problems of the New Century – in which, in Ireland as in Blair's Britain, Newness was valorised as a virtual brand name, reorientating paradigms of social purpose towards social unison, but often in superficial commercial terms designed to deflect and marginalise any *existentially significant* identification and consideration of 'difference' (and there were signs in 2001 that the foreign investments and economic boom period, dubbed 'the Celtic Tiger', were faltering if not ending).

I close this chapter with glances at four Irish dramatists who have emerged in, and responded notably to, the 1990s. Their choice of writing for one, two or three performers is informed pre-eminently by contemporary theatre economics. However, it evokes other resonances: a sense of compulsively performative and confessional, yet ultimately separated and isolated, characters; an ironic or parodic evocation of Friel's established modern Irish 'classic', *Faith Healer* (1979), or the Beckettian speaker whose defensive self-itemisation tries to keep further disintegration and entropy at bay; and the persistent dynamic of the stand-up comedian, both aggressively and defensively seeking contact with a roomful of strangers – as do we all.

Conor McPherson is best known for *The Weir* (a more export-friendly relative of Murphy's 1985 *Conversations on a Homecoming*, which similarly identifies the characteristically Irish appeal of the stretched and frozen space offered by the bar, perhaps most famously dramatised by Eugene O'Neill's *The Iceman Cometh*). However, McPherson's other plays are more original and less whimsical, with a shrewd eye for the regressive and self-compounding shame which frequently haunts Irish masculinity, and which is particularly endemic to Dublin's characteristic emphasis on boisterous evasion. The protagonist of the monologue *Rum and Vodka* (1992) immediately summarises a contemporary appetite for deliverance from complexity: 'I don't want to do the investigations, I just want the answers'. His inadvertent attachment to a girl becomes solidified because 'she was the only one who didn't criticise me', until he jumps ship from professional and domestic routine in search of the mixture of alcohol and further female company which he hopes will 'cure [his] life', release him from existential (and treacherously physical) nausea. Here and elsewhere, McPherson comically and painfully dramatises the appealing but doomed male bid to forestall consequences, to trick the body by drinking to defer the full impact of hangover, to elude a sense of enclosure with the one-night-stand who is unexpectedly adhesive and brings further demands, to escape a generalised loathing of self and others by action which ultimately fuels and compounds further degradation. Like the protagonist of Murphy's *Famine*, the central character of *Rum and Vodka* finds the sight of his children ultimately unbearable, though cannot so clearly blame external historical forces for the poverty he confronts or the violent anger and failure he feels. After all, he has lost his job through slinging a computer through a window (this is, however, a not entirely unsympathetic contemporary impulse). Another monologue, *The Good Thief* (1994), exposes the mixture of violence and sentimentality at the heart of a Dublin hard-man petty criminal increasingly embroiled in Irish gangster politics, with its virulent and neo-tribal systems of intimidation and 'protection'. However, McPherson ensures that the audience does not sentimentalise his hero, whose capacity for dispensing and enduring violence has a casual mock-heroic resolve. *This Lime Tree Bower*[24] (1995) is a notable development, three linked monologues by thwarted male romantics: a boy who idolises a schoolfriend, who responds by accusing him of rape; a philosophy lecturer who hates academics and who distracts himself alcoholically and sexually with students (whom he also dislikes); and a boy who buys into the heroic national gun culture to stage a petty robbery. In this play, brief criminality proves an enlivening release from habitual disappointment, and goes unpunished, except by becoming the substance of further romance. *Dublin Carol* (2000) shows an alcoholic undertaker struggling to rise to his daughter's request that he visit and make funeral arrangements for his estranged and dying wife. Finally, guided by a vision of directly contacting and communicating with others, he breaks the deterministic self-fulfilling prophecies of regressive shame, and prepares to keep his promise for once. *Port Authority* (2001) is a successful return to *Lime Tree Bower*'s form of three intercut monologues, depicting how three generations of Dublin men face up to the 'fear, bewilderment and disbelief' that attend the expression of emotion. However, the characters' experiences of isolation, separation and embarrassment may seem paradoxically somewhat redeemed by the public performance of theatrical confession. The youngest struggles to the recognition that there are 'people who go with the flow' and 'people who fight', and that he may be the former, set for a lifetime of accommodation unless changed by this new self-awareness. All three acknowledge their vulnerability to the surprise of love. The eldest accepts his limitations and choices, tired of 'worry and regret'. *Port Authority* is McPherson at his most adeptly Chekhovian: the characters' embarrassments have a painfully humorous proximity, even whilst their fearful insecurity ensures their stasis and isolation. The performative admission, of their own maintenance of their conventional masculine restrictions, is both critical and poignant. The theatre audience may reach out imaginatively across the moat of isolation and failed communication which the characters sense around themselves.

Enda Walsh's *Disco Pigs* (1996) is a raucous tour of Pork (Cork) city with Pig (male) and Runt (female), two cheerfully bestial and appetitive 17-year-olds. The energy of Walsh's chosen style, a phonetic patois, recalls Berkoff's, with similar opportunities for extravagant physicalisation, but with added Joycean puns. Again, violence and sentimentality are shown to be two sides of the same coin, as Pig and Runt proclaim their fierce loyalty and regressive clannishness against a wider world deemed more ludicrous and indifferent than seriously hostile. As Pig remarks dismissively of the Northern conflict: 'No one gis a fuck aboud dem nordy bas-turrds. Way bodder? News a da week is let dem do each odder in!'. Like gleefully brutal infants, Pig and Runt celebrate their own authority in a noisy urban funfair of discos, booze and telly. But, in a world (and theatre of 'drama fans') which would dismiss them as *lumpenproletariat*, they demonstrate care and support for each other, as well as determination to create self-mythologising ritual and ecstasy to raise them above the 'weekday stuff'. Crisis occurs when Pig's proprietorial violence towards prospective rivals for Runt's attentions makes her flee the disco in hope of independent solitude. Like Athdark at the end of *The Saxon Shore*, Runt watches a new day rise, severed from the comforting but brutalising animality of her tribe, left to wonder – and to ask the supposedly superior audience – 'Where to?'. What lies beyond temporary dionysia except 'weekday stuff' – and *vice versa* – for her or for them?

Walsh's *Misterman* (1999), a monologue originally performed by its author, recalls the modern gothic fiction of Flannery O'Connor and Patrick McCabe in its portrait of a childlike, socially disappointed evangelist who visits his wrath on his smalltown community – a fictional surrounding audience who perhaps never hear his thoughts – in the name of divine retribution. *Bedbound* (2000) continues Walsh's exploration of regressive but wilful characters, in his most conspicuously Beckettian drama of displacement and attempted control by self-dramatisation. A working father and his polio-stricken daughter both seek self-acceptance and displacement from pain through compensatory self-performative shadowplays (the daughter admits: 'what am I if I'm not words I'm empty space / so I learn the men and play them big / we fill the room with what he was like until he stops'). As in Beckett's *Happy Days*, the duo fight to keep panic at bay through ostensibly self-protective immurement in words and pathetically romantic images of gender roles fulfilled.

Marie Jones is from an earlier generation of writers, and active as writer and perfomer with Charabanc and other theatre companies since 1983. Her two-hander *Stones in his Pockets* (1999) is an unusual achievement, an ultimately disquieting commercially successful comedy, concerning reductive commercialisation and rural despair. *Stones* identifies a variation on the theme of the 'grotesquely self-parodic postures' I have noted as endemic in Anglo-Irish relations; in this instance, the colonising force is the American film industry. Two performers play out the American stars and local extras involved in shooting a romantic Hollywood epic in Kerry. Lucrative sentimentality rather than historical authenticity is the keynote of the film, for which 'Ireland is only one per cent of the market'; however, the Irish characters not only allow Hollywood to romanticise their land, but romanticise that very process of romanticisation, for the prospect of specifically financial salvation. The well-connected assistant director, artfully named Aisling, carries out her instructions to 'get this lot [the extras] back to work'. This work is defined as looking 'dispossessed' on cue; and Aisling is instructed, 'Use a cattle prod if you have to'. The American star, Caroline, expresses a typical American third-generation romanticism of Ireland – 'You people are so simple, un-complicated, contented' – whilst Simon, an Irish assistant director, intercedes between his rural countrymen and the new imperial forces like a latter-day Owen from *Translations*. Two extras, Charlie and Jake, enjoy the brief ecstasy of commerce, beer money and drugs afforded by the shoot, and Jake is even briefly romantically fetishised by Caroline. However, the scene is shadowed by the suicide of a young local, Sean; his childhood hopes of cow farming blasted by agrarian depression, Sean has sunk into the 'virtual reality' of drugs and movies to sustain his self-belief; when Caroline orders him ejected from his local bar, he drowns himself. The fatal irony of Sean's eviction, for a community reduced to selling their reactions of romanticised dispossession on cue, is not lost on Charlie and Jake; they conceive of an alternative filmscript which is a more authentically and imaginatively Irish demonstration of reversibility, 'a story about a film being made and a young lad commits suicide . . . in other words the stars become the extras and the extras become the stars . . . so it becomes Sean's story'. Unsurprisingly, this idea is rejected as uncommercial, but Charlie and Jake resolve to maintain their self-belief, break cycles of depressive complicity, and present their version of the story, which is the performance of *Stones in his Pockets*. Some of the show's humour undoubtedly springs from the performative agility of the actors playing Jake and Charlie, who in turn play all the other roles from their perspective, thus giving the marginalised rural 'losers' a satiric power and transformability which is literally denied them. However, Jones offers more than a brief celebration of ultimately circumscribed protean energy. Jake and Charlie's reversal of the narrative perspective indicts the reductivity both of American economic imperialism and of Irish self-parody in complicity: their final image of 'slabbery dribblin' cows' is both a threat to outsiders in 'designer trainers' and a Swiftian caricature of human degeneration in a land of brutalising economic 'facts'. The reversal of priorities regarding narrative material (centralising the marginalised, and *vice versa*) also demonstrates the possibility of imaginative subversion of artistic, commercial and social conventions (and shows how these are yoked in mutual support) which is specifically, immediately possible to *theatre*. *Stones* is a significant example of 'poor theatre', demonstrating an active and imaginative *independence* from expensive and conventional resources; it can be effectively performed by two amateur actors in a village hall. The West End success of this purposefully *anti-cinematic* and *anti-commercial* play is a delicious and encouraging theatrical irony.

Mark O'Rowe may be the most promising young Irish dramatist to emerge at the time of writing. His plays *The Aspidistra Code* and *From Both Hips* (both published 1999) depict the collision between *petit-bourgeois* suburban Dublin with the labyrinthine but casual violence of Dublin gangsterism, mocking the pseudo-respectable codes and pretensions of both. The effect is comically and disturbingly reminiscent of the world of *Abigail's Party* being broken into by that of *Lock, Stock and Two Smoking Barrels*, in Dublin. O'Rowe's best play to date is *Howie the Rookie* (1999), which develops the interlinked monologue form of McPherson's *Lime Tree Bower* to further effect. O'Rowe's two monologues recount and develop events from the separated perspectives of The Howie and The Rookie (who share the surname Lee), establishing a more vivid sense of environment and surrounding cast of unseen characters than McPherson's more self-absorbed protagonists. Style of self-presentation remains a major preoccupation of The Howie and The Rookie, but their perilous landscape, and their imaginative responses to it, are more active and foregrounded, permitting no opportunity for self-pity. *Howie the Rookie* is a blackly comic demonstration of Irish reversibility *par excellence*: not only are all relationships and alliances shown to be infinitely treacherous and transmutable to good as well as bad; but the characters' mediations of their experiences are ceaselessly inventive, elevating details to the height of heroic poetic myth and the depth of wry bathetic pragmatism in immediate succession, and constantly placing faith in survival in the agility of style, with which one adapts and responds to life's endless reversals. The deadening example of a chosen perspective (in *Howie the Rookie*, everything is Janus-faced) is how The Howie's father has retreated to viewing life, even family tragedy, constantly through the voyeuristic lens of a handicam recorder. The 'good' but fatally heroic response is that of The Howie, who chivalrously intervenes to help The Rookie to atone for his earlier beating from The Howie, and to try to expunge some of The Howie's guilt for the death of a fatally neglected brother. No wonder The Rookie goes 'all introspective an' pond'rous for a minute', striving briefly for deduction, when acts of astounding courage and generosity can emerge from a fantastic urban Boschian landscape which also conceals a hulkingly violent incestuous human 'white pudding', and a gangland spectre, Ladyboy, rumoured to possess three sets of serrated teeth like the lost fighting fish which he seeks to avenge. Even The Rookie, who can revenge himself upon his absentee father by seducing his girlfriend and brandishing her knickers triumphantly, admits that the human depth and range of response in sliding down the razorblade of life is 'all a bit fuckin' mysterious'. As in Berkoff's *West*, physical violence provides the principal means of conduct and contact between men, in a switchback nightworld of apparent dead-ends and hallucinatory disclosures, in which someone's eyes are always on your own, in constant assessment, provocation and judgment.

O'Rowe's *Made in China* (2001) develops his acumen for shamelessly artificial self-energising language, but unfortunately suggests that the premise of laddishly flippant but lurid bloodfeuds between petty criminals is ossifying into predictable cliché, not least through its resolutely *macho* denial of pain and of the disturbing power and promise of any feminine sexuality (for examples of this conspicuous 1990s stage gangster genre, see Butterworth's *Mojo* and Penhall's *Pale Horse* at best, Simon Bennett's *Drummers* and Welsh's *You'll Have Had Your Hole* at worst). However, the black wit of *Howie the Rookie* is a long way from the Chekhovian laments of Friel, McDonagh, Barry or *The Weir*. In his best play, O'Rowe offers a glimpse of the constant possibility and 'mystery' of actively discovering exhilaration alongside terror in a constantly defamiliarising landscape: perhaps the most distinctively and courageously Irish response of them all.

# Notes

1. C. Murray offers a useful introductory overview, *Twentieth Century Irish Drama* (Manchester, 1997), though Pine's single-author study, *Brian Friel and Irish Drama*, contains the most stimulating observations on cultural context.

2. By Norman Vance, forthcoming.

3. Rabey, 'The Bite of Exiled Love', *Essays in Theatre*, 13, 1 (Nov. 1994), pp. 29–43.

4. Pine, op. cit., p. 89.

5. Hugh's words, in Friel's *Translations* (1981), p. 42.

6. Pine, op. cit., p. 41.

7. Ibid., pp. 223, 221.

8. Rudkin, 'Burning Alone in the Dark', interview conducted by me in *Planet*, 114, Dec–Jan. 1995–96, pp. 91–9 (96).

9. Murray, op. cit., p. 224.

10. Murray, op. cit., p. 147; who also notes the 'significant paradox' of Tom MacIntyre's 1983 dramatic adaptation of Patrick Kavanagh's 1942 poem, *The Great Hunger*, 'the classic Irish anti-pastoral'. MacIntyre resists naturalistic form to release 'the joy and sexual release which in Kavanagh is everywhere suppressed', but this means that the play's 'traditional materials' are viewed from the perspective of the 1980s, 'when the plenitude of sex is a resource to be celebrated rather than a sin to be expunged', p. 232.

11. Pine, op. cit., repeatedly and insistently refers to Friel as 'the Irish Chekhov'; Friel has adapted Chekhov's *Three Sisters*, as well as two works by Turgenev.

12. F. O'Toole, Preface to Murphy's *A Whistle in the Dark and Other Plays* (1989), p. x.

13. Murray, op. cit., p. 191.

14. Michael Harding's *Una Pooka* (1989) might be a comparatively rare example of the 'late O'Casey model'. As in O'Casey's *Cock-a-Doodle Dandy* (1949) and *The Drums of Father Ned* (1958), Harding animates a folklore energy against the religious and moral closure and aridity he associates with contemporary Ireland.

15. Homosexuality was not decriminalised in Ireland until 1993.

16. A. Smith, quoted in Rabey, *Sacred Disobedience*, p. 61; in which, see pp. 49–53, 59–62 and 128–34 for more detailed readings of the Rudkin plays mentioned in this chapter.

17. *The Saxon Shore* was initially Rudkin's response to a commission from Friel's theatre company, Field Day. They rejected it as unsuitable for their purposes.

18. *Contemporary British Dramatists*, ed. K. A Berney (1994), p. 501.

19. Introduction to the 1994 NHB edition of the play, viii.

20. The performance (and possible genuine feeling) of extra-professional zeal by the RUC in attempting to fracture a wall of tribal complicity is also dramatised in Gary Mitchell's *The Force of Change* (RC, 2000).

21. In Berney, op. cit., p. 362.

22. In this respect, *Rat* resembles Murphy's *Whistle*; and also Thomas Kilroy's fine dramatisation of 'paradoxical significance', *Double Cross* (1986), on which see Rabey, 'The Bite of Exiled Love', pp. 34–8.

23. Rabey, 'The Bite of Exiled Love', p. 41, which includes a fuller reading of *Pygmies*.

24. The title alludes to a Coleridge poem which identifies a sense of stasis, a sense of (self-imposed?) paralysis within beauty (thanks to Michael Mangan for this observation).

# Chapter 10

# From the 1980s to the 1990s:
# Trapped Enough to Belong

By the mid-1980s, Thatcherism had concentrated highly selective investment in a prosperous London and Southern 'Home Counties'. This intensified social division and variance of economic and social conditions elsewhere through cash restraints on public services. The government's notional dedication to extending individualism and the private ethic disguised unprecedented movements towards economic centralisation and state control, exemplified by increased powers for police and security forces, restrictions on press and media, and the systematic erosion of national health and education services. American and British defence policies generated a new Cold War rhetoric based on the myth of a winnable nuclear war; and Britain's movement towards nuclear power offered a pretext for the government to bypass traditionally radical mining unions, to foster short-term entrepreneurial opportunities on the basis of the long-term ecological disaster of nuclear waste, and to reduce civil liberties in the name of 'security'.

Conservatives also applied inappropriate industrial paradigms to education (paradigms which New Labour has not subsequently displaced). Universities found difficulties in maintaining their ideal role of crucibles of innovative enquiry, when they were staffed by bitterly exhausted lecturers pressurised by Thatcherite management 'culture' and its bureaucratic invasions of time formerly designated for teaching and research (notwithstanding simultaneous accelerations in demands for quantifiable 'increased productivity' in these spheres) and populated by apathetic, politically uneducated students concerned principally about their own potential incomes. The conception and expression of imaginative alternatives was more difficult in a climate of supposedly but spuriously 'pragmatic' monetarism. However, the more alert and worldly representatives of student body and youth were politicised by the alarming policing and surveillance tactics employed by the government during the 1984–85 Miners' Strike; as were many women and miners' wives, who made important sympathetic links and imaginative links within their communities and beyond them. A particularly tenacious and imaginatively resonant instance of social protest was provided by the women who kept vigil in camps outside the arms base at Greenham Common until its decommission.

Thatcher's dictatorial and triumphalist self-presentation barely concealed more implicit forms of authoritarianism, such as arts funding, in which the discourse was changed significantly. From its 1985 prospectus ('A Great British Success Story'), the Arts Council emphasised commercial aspirations and populist justifications: investment, cost-effectiveness, product and value for an implicitly narrow-minded public's money. The fear and impact of AIDS was manipulated to valorise family, fidelity and heterosexuality (a confidence trick most searchingly dismantled by Barker's *The Bite of the Night*, written 1986, staged 1988). Section 28 of the Local Government Act outlawed the 'promotion' of homosexuality in any educational or artistic context, without specifying the terms of 'promotion'. This legal instrument of repression was more often invoked or imaginatively internalised than enforced, but it also had the effect of politicising much of the gay and lesbian communities against the government, especially the young who had no previous experience of legislative criminalisation of sexual culture. Elsewhere, many Britons internalised Thatcherite ideology in defeatist acceptance of its terms of monetarist determinism, and a 1987 election brought the Conservatives to a third term in office. English football hooligans presented themselves as demonstrating national might at home and abroad, in ways which Marwick identifies as 'however distortedly, in keeping with the values of the aggressive market-place and the Falklands War'.[1]

However, the prioritisation of short-term profits over long-term safety was exposed and questioned by a number of national transport disasters during 1987–88, including the capsizing of the resonantly-named ferry, *The Herald of Free Enterprise*. Public scepticism about the harvest of enterprise culture's ideology of consumption and unaccountable wealth creation became evident in the 'green' arguments of environmentalists, and increasing public demand for organic products. Directly interventionist musicians, such as Elvis Costello, The Style Council, The Redskins and Richard Thompson, released songs which reflected and expressed political resistance (during the 1983 election campaign, Costello's 'Pills and Soap' threatened vengeance on the governors of a tawdry England who treated the lives of their mesmerised loyal subjects as ultimately disposable; even the commercially successful mainstream band Simply Red introduced through a bestselling 1989 album a song, 'She'll Have to Go', which accused Thatcher of using money from taxes to fund murder). Whilst it seemed that for a while Thatcher had quite literally captured the nation's imagination, there were increasing signs that she had not entirely defined and enslaved it.

Unfortunately, British theatre of the late 1980s and early 1990s frequently chose to reflect, and seek commercial conciliation with, the supposed economically defined cultural priorities rather than anticipate, and help create, a future national identity. The work considered in this chapter constitutes honourable exceptions. Elsewhere, radical theatre artists were often exhausted, demoralised and stripped of resources. Whereas John McGrath's 1981 book *A Good Night Out* had offered bracingly assertive Marxist arguments for a popular (working-class oriented) political theatre, his 1989 book, *The Bone Won't Break*, reflected his bewilderment and impotence in the face of the Thatcherite priorities which had ordered withdrawal of funding for his 7:84 Theatre Company. Larger institutional theatres, such as the RSC, moved towards supposedly apolitical 'director's theatre' and away from new writing.

This generated some inventive Shakespeare productions, such as Deborah Warner's 1987 *Titus Andronicus* at the Swan, and those of Michael Bogdanov and Michael Pennington's deliberately maverick English Shakespeare Company, but many vacuous ones. Chekhov's sad humanist comedies of resignation to 'inevitabilities' became second only to Shakespeare as a favourite theatrical choices for classical revival. As Thomson observes, 'The insistence on accountability and market values had the effect of emasculating the radical companies without enhancing the potency of the "established" theatre', particularly given the Thatcherite climate's pressure towards and excuses for minimal rehearsal; and designers often collaborated with directors to conceal artistic weaknesses with vacuous visual extravagance, 'a technique which Peter Ustinov has called "veneer disease" '.[2] The RSC's bid to recreate the successful 'event theatre' of *Nicholas Nickleby* was a more anodyne adaptation, *Les Misérables* (1985), and the success of the 1982 National Theatre production of *Guys and Dolls* spawned a speight of inferior productions of musicals, which were seized upon as commercial panacea by panicky West End and provincial and amateur theatres alike, so that the popular repertoire regressed towards that of the early 1950s. Theatre was – like everything else under Thatcherism – widely held to be answerable and justifiable on financial terms alone, and alternative ideals for art were considered increasingly indefensible or irrelevant in a climate of populist philistinism. Thatcherism's presentation of everything in terms of an intrinsically reductive '*either/or*' choice sought to minimise the value and possibility of '*both/and*' alternatives.

# On the edge

I feel it appropriate to depart from my usual rule of principal concentration on the work of stage dramatists, and the specific power of shared space with the interrogatory physical presence, to glance at two examples of television drama from the 1980s. Both produced by Michael Wearing, they reflected growing moods of personal desperation and political dis-ease, and demonstrated expressive possibilities from which the medium has since retreated.

Alan Bleasdale's five-part drama series *The Boys from the Blackstuff* (BBC, 1982) followed the declining fortunes of six unemployed Liverpudlians, experiencing the disintegration of their hopes and their very identities. The last two episodes, 'Yosser's Story' and 'George's Last Ride', provide the epicentre. The former is a harrowing yet blackly humorous account of a volatile but pitifully persistent man struggling against the removal of all the fragile tokens of conventional male identity – job, wife, house, children – until even his manic perseverance crumbles, and he seeks dignity in suicide, which is also denied him by the agents of a paternalistic society. Even in depicting disintegration, the play testifies to the impulse to hit back, as when Yosser's daughter tactically ingratiates herself with the social worker who is forcibly removing her from her father. The daughter performs acquiescence, and the social worker smiles reassuringly, in mutual congratulation; the daughter smiles back, then repudiates the extension and value of this façade of patronising sentimentality by inflicting a headbutt (her father's trademark action of aggression and desperation) on the social worker's nose. This darkly comic sequence emphasises how liberal humanist sympathy – even that of the viewing audience – cannot disguise or excuse professional instrumentality in systematic dispossession. 'George's Last Ride' depicts the demise of an old socialist; his essential hope in mankind is also considered 'dead', and replaced by alarming, hysterically desperate scenes of social degeneration in a local pub, where frenetic activity attempts to conceal the admission that all involved 'wish they were dead'. Bleasdale's denial of consolation in both episodes is a deliberate subversion of televisual narrative expectations, seeking instead to unite its audience in empathy with despair.[3]

Troy Kennedy Martin's six-part drama series *Edge of Darkness* (BBC, 1985) extrapolated the initial premise of the detective thriller into an anatomy of international political collusion centred on the economic opportunism bound up in nuclear power. Craven, a Yorkshire policeman investigating his daughter's murder, discovers that she was secretly an ecological activist who broached Northmoor, a privately owned British underground nuclear storage plant, which manufactures plutonium in defiance of international law, but with government condonation. Craven's daughter was, briefly, the sole survivor of her group's expedition to steal the plutonium to substantiate their investigations, her colleagues being killed by the plant owners. Whilst a select committee in London begins legal and political hearings about this incident, Craven and Jedburgh (an idiosyncratic CIA agent with whom he has formed an ironic alliance) also break into Northmoor and seize plutonium, but are both fatally irradiated. These events create a focus for various collusions and betrayals between international covert commerce and domestic political 'security' policing; these are shown to have their surprising, labyrinthine conjunctions and occasional ironically surprising divergences (even from American political interests, as laconically represented by Jedburgh).

The closing episode, 'Fusion', draws together the multitudinous activated characters and seams of conspiracy for tragic assertions of defiance by Craven and Jedburgh. The two characters now resemble both Jacobean revengers (dislocated both politically and mortally, by the awareness of betrayal and of their limited life expectancy) and the soldiers in Arden's *Serjeant Musgrave's Dance* (disillusioned renegades seeking to 'work back' their 'wild-wood-madness' and infection to the public doorstep of those who condone it, and to strike at those in power who are protected by political–economic hierarchy). At a NATO conference, Jedburgh publicly warns that 'The future nuclear state will be an absolute state whose authority will derive not from the people but from the possession of plutonium'. He climaxes his speech by brandishing irradiating plutonium samples; this scatters the delegates who are prepared to countenance nuclear proliferation from a protected distance only, and irradiates the nuclear entrepreneur who would pronounce himself 'in charge', and in control, of the planet (Jedburgh here unites the dramatic energies of both Musgrave, dancing publicly beneath his 'flag' of skeletal death, and Vindice in

*The Revenger's Tragedy*, extending his poisoned skull towards the agents of corruption, whom *Edge of Darkness* identifies as representing 'Not democracy but despotism'). Craven, on the other hand, develops in dying a political allegiance to the planet rather than to mankind: the extreme position he once found so incomprehensible in his daughter. As in *Musgrave*, there is no overt sense that Craven or Jedburgh 'start an orchard' of wider political defiance: their actions are politically concealed, finally as throughout. However, surprising black flowers emerge at the sites of Craven's death and of his daughter's murder: flowers which may indicate a planetary ecological resistance.

*Edge of Darkness* shrewdly contextualised its apparently more fantastic events by using, in the background of its fictional scenes, immediately recent news and interview footage of Thatcher justifying national nuclear and economic policy. However, since the time of its transmission, no television drama series has implicitly raised so many questions of power and interest about the government of the day; and single, freestanding British television dramas have now become practically extinct under the ubiquitous reliance on the most (contrastingly) depoliticised forms of police and murder thrillers. Even though working in the mass medium of television, Bleasdale and Kennedy Martin thus managed, however briefly, to argue for and generate dramatic opportunities to express deeply sceptical political interrogation of immediate contemporary events and policies. They challenged imaginatively the complicit sense of dazed, mitigating public acceptance that 'things had to be as they were', under Thatcher, and that the consequences could not be so bad as supposed 'alarmist extremists' might suggest.

On the subsidised stage, the Scottish dramatist C. P. Taylor's play, *Good* (RSC, 1981) depicted a nightmarish drift, via imaginative self-mutilation, into complicity with national right-wing authoritarianism. Halder, a German lecturer witnessing the rise of Nazism in the 1930s, experiences delusions of an imaginary band as a symptom of his anxiety and its attempted suppression:[4] 'I can't lose myself in people or situations. Everything's acted out against this bloody musical background'. This anaesthetising self-preoccupation permits Halder's gradual dissociation from his Jewish friend ('He's a nice man. I love him. But I cannot get involved in his problems'). Despite his mistress's reassurances that 'we're good people', Halder finds his symptoms of unease realised when a group of prisoner musicians greets him at Auschwitz (where 'The band was *real*!'). Taylor's liberal tragedy is precariously balanced: the audience's constant sharing of the protagonist's perspective may make his adaptation to circumstances seem almost necessary or unavoidable, and the use of popular music may celebrate the energy which the play finds ultimately reductive. But if the production can establish the play's pertinence beyond Halder's viewpoint and one particular historical context, it can show the paralysis of the supposedly reasonable and broad-minded 'good' citizen to be *self-maintained*.

The motif and logic of the Nazi concentration camp, and their possible contemporary British social connections, are depicted with more searching provocation in Peter Flannery's *Singer* (RSC, 1989). Flannery's *Our Friends in the North* (RSC, 1982) had previously assembled an uncompromising, Dickensian

171

'big picture' of the pervasive networks of corruption in modern British life (and its events and characters were subsequently developed into a 1995 BBC television drama series). *Singer* is artfully conscious of its premiere audience and location – the middle and upper-middle classes, potentially if not overtly sympathetic to right-wing ideologies, who patronise the RSC Swan Theatre – in its use of the Jacobean City Comedy form and five-act structure, the use of Chorus and soliloquy, and numerous Shakespearean cross-references. However, the play begins with a shocking jump from a disingenuously amiable and familiar prologue by the Chorus into the location of Auschwitz, where a starkly reduced set of market forces determine not only dignity but survival. Two Polish Jewish prisoners, Singer and Stefan, win a precariously advantageous existence through child prostitution and the betrayal of a fellow prisoner to a brutal beating. This scene makes the subsequently-depicted complacency of the notional post-war British social order seem particularly ill-founded. Singer, Stefan and Manik – their former fellow prisoner, now traumatised and pathetically dependent – are separated in immigration, and polarised as characters. Stefan's memory is concentrated on one event: his paintings repeatedly re-present the Auschwitz experiences which dominated his life, whereas Manik has lost memories of anything since his debilitating beating. Singer strives for integration into a society which distrusts him as an outsider, and so he extends its logic at the expense of less fortunate fellow immigrants (bringing a post-war European lack of compunction into the smug civilities of English pseudo-respectability, like the Polish refugee in Cooper's *Everything in the Garden*[5]).

Throughout the play, Flannery skilfully orchestrates the indicting recurrence of visual and verbal motifs from the Auschwitz prologue. Singer attempts a chameleonic resilience, assuming and playing out others' definitions of him as he lacks any sustainable vision of himself. Significantly, he is horrified when a former camp guard fails to remember him, even when Singer has taken vengeance upon him through his daughter. Singer tries to dissociate himself from his own reduction into a political soundbite – 'Singerism' – denoting opportunistically exploitative economic strategy, but he is also seduced by the attention and energy this promises, as the play comes up to date of first performance, with the national adoption and enshrinement of neo-'Singerist' values. The scene in which his Tory disciples expound their plans to generate profits by building disciplinary housing for 'mental invalids' and 'social misfits' is startlingly framed, and exposed in its logic: Manik circumnavigates the exchange, asking (as in the first scene in the concentration camp) 'Is this the market?'. Manik's reconnection with his memory is offset by Stefan's despairing suicide. Singer extends the play's implicit Dantean parallels by escaping from the inferno of a burning building, emphasising the necessity of continuing despite all discouraging evidence. As in the stage version of *Our Friends*, Flannery builds carefully amassed detail to support a challenging conclusion: in *Singer*, the proposition that the logic of contemporary Conservatism was – when extended, or even when purposefully obscured – ultimately nothing less than analogous to that of German Nazi social policy. Whilst detractors might claim that the analogy was ill-founded and distorting, in performance the artful confluence of visual and verbal imagery proved impossible to forget. The black, damning, Protean verve of Flannery's play provides an appropriately vicious questioning of British social terms and vilification of political tendencies in the 1980s. *Singer* stands as an appropriate summation, extension and culmination of other contemporary but less incisive British neo-Jacobean epics (such as Brenton and Hare's *Brassneck* and *Pravda*) and, at the time of writing, the last fundamentally searching political play to have been attempted by the RSC.

## Engendered rage

The political climate of the 1980s and 1990s inevitably drove many dramatists to interrogate the terms of choice and permission in the national and sexual economic revolution which the Conservatives were attempting. Some of this period's most important dramatic interventions into the imagery of gender construction and sexual possibility are discussed elsewhere in this book (Churchill's *Cloud Nine* and *Top Girls*; Barker's *The Castle*, *The Bite of the Night* and *Women Beware Women*; Wertenbaker's *Mary Traverse* and *The Love of the Nightingale*). This sub-section will consider other plays of the period which focus on issues and tensions associated with national and sexual identity, with all the wider repercussions generated for the image of the British body politic.

Significantly, one of the most conspicuous commercially successful dramas of the period is Willy Russell's *Educating Rita* (RSC, 1980, filmed in 1983), which obligingly contracts its theatrical form to two characters on a single set. Mangan has observed how, like Shaw in *Pygmalion*, Russell represents social and cultural authority with some irreverence, yet 'the play leaves assumptions about the implicitly gendered nature of social and intellectual authority intact';[6] it also keeps the potential destabilisation of passion at arm's length.

A contrastingly explicit series of images of gender negotiation occurs in Nigel Williams's play *Sugar and Spice* (RC, 1980) which, like Morrison's *Flying Blind*, shows how nakedness can inflame as well as defuse antagonism. A group of teenage girls take over an older woman's flat, where they lure a boy, Steve, into a demonstration of how his laddish attitudes are a tissue of socially manufactured clichés; the girls' leader, Sharon, then levels a broken bottle at him and forces him to strip. Sharon effectively reduces Steve to his penis, which she addresses directly as a bathetic representative of the phallocentric patriarchy which she claims led her friend Carol into the trauma of an unwanted pregnancy and renunciation of the child. Sharon forces Carol to look: '*CAROL turns. Looks at first at STEVE's face and then at his prick. Initially this should be tender and at the same time threatening. She starts to shake. The violence in CAROL is suppressed and perhaps all the more frightening for that when it starts, as now, to come to the surface*'. Mesmerised by Sharon, Carol approaches Steve's genitals with the broken bottle. However, the situation is halted and reversed when Steve's friend John enters. John is as irritated as Sharon with the way that Carol and Steve edge towards a flirty amity when the tension is dispelled. When Carol does a provocative dance, John insists she continue to undress completely, then threatens her and scornfully addresses her genitals directly, a mirroring of the treatment to which Sharon subjected Steve. When Carol challenges John to look at her face, he touches '*her fanny with the bottle*'. Steve intervenes, but '*With something terribly like relief*' John '*whips round to face STEVE who, armed only with a cushion, is coming for him*'. Sharon comments on the ensuing duel of male honour, 'Iss wot they bin' waitin' for. I tell yer. They fuckin' enjoy it'. John '*grinds the bottle into STEPHEN's genitals*'; without another male adversary, John then has nowhere to direct his energy and anger except in on himself. As the teenagers try unsuccessfully to contact an ambulance, Carol tries to comfort Steve with romantic platitudes: '*The lights slowly fade so that the last thing we see is the two naked figures*'.

*Sugar and Spice* is unusual in its consideration of the *consequences* of nakedness. It transcends what it criticises: coercive associations with, and complicities in, power, maintained through titillation and fetishisation, on which social and sexual convention depend. The misandry of Sharon and the misogyny of John both, at times, fuel eloquent attacks on the imagery and conditions of consumerist permission and of social hierarchy. However, Sharon and John's attacks on the bodies of Steve and Carol, *reducing* them to representations of such imagery, are not condoned, though the violence is traced back to identifiable social pressures. The play in performance explores consequence is two powerful ways: firstly, the *duration* of nakedness demanded of the performers playing Steve and Carol is considerable (the radical opposite to the deferment, tease or glimpse of much cinematic nudity, including that of *The Full Monty*, where economic terms of permission remain fundamental). Steve and Carol may both take recourse in parodic striptease routines, attempting to retain some element of playfulness and so control their situations through irony, but both characters are made to live with the consequences of their semi-serious undressings in ways which permit no maintenance of ironic distance. Secondly, the performers (like the characters) may evoke pathos – as well as bathos – in having their genitals addressed and mocked by the antagonistic characters, but the antagonism reaches a startling level of physicality when the script specifies intimate contact. Admittedly, the audience are not likely to believe that the 'broken bottle' is any more than a specially constructed stage prop, but the contact and enacted violence involve genuine transgressions of physical boundaries normally considered intimate. Sexual antagonisms implicit in social imagery are not only identified through word and visual image but rendered *experiential*, as not only the characters but also the performers are laid vulnerable to aggression expressed through touch. Whilst maintaining its fictional frame, *Sugar and Spice* dismantles the mechanics of reductive social gender stereotyping through insisting on playing out consequences: anti-conventional immediacies of physicality which most film, theatre *and* performance chooses to ignore.

Sarah Daniels's *Masterpieces* (1983) makes a fierce attack on pornography, the damaging effects of which are linked to liberal complicity in the notion that 'looking at pictures never hurt anyone'. The play's writing and performance respond to the newly widespread availability of video recorders and pornographic videos in the early 1980s. Daniels relates events in flashback to engender audience curiosity as to how the apparently moderate social worker Rowena might find herself on trial for homicide, and to show how the apparently separatist extremist Yvonne might be justified in her anger. The specifically theatrical strengths of *Masterpieces* are in two scenes in which Rowena is approached by an inscrutable but vaguely threatening male presence (in one instance, it turns out to be her husband, but the incident demonstrates the daily imminence of sexual intimidation of woman), and in Rowena's closing description of a snuff movie which she has watched, the cruelty of which exceeds the possibly over-reactive, possibly self-defensive manslaughter of which she is guilty. The theatre audience are required to sit through the gruellingly precise description of the actual sadistic murder filmed for the snuff movie, to visualise and complete it in their personal imaginations, in a way which permits none of the distance or incredulous dismissal which might accompany abstract statistics or emotive arguments. Rowena proposes the snuff movie as the ultimate consequence of misogynist jokes. Daniels's theatrical articulation of this proposition affords no space for internal counterargument, and reduces the male characters to two-dimensional oppressors (economically complicit in their imaginative self-reductions). But both of these tactics can be rhetorically effective. The play implicitly asks why this strategically provocative two-dimensionality of characterisation should not be as legitimate in a play of female perspective as in, say, *Look Back in Anger*. It is precisely the ways that *Masterpieces* seeks to polarise its audience by gender, and to provoke argument about the legitimacy of its theatrical means, which make it an enlivening theatrical response to matters of brutal simplification. In these respects, it importantly anticipates Sarah Kane's *Blasted* (1995); *Masterpieces*, however, chooses to avoid the complications of pity, and to demonstrate the force of damning (mutual) antagonism. In *Beside Herself* (RC, 1990), Daniels's writing recalls both Churchill's *Top Girls* and Edgar's *Mary Barnes*, and her impulses seem at odds with the predominantly socially realistic form. However, the play contains powerful scenes in which the central character Evelyn, accompanied and prompted by her socially silenced self Eve, accommodates then confronts her abusive father. In this decisively expressive view of conventionally internalised despair, and the search to imagine new consequence, Daniels foreshadows some themes which Kane's *Crave* (1998) will address in more innovative and open form.

Liz Lochhead's *Mary Queen of Scots Got Her Head Chopped Off* (1987) interrogates presumptions of national, religious and sexual identity, history and realism. The play also incorporates elements of popular theatre performance techniques such as music, dance and direct address, as did John McGrath's politicising view of Scottish heritage, *The Cheviot, the Stag, and the Black, Black Oil* (1973). However, Lochhead extends these elements beyond the popular certainties of McGrath's play, to indict a 'National pastime: nostalgia' and extrapolate her tale of Reformation Scotland (when there were 'two queens in one island, both o' the wan language – more or less') into a demonic circus and blackly comic ballet of 'dream-people' acting out their repressed loves through dances of attraction and arranged marriage. The overall effect has more affinity with Arden and D'Arcy's surprising re-vision of national heritage *The Island of the Mighty,* and the dangerous, freakish, complicating vitality of Barnes's thwarted despots, than with McGrath's definite identifications of geographical communities of common political interest. Lochhead's Mary struggles to make sense of her kingdom, 'Alternately brutal and boring', whilst Dr John Knox raises opinion against the influences of 'the monstrous regiment o' women' and Catholicism. Mary's bid to marry whom she loves isolates her,[7] whereas the English queen Elizabeth quells any 'rebellion' in her own heart that might threaten her maintenance and advance of power. Finally, the play extends its tale of scapegoating, separation and elimination with the last of a series of transformations for the performers/characters, into squabbling schoolchildren. Whilst this gives a further, readily recognisable context for the scenario of rivalry and victimisation, it also may have the effect of dissolving the previous complexities into a regressive infantilism which may seem inevitably recurrent through its very familiarity. Nevertheless, Lochhead memorably develops a Scottish tradition of dramatising decisive, pragmatic female activity which can also be identified in Ena Lamont Stewart's *Men Should Weep* (1947),[8] Rona Munro's *Bold Girls* (1990) and *The Maiden Stone* (1995), and the plays of Sue Glover and Donna Franceschild.

Scottish drama is often drawn to documentary images of the historical past (such as Glover's 1990 play *Bondagers*) or socially realistic images of the urban present to characterise female resilience and male regressive dependency (often compounded by an addiction to alcohol or, increasingly, drugs: as in, for example, Henry Adam's *Among Unbroken Hearts*, 2000, in which one male character reads from *Peter Pan*, the story of a boy who wanted to avoid growing up, as a prelude to events of self-destructive irresponsibility and damaging disappointment). The most immediately dramatised and politically contextualised Scottish dramatic image of the threatening, regressive, strategically abject male body is in Tom McGrath and Jimmy Boyle's *The Hard Man* (1977), on which I have written at length elsewhere.[9] McGrath and Boyle's play shows a Glaswegian gangster's version of his own story, his contempt for the twin gods of 'authority and private property', and his skill at vengeful desecration. But the gangster, Byrne, is opposed by a vicious warder, Paisley, who maintains the separation of social space between Byrne and the audience through sadistic tactics, reminding the audience how he thus preserves their 'social sewage system' and how 'if you excuse him (*indicates BYRNE*) on the grounds that he's a product of this shit-heap system, then you'd better excuse me on the same grounds'. Byrne finally challenges Paisley's physical threats by caking his own naked body in chamberpot excrement, smearing his own face and challenging warder and audience alike: 'How much of it can you accept?'.

Byrne knows he is less defiled than any who touches him. *The Hard Man*'s continual destabilisations of sympathy and discomforting political analysis are lent force by its daunting physically theatrical immediacy. It shows up Irvine Welsh's attempt at shocking neo-Jacobean nihilism, *You'll Have Had Your Hole* (1998), as melodramatic and indulgent by comparison.

*Ironmistress* (1989) by April De Angelis uses and permits character transformation in a more open(ing) way than Lochhead's *Mary*. Like Lochhead's Elizabeth, De Angelis's Martha is a woman proudly self-defined in male terms (the title contains reverberations of Thatcher's nickname, the 'Iron Lady'). She has taken on her dead husband's nineteenth-century ironworks, challenging notions of female confinement to domesticity whilst in other respects underpinning values of social authority and property. However, Martha's daughter, dubbed Little Cog, develops a compulsion for questioning reminiscent of Wertenbaker's Mary Traverse. In response to repressive constriction, she imaginatively assumes and animates the persona of Shanny Pinns, a demonised liminal figure who haunts the edge of her mother's estate and control. De Angelis's play considers what Martha has accepted and incorporated to maintain the terms of her power, and the ultimate effects of her displacements; it also shows how Little Cog is compelled to challenge the restrictive definitions with which she is provided, and to discover how Shanny Pinns was the model for the iron statue of a woman erected and fetishised by Martha's husband, begging the question as to who was the wife and who the 'iron mistress'. De Angelis's brief two-hander permits her characters more imaginative and transformative agility than Lochhead (whose performers of Mary and Elizabeth continue to enact variations on the same theme of social hierarchy and restricted possibility). Both Martha and Little Cog become increasingly aware of human capacities for degeneration into the coldly mechanical and basely material, and learn what lies within and fuels the demonic, anarchic allure of Shanny Pinns. Little Cog finally casts herself imaginatively in the image of Shanny in order to claim an outlaw's rebellious freedom. The characters achieve a dual awarenesses, of past hauntings and supernatural mobility. *Ironmistress* offers a resonant tale: whilst mindful of the constrictions and collusions represented by the past, it also indicates the infinitely surprising reversibility of play and wilful performance, and the potential importance of these in making one's own future.

## Cartwright: dying by instalments

The most critically acclaimed British dramatist to emerge in the 1980s was Lancastrian Jim Cartwright. On the one hand, it can be argued that Cartwright was the latest in a series of Royal Court discoveries to present what John McGrath has described as the adaptation of 'authentic working-class experience' into 'satisfying thrills for the bourgeoisie';[10] and that Cartwright ultimately either reinscribes a generalised pessimistic fatalism, or escapes into sentimental fantasy. On the other hand, one can argue for Cartwright's original achievements as a dramatic poet of the underclasses who releases a nocturnal eloquence in conventionally silenced or unarticulated characters; who demonstrates how a sense of social malaise informs a sense of sexual failure; and who suggests that it is the national inclination to take refuge in mute resignation and discarded wishes that leads to the sterility at the heart of English life.

*Road* (RC, 1986) owes much of its immediate success to its artful blend of the familiar *dayenglish* television soap opera form, which offers a vicarious perspective on the irony and pathos of others' problems, with the free-associative *nightenglish* disclosures of Thomas's *Under Milk Wood*, in which the young and old alike are given a dignity of eloquent lament which cumulates in an effect of supernatural compassion. However, the inhabitant of Cartwright's *Road* are more confused and bewildered than the denizens of Thomas's Llareggub. Many of Thomas's characters seem to attain some sense of consolation in their personal separateness of space and rhythm; Cartwright's characters, here and elsewhere, are more uncomfortable in their sense of being simultaneously united and separated, often by self-interest (as one asks: 'who's spoiling life, me, us, them, or God?'). *Road*'s sense of a succession of opened doll's houses can be effectively emphasised and complicated if performed in its original Royal Court promenade format, with dramatic characters also making interrogatory incursions into the audience's physical space to problematise the conventional sense of ironic separation. Cartwright is at his most skilful in writing monologues, which provide a further, distinctly theatrical, form of direct character contact with the audience. *Road*'s volatile and unreliable narrator, Scullery – himself an outsider in the Road, a former seafarer, by turn avuncular and confrontational – guides the audience through images of characters' isolation, or of their attempted means of escape (through alcohol, fantasy, sex, 'fun', love or suicide). In the bleakest episode, 'Joey's Story', a couple, for whom romantic love is not enough, jointly retreat into starvation to confront their despair. Joey's suggestion that 'There is no solution', includes an acknowledgement that the audience are 'all adding a "maybe" aren't you?'. At such moments, Cartwright is more direct than Chekhov in his questioning of the terms of society and, though his plays offer no solutions to the characters' wish for change, they may initiate a process of heightened awareness of common, yet habitually separated and unshared, disappointment. Pathetically and perhaps naïvely, *Road*'s characters want a sense of 'magic and miracles', a Jesus, Buddha or Otis Redding to 'show the invisible' beneath the ordinary and remind them of the importantly anti-monetarist value of 'feelings you keep forgetting'.

The episodic, fragmentary structure of *Road* gives way to the rhapsodic dreamworld of *Bed* (RNT, 1989), which is nevertheless also haunted by memories of a lost and better England, and by Sermon Head, an envious imp who deprives others of sleep because he lacks it himself. A group of elderly characters – unspecified rather than stereotypical – are fantastically thrown together in their searches for sleep but again cannot break through to satisfying contact with, or assistance of, each other; they seem as self-absorbed in their nightdreams as *Road*'s characters were in their daydreams. Like *Road*'s older characters, they are drawn into nostalgia ('I love sleep but can never get deep like the old days'), joining Charles in his mythical drive to evoke an idealised 1940s/1950s England, until this falters in recognition of the dreamscape's degeneration into 'fag end and piss precincts and towns of seventies cement' where modern man is 'useless, killable. Standing in his underpants in the middle of the motorway with a personal hi-fi on'. A joint reflex into the communal sentimentality of singing 'A Hard Day's Night' briefly lifts the characters out of despair; similarly, a dream of a disco subsequently offers another fundamentally populist form of deindividuation, until Sermon Head jealously changes its atmosphere. The audience are likely to react to the characters' imaginative circumstances rather than their uninflected particularities, but the bid for the escape (escapism?) of sleep is thwarted by dreams which consistently bring intimations of negative aspects of the past (an experience with which not only the elderly will empathise). The Couple acknowledge how they have 'shared ourselves away to each other', begging the question as to what extent thay have refined self-effacement into a comfortably eroded equilibrium, or else colluded in an interlocking self-amputation. They become lost in an *Alice in Wonderland*-style dream-logic delirium, in which the scale of everything is changed, and the relief represented by a glass of water is distilled from tears. The Spinster similarly identifies the tamped fears and resentments which ossify into self-restricting rigour, whereas the Bosom Lady personifies blowsy, boisterous indulgence. Marjorie describes a life of deathly routine (the resignation to 'dyin' by instalments', identified by a character in *Road*) which culminates in the image of a lost child, which presages mute resignation and a discarded wish. One is left to ask whether the characters are simultaneously united and separated by personal inclination, imposed circumstance, or both; and how the prospect of old age as a time of restless dissatisfaction might be challenged.

*Bed*'s image of stillbirth is echoed by the dead child at the heart of the central relationship in *Two* (1989), in which two peformers incarnate all the inhabitants in, and visitors to, a Northern English pub. *Two* develops the *Coronation Street*-style Northern soap opera facet of *Road*, whereas *Bed* developed *Road*'s impulse towards shadowy expressionism. In *Two*, the Landlord and Landlady's avoidance of confronting each other with the memories of their son's death recalls the oppressive collusion at the centre of Albee's *Who's Afraid of Virginia Woolf?*, and again suggests a particularly English joint degeneration into sterility and apathy through smothering routine ('We've held ourselves for all these years, sick of our own arms, squeezing, squeezing'). *The Rise and Fall of Little Voice* (RNT, 1992) represents a more commercial direction for Cartwright, into a more conventional structure; the play is oddly reminiscent of Delaney's *A Taste of Honey* in its character configuration, but is resolutely wedded to a sentimentally upbeat ending. *Hard Fruit* (RC, 2000), on the other hand, explores the difficulties of an elderly man in confronting and expressing his homosexuality, and finally emphasises the fear and wasteful enclosure which persists within an apparently cosy Northern neighbourhood. The overall effect is similar to a downbeat version of one of Jonathan Harvey's comedies, such as *Beautiful Thing* (1994), with Cartwright emphasising pathetic and ultimately fatal self-restriction rather than reconciliation.

Cartwright's best play avoids both the sentimentality of *Little Voice* and the pathos of *Hard Fruit*. Whilst *Road*'s repeated references to the persistence of the work ethic and its lack of references to recreational drugs beyond beer may make it seem dated in twenty-first-century Britain, *I Licked a Slag's Deodorant* (RC, 1996) shows a nightmarish urban NightEngland which is threateningly immediate, painfully sad and unsentimentally predatory. Again, Cartwright foregrounds the dependency of characters who cannot deal with, or function in, the demands on which society's promises are predicated: characters who seek escape or relief through drugs, drink, television and sleep, yet who deliver monologues of surprising depth of pain, expressed through imagery which skews familiar details into startling configurations. *Slag*'s is set in a corner of contemporary London, where a barely-defined Man is adrift, lost in the supermarket of consumerist self-definition as provided by Hot Hits compilation albums and Brut aftershave. Nearby, an increasingly desperate Slag drops the price of her 'menu' of offers (and confrontationally second-guesses audience curiosity: 'Do I take it up the shitter? YES'). The Man describes how, after his mother deserted him through death, he inhabited the shell of her house, without changing anything; now, released from the 'hospital', he attempts a foray 'out', but is beaten up by drug pushers. As compliant and aimless as a large toy, he drifts into an association with the Slag, who *'punches him'* then *'loves him better'*, berates him and offers tenderness in similarly unfocused and inappropriate ways. At other moments, her concentration is completely derailed ('HANG ON MY MIND'S GONE') by the crack on which she depends to maintain her own commercial pliability. They arrive at a mutually convenient regression: the Man takes up residence under the Slag's bed while she services her clients, in awe of her as he was of his late mother. However, this synopsis of events covered by the characters' intercutting monologues does scant justice to the poetic texture of *Slag*, which is both viciously acrid and nightmarishly enveloping. It contains Cartwright's strangest and most powerful scenic image of adjacent isolation and separated longing, when the Man sits with his slashed head bound in a deodorised but increasingly bloodstained bra, humming 'Solitaire' in pain, whilst the Slag dances to the tune as she awaits her fix against a brick wall. The Man and Slag's monologues contain Cartwright's most visceral poeticisations of degeneration and desperation, which are ultimately orchestrated into a pungently detailed, yet mysteriously irreducible, configuration of isolations. Cartwright's distinctive ear for a nightenglish which exposes and explores the startling reversibilities of the ostensibly familiar – where poverty turns skin 'like ham', the night becomes 'tight beaten' against your face 'like the balloon in *The Prisoner*', pain is something to be ridden like a 'searing jelly horse', and life is 'like walking through meat in high heels' – has never been so vividly and unsparingly deployed.

# Notes

1. Marwick, op. cit., pp. 351–2.

2. P. Thomson, 'Shakespeare and the Public Purse', in *Shakespeare: An Illustrated Stage History*, ed. J. Bate and R. Jackson (Oxford, 1996), pp. 160–75 (161). This essay offers a shrewd perspective on strengths and weaknesses of representative Shakespearean productions and artistic policies of the period. Jackson's essay in the same volume, 'Shakespeare in Opposition: From the 1950s to the 1990s', provides an important account of how 'In companies with explicit political agendas the performance of Shakespeare has often featured as an attack on what is seen as the harmful dominance of British culture either by the plays themselves or the attitudes that have become attached to them', pp. 211–30 (213).

3. Bleasdale's stage play *On the Ledge* (RNT, 1993) depicts ambivalently the chaotic humour to be found in social disintegration. Disappointingly, this black farce of internalised brutalisation ultimately lapses into a cartoon miserabilism, reducing the desperation which fuels outrage.

4. Taylor's ironic contrapuntal use of anodyne popular music, a 'strategy for survival' through 'turning reality into fantasy', reflects Dennis Potter's similar motifs in his television plays, *Pennies from Heaven* (1978) and *The Singing Detective* (1986). However, Potter's stylistic disjunctions are psychologically, rather than also politically, contextualised.

5. *Singer*'s address to the experience of the immigrant in Britain may also be compared to Harwaint S. Bains's *Blood* (RC, 1989). Bains's Asian characters similarly struggle to read a heritage out of their traumatic experiences and subscribe to prevalent British corruption, extending its logic into gangster violence and artistry in evil.

6. M. Mangan, *Staging Masculinities* (forthcoming).

7. Lochhead's *Mary* might be linked to Pam Gems's *Queen Christina* (RSC, 1977), another consideration of the limited freedom of a mythologised female monarch seeking to reconcile personal impulse with the dominant, externally-imposed terms of power. Aston identifies 'the gender-based conflict between marriage, reproduction, and disempowerment on the one hand, and monarchy, non-childbearing body, and power on the other', in *The Cambridge Companion to Modern British Women Playwrights*, ed. Aston and Reinelt (Cambridge, 2000), p. 160.

8. Lamont's play, written in the early 1940s and revised in the 1970s, is considered in detail in the preceding volume in this series, Chothia's *English Drama of the Early Modern Period, 1890–1940* (1996), pp. 221–5.

9. Rabey (1986), pp. 95–8.

10. J. McGrath, *A Good Night Out* (1981, 1996), p. 11.

# Chapter 11

# Barker: Appalling Enhancements

More than any other dramatist of this period, Howard Barker has striven to reclaim language from a sense of social crisis expressed as fatalistic determinism (the presumption that there is only one possible way that things can turn out). Through a unique combination of style, content, theoretical argument and *mise-en-scène*, he has countered the implicitly authoritarian presumption and proposition of supposedly 'natural' diminutions or 'inevitable' restrictions of the options whereby one might think, feel, speak, act, love and exist. His drama, poetry and direction of his own work offer a consciously and purposefully anti-naturalistic expansion of vocabulary: of language, terms of experience, scenic and physical expression, and being. His compulsive re-evaluations aim to reveal radical experience of how the imagined, unlived life can inform and transform the diminishing returns of received wisdom and prescribed action ('Writing now has to engage with what is not seen . . . because real life is annexed, reproduced, soporific'[1]). He provokes dissociations, polarisations and surprising admissions within the theatrical experience, culture and discourse, which expose their replications and service of management of power; he also insists on the capacity of the individual to reverse such constrictions, and the importance of the ability of the actor and the dramatist-director to lead by imaginative example.

Barker's instincts are, crucially, opposed to all forms of reconciliation, in a society and a medium which attempt to reconcile people to their predetermined roles and actions in traditional social and artistic symbolic ritual:

> The deterioration of habitual moral and political assumptions was the sole means by which a change in form became possible. This was inevitable at a time of political collapse. But the resistance had to lie in questions of first principle, which is the theatre's special territory. For example, our participation in acts of violence . . . I believe in a society of increasingly restricted options that a creative mind owes it to his fellow human beings to stretch himself and them, to give others the right to be amazed, the right even to be taken to the limits of tolerance and to strain and test morality at source.[2]

Barker is the most relentlessly prolific dramatist under survey, often writing four plays a year, in addition to his work as a poet and painter. He named and formed his own theatre company, The Wrestling School (in 1988, initially with the actor/director Kenny Ireland), for the first productions of his own plays. These productions have increasingly been examples of Barker's own distinctively powerful direction, which reflects the precision and boldness of his other work as a visual artist, and combines this with a compositional

emphasis on surprising physical movement and imagery and disturbingly unforeseeable sound. Like Beckett, Barker's ballets of precise reversibility suggest
a self-conscious acceptance of isolation and solitude but, unlike Beckett, Barker
suggests this disengagement may testify to discovery, as well as loss, of power.
Barker observes how his characters 'are not forgiving, but they master and
incorporate pain into their continued existence; it is the struggle that dignifies,
and that is usually located in sexuality. Only in the darkest recesses of sexuality
can some peace be discovered – and by peace, I don't mean tranquillity, but
some sort of struggle which enhances the human; so the texts are excoriating,
but I suppose they're also redemptive, to that extent'.[3]

With a unique and purposeful eloquence, Barker consciously identifies and
manifestly breaks step with the British theatrical presumptions and trends
around him, as in this denunciation of the complicit contractions of 1980s
British theatre: 'The culture . . . permitted philistinism to parade as democratic
art. The managers leapt to sham renaissance postures, wanting power, gold
and spectacle, while the fringe, which had sheltered even those whose aesthetic
was not oppositional, suffered a double relapse, a miniaturist art no longer
fitting the ambition of writer or actor and shrivelling again into scenes of
domestic life'.[4]

More seriously and persistently than his peers, Barker has extended, elaborated and refined his propositions for a practically and morally experimental
theatre, in his expanding collection of *aperçus, Arguments for a Theatre*. These
writings demonstrate how his distrust of social authority is nevertheless
informed by a revolutionary faith in individual imaginative capacity:

> The notion of the stable audience is a reactionary one, a blunt weapon used against
> the revolutionary text. It is a notion of the people used against the people, and the
> sing-song of the populist state. The cultural managers will demonstrate the frivolity,
> the absence of concentration, the impatience, the dictatorship of television habits
> over the minds of the audience, but never the appetite for challenge, truth or dis-
> crimination. The Public, as an invention, becomes the enemy of the artist, a solid
> block of immovable entertainment-seekers whose numbers and subsequent economic
> power forbid intelligence. I refused this as a description of the audience and [found]
> the audience for the work, sometimes half-hostile, but wanting. The tension between
> the audience and the play became for me an aesthetic, the nature of experience. This
> involved challenges to common morality, common socialism, even what passes for
> common humanity.[5]

This testing of morality and fundamental questioning of the social terms
of existence is manifest even in early Barker plays, which frequently centre
on 'moments of decay, the melancholia of lost power or mistaken judgements
as to where power lies'.[6] *Downchild* (written 1977, RSC, 1986) tries and
condemns the imaginative imprisonments of English Wilsonian social democracy 'which made stupor rhyme with socialism', finds it 'guilty of humanity'
which, in order to spare 'pain' and secure power, murders the instinctive
self and consigns the young to meanness. Crucially, the apparent infanticide
in Barker's play emphasises its divergences from the inarticulate persistence
ultimately re-presented in Bond's *Saved*; Barker's protagonist assumes the rights

of direct confrontation, Wildean eloquence and fatally unforgivable perform-ance. *Fair Slaughter* (RC, 1978) also features a *King Lear*-like tribunal of liberal humanism, which spills into poignant self-deception. It also features Barker's first assembly of what will prove characteristic motifs. The tribula-tions of an English music-hall comedian (played by Max Wall, a performer associated with both Osborne's Archie Rice and Beckett's Krapp) are extended and recontextualised within the nightmare of international history, where the interpretative invocation of 'the people', the broken body, and the work of art, become oppositional talismans in the duel between those conciliators who would extirpate pain (through anaesthetising trivia and retention) and those who (however ineptly, irritatingly or disingenuously) strike a flame of unforgiv-ing disobedience in the succeeding generation. *The Love of a Good Man* (1978) shows characters working a battleground, a landscape 'not ground so much as flesh', into a suitable form to be consecrated as a monument to national investment. Fascination and authority persist beyond – even because of – death and dismemberment.

Barker's drama quickly moves away from contemporary settings into explora-tions of past or future mythic history, inventing rather than describing, seeking:

> not the reproduction of reality, critical or otherwise (the traditional Royal Court play, socialistic, voyeuristic), but speculation – not what is . . . but what is *imaginable*. The subject becomes not man-in-society, but knowledge itself, and the protagonist not the man-of-action (rebel or capitalist as source of pure energy) but the struggler with self. So in an era in which sexuality is simultaneously cheap, domestic and soon-to-be-forbidden, desire becomes the field of enquiry most likely to stimulate a creative disorder.[7]

Barker's drama increasingly testifies to the essential importance of aware-ness of location and manipulation of power through sexuality, and sexuality through power. The subversive power of this foregrounding of sexuality and desire, the personal pain and poetry of wanting, cannot be underestimated by any society which depends upon regimentation in deference to an ideology of abstraction and deferral (as do all societies).

*Crimes in Hot Countries* (written 1978, staged 1983, RSC, 1986) repres-ents the first flourishing of this theme in the unlikely liaison between Toplis, a subversive juggler, and Erica, a woman stranded in a wartime imperial outpost. Soldiers determine to mutiny and invent a 'new England' from scratch, but Toplis's provocation of disobedience becomes itself destabilised as he and Erica become mutually spellbound by making each other 'feel [their] pain', admitting the limitations of this precarious and unlikely Utopia. Erica finds New England, like the Old, maintains an 'unnatural capacity for understand-ing one another' when she thrills to contradiction, antagonism and the pain of obsession ('I love . . . I'll die for it. Or of it. Nothing else') in ways which make their union unforgivable to all ideological forces which would (re)claim them. The immediacies of physical and sensual experience are extended into a com-pulsive alienation from socialising forces.

*No End of Blame* (1981) begins a trilogy of plays – with *Pity in History* (1984) and *Scenes from an Execution* (1985) – examining the ownership of art, the reclaimability of the artist, and the fight against surrender of work and self to annexing assimilation, by which the state aims to defer, displace or digest criticism. Barker's artists strive to perform contradiction (in Barker's world, the essence of the human condition) and locate blame, but occasionally in ways which threaten to make them heroic, and therefore vicarious for others. *Victory* (1983) consequently offers a more dislocating moral experience in a more chaotic post-Restoration social landscape, with a resolutely unheroic and contradictory protagonist who decides to endure and hasten the breakings of all forms of her former faith, love and duty. *Victory* marks Barker's breakthrough into a form of anti-reconciliatory tragedy he calls Theatre of Catastrophe:

> At the end there is no restatement of collective principles such as justify Greek and Shakespearean work; the individuals who break the social code, in the essential moment of tragic action, do not apologise, are not brought back into the *polis*, nor do they necessarily die; they possibly wander off into solitude, into a very empty landscape, and disappear into that.[8]
>
> The audience participate in the struggle to make sense of the journey, which becomes their journey also. Consequently, what is achieved by them is achieved individually and not collectively. There is no official interpretation.[9]

Barker's dramatic insistence on gruellingly and enticingly explicit verbal and physical expressive imagery extends his work into a realm where the *poetic* is the *political*, through its insistence on infinite capacity, transformability and reversibility, in which language can be decisive power: 'I wanted to take advantage of fiction, to permit more articulation than nature would permit . . . and to do so with a form of language which was – despite the actor's ease – contrived, dense, poetic, in a way common speech rarely can be, so both the content and the mode of expression were unhindered by the considerations of truth-to-life':[10] as in poetic drama of the Renaissance. Barker's language 'never denies articulation, is not repressive, implicatory or suggestive but describes, expostulates, seduces; language is the means by which the characters repel the misery of existence, and in the beauty of their speech, through both poetry and abuse, will themselves new life'.[11]

*The Castle* (RSC, 1986) shows Barker's verbal and scenic poetic density at their most concentrated, in a harrowing medieval tragedy of gender opposition, the exclusivity of which is characteristically both intensified and undermined by sexual obsession and the pain of irrevocable loss. The eponymous edifice serves as an image for all self-perpetuating aggression – 'by definition, not definitive', although a surprising confluence of characters finally gather to consider the possibility of its demolition. In *Women Beware Women* (1986), Barker hi-jacks Middleton's Jacobean tragedy to explore how sexuality can cement, but also unlock, civil discipline; the discovery of sexual transformation drives characters, formerly complicit, to disrupt the voyeuristic pageantry of state through desecration of those who would be its instruments. The provocative sexual lengths of expression and action are both alluring and shocking here, memorably suggesting the political dimension of the metaphorical imagination, its capacity both to dissolve literal or conventional polarities, and to force new distinctions: the delimitation of the body releases the imagination to wreak havoc in the finite allocation of power which official definition pretends.

Barker's compulsorily performative characters strive to undercut each other's performances and occasionally undercut their own (either inadvertently, through pain, or strategically, through abjection). Their existential *modus vivendi* is thus a demanding but charismatic analogue for that of the process of her/his stage incarnation, in which 'The actor is elevated, through language and through the extent of the pain he embodies, to a dominant status, one which obviates pity or judgement'; the seductive criminality of the performer is required to entice and compel the audience beyond shame into a realm of deliberate and conscious excess, in which 'The production must become, in essence, a poem and, like a poem, not reducible to a set of statements in other forms' and 'The liberating of pain from its . . . so-called objective conditions . . . affirms the individual's right to chaos, extremity and self-description'.[12]

*The Bite of the Night* (RSC, 1988) is one of Barker's most formally innovative works, a four-and-a-half-hour odyssey into personal and mythic imagination, beginning with a Prologue which seeks to free the audience from dependence on conventional narrative coherence, even as it demands 'what are theatres for'. Barker has suggested that the specific power and potential of theatre in fact has little in common with either television or film:

> The sterility of the commonplace theatre, and its imminent extinction, follows from the theatre's sense of itself as an industry with a market, on the one hand, or a social service with a popular obligation on the other. . . . Both of these positions require that the dramatist satisfy an audience in its perceived *demands* – entertainment or education. In attempting to satisfy these demands, the theatre slavishly performs functions more efficiently provided elsewhere and diminishes its particular powers, poetry, the spoken voice, the hypnotism of the actor. The Catastrophic Theatre on the other hand, does not address itself to demands at all . . .

Rather, it addresses needs 'not articulated in the wider culture', through Tragedy, which 'is inherently irrational' and 'affirms the *limits of social action*'.[13]

In *The Bite*, Savage, a university lecturer, pushes his enquiries into self and others to 'breaking point', finds he does not break, and pushes further. Accompanied by his sole remaining student, he tears through to the psychic and historical omphalos of mythic Troy, where his estranged wife and the historical figures of Helen and Homer appear in surprising new forms. Whilst *The Bite* resembles a dream or nightmare play, it is a relentlessly political exploration of various contemporary publicly fetishistic prescriptions, charting the feverish rising and falling of numerous Trojan political regimes which are in fact successive manifestations of a given character's psyche and sexuality. The exhaustive permutations which the characters willingly and unwillingly explore provide an excellent example of Barker's technique: 'it overwhelms the audience by the *plethora* of what it experiences. The sense of witnessing *too much*, of being *out of control* is essential to the Catastrophic play.... This quality of plethora invites new ways of seeing and witnessing since lineal narrative is regarded as reactionary and the experience is one of constant digression and a multitude of spectacles which are related not by theme but by tension, psychology or atmosphere'.[14] Helen of Troy, an embodiment of shameless beauty, is mutilated as offensive by each successive regime, yet retains her disruptive magnetism, not least by her 'elitist' insistence 'I want to be unforgivable! How could I ever forgive myself if I were forgivable?'. This connects her to Katrin, the war-desecrated heroine of *The Europeans: Struggles to Love* (written 1987, staged 1991), who discovers her own power to disturb the morality of sexual and ethical convention. In the aftermath of Islamic–Christian cultural war, Leopold, the artfully unstable Emperor of the Hapsburg state, tries to harness her image to the symbolic order of his own conciliatory regime, but Starhemberg, a melancholy former defender of Vienna, expresses his adoration for Katrin by assisting her towards the defiant performance of her own unassimilability. Their joint project, to reperform and subvert the mayhem which political systems impose on people, is, in the most literal of senses, hopelessly (and therefore fearlessly) romantic, and triumphs, if only briefly. Both dislocated, Katrin and Starhemberg discover together the strength to act out through their lives one of Barker's observations:

> The secret of tragedy – its inviolable secret – its terrible power of dislocation – lies in the forbidden knowledge [of] fatal susceptibility to instincts which are perfectly incompatible with collective discipline. Whilst it is possible to wring pity from the spectacle of the sad, the spectacle of the tragic penetrates beyond pity and achieves its effects in that place of irrationality which is also home to desire . . . its seductive authority reaches always to the self-determining, the self-describing, and the erotic. It is the private, the occluded, to which it addresses its disruptive powers.[15]

Barker's poetic monologues – *Don't Exaggerate* (1984), The *Breath of the Crowd* (1986) and *Gary the Thief/Gary Upright* (1987) – develop the focus on the individual foregrounded against the crowd, and the compulsion of instinct (for death in the first, for shamelessly continued life in the third) to break through socially imposed form and received wisdom. Gary Upright proposes the possibility that each man and woman might be their own divinity, a form of self-accepting refinement and sense of charismatic power which will recur in Barker's work. *The Last Supper* (1988) develops this theme in depicting the twilight of a prophet, Lvov, set against the reflexive demands of the crowd (incarnated as a disembodied and spasmodic chorus) and a series of parables (whose scenes of disingenuous abjection invite, only to disrupt, comparisons with Brecht's *Lehrstücke*; as does Barker's 1987 collection of short plays, *The Possibilities*, in which the apparent possession of irrefutable 'truth', as conventionally and ideologically defined, is exposed as insufficient reason for acquiescence). Witnessing 'the death of complexity', Lvov's ultimately predictable followers are outstripped only by Judith, who can remind him 'You taught me that information is nothing, and expression, all'. Judith's relentless appetite for knowledge and skill in performance rescues Lvov from his residual impulses towards 'the mundane satisfactions of the common life' by challenging him to go where he must – into death – in order to seal his immaculate artificiality of will. She initiates his murder by his fatally haunted disciples. *Seven Lears* and *Golgo* (both 1990) continue the examinations of wilful performance and relentless self-overcoming ('God give us the courage of our cruelty' is a concluding line in *Golgo*). *Seven Lears* speculates about the early life of Shakespeare's Lear, a monarch flayed by his own acuteness of philosophical sensibility, haunted by victims of injustice yet aware that the appeal to all that is good in a man is a strategy for weakening an adversary into 'anybody's fool'. Unusually for Barker, the effect can be to adumbrate and rationalise aspects of Shakespeare's play.

Barker's subsequent reanimation, *(Uncle) Vanya* (written 1990, staged 1993), contrastingly explodes out of the husk of naturalistic constriction and of British theatre directors' contemporary fetishisation of invocations of Chekhov's 'classical' determinism, entropy and pathos (the preponderance of English productions of Chekhov in the 1980s and 1990s seemed to suggest he had taken over as national dramatist). In Barker's version, we share Vanya's viewpoint to the extent that the action can stop and freeze around Vanya whilst he steps out of the 'frame' of the Chekhov world, to comment on it, albeit impotently; thus, the familiar tactics of Chekhovian evasion through small-talk are counterpointed by dream-like moments of eloquent and shameless expression: Helena taunts him with the reminder that the ageing patronising husband of this listless beauty can nevertheless enter her bedroom where he 'fucks her hard'. Vanya's repeated proclamation 'I have a gun' tries to establish his desperation in a way that will make them take him seriously but fails, until he shoots Serebryakov and becomes committed to a life of transgression, into which he and Helena enter, in mutual enticement and sexual assertion. Serebryakov and Astrov appear posthumously as ghosts, forming a chorus of fearful, conventional voices praising Chekhov and trying to subordinate the transgressive characters' confidence; even the moribund dramatist himself intervenes, attempting to subdue his creations with empathy. In differing repudiations of Chekhovian 'melancholy compromise', Helena initiates the tragic gesture of a suicide pact, but Vanya chooses not to yield, even to his grief at the loss of Helena. In stepping beyond the boundaries of externally prescribed identity, Vanya finds himself, in the last words of Barker's previous play *Rome* (written 1989), 'perfectly alone'. Barker's liberationist repudiation of social determinism, through his artful subversion of analogous theatrical convention, is here at its most incisive, emotionally demanding and resonant. *Vanya* is an excellent example of catastrophism in its demonstration that, albeit through unforgivable transgression and unforeseeable pain, the world unlocks, although the self that comes through may be unnatural, inhuman, unrecognisable even to the self. Contrastingly, *Ten Dilemmas* (written 1991; unstaged) is perhaps Barker's most unremittingly tragic play in its demonstration that some passions permit neither redemption nor relief, and that incarceration can occur on every conceivable level of being.

*Hated Nightfall* (1994) offers in many ways a classical example of Barker's work: a figure usually submerged by history – the tutor of the Romanoff children – pursues his own apotheosis of absolute play, murderous abandon and vengeful erotic dedication, with wry but lethal disregard for the agents of ideological discipline and historical order who attempt to interrupt him. *He Stumbled* (written 1998, staged 2000) depicts an anatomist embroiled in a Jacobean intrigue, brought to question the distinction between flesh and identity. *A House of Correction* (1998) shows characters caught in paroxysms of procrastination, attempting to fathom the relation between consciousness of freedom and unconscious will to catastrophe. *Und* (1999) stretches and specifies this experience of 'killing time' in a one-woman show for one of Barker's 'perfect liars', awaiting extermination but wilfully eroticising the unseen, malevolently deterministic executioner. With nothing to lose, Und (whose very name suggests continuation, a refusal to reach a full stop until she is compelled to) indulges in a wilful fabrication: a scenario of imaginative invention and complication, while waiting for the call of a lover. She opposes the imposition of brutal simplification (the label of 'Jew' and her consequent death) by endowing the experience with a defiant sensuality and mutuality of determination. Thus she, and Barker, avoid the sentimental platitude of the victim who possesses the sole authentic perspective on the Holocaust or on any other example of ethnic cleansing; the experience of elongated, tenuous concentration recalls Beckett (particularly *Happy Days*) but with malevolence characterised historically rather than metaphysically.

This characteristic sense of the gratingly beautiful and the desperately erotic – and of the promise of their discovery, in both refinement and disarray – is carried through from *Und* into the more innovative next phase of Barker's writing, commenced by *Ursula* (1998): a parable of longing and sacrifice in which the self-conscious executioner is at least as compelling as the self-conscious martyr in their mutual drive into unforgivability. The narrative has a crystalline transparency (which invites, but remains invulnerable to, allegorical interpretation), invested with a strange necessity and curiously powerful, especially in the tensile foreboding and balletic suspense of Barker's own choreographic production.[16] *Albertina* (BBC Radio 3, 1999) is similarly a deceptively clear, harrowing investigative pursuit of the reversibility of all things ('nothing is ever as simple as you say'). *Ursula*'s investigations of expectation, longing and completion are extended and elaborated, both grotesquely and gracefully, in *The Twelfth Battle of Isonzo* (written 1998, staged 2001). A young blind woman awaits the arrival of an old blind man to whom she is betrothed. On appearing he initiates a duel of deception 'stretching the pleasures of anticipation to their breaking point'. In this archaeology of strategy, evasion, refuge, the intrinsic artificialities of desire and agonised devotion become 'wound more tightly than a spring'. Their contesting negotiations towards sexual fulfilment make them occasionally enthralled by one another, but unwilling to submit to each other, their dealings crystallising one of Barker's central metaphorical propositions 'that out of the agony of something comes a particular form of ecstasy, and vice versa'.[17] *Found in the*

*Ground* (published 2001) is perhaps Barker's furthest attempt to open up a landscape, rather than a narrative, with the details of the text demanding painterly, operatic and choreographic precision in realisation, through imagery enacting notional impossibility, excavating and remaking notions of moral consequence. No dramatist of the period under review has questioned and extended the possibilities of theatre so restlessly, eloquently and purposefully as Barker.

## Notes

1. Barker, *Arguments for a Theatre* (3rd edition, Manchester, 1997), p. 23.
2. Ibid., pp. 21, 37.
3. Barker, in the radio documentary 'Departures from a Position', BBC Radio 3, 14/2/99.
4. *Arguments*, p. 20.
5. Ibid., p. 22.
6. 'Departures from a Position.'
7. *Arguments*, p. 38.
8. 'Departures from a Position.'
9. *Arguments*, p. 46.
10. Ibid., p. 96.
11. Ibid., p. 133.
12. Ibid., p. 123.
13. Ibid., p. 146.
14. Ibid., p. 147.
15. Ibid., p. 173.
16. Barker, on his directing style: 'I continually try to create pictures of mobility, with significant, often emblematic kind of moves', more akin to performance art than naturalistic theatre, *In Dublin*, 9–22/8/01, p. 43.
17. 'Departures from a Position'. In Barker's own production of *Isonzo* (Dublin, 2001), Tenna finally escaped from Isonzo's room, albeit bruised and bleeding. Whilst her guidance of Isonzo into death recalled Judith in *The Last Supper*, her flight into an unknowable world elsewhere thus reflected Barker's Vanya.

# Chapter 12

# A Blasted F£££ing Difference?: The 1990s and Beyond the Big Zeros

Thatcher's dogmatic rhetorical assurance, 'There is no alternative', was decisively challenged in 1990. Her own Cabinet perceived her as an electoral liability in a changing national mood: economic recession was affecting previously sheltered Southern England as well as the North, challenging the balance of power in the country's geographically schematic division of loyalty. Public opposition to a proposed Poll Tax had rendered the scheme unworkable. Her Conservative successor John Major won a rather apathetic general election in 1992, but the moralising of his 'Back to Basics' campaign (another vacuous appeal to supposedly traditional family values) was ironically discredited by a series of scandals in which Conservative Ministers and MPs were caught embroiled in financial corruption or sexual scandals, which made Barnes's *The Ruling Class* seem closer to social realism. In 1993, 10 per cent of the population owned 48 per cent of its wealth,[1] and public disaffection with the manifest gap between government and governed grew. The youthful ascendant Labour leader Tony Blair promised a 'New Labour' to lead a 'New Britain' in generalised invocations of moral values (more often than policies) which suggested freedom from desperate and disintegrating clichés associated with Conservatism or socialist Labour. His resounding success in the 1997 General Election was a startling but overdue refutation of Conservative authoritarianism and its dismissal of alternatives.

However, Blair's invocations of renewal, novelty, youth, access and inclusiveness sat oddly with the instigation of neo-Conservative policies, such as the abolition of student grants and the introduction of charging students for university tuition fees, ironically dismantling the very educational grant system from which many of the government (and its supporters) had benefited in their youth. His association with the sentimentality surrounding the shadowy death of Diana, Princess of Wales, indicated his willingness to maintain the Thatcherite mould of a populist society yoked by the cult of personality (and similarly to attempt to 'take the politics out of politics', in terms of policy articulation and discussion). The first stages of Welsh and Scottish devolution were permitted, and the ill-fated 1998 Good Friday agreement briefly promised hope for agreed terms of peace between Britain and the various factions of Ireland. However, any support for the Arts continued to be expressed either through (a) Thatcherite commercial terms of readily identifiable markets of homogeneous passive consumers, thus refusing to acknowledge art as an intrinsically worthwhile or valuable pursuit, or (b) notions of 'accessibility': something to be extended primarily through provisions for the young, the community and the disabled. Rather than make an argument for (theatre) art on its own terms, or suggest confidence that it might play a meaningful, central or distinctive part in the creation of a national aesthetic consciousness, strategy statements (exemplified by the Arts Council of Wales's 'The Arts Work') attempted half-heartedly to justify 'cultural industries' in fundamentally industrial terms of commercial management answerability. This pseudo-democratic rhetoric masked a narrowing and limitation of provision for an increasingly infantilised audience, in order to maintain the dominant consumerist terms of their social controllability.

Blair's continued attempted self-association with renewal floundered conspicuously with the Millennium Dome, the centrepiece of national celebrations which was insufficiently attended. The dawn of a new millennium brought natural and widespread hope for renewal, but this was better expressed and experienced by people's brief rejections of the restrictive habits of industrial timetables, than by profligate orchestrated spectacle. In 2001, New Labour was returned to office for a second term, but it still remains to be seen whether Blair can prove capable of encouraging hope beyond the terms of a national character defined by a populist sentimentality which still carries many imprints of Conservative constrictions. Blair's nominally socialist celebrations of diversity and welcoming of difference are frequently predicated on the terms of the pseudo-accessibilities of commercial popular culture and municipal utilitarianism.

The first seismic political developments of the new millennium were international rather than British. In 2000, the Republican George Bush Jr. became the new American President, after a narrow and controversial election, and led a return to the hawkish foreign policy rhetoric of the Reagan era. On 11 September 2001, terrorists deployed hijacked planes for air attacks on the New York Trade Center and the Pentagon. American and British forces traced the blame back to Osama Bin Laden in Afghanistan, and commenced military reprisals in a self-styled 'War Against Terrorism' which was implicitly extendible to other Islamic countries such as Iraq. Reinflammations of relations between Israel and Palestine, and India and Pakistan, made for an alarmingly volatile world climate, in which a British ostensibly left-wing Prime Minister was thrust into close international military alliance with the interests of a right-wing American President. Plays such as Barker's *The Europeans* and *Judith*, Sarah Kane's *Blasted* and even Bond's *The Worlds* assumed ominous new immediacies of resonance.

## The terrible force of inconsequence

The 1990s wave of British dramatists was collectively characterised by a more widespread emphasis on challenging physical and verbal immediacy, and bleak (arguably nihilistic) observations of social decay, severed isolation and degradation into aimlessness: an abiding image of which is provided by Martin Crimp's play *The Treatment* (RC, 1993), in which socially sanctified processes of spiritual plunder are concluded by a blinded man committing himself to a taxi with a blind driver.[2] Much British drama of the 1990s showed the influence of Beckett and Pinter applied to naturalistic or socially realistic situations, and of Bond's *Saved*, in which the sense of loss of consequence is more often socially located, rather than metaphysically interpreted (as in Absurdist drama) or even politically debated (as in the work of Brenton, Hare or Edgar).

Gregory Motton dramatises an estranging interpersonal poetics of dislocation: his early plays *Ambulance* (RC, 1987) and *Downfall* (RC, 1988) depict the predatory entanglements and obsessive negotiations of self-deceiving human jetsam. *A Message for the Broken Hearted* (1993) shows a triangular relationship presided over by an incestuous father, a disarmingly explicit dysfunctional *ménage* with echoes of Orton's *Sloane* but without the resilient criminality. Rather, Motton shows how his characters 'always want what they can't have, while at the same time they destroy what they're attracted to', because of their regressive fear of change. *The Terrible Voice of Satan* (RC, 1993) shows Motton's writing flourishing into a darkly comic surrealism: an Irish–Goonish odyssey which echoes *Peer Gynt*, the play shows imaginatively benighted characters demonising and recoiling from intimations of the truth, self-aggrandising ('My inner landscape has to be seen to be believed') yet self-defeating ('All my energies are spent watching my loved ones suffer and myself suffer at their hands'). Motton's most powerful play, *Cat and Mouse (Sheep)* (Paris, 1995), begins as a satire on the British shopkeeper mentality as a self-distorting response to political rhetoric of the 1980s and 1990s. However, Motton writes with a moral tenacity which takes the premise of the imaginative mutilation of self and others beyond mere satirical irony and into harrowing, monstrous tragicomedy (like plays by Barnes and Dic Edwards). Motton's characters, both vicious and mesmerised, construct exhaustive expositions of attempted meaning and self-confirmation: a greengrocer attempts to remake himself as a philosopher–king in redemption of his social and marital disappointments, and his servile relatives conceal their childish self-interest beneath postures of moral superiority. The increasingly strenuous performance of self-justification is shown as politically symptomatic self-deception and destruction, making *Cat and Mouse (Sheep)* the most searching satire on how the lure of authoritarianism misshaped the *fin de siècle* British political unconscious.

Joe Penhall's plays, like Motton's, show the frequently cruel survival tactics adopted by social derelicts who are pushed beyond the promise of conventional social consequences. However, Penhall places his idiosyncratic, potentially explosive characters in more socially recognisable (though challenging) dramatic situations, usually that of a disintegrating, unsympathetic London (linking his work to Poliakoff's, as well as to *Saved*). Penhall's stories, of how an uncaring society predicated on self-interest compounds problems of alienation and identity, might be criticised as demonstrations of the failures of the social services rather than tragedies. On the other hand, he raises important questions, such as what is 'a rational response to life's chaos' and when does 'the obsessive quality of love step over into a psychotic state'.[3] *Pale Horse* (RC, 1995) shows a man existentially dislocated by the death of his wife. Contemptuous of the social, religious and legal platitudes of mainstream social 'purpose', he is propelled into an underworld of nihilism enlivened by risk-taking and violence. The bleak humour of Penhall's exposures here resembles a 1990s British version of Büchner's *Woyzeck*. In *Love and Understanding* (1997) Penhall further dramatises the male potential for unsettling reversibilities in identity, strategy and status, when the incursion of an old friend destabilises not only a relationship but his reluctant host's entire personality. The threat of eruptive violence in *Some Voices* (1994) and *Pale Horse* might initially seem to align Penhall with a fetishisation of criminality discernible in other 90s dramatists (Neilson, Butterworth, Ravenhill, with lethal flippancy and homoerotic violence ossifying into clichés in the plays of Simon Bennett and Irvine Welsh). However, Penhall's enquiry is more humanistic: 'I think a lot of men are far more sensitive and perverse and individual than they'd like to admit'.[4]

Like Motton, Stephen Jeffreys works within the comic genre whilst pushing its peramenters. *The Clink* (1990) questions the efficacy and purpose of comedy in an openly brutalised climate which renders satirical exposure redundant (a question persistently posed by Peter Barnes). *The Libertine* (RC, 1994) reinvents the Earl of Rochester in theatrical challenge to Etherege and to presumptions surrounding his Restoration play *The Man of Mode*. This savage comedy of articulate excess explores the relationship between power and impotence – personal, political and theatrical – through Barkerian painful humour, in which characters rack themselves to express and know, subvert themselves or falter painfully, yet persist. It maintains the form of a comedy of manners yet ultimately suffuses the very project of self-performance in the contexts of sexuality, theatricality and power with a deep melancholy which displaces cynicism. The ingenuity of *The Libertine* is how it makes the audience, like Rochester, fall into the trap of feeling directly, rather than ironically.[5]

Two Scottish plays provide notable examples of the power of language in undermining and constructing different versions of the self. Chris Hannan's *Shining Souls* (1996) is a comedy of self-contradiction played out by disconnected but resilient figures from the Glaswegian underclass, who frequently interrupt themselves to undercut or mitigate their own statements – 'I'll be fine. (If I don't fall to pieces.)' – or develop them into unpredictable digressions. The effect, though humorous, reiterates a sense of qualified possibility, lost momentum and bewildered, disorientated isolation. David Harrower's *Knives in Hens* (1995) shows a young woman in a pre-industrial rural community struggling towards an authentic sense of self-expression, distinction, consequence and possibility through language (a process of pushing 'names into what there is there as when I push my knife into the stomach of a hen'). Harrower's unforced but resonant naturalism shows restricted language to be a means of entrapment, but also depicts the development of speech as an essential index of personal individuation and social discovery (in a way which recalls Rudkin's drama).

# Coming closer

fear is really the dullest side of horror's coin

(Anthony Neilson, *Normal*)

Aleks Sierz's account of 1990s British drama, *In-Yer-Face Theatre* (2001), notes the fashionable emergence of an experiential theatre – as it might be termed more gracefully and precisely – which challenges the conventional responses of both audience member and performer, through emphasis on 'confrontation brought to its physical conclusion'.[6] This form of drama offers an experience rather than a description or explanation of experience (and, if ever analytical, it is subjectively rather than objectively so). It interrogates the binary oppositions involved in the distinctions of being human ('human/animal; clean/dirty; healthy/unhealthy; normal/abnormal; good/evil; true/untrue; real/unreal; right/wrong; just/unjust; art/life'); it shows existential definition confronting an abjection which animates 'ancient fears about the power of the irrational and the fragility of our sense of the world',[7] often through 'images of violated intimacy'.[8] As Sierz acknowledges, there is a long and important (perhaps *the most* important) tradition of theatre which disrupts and renegotiates the relationship between audience and performers, which breaks taboos in open ways which provoke an unsettling and divisive self-consciousness (Sierz: 'When you're watching a play, which is mostly in real time with real people acting just a few feet in front of you, not only do you find yourself reacting but you also know that others are reacting and are aware of your reaction';[9] compare Barker's ideal of the perceptibly divided audience in *Arguments for a Theatre*). Aspects of this tradition can be traced through Greek, Shakespearean and Jacobean tragedy, to Grand Guignol and Schnitzler's *Reigen* and Genet, to Rudkin, Bond, Barker and many of the distinctive dramatists considered in the book you are reading. Sierz notes how many of the 1990s experiential plays often sought to 'seduce the audience with a naturalistic mood and then hit it with intense emotional material',[10] but then so does Ibsen's *Ghosts*.

More precisely, Sierz notes how 1990s British experiential plays provided a deliberately conspicuous break with 'politically correct "victim drama" where perpetrators were bad and victims good. . . . By emphasising such troubling notions as the complicity of victims in their victimisation, provocative drama became more complex, less ideological. Instead of a morally black and white world, theatre offered grey areas and ambiguous situations'.[11] This is a particular break with the rhetorical drama of political morality developed by Hare and Edgar (and Edgar's *The Prisoner's Dilemma* can be seen as a riposte against the glamorisation of violence and an assertion of the importance of verbal negotiative discussion). Moreover, it shows younger writers experimenting with the freedoms of the theatrical encounter, away from the commercial pressures of television writing (the near extinction of the single television play may have pushed more writers towards the theatre[12]), and in less commercial smaller auditoria (many of this wave of writers had their work initially performed in small and upstairs theatres, performance circumstances in which the audience can not only touch but even *smell* the performers, and which may be the anti-commercial ideal setting for drama which involves disruptively cruel confrontations and physical and imaginative exposure).

Philip Ridley's anatomies of menace helped to define this 90s vogue. Ridley attempts to use 'elements of melodrama in a postmodernist way',[13] and his plays begin with splendidly energetic monstrous characters, whose names combine the self-styled extravagance of graphic novel hero/villains with the suggestive but imperfectly definable resonances of Dickens. However, the dramatic premise and development of Ridley's plays are often confined to paradigms strongly reminiscent of early Pinter and Orton, with solipsistic but insecure characters responding violently to invasive threats, but ultimately contracting into regression. Ridley also demonstrates a Beckettian sense of the power (and fragility) of the narrative of displacement, whereby a character attempts to (re-)order their past through a repeated activity of storytelling which wilfully obscures any reliable boundaries between truth and fiction. Thus the extravagant but infantile 'superselves' which the characters construct for themselves, with the support of subordinates, are tenuous and ultimately flawed. In *The Pitchfork Disney* (1991), one character fearfully deduces 'I don't think it makes any difference if I'm good or not. Not when so much in life can explode. So many things can burn us up through no fault of our own. There's nothing we can do to save ourselves'. An alternative sense of purpose is represented by self-styled dark angels of corruption, who take an adolescent pleasure in the desecration of the falsely preserved innocence of the 'Ancient children with no vocation', whose invented worlds aspire towards a privileged 'oblivion'. *The Fastest Clock in the Universe* (1992) shows the Ortonian equilibrium of Cougar Glass and Captain Tock threatened, when the schoolboy object of Cougar's predatory paedophilia is claimed by Sherbet Gravel, an equally proprietorial agent of heterosexual kitsch (preaching 'the value of traditional things'). At the end of an enforced ritual strongly reminiscent of Pinter's *The Birthday Party*, Cougar beats Sherbet (a latter-day Lulu) until she loses her unborn baby, and Cougar and the Captain are free again to shrug off the external threat and preserve their own time-defying artificial idyll of 'love'. *Ghost from a Perfect Place* (1994) shows Travis, a self-styled 'gentleman gangster' of a bygone 'heyday', visiting Torchie (a latter-day Meg) and rekindling her memories of 'A perfect place I visited once, but can never visit again'. Travis is pinioned by Rio, Torchie's prostitute granddaughter, and tortured by Rio's girl gang; his selective memory and glamorisation of violence is challenged by these youthful female monsters, dedicated to 'domination'. However, Travis abjectly confesses his revisionary self-authorisation, and disingenuously involves Rio in the narration of his rape of her mother. With Travis and Rio jointly confirmed in new versions of their identities, as father and daughter, she releases him. Ridley's nightmarish fables of predatory searches for the confirmation of identity demonstrate linguistic verve and, superficially, an almost Expressionist energy; but I emphasise the 'almost'. His plays ultimately reiterate early-Pinteresque contractions, into defensively reductive withdrawal. Apparently, Ridley considers the breakthrough effects of his excellent children's stories – in which adventurous children educate their dysfunctional, regressive elders through demonstrating imaginative possibilities of transformation – to be inappropriate to his drama for adults.

Scottish dramatist–director Anthony Neilson has purposefully explored his sensed distinction between film and television, which the audience watch more passively, and theatre, where people go to place themselves in 'a situation which is halfway between watching and participating'.[14] *Normal* (1991) recalls both Brenton's *Christie in Love* and Taylor's *Good* in its pre-war confrontation of a German serial killer and psychologist. The killer, like Thatcher, asserts 'There is no such thing as society' and, less glibly, asks the psychiatrist how he has arrived at his conventional definitions of love. The psychiatrist looks back on his own behaviour in Nazi Germany: 'In the years that followed . . . I / and a great many "normal" men / were to do things we had never thought ourselves capable of . . . I can only hope that [God] will judge us / not as the monsters we have become / but as the children / we once were'. As in McGrath and Boyle's *The Hard Man*, the self-confessed killer's taste for blood finds a discomforting echo in socially directed orders for 'good, normal' behaviour. Even Neilson's minor work, such as the ultimately melodramatic comedy *Year of the Family* (1994), plays out a confrontational, insistent and socially contradictory physicality: in this case, a memorable sadomasochistic exchange involving tabasco sauce. *The Censor* (1997) is Neilson's best stage examination of the unsettling immediacy of the physical presence, of both character and performer. An inured, disenchanted film censor finds his imagination ignited by the seductive personal presence of Fontaine, a film director whose work he has dismissed as unexceptionally pornographic. She insists on the way that the explicit sexuality of her film represents a whole language of 'engagement', and how her physical contact with the Censor can articulate trust, curiosity and even sly humour. They progress to his admission of arousal at watching her defecate; this poses a challenge to the theatre audience to discover, with the Censor, a beauty in the performance of the simulated(?) action. Like *The Hard Man, The Censor* involves the theatre audience in a startling confrontation with the performers' contact with excrement (*presumed* artificial but necessarily *practically* convincing), perhaps even more challenging in Neilson's play for its location in an erotic rather than violent context. When Fontaine is killed, the Censor remains pleasurably haunted by her provocations, her expansion of his vocabulary of possibility, and his discovery of capacities for tragic love. Neilson's movement into film might seem unlikely, but represents the full flourishing of the apparent influence of McGrath and Boyle's play: Neilson's *The Debt Collector* (Film Four, 1999) is not only resonantly powerful but also a virtual sequel to *The Hard Man*. Dryden, a reformed gangster turned writer and sculptor (strikingly similar to Boyle), is hounded by Keltie, the policeman who arrested him and who continues to despise Dryden as 'a traitor to his country and his class'. The isolated, sexually constrained and morally vengeful Keltie insists that 'killing doesn't take guts, trying to live a decent life is what takes guts', and sees Dryden's celebrity as symptomatic of destructive Scottish paradigms of heroism: 'your national heroes are junkies, drunks and whores'. Keltie assumes an attack upon his mother to be Dryden's return to 'the Policy' – a strategy of striking at defiant men through their partners and families – and reverses the strategy by attacking and raping Dryden's wife. Keltie taunts Dryden that 'All she'll see when she looks at you is fear and pain and loss, and me, and what we did tonight', as they engage in brutal physical struggle, to the ironic counterpoint of the Edinburgh Tattoo and 'Scotland the Brave'. *The Debt Collector* is one of the most harrowing recent dramatic excavations of contemporary masculinity in its stark images and articulations of the abject male, erotically vulnerable and provocatively vicious, seeking to appease women whilst threatening other men. *The Debt Collector* and *The Censor* indicate Neilson's notable promise for the future, through their physically immediate discoveries and manifestations of tragic compulsions.

Jez Butterworth's *Mojo* (RC, 1995) echoes Neilson's awareness of the lure of violence which invites regression into childish monstrosity, and Ridley's sense of desecrated infantile vulnerability on collision with (and mutating into) adolescent predatory homerotic glamour. The cover blurb of the NHB script locates *Mojo* succinctly: 'Soho, summer 1958. British youth, seduced by the speed and optimism of a glittering American future, have swapped their ration books for rock'n'roll records'. However, *Mojo* is not a socially realistic account of the *Look Back in Anger* era, and its ditching of deferentiality; like Ridley's drama, it is a postmodern, blackly humorous melodrama celebrating masculine performative duels of charismatic and intimidating but defensive style. The 'speed and optimism' of *Mojo*'s boys is more informed by Tarantino films and Britpop style (a mid-90s vogue for recycling with attitude, expressed through music, fashion and posture-striking, and briefly endorsed by the Blair administration as the exportable flowering of a youth culture parallel to that of the 1950s and 1960s). For the *cognoscenti* of self-consciousness, the play's references are fluid, mischievously light and knowing: a body separated into dustbins recalls Beckett's *Endgame*, a box apparently containing a head raises the spectre of Emlyn Williams's *Night Must Fall*, and the protagonist Baby likens himself to Spiderman (a character invented in 1962). *Mojo* depicts a gangland war in the backrooms of showbiz hustle, in which the characters fight over a precocious young rock'n'roll potential star, Silver Johnny, the voodoo talisman of the title. A gangster boss, Ross, kills and cuts in half his rival, Ezra. The fast-talking lads who inhabit Ezra's club swap defensive wisecracks and reflex into playground scapegoating to cover their fear of further reprisals. Ezra's heir apparent, Baby, is the wild card: sexually abused by his father, Baby demonstrates a childlike volatility reminiscent of Richmal Crompton's William Brown rewritten by Philip Ridley, and *Mojo* shows his flourishing into murderous avenger. Baby does not stop at killing Ross and retrieving Silver Johnny (whom Baby suspends upside down, like butcher's meat, in the style of the gangster tactic in Barrie Keeffe's 1981 film, *The Long Good Friday*). Baby also discovers the identity of a traitor in the surrounding gang, Mickey. However, Baby's violence is displaced, bathetically, onto the least formidable member of the lads, Skinny, whom Baby has regularly bullied. When Skinny sides with Mickey and denounces Baby as a 'Jew', and rejects him in playground language ('None of us want you. You're nasty and you lie'), Baby shoots Skinny. The gang's former bonds of faith in homoerotic love and loyalty are shattered, but Baby and Silver Johnny walk off in search of a world elsewhere, together, discarding the talismanic silver jacket which they have both donned, like a superhero costume, in their most powerful moments. *Mojo* is a celebration of the amoral energy and (potentially casually lethal) style of the self-mythologising adolescent male (in the theme, but not the mock-heroic poetic form, of Berkoff's drama). Nevertheless, its comedy of menace offers surprising twists through the unpredictability of its disturbingly damaged and attractive protagonist, Baby, who is by far the most substantial and memorable characterisation in the play. He is a mid-1990s refraction of the Coriolanus complex I have identified earlier as being repeatedly played out in 1940s and 1950s British drama: an imperfectly individuated manchild who interprets neo-parental injunctions to maturity in self-consciously shockingly excessive actions, embarrassing to the society who finds its own ethos of achievement played out appallingly, to the hilt and beyond. Butterworth's film version of *Mojo* (BBC, 1998) emphasises the predatory childishness of all the characters, including Ezra and Ross (and contains another postmodern joke by having Harold Pinter play the latter ageing gangster, sexually plunderous and as testingly manipulative as the unseen boss of *The Dumb Waiter*).

Patrick Marber is a former stand-up comedian, and his play *Closer* (RNT, 1997) contains lines and scenes that are in many ways humorous: in many ways, but not in all ways. As in Noel Coward's *Private Lives*, we watch as two couples who have swapped partners, then swap back. *Closer* observes the traditional, even classical realistic structure of dialogues moving the story onward. However, the intensity of the feelings which the characters voice demonstrates an uncontrolled, even uncontrollable eloquence; the emphasis is not so much on submerged feelings and subtext, as on a fierce, even brutal honesty. Unlike Kane's *Blasted* or Ravenhill's *Shopping & F£££ing*, the shock resides in the verbal rather than the visual images. The characters speak straight from the heart (or gut, or groin), but the (particularly male) insistence upon honesty and explicitness tends to inflame their jealousy rather than draw them together, and by the end of the play, the characters are less 'closer' than ever before, deliberately flouting romantic hopes (at the end, the characters are not even friends, just acquaintances). The cybersex scene provides comedy of escalating mistakes and deception, exploiting the ironic gap between the virtual and the actual; it is also a wry demonstration of how technology does *not* 'shrink the world', but maintain and extend the distance between people; Dan and Larry are separated by computers so that they can exchange fantasies without embarrassment, but the situation is complicated by Dan's impersonation. The Internet's promises of access, possibility, democracy and future in fact bathetically reduces them to 'two boys tossing in cyberspace'.

The imagery of the play frequently refers to skin, surfaces and what might lie beneath them: this is, after all, a story involving a dermatologist, a photographer and a lap dancer, and which is punctuated by references to an underground river which might course beneath the surface of the modern city, and finally suggests that the human heart both literally and metaphorically resembles 'a fist wrapped in blood'. Dan seems to desire the woman he is *not* with, whom he is less close to; Larry tries to get physically 'closer' to a woman in a lapdancing club, but is ultimately separated from her by security regulations, so he sinks deeper into depression even as he goes through the motions of extending their formalised relationship, in terms which are financially regulated, and financially limited. Act I Scene 6 uses a technical trick also found in Alan Ayckbourn's *How the Other Half Loves*: of dividing a stage space in order to present alternate moments from two separated yet entwined households; both situations are sharply ironic, but Marber's willingness to explore the pain of the situation lifts *Closer* out of the comic tradition within which Ayckbourn remains, by refusing to permit the audience distance and detachment upon which comedy depends. This is an experience *closer* to home, and *closer* to the bone. Unlike Coward's *Private Lives, Closer* exposes the painful complication of being in love with two people, and of having to persist in the knowledge of one's own destructiveness to others and to oneself.

Though the play is importantly about the vocabulary and style of verbal strategy and self-expression, it also emphasises the importance and eloquence of body language and physical choreography. Artfully, the script only prescribes physical actions and attitudes incompletely; as with Shakespearean texts, the onus to develop an expressive physical vocabulary lies with the director and performers. The characters' physical expressiveness or concealment becomes an increasingly fascinating counterpoint to what they say, as the audience, like the other characters, scrutinises them particularly closely to see if they can detect if and when the characters are lying. On the one hand, the play suggests that 'lying is the currency of the world', in the manner of a satirical exposé which we might expect of a comedy of manners. On the other hand, the play shows the seductive power of incompletion, how the *pain* and the *piquancy* of *uncertainty* can be unbearably exciting, compulsively destructive and repeatedly addictive. Seduction is shown to be a game in which players do not disclose themselves, but ignite their fellow players' imaginations, only to leave those players to the ravages of their imaginations' capacities for infinite activity. Alice initially introduces herself by saying she knows what men want, and that she is both a 'waif' and a stripper. Larry admits that he is fascinated by her indefiniteness, her ability to ignite the imagination. Significantly and artfully, we never actually see the character (or performer) of Alice strip; in the 1999 RNT production, we also saw the characters of Larry and Alice simultaneously back-projected from the 'camera in the ceiling', compounding the sense of voyeurism and of heightened self-consciousness. Larry's shout, 'WHAT DO YOU HAVE TO DO TO GET A BIT OF INTIMACY ROUND HERE?', is, fictionally, directed into a two-way mirror; theatrically, it is directed towards the theatre audience, in a way that both acknowledges and momentarily blasts the fiction of the invisible audience, who nevertheless are never granted Alice's nakedness for (what Larry terms) their 'viewing pleasure'. Larry says he wants to know details 'Because I want to know everything because I'm a loony'. Dan's insistence on knowing the truth about Alice and Larry ultimately makes Alice stop loving Dan. Did Larry know this would happen when he told Dan about him and Alice? Is this a vindication of his strategy?

*Closer* often has the sharp reflecting surface of a comedy, with its trick questions and cut-and-thrust repartee, in which one good line is topped by an even better one: 'Please don't hate me'/ 'It's easier than loving you'; 'If you love her, you'll let her go so she can be happy'/ 'She doesn't want to be "happy"'; 'It's not a competition'/ 'Yes it is'; or extended further into three-way volleys: 'Everything's a lie, nothing matters'/ 'Too easy, it's the cop-out of the age'/ 'Yeah, well, you're old'; 'They [men] spend a lifetime fucking and never know how to make love'/ 'So eat pussy, Anna'/ (*weary*) 'Oh, I have'. But the play invites and draws the imagination beneath surfaces, and identifies potential tragic compulsions to which the audience might sense their own disturbing proximity and susceptibility. It suggests that it is indefinite possibility, rather than definite qualities, which attract, compulsively; that this attraction sparks the appetite for the sexually definite, compulsively; and that discovery of the definite ultimately separates people, compulsively. When Anna asks Larry why it is so important for him to know the details of her sexual actions, he replies 'BECAUSE I'M A FUCKING CAVEMAN'; and, whilst this is a wryly funny line, it contains a confrontation with the vicious possibility that, one way or another, we might all be fucking cavemen. Finally, characters and audience discover that Alice made herself up. But then, the play invites us to ask: Don't we all? And don't we all make each other up? The question is, how well? And who and what do we fall in love with, and why? And what do we risk?

Mark Ravenhill's plays also contain elements of the comedy of manners, but extend into darker social satire which ambivalently exposes contemporary reflexes into stylish heartlessness. Leggatt has noted how comedies (from *The Taming of the Shrew* to Cooper's *Everything in the Garden*) frequently show society as a market for the display and sale of people: 'As the necessity of display in the arena can reduce people to performances, so the materialism of social life reduces them to commodities'.[15] *Shopping and F£££ing* (RC, 1996) literalises this, when Mark 'buys' Robbie and Lulu, disposable human 'trash' whom he adopts as housemate-pets to join him in the 'comfort' of cheeseburgers, chocolate and ready meals. Lulu is a petty thief passing herself off as an actress: at her audition for Brian, a businessman, he reduces her to speaking Chekhov ('One day people will know what all this was for') without her blouse to activate his voyeurism and sentimentality. Robbie is stabbed with a plastic fork when he emphasises the possibility of choice to an offended customer in a burger bar. Mark is trying to wean himself off the emotional dependencies he finds just as addictive as drugs, seeking instead 'a transaction' with Gary; 'the important thing . . . for my needs, is that this doesn't actually mean anything'. However, after rimming Gary, Mark discovers '*There's blood around his mouth*'. Indeed, the surprising persistence of blood is a running motif in the play, compounding the sense of others as a source of danger and infection: Lulu finds 'too much choice' of chocolate at the local supermarket, and also gets blood on her face when a wino stabs the checkout girl; Lulu's response is to walk away and eat her chocolate bar very quickly. Robbie is the next to be bloodied: he and Lulu are charged by Brian to sell a bag of ecstasy tablets to clubbers, but Robbie gets high and distributes them freely to the potential customers; he feels euphorically benevolent, until the crowd becomes more greedily demanding and beats him up. Mark recognises that he has 'no definition' of himself, so becomes addictively attached to others as a 'potentially destructive' avoidance of knowing himself, but Gary wants a 'a dad . . . all the time, someone watching me'. Contrastingly, Mark admits he does not know what he wants; for years everything he has felt has been 'chemically induced', now 'I want to find out, want to know if there are any feelings left'; in reply, Gary offers a choice of Pot Noodles. When Brian demands recompense for the ecstasy tablets, he tells Robbie and Lulu how behind the ideals of 'beauty, God and Paradise' is money: he shows them sentimental video images of a boy with a cello, which are succeeded by the threatening images of a household drill moving towards a transgressor's face. In desperation, Robbie and Lulu open a phone sex business, surprised that there are 'so many sad people in the world', but reassured that they are 'making money' from this and so are 'going to be all right'. Gary has to reassure Mark that their kiss meant nothing to him to stop Mark falling in love. Lulu discovers that one of her customers masturbates to the security video of the supermarket knifing, but is undaunted: she scorns Robbie's anxiety, pushing his face into his food when he claims he 'can't taste' for fear, and uses the word 'darling' as a strategic weapon. However, Gary's entrance upsets their *ménage à trois*. Robbie claims the 'big stories' of religion and social progression have died or been forgotten, but that 'we all need stories . . . so that we can get by', 'so now we're all making up our own': Mark's epiphanic story is the revelation of sex in a toilet, which was apparently interrupted by Princess Diana and Sarah Ferguson, cruising and 'slumming it' sexually, disguised as policewomen. Gary's story is the account of his own fantasy, which involves his being penetrated by Robbie, then Mark, and ultimately by a kitchen knife; in exchange for money, Mark fulfils his request. Now that the trio can repay Brian, he welcomes them with his own words of comfort: 'the first few words in the Bible are . . . get the money first'; 'Money is civilisation'. This informs Brian's sense of duty, 'we must work' for the 'purity' of money for ensuing generations (a parodically neo-Chekhovian self-transcendence which always proceeds *exploitatively*, and thus promises a *highly selective* purity; Brian even reads a sense of exploitative conservatism out of *The Lion King*, but his references to the 'Cycle of Being' show he cannot even remember 'The Circle of Life' accurately!). Mark indulges in the fantasy of complete control of another, and the trio finally contentedly infantilise each other and themselves by feeding each other junk food.

It is worth recounting the mosaic of details which constitutes *Shopping and F£££ing* to give some sense of its loosely but rhetorically connected, nihilistically comic juxtapositions. Its studied observations of resolute superficiality, which rebrands love as dependency, show up the reductivity of 1990s consumerism as both blackly humorous and ultimately lethal. Unlike *Closer*, with its reverberative verbal barbs, *Shopping and F£££ing*'s power resonates through its visual images, of blood and sex acts and junk food, which are welded to an engagingly familiar thriller scenario (how to clear a debt to a threatening gangster within a lethal deadline: compare *Lock, Stock and Two Smoking Barrels* and *Things to Do in Denver When You're Dead*). Its bleakly presentational delineation of degradation and sudden shocking developments of scenic form and detail also (like Kane's plays) demonstrate the influence of early Bond, particularly *Saved*. But as Sierz observes, Ravenhill's young characters are not representatives of an inarticulate underclass, they are 'the children of middle-class, middle Britain, and their crisis is part of a country's redefinition of its self-image'.[16] One might ask whether its ironic observation of nihilistic subsidence into apathy and ubiquitous desperation for comfortable numbness and infantile gratification is more or less subversive than, say, Williams's *AC/DC* (1970)?

Ravenhill's *Faust Is Dead* (1997) is a more abstract satire on abstraction, particularly the way that, as in *Shopping and F£££ing*, pain is either ignored and avoided, or turned into a virtual commodity for transaction. Alain (a character based on the postmodernist philosopher Jean Baudrillard) and his pick-up boyfriend Pete pursue their own romance with the ironic and the unseen. This is problematised by a website encounter with Donny, who fascinates Alain, and makes him rhapsodise: 'He scars himself. He submits to a moment of intense . . . to a tribal agony. He creates his art. A testament of suffering', involving 'A moment of power, of control over the self as he draws the blade through the body' in 'An initiation rite for the end of the twentieth century'. Pete counters prosaically 'Either that or he's a loser who cuts himself . . . he hurts real bad inside and wants the outside to kinda match'.

Pete and Donny meet in person, to compete in self-mutilation, and Donny wins by slashing his jugular; even Alain, the ironic observer, is driven to cry out 'Stop the blood'. Nevertheless Alain maintains his theory, that any event is 'just a shadow, a reflection of our analysis', despite the challenging physical immediacy of Donny and his irrevocable act. This drives Pete to shoot Alain, in a pointed demonstration of how some aspects of cruelty and agency cannot be theorised away into abstraction. *Faust Is Dead* presents Ravenhill's further observations of the mesmeric promise and deathly poise of unfeeling irony, as encapsulated by the Chorus: 'I'm the kind of person who can stand in the middle of an earthquake and I'm just like "whoa, neat earthquake". And I wonder what made me that way'. Ravenhill also invites the audience to wonder what makes people how they are, and wisely chooses not to supply a single definitive formulaic answer. However, his own posture – that of an ironic observer inviting the audience to be ironic observers of the actions of characters who are ironic observers – may appear (or threaten) to enfold into that of his characters. *Handbag* (1998) is an unengaging amalgam of *The Importance of Being Earnest*, Churchill's *Cloud Nine* and Bond's *Saved* which is peopled by self-numbing stereotypes and is finally less than the sum of its parts.

*Some Explicit Polaroids* (1999) is Ravenhill's best play to date, a contemporary comedy of manners which reprises and questions motifs from his previous drama (the purchase of the self-conscious human 'trash', the dying boyfriend who refuses to take his pills). *Polaroids* assembles various *fin de siècle* neo-Restoration types around a modern 'plain dealer', Nick, a volatile political activist released from prison for the first time since the 1980s. The character of Nick is partly inspired by Ernst Toller's *Hoppla! Such Is Life!* (1927), but also reflects Brenton's *Magnificence* (1973), in which a 'honed-down' Marxist is shocked by his former comrades' subsidence into compromise, and questions the prevalent desperate appetite for vogueish numbness. Victor scorns the search for meaning perpetuated by those who are 'loving, spiritual, vulnerable, ill', preferring 'crazy' enjoyment and 'fun'; Nadia spouts New Age platitudes to cancel any sense of traceable blame ('He is a child inside. And we're all children inside'); Helen proffers the fashionable combination of money and excuse ('Sorry') to her former class enemy, Jonathan, but he eloquently repudiates the moral bankruptcy of her pose; Tim withdraws into the liberalism of consumerist *laissez-faire* ('We're all responsible for our own actions, okay? We don't blame other people. That's very nineteen eighty-four'). Nick challenges them: 'You look at me and you see bitter and ugly, alright then, but I look at you and see.... Nothing's connected, you're not connecting with anything and you're not fighting anything'. The 1990s kids blithely reply: 'But we're happy . . . content with what we've got . . . at peace with ourselves . . . our own people . . . and we're not letting the world get to us'. However, the immediacy of Tim's fatal illness dislocates Victor out of his 'promised happy world' into the dangerous mutuality of love and loss, and Jonathan's scars mock Nadia's bid for self-abasing atonement (when she offers, 'I'll kiss it better', he ripostes 'Don't be so fucking stupid. That's not going to work, is it?'). Jonathan's disingenuous civility even draws the fire from Nick's antagonism (a subversion of the violent vengeful confrontation implied by the play's resemblance to *Magnificence*). As Nick proposes to abandon his anger, Helen admits she finds it represents something 'missing', and something sexually attractive; Nick and Helen appear to settle knowingly into their own variation on the Porters' game of bears and squirrels. *Some Explicit Polaroids* wittily interrogates the allure and expectations of being 'old' or 'grown up', as defined from various perspectives, and represents Ravenhill's development from ironic satire to satirical comedy.

## The mark of Kane: how should we die?

Silence or violence / The choice is yours

(*Crave*)

Sarah Kane, the major writer to emerge from the 90s wave of British experiential drama, startlingly intensifies her audience members' awareness of the choices they make, even as she ambivalently dramatises attempts to transcend the oppression of physicality. Ian and Cate, the central characters of *Blasted* (RC, 1995), are both physically inscribed by aggression: Cate has blackouts 'Since dad came back', probably a reference to an abusive family relationship. Ian's reductive attitudes are reflected by his conscious reduction of his own immediate life expectancy through heavy drinking and smoking. He is aware that his repeated showering does little to suppress his tendency to 'stink'; when he asks Cate to 'put [her] mouth on' his naked body, he presumes she refuses for this reason. He is, however, as politically deterministic towards others as he is towards himself, both in his professional capacities as tabloid journalist and armed, bigoted government agent, and in his dismissive appraisals of Cate's intelligence, capabilities and chances in life. In Scene 1, their relationship, predicated on implied provocation, romantic sentimentality, bathos and masturbation, has a bleakly comic equilibrium. Scene 2 opens by demonstrating the extent of Ian's physical decline: he collapses ('*his heart, lung, liver and kidneys are all under attack*') but recovers through recourse to more neat gin and cigarettes. He has also apparently bitten and sodomised Cate; she bleeds from both orifices and abuses him in his own terms of disgust ('Cunt'). He takes no responsibility for his own actions ('Don't worry, I'll be dead soon') except by inviting her to shoot him with his own pistol; she faints. He, on the other hand, is excited by the prospect of armed domination, as shown when he masturbates on her unconscious figure, '*gun to her head*'. Her sudden awakening is blackly comic, as is her subsequent bid to regain power, in a scene very characteristic of Kane's insistence on physical explicitness as a manifestation of vulnerability for characters and performers alike: Cate encourages Ian to reflect on his own status through 'the real job' of homicidal covert action, whilst '*kissing his neck*', '*undoing his shirt*', '*kissing his chest*', '*massaging his neck*'; she then '*strokes his stomach and kisses between his shoulder blades*', '*licks . . . claws and scratches . . . bites his back*', '*sucks his nipples*', '*begins to perform oral sex*'; '*On the work "killer" he comes. As soon as* **Cate** *hears the word she bites his penis as hard as she can.* **Ian's** *cry of pleasure turns into a scream of pain. He tries to pull away but* **Cate** *holds on with her teeth. He hits her and she lets go*'. This is a good example of how, in Kane's drama, both violence and the desperate bid to survive violence rip into and evacuate the most intimate and sacramental body sites. The notorious scene in which the Soldier buggers and blinds Ian is accounted for by the Soldier's final impulse to visit on another what was visited upon his own lover, just before he kills himself in despair. Ian's continued existence is bleak, but blackly comic in its insistent *consequentiality*: still driven to masturbate, seek death, seek sleep, seek food, he thinks he finds a place to '*die with relief*', only to be rained on as proof of his bathetically prolonged residual existence. Finally, Cate returns, still marked, perhaps terminally, by contact with Ian: '*There is blood seeping from between her legs*'; in imitation of him, she now eats meat and drinks neat gin, which she shares with him, then '*sits apart . . . sucks her thumb*'. Ian's continued existence, with its mockery of desecrated absolutes, is a *tour de force* example of the tragedy of the grotesque, and is curiously, bleakly uplifting. However, the decline of Cate, eking out a brief survival through imitation of her oppressor, is a bleakly deterministic counterpoint, suggesting – like the Soldier's story – people's tendency to be enveloped by atrocities inscribed upon them, in fatal mutual infection (the Judas Kiss is a significantly recurrent motif in Kane's drama). Like Sarah Daniels's *Masterpieces*, *Blasted* suggests that the logic of (even casual) sexual behaviour – here predicated on the (predominantly male) notion of sex as a promise of a relief from self-consciousness – can be extended and projected into (inter)national institutionalised atrocity, as abuse in a hotel room in Leeds opens up to connect with battlefield atrocities reminiscent of Bosnia.[17] The entry of the soldier presages the unforeseeable violatation, not only of Ian, but of the apparently naturalistic form of the play, in a subversive and discomforting enfolding of form and content: the play is disturbing not just for *what* happens, but *how* it happens. *Blasted* also suggests people's capacities for resilence and adaptability in persistence with some form of life, however gruelling and removed from the form of life they might have wished for;[18] even here, as elsewhere in Kane's work, the surprising eruptions of black humour should not be avoided.[19]

Kane's *Cleansed* (RC, 1998) goes even further in depicting the systemisation of oppressive abuse which searches out precise means to rip people apart in their holiest places. Grace visits 'the university': an institution of social and probably ethnic cleansing, where inmates are spiritually and physically reduced on each occasion when they profess defiant affection. Grace comes in search of the dead Graham, a lover who may or may not also be her brother: she insists on the right to '*undress completely*', don his former clothes and stay. Her command 'Love me or kill me' initiates a sequence in which she and Graham's ghost undress, '*he sucks her right breast*', '*she touches his penis*', '*They begin to make love, slowly at first, then hard fast, urgent*'. An injury to the actress playing Grace necessitated Sarah Kane herself stepping in to assume the role during some performances of the premiere production. Kane consequently experienced the full range of demands she made in playing a character who twice undresses, copulates, is beaten with baseball bats, electrocuted and finally subjected to human vivisection which leaves male organs grafted onto her naked body. Thus, Kane demonstrated the necessary preparedness and courage to play out the part, taking responsibility for her drama not only imaginatively but physically. Nevertheless, *Cleansed* is imaginatively limited. The only affirmation which it offers is proposed through the analogy of the performers' physical courage. But, in dramatising repression, Kane mainly asks the performers to enact states of victimisation. The performers' courage is demonstrated by their *submission*, both enacted and real, to exposed vulnerability: potential embarrassment, mockery, even physical harm (as the injury to the original performer of Grace attests). Like Pinter's *One for the Road* and *Mountain Language*, in which the oppressors can do anything that their victims cannot stop them doing, *Cleansed* presents power as a one-way street: oppressive and predatory towards the individual, remorseless, searching, deterministic, unstoppable.

Kane, like Ravenhill, is manifestly influenced by Bond, and his materialist demonstrations of how characters are often primarily defined by a systematic degradation, and sometimes choose to compond their own reductions to mean simplicities. However, Kane and Ravenhill explore the sexuality of violence in ways which Bond does not. Moreover, Ravenhill presents the Jonsonian reduction of his characters to bestial or mechanical ambulant appetites; Kane has a more Marlovian (and occasionally Barkerian) imaginative sympathy with the self-conscious and purposefully self-dramatising seeker of excess, who poeticises the briefly incandescent flourish of passion, the pain of wanting. Kane's re-vision of the myth of Phaedra and Hippolytus, *Phaedra's Love* (1996), shows Hippolytus demonstrating an unconventionally explicit and persistent refusal of shame which enhances his regal sense of sexual privilege, whilst Phaedra poeticises her own sense of searing, powerless rapture of passion for him ('Can't switch this off. Can't crush it. . . . Wake up with it, burning me. Think I'll crack open I want him so much'). Hippolytus is insistently heartless as he infantilises himself through shopping and oral gratification (in ways which outperform even Ravenhill's characters); Phaedra's passion is unreciprocated and unrelieved (and yet intensified) because Hippolytus recognises she is crippled by a self-hatred, from which he (however bored and cynical) is charismatically free. Many of the play's effects of imaginative freedom – something deliberately denied in *Cleansed* – are generated through black humour based on bathetic and casual attitudes to the persistence and immediacy of physicality. Hippolytus maintains a political and theatrical power through his stance, 'If I've lived by honesty let me die by it', and his insistence on playing out his distinctive terms of 'free will'. This makes him the focus of rage for a populist mob, but he finds an affirmation even in this.

Kane makes her audience *choose to look differently* in unusually immediate terms: faced with startlingly explicit physical images of abjection and attack, the audience has to choose: to look *directly* or to look *away*.[20] *Crave* (1998) changes the focus by demanding confrontation with psychic rather than physical pain (whilst insisting the one involves the other), and represents a further dissolution of dramatic setting as four voices contend with each other. *Crave* amplifies Artaudian and Beckettian resonances, concerning the destruction of the defence mechanisms of the ego, the surfacing of the warring forces and internalised voices within the individual psyche, and provoking and accelerating of impulses to radical separation.[21] *Crave* is Kane's most searching and poetic text, with an absolutely playful sense of reversibility: the text is alternately aphoristic and desperate, associative and wryly separated, self-mockingly ironic and proudly obsessive: 'And if this makes no sense then you understand perfectly'. On the one hand, the text reflects a breakdown in consequence ('What's anything got to do with anything?' / 'Nothing') whilst simultaneously suggesting an inescapable determinism ('What ties me to you is guilt', 'God has blessed me with the mark of Cain'); it also deduces 'Only love can save me and love has destroyed me' whilst insisting 'this has to stop'. An apparently abusive older man, A, delineates his passion with an overwhelming extensiveness; a younger woman, C, explores her own wracked sensibility, 'I hate these words that keep me alive / I hate these words that won't let me die'; M seems a thwarted maternal figure, and B casually self-destructive. However, the narrative of characteristics (rather than events) slides across from one character to another (C: 'I am an emotional plagiarist, stealing other people's pain, subsuming it into my own until / A: I can't remember / B: Whose / C: Any more') so that they seem to merge into a choric Hydra contraption for perpetual momentum in the exploration of pain and wry black humour (in performance, *Crave* is importantly rhythmic, even incantatory, in its momentum). The characters recall the speakers of Beckett's *Play*, except that *Crave* further emphasises how hell is not only other people but also one's inextricable and inescapable self. Kane's pessimism here seems not cosmic, because so intensely personal, but nevertheless mortal: being born is the crime and the sentence is living ('Why did I not die at birth'). C seems to deduce that attempted freedom from memory and desire may involve freedom from life, and the closing words are a hymn to embracing definition and infinity.

A line in *Crave* – 'My entire life is waiting to see the person with whom I am currently obsessed, starving the weeks away until our next fifteen-minute appointment' – seems to refer directly to part of the predicament explored in the posthumous work, *4.48 Psychosis* (RC, 2000), a first-person exploration of emotions culminating in suicidal depression ('I sing without hope on the boundary'). A doctor insists 'we have a professional relationship . . . a good relationship. But it's professional . . . I know you'll be okay because I like you and you can't like someone who doesn't like themself'; speaking from their simultaneously vital and terminal state of guilty despair, the patient counters 'I hope you never understand / Because I like you'. The text echoes with a grim certainty that 'Body and soul can never be married'. Notwithstanding its apparent status as dramatic suicide note, *4.48 Psychosis* is profoundly (perhaps uniquely) self-dramatising, and part of its poignance resides in the physical paradox of performance, whereby performers – physically immediate for the audience yet conventionally separated from them – stand in for a voice which insists the audience 'watch me vanish', and partially represent 'a myself I have never met, whose face is pasted on the underside of my mind'. The audience's choice of interpretation and response is opened out by the artfully incomplete prescription of the last line: 'please open the curtains'. This invites them to acknowledge an imaginative kinship with a self they have never met (Kane's) or at most briefly confronted (their own self-destructive impulses). The release of light in the theatre – or else, the release from the theatre into light – ritualises the audience's further release into conventional daily imaginative and physical separation: into the choices of ongoing life, and away from theatrical conclusion.

# Epilogue: words*kill*

OH THIS MONOTONOUS HOSTILITY WHAT COULD BE WORSE ONLY MONOTONOUS LOVE

(Howard Barker, 'Mates of Wrath'[22])

Kane's depression cannot be entirely blamed on the irresponsible reductivity of journalists (which she depicts critically in *Blasted*) and critics. However, she manifestly felt crucially unsupported by, and despairing of, the theatrical and social discourse of turn-of-the-millennium Britain. The focus of her work consequently turned, from the question *How should we live?* to the question *How should we die?* Nevertheless, her drama reminds us that we – like Mock at the end of Ed Thomas's *Flowers of the Dead Red Sea* – are still here, with choices to make.

In 1956, John Whiting wrote:

> No art exists by any man's favour. Public entertainment certainly does so, but art exists in its own right as something worth doing for its own sake. A play, like any other created work, must have the arrogance of its convictions . . .
>
> A playwright must not think that he will extend his audience beyond that of the novel or poetry. It was a mistake to see the theatre as a popular art. It may have been fifty years ago, but new mediums have changed all that. *The play must now be directed towards a specialised audience. That may well be the theatre's salvation.* Physically, it is having to pull in its boundaries. Within a few years it will be in a state of final siege in the West End of London. In all ways it must become smaller, but more concentrated.[23]

Or, I suggest, more concentrated but less dependent on commercial formulations of justification. Experiential 90s theatre discovered some freedom in small, constricted playing spaces, with their possibilities of physical immediacy. But it is restrictive to insist that an artist always paint on a miniature canvas. University theatre, usually freed from commercial dictates, can still provide a context for unusually exciting experimentation, and should be used as such. Whiting may be right that it is a fallacy to maintain that 'any art is infinitely communicable to an unlimited number of people';[24] on the other hand, when presented with an unusual freedom of choice beyond conventionally infantilising fare,[25] an unexpected number of people (young or otherwise) may find their appetites extended, to mutual surprise. Drama only finds its own audience – and thereafter the possibility of enlarging or redefining that audience – when it follows no laws, and no morality, but those of its own constant restlessness.

# Notes

1. Morgan, op. cit., p. 528.

2. Crimp experiments with various forms: *The Treatment* is a memorable fable of commercial and personal rapaciousness in New York, reminiscent of Mamet; *Attempts on Her Life* (RC, 1997) is an open text for ensemble choreography, anticipating Kane's *4:48 Psychosis* (2001); *The Country* (2000) is strongly reminscent of mid-period Pinter.

3. L. Hoggard, 'Extraordinary Joe and his Cast of Plain Men', *The Independent on Sunday*, 20/8/2000, p. 6.

4. Penhall, quoted in ibid.

5. Thanks to Charmian Savill for this observation. *The Libertine*'s power as a drama of political disappointment has, if anything, increased since its date of first performance. In my 1998 production of the play, I suggested in rehearsal that the Rochester performer,

Hannah Lavan, deliver the speeches to Charles in Scene 11 as if to Tony Blair. The results were impressive.

6. Sierz, op. cit., p. 56.

7. Ibid., p. 6.

8. Ibid., p. 233.

9. Ibid., p. 7.

10. Ibid., p. 5.

11. Ibid., p. 231.

12. A suggestion by J. Meth, in ibid., p. 234.

13. Ridley, quoted in ibid., p. 45.

14. Quoted in ibid., p. 79.

15. Leggatt, op. cit., p. 49.

16. Sierz, op. cit., p. 132.

17. Kane: 'I do think that the seeds of full-scale war can always be found in peacetime civilisation and I think the wall between so-called civilisation and what happened in central Europe is very, very thin and it can get torn down at any time'; quoted in Sierz, op. cit., p. 101.

18. Thanks to Charmian Savill for this observation.

19. Miranda Hughes has remarked upon the importance in Kane's work of 'psychotic humour', when a perpetrator finds his action amusing whilst those around find it terrifying, situations of unnerving laughter where 'crying is rarely an option because tears are like pity, a luxury you cannot afford'.

20. Thanks to Claire Eriksson for this observation.

21. Vicky Featherstone's premiere production of *Crave* chose to visualise the play by imbuing the banal form of the television chat-show with a Beckettian relentlessness and wry humour in delivery. However, the open form of the play does not preclude physicalisation, as demonstrated by Charmian Savill's practical exploration of the text with students at the University of Wales, Aberystwyth, in 1999. This interpreted the text as relentlessly physicalised and dangerously athletic 'black circus'.

22. Barker, *The Ascent of Monte Grappa* (1991), p. 77.

23. Whiting, *At Ease . . .* , pp. 88–9 (my italics).

24. Ibid., p. 99.

25. Which, however well-meaning, can only offer a totalitarian reductivity of the cultural ethos – as depicted in Ridler's *The Shadow Factory*.

# Chronology

*Note*: Dates of plays refer to first British production unless otherwise stated; reference to date of composition is signalled by **wr**. Place of production is London except where noted.

Other abbreviations used are as follows: **B** Birmingham; **C** Cardiff; **D** Dublin; **E** Edinburgh; **G** Glasgow; **L** Liverpool; **M** Manchester; **S** Sheffield; **SuA** Stratford-on-Avon; **Z** Zurich; **NY** New York; **LA** Los Angeles; **Bn** Berlin; **P** Paris; **wr** play written, not yet produced; **n** novel; **f** film; **p** poetry; **tr** English translation performed or published; **tv** broadcast on television; **r** broadcast on radio; **gn** graphic novel; **lp** record album; **45** record single; **cd** compact disc; **GE** General election victory for stipulated party; **PM** Prime Minister; **d** died; **b** born.

| DATE | PLAYS | FOREIGN PLAYS AND OTHER WORKS | CULTURAL AND HISTORICAL EVENTS |
|------|-------|-------------------------------|-------------------------------|
| 1940 | O'Casey *The Star Turns Red*  Willliams *The Corn is Green* | | Occupation of Paris Battle of Britain Churchill forms Coalition Government CEMA founded to sponsor amateur, touring and regional drama |
| 1941 | Coward *Blithe Spirit* | Orwell *The Lion and the Unicorn*  Brecht *Mother Courage* **Z**  Welles *Citizen Kane* **f** | Japanese attack Pearl Harbor. USA enters war. |
| 1942 | Ackland *The Dark River* | Eliot *Four Quartets* **p** | |
| 1943 | O'Casey *Red Roses for Me* **D** | Genet *Notre Dame des Fleurs* **n**  Brecht *The Good Person of Szechwan* **Z**  Powell & Pressburger *The Life and Death of Col. Blimp* **f** | |

211

| 1944 | | Cary<br>*The Horse's Mouth* n<br><br>Olivier<br>*Henry V* f | D-Day: Allied Forces<br>land at Normandy<br>Butler Education Act |
| 1945 | O'Casey<br>*Purple Dust* L<br><br>Ridler<br>*The Shadow Factory* | Orwell<br>*Animal Farm* n<br><br>Lean<br>*Brief Encounter* f | Germany surrenders<br>Atomic bomb dropped<br>on Hiroshima. Japan<br>surrenders.<br>World War Two ends.<br>Conservative<br>Government under<br>Churchill formed as<br>'caretaker'<br>administration.<br>**GE:** Labour<br>**PM:** Attlee |
| 1946 | Priestley<br>*An Inspector Calls*<br><br>MacNeice<br>*The Dark Tower* r | O'Neill<br>*The Iceman Cometh* NY<br><br>Reed<br>*Odd Man Out* f<br><br>Sartre<br>*In Camera* tr | BBC resumes TV<br>broadcasting<br>British nuclear<br>programme begins, at<br>Sellafield<br>Independence for<br>Burma |
| 1947 | | Rodgers & Hammerstein<br>*Oklahoma!*<br><br>Brecht<br>*The Life of Galileo* LA<br><br>Miller<br>*All My Sons* NY<br><br>Camus<br>*The Plague* tr n | Nationalisation of coal,<br>rail and electricity<br>industries and Bank<br>of England<br>Two years' national<br>service mandatory for<br>all 18-year-old men<br>Independence for<br>partitioned India |
| 1948 | Fry<br>*The Lady's not for<br>Burning*<br><br>Rattigan<br>*The Browning<br>Version*<br>*Harlequinade* | Waugh<br>*The Loved One* n | Czechoslovakian<br>government<br>overthrown<br>Stalin cuts off land<br>corridor to West<br>Berlin<br>US Air Force<br>established at British<br>bases<br>Last British troops<br>withdraw from<br>Palestine<br>Antonin Artaud d |
| 1949 | O'Casey<br>*Cock-a-Doodle<br>Dandy* | Williams<br>*A Streetcar Named Desire* | North Atlantic Treaty<br>(NATO) signed |

| | | |
|---|---|---|
| Eliot<br>*The Cocktail Party* | Brecht<br>*Mother Courage* **Bn**<br><br>Miller<br>*Death of a Salesman* **NY**<br><br>Hamer<br>*Kind Hearts and Coronets* **f** | State of Israel<br>recognised<br>Foundation of Berliner<br>Ensemble |
| **1950** | Anouilh<br>*Ring Round the Moon* **tr** Fry | Korean War begins<br>Bernard Shaw **d** |
| **1951** | Whiting<br>*A Penny for a Song*<br>*Saint's Day*<br><br>Hunter<br>*The Waters of the*<br>*Moon* | Greene<br>*The End of the Affair* **n**<br><br>Ionesco<br>*La Leçon* **P** | **GE**: Conservative<br>**PM**: Churchill<br>Festival of Britain |
| **1952** | Ackland<br>*The Pink Room*<br><br>Rattigan<br>*The Deep Blue Sea* | Ionesco<br>*Les Chaises* **P** | |
| **1953** | Greene<br>*The Living Room* | Loesser<br>*Guys and Dolls*<br><br>Beckett<br>*En Attendant Godot* **P** | Coronation of<br>Elizabeth II<br>Theatre Workshop<br>moves to London |
| **1954** | Thomas<br>*Under Milk Wood* **r**<br><br>Fry<br>*The Dark is Light*<br>*Enough*<br><br>Whiting<br>*Marching Song*<br><br>Neale and Cartier<br>*1984* **tv** | Amis<br>*Lucky Jim* **n** | Food rationing ends |
| **1955** | Beckett<br>*Waiting for Godot*<br><br>Bagnold<br>*The Chalk Garden* | Ionesco<br>*The Lesson* **tr**<br><br>Genet<br>*The Maids* **tr NY** | **PM**: Eden<br>ITV begins broadcasting |
| **1956** | Osborne<br>*Look Back in*<br>*Anger* **tv**<br><br>Behan<br>*The Quare Fellow* | O'Neill<br>*A Long Day's Journey into*<br>*Night* **NY**<br><br>Baldwin<br>*Giovanni's Room* **n**<br><br>Ellington<br>*At Newport* **lp** | Suez crisis<br>Russia suppresses<br>Hungarian revolution<br>Berliner Ensemble's<br>*Mother Courage* in<br>London<br>Brecht **d** |

213

| | | | |
|---|---|---|---|
| 1957 | Beckett<br>*Fin de Partie*<br><br>Osborne<br>*The Entertainer* | Genet<br>*The Balcony*<br><br>Ionesco<br>*The Chairs*<br><br>Hoggart<br>*The Uses of Literacy*<br><br>Kerouac<br>*On the Road* **n**<br><br>Basie<br>*The Atomic Mr Basie* **lp** | Eden resigns as PM in<br>response to Suez<br>crisis<br>Macmillan succeeds him<br>Government sanctions<br>drowning of Welsh<br>village Treweryn to<br>supply reservoir for<br>Liverpool |
| 1958 | Beckett<br>*Krapp's Last Tape*<br><br>Pinter<br>*The Birthday Party*<br><br>Behan<br>*The Hostage*<br><br>Delaney<br>*A Taste of Honey*<br><br>Jellicoe<br>*The Sport of My<br>Mad Mother*<br><br>Shaffer<br>*Five Finger Exercise*<br><br>Greene<br>*The Potting Shed* | Sinatra<br>*Only the Lonely* **lp** | Foundation of CND<br>First march from<br>London to<br>Aldermaston |
| 1959 | Arden<br>*Serjeant Musgrave's<br>Dance*<br><br>Simpson<br>*One Way Pendulum* | Burroughs<br>*The Naked Lunch* **n**<br><br>Peake<br>*Titus Alone* **n**<br><br>Davis<br>*Kind of Blue* **lp** | Khrushchev begins<br>educating Russia<br>from Stalinism<br>Billie Holiday **d**<br>**GE**: Conservative |
| 1960 | Wesker<br>*The Wesker Trilogy*<br><br>Pinter<br>*The Caretaker*<br><br>Bolt<br>*A Man for All<br>Seasons* | Ionesco<br>*Rhinoceros*<br><br>Coltrane<br>*My Favourite Things* **lp** | Macmillan agrees to<br>station American<br>nuclear submarines at<br>Holy Loch, Scotland<br>Penguin Books win trial<br>to permit publication<br>of *Lady Chatterley's<br>Lover* |
| 1961 | Whiting<br>*The Devils*<br><br>Murphy<br>*A Whistle in the<br>Dark* | Williams<br>*Culture and Society*<br><br>Heller<br>*Catch-22* **n**<br><br>Spark<br>*The Prime of Miss Jean<br>Brodie* **n** | Construction of Berlin<br>Wall<br>RSC established and<br>opens Aldwych base;<br>Hall appointed<br>director |

| 1962 | Rudkin<br>*Afore Night Come* | Albee<br>*Who's Afraid of Virginia Woolf?* | Cuban missile crisis |
|---|---|---|---|
| | Bond<br>*The Pope's Wedding* | Burgess<br>*A Clockwork Orange* **n** | |
| | Cooper<br>*Everything in the Garden* | Kesey<br>*One Flew Over the Cuckoo's Nest* **n** | |
| 1963 | Theatre Workshop<br>*Oh! What a Lovely War* | Jung<br>*Memories, Dreams, Reflections* **tr**<br><br>Hitchcock<br>*The Birds* **f** | **PM:** Douglas-Home<br>J. F. Kennedy<br>assassinated<br>Independence for Kenya |
| 1964 | Orton<br>*Entertaining Mr Sloane* | Weiss<br>*Marat/Sade*<br><br>Golding<br>*The Spire* **n** | **GE:** Labour<br>**PM:** Wilson<br>National Theatre<br>company under<br>Olivier moves into<br>Old Vic<br>BBC2 starts<br>transmitting<br>Mnouchkine founds<br>Théâtre du Soleil |
| 1965 | Osborne<br>*A Patriot for Me*<br><br>Pinter<br>*The Homecoming*<br><br>Bond<br>*Saved*<br><br>Orton<br>*Loot*<br><br>Keane<br>*The Field* | Plath<br>*Ariel* **p**<br><br>The Who<br>*My Generation* **45**<br><br>Gilbert<br>*Alfie* **f**<br><br>Tracey<br>*Under Milk Wood* **lp** | Death penalty abolished |
| 1966 | Sandford<br>*Cathy Come Home* **tv** | Lorenz<br>*On Aggression* **tr**<br><br>Pynchon<br>*The Crying of Lot 49* **n** | English football team<br>win World Cup<br>**GE:** Labour |
| 1967 | Wood<br>*Dingo*<br><br>Nichols<br>*A Day in the Death of Joe Egg* | O'Brien<br>*The Third Policeman* **n**<br><br>McGoohan<br>*The Prisoner* **tv**<br><br>The Beatles<br>*Sgt Pepper* **lp**<br><br>Laing<br>*The Politics of Experience* | British legalisation of<br>homosexual acts<br>between privately<br>consenting adults<br>Irish Catholic Civil<br>Rights movement<br>Welsh Language Act |

Foucault
*Madness and Civilization* **tr**

| | | | |
|---|---|---|---|
| 1968 | Arden & D'Arcy<br>*The Hero Rises Up* | Brook<br>*The Empty Space* | Abolition of<br>requirement of Lord<br>Chamberlain |
| | Barnes<br>*The Ruling Class* | Grotowski<br>*Towards a Poor Theatre* | licensing plays for<br>production |
| | Bond<br>*Early Morning* | Morrison<br>*Astral Weeks* **lp** | Enoch Powell's 'Rivers<br>of Blood' speech |
| | Bennett<br>*Forty Years On* | Didion<br>*Slouching Towards Bethlehem* | |
| | Murphy<br>*Famine* | | |
| 1969 | Orton<br>*What the Butler Saw* | Peckinpah<br>*The Wild Bunch* **f** | British army 'peace-<br>keeping force'<br>dispatched to N. |
| | Wood<br>*H* | Vonnegut<br>*Slaughterhouse-5* **n** | Ireland<br>US Moon landing |
| | Nichols<br>*The National Health* | Springfield<br>*Dusty in Memphis* **lp** | |
| 1970 | Williams<br>*AC/DC* | Handke<br>*Offending the Audience* **tr** | GE: Conservative<br>PM: Heath |
| | Mercer<br>*Flint* | Fo<br>*Morte accidentale di un<br>anarchico*, Milan | |
| | Wesker<br>*The Friends* | | |
| 1971 | Bond<br>*Lear* | Greer<br>*The Female Eunuch* | Internment without trial<br>introduced in N.<br>Ireland |
| | | Russell<br>*The Devils* **f** | |
| | | Gaye<br>*What's Goin' On* **lp** | |
| 1972 | Beckett<br>*Not I* | Hughes<br>*Crow* **p** | 'Bloody Sunday',<br>suspension of<br>Stormont government |
| | Arden & D'Arcy<br>*The Island of the<br>Mighty* | Carter<br>*The Infernal Desire Machines<br>of Dr Hoffman* **n** | Miners' strike |
| | Wesker<br>*The Old Ones* | Roxy Music<br>*Roxy Music* **lp** | |
| | Ayckbourn<br>*Absurd Person<br>Singular* | | |
| 1973 | Brenton<br>*Magnificence* | Ballard<br>*Crash* **n** | Britain joins EEC<br>Miners' overtime ban |

Friel
*The Freedom of the City*

Schaffer
*Equus*

Schechner
*Environmental Theater*

Barthes
*Mythologies* **tr**

1974 Barnes
*The Bewitched*

Mercer
*Duck Song*

Rudkin
*Ashes*

Storey
*Life Class*

Ayckbourn
*Absent Friends*

Hare
*Knuckle*

Three-day Week. 'Who Governs Britain'
**GE**: Labour
**PM**: Wilson
Second **GE** est. overall Labour majority
Birmingham pub bombings: 20 dead
The Other Place opens in Stratford

1975 Griffiths
*Comedians*

Berkoff
*East*

Lodge
*Changing Places* **n**

Dylan
*Blood on the Tracks* **lp**

Referendum confirms Britain's continued membership of EEC

1976 Edgar
*Destiny*
*Ball Boys*

Rudkin
*The Sons of Light*
Newcastle

Wilson
*Einstein on the Beach* **NY**

Scorsese
*Taxi Driver* **f**

Mitchell
*Hejira* **lp**

**PM**: Callaghan
National Theatre opens on South Bank

1977 Leigh
*Abigail's Party*

Poliakoff
*Strawberry Fields*

Stoppard
*Every Good Boy . . .*

Morrison
*Flying Blind*
Liverpool

T. McGrath & Boyle
*The Hard Man* **G**

Barker
*Downchild* **wr**

Müller
*Die Hamletmaschine*
Munich

C. Barker
*Theatre Games*

The Sex Pistols
*God Save the Queen* **45**

Steely Dan
*Aja* **lp**

Costello
*My Aim is True* **lp**

Silver Jubilee

| | | | |
|---|---|---|---|
| 1978 | Pinter<br>*Betrayal*<br><br>Mercer<br>*Cousin Vladimir*<br><br>Bond<br>*The Bundle*<br><br>Hare<br>*Plenty*<br><br>Edgar<br>*The Jail Diary of*<br>*Albie Sachs*<br>*Mary Barnes* **B**<br><br>Barker<br>*Fair Slaughter* | | |
| 1979 | Churchill<br>*Cloud Nine* | Boal<br>*Theatre of the Oppressed*<br><br>Johnstone<br>*Impro*<br><br>Coppola<br>*Apocalypse Now* **f** | 'Winter of Discontent'<br>**GE**: Conservative<br>**PM**: Thatcher<br>Seizure of US Embassy<br>   in Iran<br>Russia invades<br>   Afghanistan |
| 1980 | Edgar<br>*Nicholas Nickleby*<br><br>Brenton<br>*The Romans in*<br>*Britain*<br><br>Friel<br>*Translations*<br>Derry<br><br>Schaffer<br>*Amadeus*<br><br>Bennett<br>*Enjoy*<br><br>Poliakoff<br>*The Summer Party* **S**<br><br>Russell<br>*Educating Rita*<br><br>Williams<br>*Sugar and Spice* | Shepard<br>*True West*<br>San Francisco | SAS storms Iranian<br>   Embassy, London,<br>   freeing hostages<br>Callaghan resigns as<br>   Labour leader,<br>   replaced by Foot<br>Reagan elected US<br>   President |
| 1981 | Barker<br>*No End of Blame*<br><br>Brenton<br>*Thirteenth Night*<br><br>Rudkin<br>*The Triumph of*<br>*Death* **B** | McGrath<br>*A Good Night Out*<br><br>Rushdie<br>*Midnight's Children* **n**<br><br>Moving Hearts<br>*Moving Hearts* **lp** | Riots in Brixton,<br>   Toxteth, Moss Side<br>Hunger strikes by IRA<br>   'H' block prisoners<br>Death of Bobby Sands<br>Martial law imposed in<br>   Poland |

Taylor
*Good*

Wesker
*Caritas*

Poliakoff
*Favourite Nights*

| | | | |
|---|---|---|---|
| 1982 | Beckett<br>*Catastrophe* | Mamet<br>*Edmond*<br>*Chicago* | Falklands War |
| | Flannery<br>*Our Friends in the*<br>*North* | | |
| | Nichols<br>*Poppy* | | |
| | Stoppard<br>*The Real Thing* | | |
| | Churchill<br>*Top Girls* | | |
| | Bleasdale<br>*The Boys from the*<br>*Blackstuff* **tv** | | |
| 1983 | Brenton<br>*The Genius* | Mamet<br>*Glengarry Glen Ross* | **GE:** Conservative<br>Foot resigns as Labour<br>   leader, succeeded by<br>   Kinnock |
| | Edgar<br>*Maydays* | Walker<br>*The Color Purple* **n** | Cruise missiles arrive<br>   at Greenham |
| | Barker<br>*Victory* | | Draught and famine<br>   in Ethiopia |
| | Berkoff<br>*West* | | Iran attacks Iraq |
| | Daniels<br>*Masterpieces* | | |
| | Murphy<br>*The Gigli Concert* **D** | | |
| 1984 | Pinter<br>*One for the Road* | Kundera<br>*The Unbearable Lightness of*<br>*Being* **tr** | Miners' strike begins<br>IRA attempt to<br>   assassinate Thatcher<br>   at Brighton |
| | Hutchinson<br>*Rat in the Skull* | The Impostor (Elvis Costello)<br>*Pills and Soap* **45** | Reagan re-elected |
| | Poliakoff<br>*Breaking the Silence* | | |
| 1985 | Barnes<br>*Red Noses* | Kramer<br>*The Normal Heart* **NY** | Miners' strike ends<br>Band Aid concerts in<br>   Britain and America<br>   in aid of famine relief |
| | Barker<br>*The Castle*<br>*Scenes from an*<br>*Execution* **r** | Allende<br>*The House of the Spirits* **n** | |

219

Ayckbourn
*Woman in Mind*

Brenton & Hare
*Pravda*

Bond
*The War Plays*

Wertenbaker
*The Grace of Mary Traverse*

Kennedy Martin
*Edge of Darkness* **tv**

| | | | |
|---|---|---|---|
| 1986 | Rudkin<br>*The Saxon Shore*<br><br>Barker<br>*Women Beware Women*<br>*The Bite of the Night* **wr**<br><br>Cartwright<br>*Road*<br><br>Churchill & Lan<br>*A Mouthful of Birds* | Francis<br>*Milwr Bychan* **f**<br><br>Miller<br>*The Dark Knight Returns* **gn**<br><br>Davis<br>*Tutu* **cd** | American air raid on Libya |
| 1987 | Edgar<br>*Entertaining Strangers* (NT version)<br><br>Lochhead<br>*Mary Queen of Scots . . .* **E**<br><br>Ayckbourn<br>*Henceforward . . .*<br><br>Barker<br>*The Europeans* **wr** | Karge<br>*Man to Man* **tr E**<br><br>Kennelly<br>*Cromwell* **p**<br><br>Gleick<br>*Chaos* | **GE:** Conservative<br>288 killed as *Herald of Enterprise* sinks<br>32 die in King's Cross tube fire<br>11 killed by IRA bomb at Enniskillen Remembrance Service |
| 1988 | Ackland<br>*Absolute Hell*<br><br>Pinter<br>*Mountain Language*<br><br>Barker<br>*The Last Supper*<br><br>Hare<br>*The Secret Rapture*<br><br>Wertenbaker<br>*Our Country's Good*<br>*The Love of the Nightingale* **SuA**<br><br>Thomas<br>*House of America* **C** | Lodge<br>*Nice Work* **n**<br><br>Kearney<br>*The Wake of the Imagination* | Clause 28 becomes Section 28 of Local Government Act<br>Iran accepts UN resolution calling for end of war with Iraq Act<br>275 killed in bomb explosion in plane over Lockerbie<br>Bush (Sr) US President |

| 1989 | Flannery<br>*Singer* **SuA** | Clarke<br>*The Chymical Wedding* **n** | Tianamen Square<br>massacre by troops of<br>over 1000 pro- |
| | Cartwright<br>*Bed* | Moore & Lloyd<br>*V for Vendetta* **gn** | democracy<br>demonstrators |
| | De Angelis<br>*Ironmistress* | | Havel freed, becomes<br>Czechoslovakian<br>President |
| | Cullen<br>*Frida and Diego* | | |

| 1990 | Hare<br>*Racing Demon* | Baudrillard<br>*Seduction* **tr** | Thatcher resigns<br>**PM**: Major<br>Mandela released |
| | Daniels<br>*Beside Herself* | Surman<br>*The Road to St Ives* **cd** | Germany reunified |
| | Barker<br>*(Uncle) Vanya* **wr** | | |

| 1991 | Osborne<br>*Déjà Vu* | Kushner<br>*Angels in America 1* **LA** | S. Africa abolishes<br>apartheid laws<br>UN deadline expires for |
| | Pinter<br>*Party Time* | Greenaway<br>*Prospero's Books* **f** | Iraq's withdrawal<br>from Kuwait; US |
| | Hare<br>*Murmuring Judges* | Kundera<br>*Immortality* **n** | launches air strike on<br>Baghdad: Gulf War |
| | Hutchinson<br>*Pygmies in the Ruins* | Tarantino<br>*Reservoir Dogs* **f** | Croatia and Slovenia<br>declare independence<br>from former |
| | Thomas<br>*Flowers of the Dead*<br>*Dead Sea* **C** | | Yugoslavia |
| | Ridley<br>*The Pitchfork Disney* | | |

| 1992 | Brenton<br>*Berlin Bertie* | Boal<br>*Games for Actors and*<br>*Non-Actors* **tr** | **GE**: Conservative<br>US President: Clinton<br>Serbian and Croatian |
| | Thomas<br>*East from the Gantry*<br>**C** | Kushner<br>*Angels in America 2* **LA** | forces at war: more<br>than half a million<br>killed |
| | Ridley<br>*The Fastest Clock in*<br>*The Universe* | Mamet<br>*Oleanna* **NY** | |

| 1993 | Hare<br>*The Absence of War* | Welsh<br>*Trainspotting* **n** | US attack on Baghdad,<br>with British and<br>French backing |
| | Morrison<br>*A Lovesong for*<br>*Ulster* | | Deaths and atrocities<br>mount in Serbian–<br>Bosnian war |
| | Edwards<br>*Wittgenstein's*<br>*Daughter* **G** | | |

Motton
*A Message for the
Broken Hearted* L
*The Terrible Voice
of Satan*

| | | | |
|---|---|---|---|
| 1994 | Churchill<br>*The Skriker* | Auster<br>*Mr Vertigo* n | IRA declare (2-year)<br>ceasefire<br>Blair elected Labour<br>leader, launches<br>slogan 'New Labour,<br>New Britain' |
| | Barker<br>*Hated Nightfall* | | |
| | Edgar<br>*Pentecost* | | |
| | Jeffreys<br>*The Libertine* | | |
| | Penhall<br>*Some Voices* | | |
| | Ridley<br>*Ghost from a<br>Perfect Place* | | |
| 1995 | Bond<br>*Coffee* wr | Barba<br>*The Paper Canoe* tr | President Clinton visits<br>N. and S. Ireland |
| | Kane<br>*Blasted* | McCabe<br>*The Dead School* n | |
| | Hare<br>*Skylight* | Weller<br>*Stanley Road* cd | |
| | Edwards<br>*Utah Blue* C | | |
| | McPherson<br>*This Lime Tree<br>Bower* D | | |
| | Butterworth<br>*Mojo* | | |
| | Harrower<br>*Knives in Hens* E | | |
| | Motton<br>*Cat and Mouse<br>(Sheep)* P | | |
| | Penhall<br>*Pale Horse* | | |
| 1996 | Pinter<br>*Ashes to Ashes* | Hill<br>*Canaan* p | IRA bomb in<br>Manchester: 220<br>injured |
| | Cartwright<br>*I Licked a Slag's<br>Deodorant* | Heaney<br>*The Spirit Level* p | |

Poliakoff
*Blinded by the Sun*

Kane
*Phaedra's Love*

Ravenhill
*Shopping and*
*F£££ing*

Walsh
*Disco Pigs* **D**

| 1997 | Hare | Barker | **GE**: Labour |
| | *Amy's View* | *Arguments for a Theatre* | **PM**: Blair |
| | Marber | (3rd edn) | Princess Diana dies in |
| | *Closer* | Jackson | car crash |
| | McPherson | *The Underground Man* **n** | Devolution referenda in |
| | *The Weir* | Gaiman | Wales and Scotland |
| | Ravenhill | *Sandman: The Wake* **gn** | |
| | *Faust is Dead* | | |
| | Neilson | | |
| | *The Censor* | | |
| 1998 | Kane | Hughes | Good Friday agreement |
| | *Cleansed* | *Birthday Letters* **p** | on plan for elected |
| | *Crave* **E** | McCarthy | assembly for Ulster |
| | Barker | *Cities of the Plain* **n** | |
| | *Ursula* | | |
| | Thomas | | |
| | *Gas Station Angel* | | |
| | Hare | | |
| | *Via Dolorosa* | | |
| | Poliakoff | | |
| | *The Tribe* **tv** | | |
| 1999 | Barnes | Doyle | Massacres and |
| | *Dreaming* | *A Star Called Called Henry* **n** | atrocities in Kosovo |
| | O'Rowe | | NATO air attacks on |
| | *Howie the Rookie* | | Yugoslavian military |
| | Jones | | sites |
| | *Stones in his Pockets* | | |
| | Barker | | |
| | *Und* | | |
| | Ravenhill | | |
| | *Some Explicit* | | |
| | *Polaroids* | | |
| | Edwards | | |
| | *Over Milk Wood* | | |
| | Porth | | |

223

Poliakoff
*Shooting the Past* **tv**

Neilson
*The Debt Collector* **f**

| | | | |
|---|---|---|---|
| 2000 | Kane<br>*4:48 Psychosis*<br><br>Edgar<br>*Albert Speer*<br><br>Cartwright<br>*Hard Fruit* | Hawes<br>*Dead Long Enough* **n** | Good Friday agreement<br>  falters<br>Controversy over<br>  Millennium Dome<br>Bush (Jr) elected US<br>  President |
| 2001 | Barker<br>*The Twelfth Battle<br>of Isonzo* **D**<br><br>Edgar<br>*The Prisoner's<br>Dilemma* **SuA**<br><br>McPherson<br>*Port Authority* **D**<br><br>O'Rowe<br>*Made in China* **D**<br><br>Poliakoff<br>*Perfect Strangers* **tv**<br><br>Ravenhill<br>*Mother Clap's Molly<br>House* | Sinclair<br>*Landor's Tower* **n**<br><br>Miller<br>*The Dark Knight Strikes<br>Again* **gn**<br><br>Henry<br>*Scar* **cd** | **GE**: Labour<br>Terrorist air attacks on<br>  New York World<br>  Trade Center and<br>  Pentagon<br>Bush (Jr) declares 'war<br>  on "terrorism"' |

# General Bibliographies

*Note*: Each section is arranged alphabetically. The place of publication is London unless otherwise stated.

## (i) Historical and cultural context, 1940–2001

Campbell, B.
*Wigan Pier Revisited: Poverty and Politics in the Eighties* (1984). (Powerful account of underclasses under Thatcherism.)

Childs, D.
*Britain Since 1945* (Fifth edition, 2001). (Clear and succinct, with distinctive sub-headings.)

Clarke, P.
*Hope and Glory: Britain 1900–1990* (1996). (Both readable and substantial. Impressively marshalled.)

Marwick, A.
*British Society Since 1945* (Third edition, Harmondsworth, 1996). (Detailed, lively and forceful.)

Morgan, K. O.
*The People's Peace: British History Since 1945* (Oxford, 1990, 1999). (Excellently thorough and incisively reflective on national culture.)

Sinfield, A. (ed.)
*Society and Literature, 1945–1970* (1983). (Concise, provocative, radical, questionable, cultural study.)

——
*Literature, Politics and Culture in Post-War Britain* (Oxford, 1989).

## (ii) Theatrical context of drama in the period

Browne, T.W.
*Playwrights' Theatre: The English Stage Company at the Royal Court* (1975). (Enthusiastic documentary history.)

Chambers, C.
*Other Spaces: New Writing and the RSC* (1980). (Brief in-house account of the RSC's days of convincing commitment to new writing.)

Craig, S. (ed.)
*Dreams and Deconstructions: Alternative Theatre in Britain* (1980). (An account of and for the time. Contains parallel consideration of 70s drama.)

Davies, A.
*Other Theatres: The Development of Alternative and Experimental Theatre in Britain* (1987). (Broadly informative survey.)

Doty, G. & Harbin, B. (eds)
*Inside the Royal Court, 1956–1981: Artists Talk* (Baton Rouge, 1990). (Useful complement to Browne and Roberts.)

Elsom, J.
*Post-war British Theatre* (1976).

——
*Cold War Theatre* (1992). (Location of British and American theatre since World War Two in cultural context.)

| | |
|---|---|
| Findlater, R. (ed.) | *At the Royal Court* (1981). (Testimonials by actors, dramatists and directors; celebratory, but strong on production photographs.) |
| Roberts, P. | *The Royal Court Theatre and the Modern Stage* (Cambridge, 1999). (A documentary study from inception to the present.) |
| Shellard, D. | *British Theatre Since the War* (1999). (Factually informative rather than critical.) |
| Tynan, K. | *A View of the English Stage, 1944–63* (1984). (Collection of the most eloquent newspaper reviews of the period, testifying to important events and transitions.) |

## *(iii) English drama 1940–2001*

| | |
|---|---|
| Acheson, J. | *British and Irish Drama Since 1960* (Basingstoke, 1993). (Good range of essays on principal individual dramatists.) |
| Armstrong, W. A. (ed.) | *Experimental Drama* (1963). |
| Aston, E., and Reinelt, J. (eds) | *The Cambridge Companion to Modern British Women Playwrights* (Cambridge, 2000). |
| Berney, K. (ed.) | *Contemporary British Dramatists* (1994). |
| Bigsby, C. W. E. (ed.) | *Contemporary English Drama* (1981). (A high-handed and suspicious introduction, defensively sensing cultural decline in theatre writing; limited and limiting collection of essays.) |
| Bock, H., & Wertheim, A. (eds) | *Essays on Contemporary British Drama* (Munich, 1981). |
| Boireau, N. (ed.) | *Drama on Drama: Dimensions of Theatricality on The Contemporary British Stage* (New York, 1997). |
| Bull, J. | *New British Political Dramatists* (Basingstoke, 1984). (Lucid introductions to Brenton, Hare, Edgar and Griffiths.) |
| —— | *Stage Right: Crisis and Recovery in British Contemporary Mainstream Drama* (Basingstoke, 1994). (Pithy readings of mainstream comedy in cultural contexts.) |
| Bull, J. (ed.) | *Dictionary of Literary Biography, Volume 233: British and Irish Dramatists Since World War II, Second Series* (2001). |
| Brater, E., & Cohn, R. (eds) | *Around the Absurd: Essays on Modern and Postmodern Drama* (Ann Arbor, 1990). |
| Brown, J. R. (ed.) | *Modern British Dramatists* (Englewood Cliffs, N. J., 1968). |
| Cave, R. A. | *New British Drama on the London Stage 1970–1985* (Gerrards Cross, 1987). |
| Clum, J. M. | *Acting Gay: Male Homosexuality in Modern Drama* (New York, 1994). |
| Cohn, R. | *Retreats from Realism in Recent English Drama* (Cambridge, 1991). (Loosely thematic approach to drama 1956–86; usefully updates Worth by acknowledging and considering 80s drama.) |

Cousin, G.

*Women in Dramatic Place and Time: Contemporary Female Characters on Stage* (1996). (Readings of Churchill, Lochhead, De Angelis, Wertenbaker and other women dramatists.)

Demastes, W. A. (ed.)

*British Playwrights, 1956–1995: A Research and Production Sourcebook* (1996). (A most useful collection of biographical summaries, recordings of critical receptions, career assessments and bibliographies on thirty-six dramatists. Unusually thorough and informed.)

Donoghue, D.

*The Third Voice: Modern British and American Verse Drama* (1959). (Terse if pedagogic argument for the merits of Eliot over Fry, and wider discussion of poetic drama from the literary rather than theatrical viewpoint.)

Griffiths, T. R., &
Llewellyn-Jones, M. (eds)

*British and Irish Women Dramatists since 1958: A Critical Handbook* (Buckingham 1993). (Wide-ranging, readable and provocative.)

Hinchcliffe, A. P.

*British Theatre 1950–70* (Oxford, 1974). (Some reductive categorisations, but a succinct, provocative complement to Taylor.)

——

*Modern Verse Drama* (1977).

Hawkins-Dady, M. (ed.)

*International Dictionary of Theatre – 2: Playwrights* (1994).

Hayman, R.

*British Theatre Since 1955* (Oxford, 1979). (A critic significantly out of step with then-contemporary developments: reductive, bemused and curious, but ultimately dismissive from a great cultural height.)

Itzin, C.

*Stages in the Revolution* (1980). (Oddly structured but wide-ranging impressions of British history, drama and alternative political theatre 1968–79.)

Jacobs, J.

*The Intimate Screen: Early British Television Drama* (Oxford, 2000).

Kennedy, A. K.

*Six Dramatists in Search of a Language* (Cambridge, 1975). (Attentive study of Shaw, Eliot, Beckett, Pinter, Osborne and Arden.)

Lacey, S.

*British Realist Theatre: The New Wave in its Context, 1956–1965* (1995). (Excellent consideration of both theatrical and contemporary cultural factors, the best current volume on its period.)

Leeming, G.

*Poetic Drama* (1989).

Kerensky, O.

*The New British Drama* (1977).

Kitchen, L.

*Mid-Century Drama* (1960).

Mikhail, E. H.

*Contemporary British Drama 1950–1976* (1976).

O'Connor, S.

*Straight Acting: Popular Gay Drama from Wilde to Rattigan* (1998). (Lively if anecdotal study.)

Page, A. (ed.)

*The Death of the Playwright?: Modern British Drama and Literary Theory* (Basingstoke, 1992). (An uneven collection, with some awkward attempts to theorise dramatic texts.)

227

| | |
|---|---|
| Peacock, K. | *Radical Stages: Alternative History in Modern British Drama* (Westport, 1991). |
| Rabey, D.I. | *British and Irish Political Drama in the Twentieth Century* (Basingstoke, 1986). (Introductory study with a wide range which is both its strength and its limitation.) |
| Rebellato, D. | *1956 And All That* (1999). (Highly intelligent, polemic and provocative revaluation of 1950s theatre mythologies, the 1956 'renaissance' and cultural contexts.) |
| Reinelt, J. G. | *After Brecht: British Epic Theatre* (Ann Arbor, 1994). (Accessible exposition and cultural contextualisation of Brenton, Hare, Griffiths, Bond, Churchill and McGrath within a tradition of dialectical drama.) |
| Riggs, T. (ed.) | *Contemporary Dramatists* (Sixth edition, Detroit and New York, 1999). |
| Rusinko, S. | *British Drama 1950 to the Present: A Critical History* (Boston, 1989). |
| Shank, T. (ed.) | *Contemporary British Theatre* (Basingstoke, 1994, 1996). (A broad bid to contextualise dramatists and themes alongside impressions of emergent theatre groups, musicals, directors and design from a distinctly 90s perspective. Good essays by Cohn and Dunn.) |
| Sierz, A. | *In-Yer-Face Theatre* (2001). (Provocative, rhetorical view of 1990s emergent British dramatists and trends, with acknowledgment of some important forerunners.) |
| Sinfield, A. | *Out on Stage: Lesbian and Gay Theatre in the Twentieth Century* (1999). (Well-researched, internationally-ranging, ambitious and energetic.) |
| Stephenson, H. and Langridge, N. (eds) | *Rage and Reason: Women Playwrights on Playwriting* (1997). (Interviews with Daniels, De Angelis, Kane, Wertenbaker and others.) |
| Taylor, J. R. | *Anger and After* (1962, 1969). (An informative immediate response to the '56 generation, with useful identifications of discourse, if now rather dated impressions of dramatists.) |
| | *The Second Wave* (1971, 1978). (Complementary sequel, on emergent dramatists of the 60s and early 70s. As above.) |
| Wandor, M. | *Look Back in Gender* (1987) |
| —— | *Post-War British Drama: Looking Back in Gender* (2001). (Theoretically linear feminist studies, simplifyingly selective.) |
| Winkler, E. H. | *The Function of Song in Contemporary British Drama* (Delaware, 1990). |
| Worth, K. | *Revolutions in English Drama* (1972). (Still the best single critical volume on the period 1930–70; attentive to issues of style, language and scenic form.) |

# Individual Authors

## Notes on biography, works and criticism

Entries are divided into two sections:
(a) *Brief outline of author's life and career (including, where relevant, selected non-dramatic work).*
(b) *Selected critical studies of author's drama (place of publication is London unless otherwise noted).* Works of criticism and dramatic history in the General Bibliography should also be consulted.

The following abbreviations are used:
b. = born; d. = died; educ. = educated; Uni. = University; perf(s).; f. = founded; pub. = published; rec. = recipient; RC = Royal Court; RSC = Royal Shakespeare Company; (R)NT = (Royal) National Theatre.

ACKLAND, Rodney (1908–91), b. Westcliffe-on-Sea, Essex; educ. Central School of Speech Training and Dramatic Art, London. Worked in retail and advertising, 1924–5; f., with Roland Gillett, Kinsmen Pictures, 1946. Worked as stage actor and director in the late 1920s and 30s, and wrote many screenplays in the 1930s and 40s. The awareness of compulsive self-destructiveness and critical but deeply sounded depiction of emotional addiction characterises Ackland's best work, such as *The Dark River* (1941) and *The Pink Room* (1952), revised in 1988 as *Absolute Hell*. Autobiography, with Elspeth Grant: *The Celluloid Mistress* (1954).

See: Spurling, in Berney (1994).

ARDEN, John (1930– ), b. Barnsley, Yorkshire; educ. King's College, Cambridge; BA in architecture 1953; Edinburgh College of Art, 1953–55. Served in British Army Intelligence Corps, 1949–50. Married Margaretta D'Arcy (see separate entry) in 1957. Founding member: Committee of 100 anti-nuclear group, 1961; Corrandula Arts and Entertainment, County Galway, 1973; Theatre Writers' Group (now Theatre Writers' Union), 1975. Rec. *Evening Standard* award, 1960; John Whiting award, 1973; PEN Macmillan Silver Pen award, 1992. Lives in Galway. Arden, with and without D'Arcy, excels at subjecting traditional forms of heroism and national creation myths to cool, pragmatic enquiry, with a shrewd sense of surprising reversal, as shown in *The Island of the Mighty* (1972). However, Arden and D'Arcy's dispute with the RSC over the persistently conservative emphasis of their production proved a turning point. Arden and D'Arcy withdrew their energies from the institutionalised British theatre and drama, to concentrate on a more Marxist and Irish nationalist form of popular political theatre in Ireland. Since the 80s Arden has concentrated principally on radio plays (*Pearl*, 1978; *Whose is the Kingdom?*, with D'Arcy, 1988) and novels. Other work: *To Present the Pretence* (essays on the theatre, 1977); *Silence Among the Weapons* (novel, 1982); *Books of Bale* (novel, 1988); *Awkward Corners* (essays, with Margaretta D'Arcy, 1988); *Cogs Tyrannic* (short stories, 1991).

See: Dahl, M.K., *Political Violence in Drama* (Michigan, 1987). (Contains incisive account of *Musgrave* as 'antisacrificial' play.)

Gray, F., *John Arden* (Basingstoke, 1982) (Unusually thoughtful and sympathetic account of Arden and D'Arcy's development.)

Hunt, A. *Arden: A Study of his Plays* (1974) (Excellent study of how Arden and D'Arcy develop in and from a theatrical tradition which is opposed to, and often unrecognised by, the conventional dramatic mainstream.)

Wike, J. (ed.) *John Arden and Margaretta D'Arcy: A Casebook* (1995). (Variable, but aptly various and timely, update on and consideration of their full breadth of purpose and activities.)

AYCKBOURN, Alan (1939– ), b. London, educ. Hertford. Stage manager and actor, Donald Wolfit's touring company, 1956–7; actor and stage manager, Stephen Joseph Theatre, Scarborough, 1957–62; associate director, Victoria Theatre, Stoke-on-Trent, 1962–4; drama producer, BBC Radio, Leeds, 1964–70. 1970–Present, Artistic Director, Stephen Joseph Theatre. 1986–88, Associate Director, NT. 1987, C.B.E. 1991–2, Professor of Contemporary Theatre, Oxford University. Since the production of his first play, *The Square Cat*, in 1959 at Stephen Joseph's theatre-in-the-round, Ayckbourn's plays have regularly premiered at this venue prior to transfer to London. Perhaps the most popularly and commercially successful of living British dramatists, Ayckbourn depicts the casually damaging emotional obtuseness of the English middle classes through a series of increasingly dark comedies.

See: Billington, M., *Alan Ayckbourn* (Basingstoke 1990) (Pertinent, if repetitive, identification of themes.)

Dukore, B. F. (ed.), *Alan Ayckbourn: A Casebook* (New York, 1991).

Holt, M., *Alan Ayckbourn* (Plymouth, 1999) (Concise, direct introduction.)

Kalson, A. E., *Laughter in the Dark: The Plays of Alan Ayckbourn* (1993).

White, S. H., *Alan Ayckbourn* (Boston, 1984).

BARKER, Howard (1946– ), b. London, educ. Sussex University (MA in History). His radio play *Scenes from an Execution* was awarded the Prix Italia in 1985, the same year that three of his plays (*Downchild, Crimes in Hot Countries, The Castle*) were staged by the RSC at the Barbican Pit Theatre (as the 'Barker at the Pit' season). The Wrestling School Theatre Company was formed in 1988 to produce Barker's plays. Since their 1994 production, *Hated Nightfall*, Barker has usually directed the first productions of his own plays for The Wrestling School, and proved one of the most distinctive and powerful British directors as well as dramatists. His work was the subject of two documentaries, *Refuse to Dance* (Channel 4 TV, 1986) and *Departures from a Position* (BBC R3, 1999). Also a poet, artist (with a major retrospective of paintings scheduled for 2002) and a purposefully eloquent theatre essayist. Tomlin notes the vital position in British theatre of Barker's 'world-written-as-theatre' in which performative virtuosity permits protagonists to 'construct their desires through their own artifice of performance and the colluding opposition of their audience . . . where reality is recognised as an illusion created and sustained between actor and spectator, both on stage and off'. His collection of essays, *Arguments for a Theatre*, had its first edition in 1989, and its third expanded edition in 1997. Poetry: *Don't Exaggerate* (1984), *The Breath of the Crowd* (1986), *Gary the Thief/Gary Upright* (1987), *Lullabies for the Impatient* (1989), *The Ascent of Monte Grappa* (1991), *The Tortmann Diaries* (1996).

See: Lamb, C., *Howard Barker's Theatre of Seduction* (Amsterdam, 1997). (Excellent, provocative study.)

Rabey, D. I., *Howard Barker: Politics and Desire* (1989) (Authorised and exhaustive exposition of all drama, poetry and archival work to 1989.)

Wilcher, R., 'The Theatre of Howard Barker', in Acheson (1993), pp. 176–89.

Tomlin, L., in Bull (2001), pp. 9–21.

BARNES, Peter (1931– ), b. London. One year of military service with Royal Air Force (1949–50), before and after which he worked for the Greater London Council, until leaving to become a freelance reviewer (including work for *Films and Filming*). 1956, story editor for Warwick Films. Rec: John Whiting, *Evening Standard*, Sony Best Play, Olivier, Royal Television Society awards; Oscar nomination (for 1993 screenplay adaptation *Enchanted April*). Has also adapted Wedekind, Jonson and other Jacobean dramatists, and directed some of his own work for television (*Nobody Here But Us Chickens*, 1989; *The Spirit of Man*, 1990). Barnes is an unusually and admirably bold theatre imagist, whose blackly comic defiances of institutional authority achieve a peculiarly English, even Shakespearean, mixture of high and low cultural references, and an anarchic generosity of spirit.

See: Dukore, B., *Barnestorm* (1995)
—— 'Red Noses and Saint Joan', *Modern Drama* 30.3 (Sept. 1987), 340–51.
Woolland, B., in Bull (2001), pp. 22–34.

BECKETT, Samuel (1906–89), b. Foxrock, educ: Trinity College, Dublin. Lecturer at École Normale Supérieure, Paris (1928–30) and Trinity College, Dublin (1930–1). Translator and writer in Dublin, London and Paris prior to war; joined French Resistance; worked in Irish Red Cross Hospital in France, 1945. Rec. Croix de Guerre and Médaille de la Résistance for war service, 1945. Published many of his works in both French and English versions, and latterly directed many productions of his own work. Many artistic awards include 1969 Nobel Prize for Literature. An innovatory dramatist of remorseless concentration, in both verbal and visual stage imagery. Like his prose work, his plays often depict experientially the fragmentary sub-division of a consciousness turning inwards and against itself, and consequences of repressed expression. Fiction includes *Molloy, Malone Dies, The Unnameable* (pub. in French individually 1951–3, pub. in English as a trilogy of novels, 1960), *How It Is* (1964; novel, pub. as *Comment C'Est*, 1961) and many shorter prose works.

See: Birkett, J. and Ince, K. (eds), *Samuel Beckett* (2000). (Summary of shifting and recent theoretical perspectives of the huge Beckett critical industry.)
Brater, E., *Beyond Minimalism* (Oxford, 1987). (Incisive study of Beckett's late dramatic developments.)
Cohn, R., *Just Play: Beckett's Theatre* (Princeton, 1980). (Fine introduction to themes, motifs and issues in performance.)
Connor, S. (ed.), *New Casebooks: Waiting for Godot and Endgame* (Basingstoke, 1992).
Fletcher, J. and Spurling, J., *Beckett: A Study of his Plays* (1972, 1978). (Lucid introductory study.)
Kalb, J., *Beckett in Performance* (Cambridge, 1989). (Good consideration of Beckett's theatricality, particularly in the late work, with interviews with practitioners.)
Pilling, J. (ed.), *The Cambridge Companion to Beckett* (Cambridge, 1994). (Very good selection of essays on his drama and prose.)
States, B., *The Shape of Paradox* (Berkeley, 1978). (Excellent essay on *Godot*, with many reverberations for other Beckett drama.) Worth, K. (ed.), *Beckett the Shape Changer* (1975). (Very good essay on space and sound in Beckett's theatre, by Worth herself.)

BENNETT, Alan (1934– ), b. Leeds, educ: Exeter College, Oxford. National Service: Joint Services School for Linguists, Cambridge and Bodmin. Temporary junior lecturer in History, Magdalen College, Oxford, 1960–2. Thereafter, writer, actor, director and broadcaster. Rec: Tony award, *Evening Standard* award, Guild of Television Producers award, Broadcasting Press Guild award, Royal Television Society award, Olivier award. His television monologues, *Talking Heads* (1988 and 1998), are his best known work, playing the apparent intimacy of the medium off against perceptual limitations reflected by the restricted or fixed camera angle, often suggesting frailty and the poignance of diminishing capability.

See: Turner, D., *Alan Bennett: In a Manner of Speaking* (1997).

BERKOFF, Steven (1937– ), b. London, educ. Webber-Douglas Academy of Dramatic Art and École Jacques LeCoq, Paris. Actor in Repertory in Nottingham, Coventry, Liverpool and Glasgow. 1973, f. London Theatre Group, which has produced many of his plays, such as *East* (1975) and *West* (1980). Continues to act in and direct his own plays, and act in films. Berkoff frequently celebrates (rather than analyses) the release of repressed energy, and has developed a distinctive directorial and production style through which to give formalised expression to instincts and impulses.

See: Berkoff, S., *The Theatre of Steven Berkoff* (1992). (A striking pictorial documentary, not a critical book.)

BLEASDALE, Alan (1946– ), b. Liverpool, educ: Widnes and Padgate. Teacher 1967–75. Joint Artistic Director, 1981–4, and associate director 1984–6, of Liverpool Playhouse. *Boys from the Blackstuff* (BBCTV, 1982) remains the best of Bleasdale's 'deadpan farces' of the tragicomedy of desperation.

See: Millington, B. and Nelson, R., *Boys from the Blackstuff: The Making of Television Drama* (1986).

BOND, Edward (1934– ), b. London, educ: Crouch End. National Service: British Army, 1953–5. Rec: George Devine, John Whiting and Obie awards. Moving from bleak social realism (*The Pope's Wedding*, 1962; *Saved* 1965) through political expressionism (*Early Morning*, 1968) to a socially parabolic form of mythic history (*Narrow Road to the Deep North*, 1968; *Lear*, 1971), Bond has developed a drama which combines Brechtian analyses of social pressure with particularly shocking exposures of human consequences. *Saved* and *Early Morning* were the subjects of legal action, but the controversy generated resulted in the British laws of stage censorship becoming liberalised. *The War Plays* were produced as a trilogy by the RSC in 1984, but Bond's increasing dissatisfaction with the aesthetic politics of British subsidised theatre has led him to withdraw from this arena (like Arden), preferring to offer the strength of his writing to the bolder artistic ambitions and social immediacy of student and theatre-in-education companies. His poetry is collected in *Theatre Poems and Songs* (1978) and *Poems 1978–1985* (1987).

See: Hay, M. and Roberts, P., *Bond: A Study of his Plays* (1980). (Admirably attentive to scenic form, and well documented.)
Hirst, D., *Edward Bond* (Basingstoke, 1985).
Mangan, M., *Edward Bond* (Plymouth, 1998). (Succinctly introductory, and also good on recurrent story patterns and effects.)

BRENTON, Howard (1942– ), b. Portsmouth, educ: St. Catharine's College, Cambridge. Rec: John Whiting and *Evening Standard* awards. Stage manager in several repertory companies. Early experiments with self-consciously 'rough', provocative alternative theatre forms and styles led Brenton to a series of plays which all attempt to discern and examine the estranged postures of counter-cultural deviancy or revolt in a slumbrous, conciliatory but unjust English climate of presumption. *The Romans in Britain* (NT, 1980) was the subject of prosecution under the Sexual Offences Act because of its simulated buggery of a Celt by a Roman soldier, Brenton's metaphor for the insistencies of imperial power. Brenton has translated and adapted work by Büchner, Brecht and Shakespeare, and collaborated with other dramatists including David Hare (*Brassneck*, 1973; *Pravda*, NT, 1985), Tunde Ikoli and Tariq Ali. The latter seems to have led Brenton's writing increasingly towards satire and farce. His collection, *Hot Irons: Diaries, Essays, Journalism* (1995), is illuminating and informative on the cultural contexts, ambitions and rehearsals of his writing.

See: Boon, R., *Brenton the Playwright* (1991). (Substantial and detailed study, with authorised archival references.)

BUTTERWORTH, Jez (1969– ), b. St. Alban's, educ: Cambridge University. Rec: George Devine, *Evening Standard*, Writers Guild, Critics Circle and Olivier awards for *Mojo* (RC, 1995; film adaptation, 1998).

See: Sierz (2001).

CARTWRIGHT, Jim (1958– ), b. Farnsworth, educ. Royal Academy of Dramatic Art. Rec: George Devine, Monte Carlo Golden Nymph and *Evening Standard* awards. Cartwright emerged as a purposefully surprisingly poetic observer of the Northern underclasses in *Road* (1986) and *Two* (1989), which both use the episodic form of the television soap opera. *Bed* (NT, 1989) gave rein to his more surreal impulses, in a dream-play which nevertheless maintains and develops his compassion for those bewildered by the sterility and disappointments at the heart of modern Britain. *The Rise and Fall of Little Voice* (RNT, 1992), like the television play *Strumpet* (2001), reveals a weakness for wish-fulfiment endings, which the pathos of *Hard Fruit* (RC, 2000) resists, but without avoiding sentimentality. *I Licked a Slag's Deodorant* (RC, 1996), however, is a memorable depiction of urban futility and regressive intimacy.

CHURCHILL, Caryl (1938– ), b. London, educ. Lady Margaret Hall, Oxford. Rec: Obie, Susan Smith Blackburn, Olivier and *Evening Standard* awards. Churchill has distinguished herself as one of the most restlessly formally experimental non-realistic dramatists of her time, who is nevertheless always interrogatory about what might constitute the terms of social identity. Work with the companies Joint Stock and Monstrous Regiment in the 1970s seemed to accord with her own appetites for research, improvisation and the application of multiple perspectives. *Cloud Nine* (1979) employs aspects of satire and farce, but also generates more delicate and poignant effects, in considering links between British imperialism and sexual restriction. Her most original work, *The Skriker* (NT, 1994), depicts Dionysian forces of release which border conventional rationality, to both positive and destructive effect. Here, as elsewhere, Churchill foregrounds the crucial element of choice in social reaction.

See: Cousin, G., *Churchill the Playwright* (1990). (Useful introductory survey.)
  Kritzer, A. H., *The Plays of Caryl Churchill* (Basingstoke, 1991). (Intelligent and lucid detailed readings of themes and techniques.)
  Randall, P. (ed.), *Churchill: A Casebook* (New York, 1990).

CULLEN, Greg (1954– ), b. Kilburn, educ. St. Mary's College, London. Rec: Time Out award for New Expressionism. Cullen weaves artful subversive fables which are grounded in the visceral realities of political repression, and which identify the fear at the heart of control-orientated social presumptions and systems. His plays offer a frank recognition of the centrality of love and sexuality in people's powers to surprise themselves, their peers and those who would maintain a deadening social orthodoxy. Cullen set up Mid Powys Youth Theatre in 1987 (winners of the Lloyd's Theatre Challenge, BT National Connections Award, BBC Arts Award, Barclays Youth Action Award) and worked as its Artistic Director and Dramatist for over ten years. His radio play about the Falklands War, *Taken Out* (1985), was the vanguard play in a Sony Award-winning season of Welsh radio plays. *Mary Morgan* (1987) and *Tarzanne* (1988) question terms of social integration, and *Frida and Diego* (1989) identifies a vital duality as expressed through the lives, loves and work of the painters Frida Kahlo and Diego Rivera.

See: Davies, H. W. (ed.), *State of Play* (Llandysul, 1998).

DANIELS, Sarah (1957– ), b. London. Rec: George Devine Award. Daniels's consciously redressive and challenging feminist drama aims to provoke argument, above all. She reverses conventions of history and narrative to centralise women and their responses to traditional repression. Indeed, much of Daniels's drama works to expose what is conventionally hidden or obscured by male terms of definition: women's history (*Birthryte*, 1986), sexual orientation in the face of professional discrimination (*Neaptide*, NT, 1986), and sexual abuse (*Beside Herself*, 1990).

See: Griffin, in Aston and Reinelt (eds, 2000).

D'ARCY, Margaretta (1934– ), b. London, educ. Dublin. F. Galway Theatre Workshop, Women in Media and Entertainment, Women's Sceal Radio and Radio Pirate Women. Wife of, and frequent collaborator with, John Arden. Her work in Ireland (also as a co-director, with Arden) works to harness and assert popular and community energies against the power structures that would be imposed upon them. Also works as a video and documentary maker.

See: Arden, John, for bibliography of collaborative work and criticism; and Turner, in Berney (1994).

DeANGELIS, April. Educ: East 15 Acting School. *Crux* (1989) and *Ironmistress* (1989) are particularly powerful dramatisations of women struggling to overcome a repression compounded by internalised shame.

See: Stephenson and Langridge (1997).

EDGAR, David (1948– ), b. Birmingham, educ: Manchester Uni. Worked as a reporter in Bradford prior to playwriting career. 1989, appointed Chair of Birmingham Uni.'s MA in Playwriting course. 1970s work in agitprop and alternative political theatre led on to *Destiny* (RSC, 1976), a trenchant and artfully situated critical dramatic analysis of the appeal of the political far Right. Has demonstrated his ability to be a shrewd and powerful adaptor of non-dramatic sources (*The Jail Diary of Albie Sachs and Mary Barnes*, both 1978; *Nicholas Nickleby*, RSC, 1980), situating resonant stories in wider political and historical contexts. Recent work, best represented by *The Prisoner's Dilemma* (2001), continues to develop the drama of purposeful argument and negotiative politics, unspectacular events on which lives nevertheless hang. His collected essays and articles, *The Second Time as Farce* (1988), provide eloquent commentaries on political and dramatic issues.

See: Painter, S., *Edgar the Playwright* (1996).
  Braun, E.., in Bull (2001), pp. 96–111.
  Rabey, D. I., *Contemporary Writers: David Edgar* (British Council/Book Trust pamphlet, 1989).
  Swain, E., *David Edgar: Playwright and Politician* (New York, 1986).

EDWARDS, Dic (1953– ), b. Cardiff, educ: Lampeter University and University of Wales, Aberystwyth. Has also written opera libretti and poetry. A protégé of Edward Bond, Edwards consistently debates morality and demonstrates how social conventions demand and compound the imaginative restrictions of stupidity and myopia.

See: Davies, H. W. (1998) (includes examples of Edwards's correspondence with Bond).

FLANNERY, Peter (1951– ), b. Jarrow, educ. Manchester Uni. Rec: John Whiting and Beckett awards. Planned to be a director, but turned to writing. The BBCTV version of *Our Friends in the North* (1995) expands and updates the chronological sweep of the stage into the best example of televisual social realism in the 90s. Flannery combines Edgar's skill at dramatising researched events from recent history and Dickensian deftness at interweaving apparently abandoned plot strands with a keenly varied sense of social and emotional consequences, and a challenging immediacy in proposing terms of defiance which are fiercely critical of liberal humanist postures.

See: Llewellyn-Jones, M., in Bull (2001), pp. 120–127.

FRAYN, Michael (1933– ), b. London, educ: Emmanuel College, Cambridge. Served in Royal Artillery and Intelligence Corps, 1952–4. Reporter and columnist, 1957–68. Rec:

*Evening Standard*, Society of West End Theatre, British Theatre Association, Olivier, New York Drama Critics Circle, Emmy awards. Has published eight novels. Frayn presents an ironic view of the English middle-class's innate but ill-fated compulsion to impose order on existence.

See: Blansfield, K. C., in DeMastes (1996), pp. 143–157.

FRIEL, Brian (1929– ), b. Killyclogher, educ. Maynooth and Belfast. Teacher 1950–60. 1960, f. Field Day theatre company with Stephen Rea. Rec: New York Drama Critics' Circle, Olivier, *Evening Standard*, Writers' Guild of Great Britain and Tony awards. Language, identity, history and obstructions to communication are Friel's favourite themes. Like Chekhov, he is concerned to trace the disintegration of 'the images of the past embodied in language' whilst considering the need for, and terms of, renewal. *The Freedom of the City* (1973) and *Translations* (1980) are his most searching interrogations of the mechanics of historical definition, the ways that people, places and events are commonly, rigidly fixed in an 'official' or habitual reading of them. The plays more often emphasise irony, poignance and tragic separation than the sense of alternative possibilities.

See: Pine, R., *Brian Friel and Ireland's Drama* (1990) (The best of several critical studies of Friel: an ambitious and eloquent cultural contextualisation.)

FRY, Christopher (1907– ), b. Christopher Fry Harris, Bristol; educ. Bedford. Served in Non-Combatants Corps, 1940–44. Actor, teacher, secretary and composer. F. Tunbridge Wells Repertory Players, 1932. Rec: New York Drama Critics Circle, Royal Society of Literature awards, Queen's Gold Medal. Fry's drama often examines the aftermath of war in a spirit of redemptive philosophical comedy, seeking to find a delight and dignity at the unfathomable strangeness and variety of existence.

See: Leeming, G., *Christopher Fry* (Boston, 1990).

GRAY, Simon (1936– ), b. Hayling Island, educ: Trinity College, Cambridge. Lecturer in English, University of British Columbia, Vancouver, 1963–4; supervisor in English, Trinity College, 1964–6; lecturer in English, Queen Mary College, London, 1965–85. Rec: *Evening Standard*, New York Drama Critics Circle, Cheltenham awards. Gray presents, ironically but sympathetically, characters whose social advantage is self-consciously vulnerable to the erosion of passing and changing time. Their persistence, in spite of this awareness, is often depicted as an awkward, unfashionable, but frank, integrity. Many of Gray's plays have been directed by Harold Pinter, making for a surprisingly resilient artistic partnership, given the right-wing instincts and determinism discernible in Gray's work, and Pinter's increasingly explicit left-wing standpoint.

See: Burkman, K. H., *Simon Gray: A Casebook* (1992).
Stafford, T., in Demastes (1996), pp. 169–182.

GRIFFITHS, Trevor (1935– ), b. Manchester, educ. Manchester Uni. Served in British Army 1955–57. Teacher 1957–61; Lecturer at Stockport Technical College, 1962–65; Further Education Officer, BBC Leeds, 1965–72. Griffiths remains committed to the possibilities of film (*Reds*, with Warren Beatty, 1981; *Fatherland*, 1987) and television work (*Collected Plays for Television*, pub. 1990) as well as theatre. His theatre work nevertheless presents his most enduring images of the vitality of dialectic debate, and the priority of individual political integrity in the face of unjust social conciliation.

See: Garner, S. B., *Trevor Griffiths: Politics, Drama, History* (Michigan, 1999). (A comprehensive and highly politically literate study.)

HANNAN, Chris (1958– ), b. Glasgow, educ: University College, Oxford. Voluntary worker, Simon Community, Glasgow, 1975–8.

HARE, David (1947– ), b. St. Leonard's-on-Sea, educ. Cambridge. Co-founder of Portable Theatre (1968), Joint Stock theatre company (1973) and Greenpoint Films (1982). Rec: BAFTA, New York Critics Circle, Olivier and London Theatre Critics awards. Hare explores the effect of British institutions and culture on the spiritual life of his characters. From his collaboration with Howard Brenton, *Brassneck* (1973), Hare aspires towards dramatic diagnoses of the state of the nation, sometimes complex (*Plenty*, 1978), sometimes schematic. Television and film works such as *Licking Hitler* (1978) and *Wetherby* (1985) explore issues of compromise, truthfulness, individual idealism and unspoken emotion. A second collaboration with Brenton, *Pravda* (1985), was a rather obvious satire on tabloid journalism; his subsequent Trilogy on national institutions, also written for the National Theatre, similarly explored the defeat, by the energy of the mendacious, of liberals unable to articulate their beliefs (*Racing Demon*, 1990; *Murmuring Judges*, 1991; *The Absence of War*, 1993). Hare's performance of his own monologue, *Via Dolorosa* (1998), showed him subjecting his own liberal unease about the Israeli–Palestine conflict to both critical scrutiny and disarming parody. Prose work includes *Writing Left-Handed* (collected essays, 1991), *Asking Around* (account of researching *The Absence of War* with professional politicians, 1993) and *Acting Up* (diary of performing *Via Dolorosa*, 1999).

See: Dean, J. F., *David Hare* (Boston, 1990). (Succinct and continuingly pertinent introductory study.)
    Donesky, F., *David Hare* (Westport, 1996). (Excellent location of subject within historical and cultural contexts; sympathetic, but increasingly and eloquently critical.)
    Homden, C., *The Plays of David Hare* (Cambridge, 1995). (Oddly structured thematic survey.)
    Olva, J. L., *David Hare: Theatricalising Politics* (Ann Arbor, 1990).
    Zeifman, H. (ed.), *David Hare: A Casebook* (New York, 1994).

HUTCHINSON, Ron, b. Lisburn, educ. Coventry. Various jobs, incl. clerk, bookseller, social worker and DHSS claims investigator. Rec: George Devine, John Whiting, Emmy awards. Moved to Los Angeles, 1988. Hutchinson's plays, such as *Says I, Says He* (1977), *Eejits* (1978) and *The Irish Play* (RSC, 1980), depict self-consciously performative Irishmen struggling to understand the influence of their country on their own identities when they find themselves outside their native Ireland. Their dislocation tends to throw both their problematic terms of masculinity and their defensive strategies into relief. Hutchinson excels at creating blazingly articulate characters who achieve a distinctly Protestant form of arrogant defiance, reproaching the authority which implictly demands, and even incites, their transgression.

See: Rabey, D. I., 'The Bite of Exiled Love', *Essays in Theatre* 13, 1 (Nov. 1994), 29–43.

JEFFREYS, Stephen (1950– ), b. London, educ. Southampton Uni. Teacher, 1974–5; Lecturer in English and Drama, Cumbria College, 1975–8. Rec: *Evening Standard* and Critics Circle awards. Work with the small-scale touring company, Pocket Theatre Cumbria, included an adaptation of *Hard Times* (1982). *Desire* (1986) was a more politically immediate version of Stevenson's *The Bottle Imp* for Communicado theatre company. *Valued Friends* (1989) and *A Going Concern* (1993) are naturalistic views of the erosive effect of Thatcherism on human relations; more distinctive are his mischievously anachronistic period comedies on the efficacy of theatre, *The Clink* (1990) and *The Libertine* (RC, 1994), the latter a startling and hilarious melancholy comedy of personal and political disappointment. *I Just Stopped By to See The Man* (RC, 2000) continues his exploration of the nature of the relationship between performance and its political ramifications, in an American setting.

JELLICOE, (Patricia) Ann (1927– ), b. Middlesbrough, educ. Central School of Speech and Drama. Founding director, Cockpit Theatre Club, 1952–4, and Colway Theatre Trust, 1979–85. Rec: OBE, 1984. Jellicoe's early training and work as an actress and director informs her distinctly theatrical (rather than merely verbal or literary) imagination, which deals in large and unusual stage imagery, verbal rhythm, the keenly instinctive animality which impels human negotiations, and directness of contact between performer and audience. *The Sport of My Mad Mother* (RC, 1958) remains a bold drama, with self-consciously improvisatory characters (or perhaps 'energies') in competition, which has aged well. *The Knack* (1961) is a more naturalistic address to the theme of intuition and ritual in human dealings. She has also written plays for children, and community plays for various locations in Devon. Her work in the latter field is recounted and theorised in *Community Plays* (1987).

See: Oliver, J., in DeMastes (1996), pp. 220–226.
    Kershaw, B., in Bull (2001), pp. 159–166.

JONES, Marie, b. Belfast. Rec: John Hewitt Award. Actor; Writer-in-Residence for Charabanc Theatre Company, 1983–90. Plays include *Lay Up Your Ends* (with Martin Lynch, 1983), on the growth of Belfast mill workers' trades unionism in 1911; *Oul Delph and False Teeth* (1984), set during the Northern Irish election of 1949, charting the problems of autonomy for characters planning their futures with British state aid; *A Night in November* (1994), about an Ulster Protestant who discovers a new sense of national identity and freedom through supporting the Irish Republic football team; *Stones in his Pockets* (1999), an artful comedy which depicts Irish complicity in, and defiance of, Hollywood cinematic imperialism.

See: Maguire, T., in Bull (2001), pp. 182–187.

KANE, Sarah (1971–99), b. Brentwood, educ: Bristol Uni., Birmingham Uni. Performer and director (plays by Barker, Beckett, Shakespeare) whose form-shattering explorations of experiential drama skilfully transmuted her acknowledged influences (Beckett, Bond, Pinter and Barker: Kane played Bradshaw in a production of Barker's *Victory*, and professed an ambition to play Skinner in *The Castle*) into original, increasingly poetic style, which pushed theatre towards explicit body performance and disintegratory art installations. With a fierce black humour, her plays identify ways in which people consign themselves and each other to emotional hell through the disturbing demands of passionate love.

See: Saunders, G., *Love Me or Kill Me: Sarah Kane and the Theatre of Extremes* (Manchester 2002).
    Sierz (2001).
    Stephenson and Langridge (1997).

KEANE, John B(rendan)., (1928– ), b. and educ. Listowel. Chemist's assistant, 1946–51; street sweeper and furnace operator, Northampton, 1952–4; since 1955, pub owner, Listowel. Listowel Drama Group won the 1959 All-Ireland Drama Festival in Athlone with Keane's *Sive*. His plays show an apparently familiar rural Ireland with characters, drawn in broad mythic strokes, who self-consciously intensify rather than develop conventionally. Has also written novels, short stories, poetry and prose.

LOCHHEAD, Liz (1947– ), b. Motherwell, educ. Glasgow School of Art. Teacher, 1970–8. Wrote and toured as a performance poet. *Blood and Ice* (1984) considers social construction and expectation through the motif of Frankenstein's monster. *Mary Queen of Scots Got her Head Chopped Off* (1987) is an eclectic, epic and transformative view of Scottish history, in which social presumption is interrogated by the potential reversibility of character and terms of address. *Perfect Days* (1998) is a more conventionally comic meditation on possibility. Her poetry includes *Memo for Spring* (1972), *The Grimm Sisters* (1981) and *Dreaming Frankenstein, and Collected Poems* (1984).

See: Scullion, A., in Berney (1994), pp. 434–438.
    Koren-Deutsch, I., in DeMastes (1996), pp. 237–245.

McGRATH, Tom (1940– ), b. Rutherglen, educ. Glasgow Uni. Director, Third Eye Centre, Glasgow; f. *International Times* newspaper; jazz pianist. Associate literary director, Scottish Arts Council, 1990. As well as his collaboration with Jimmy Boyle, *The Hard Man* (1977), McGrath's work includes *Mr Laurel and Mr Hardy* (1976), examining the former's Glaswegian roots, *Animal* (1979), the trilogy *1-2-3* (1981) and *Kora* (1986): diverse plays analysing social, national and sexual identity.

See: Chaillet, N., in Berney (1994), pp. 467–470.

McPHERSON, Conor. His most digestible and commercially successful play, *The Weir* (1997), won the *Evening Standard*, Critics Circle and Olivier awards. His less comfortable plays, *This Lime Tree Bower* (1995) and *Port Authority* (2001), manifest the simultaneity of compulsive storytelling and essential isolation, and are the best of recent neo-Chekhovian Irish drama.

MARBER, Patrick. Rec: Writers' guild, *Evening Standard*, Critics' Circle, Olivier and New York Drama Critics' Circle awards. *Dealer's Choice* (RNT, 1995) depicts male compulsion as focused on a poker circle. *After Miss Julie* (BBC2, 1995) imaginatively relocates Strindberg's duel to an English country house in 1945, on the night of the Labour Party's election victory. *Closer* (RNT 1997, 1999) has proved one of the most critically and commercially successful British plays of the 1990s.

MERCER, David (1928–80), b. Wakefield, educ: Durham Uni: Served as laboratory technician in Royal Navy, 1945–8.; teacher, 1955–61. Rec: Writers Guild, BAFTA, French Film Academy, Emmy awards. Author of many astute, discomfortingly interrogatory and formally adventurous works for stage and television, probing the (frequently contradictory) demands of political principles and personal freedom.

See: Dunn, T., in Berney (1994), pp. 476–480.
    Jarman, F., Noyce, J. and Page, M., *The Quality of Mercer* (1974). (Bibliography of writings by and about Mercer.)
    Madden, P. (ed.), *David Mercer* (1981)
    Taylor, D., *Days of Vision: Working with David Mercer* (1990). (Critical memoir of Mercer and working on his television plays.)

MORRISON, Bill (1940– ), b. Balleymoney, educ: Queen's Uni, Belfast. Actor, writer and radio producer. Artistic Director, Liverpool Playhouse, 1983–5. Chair, Merseyside Arts Drama Panel, 1985. Morrison is a restless, formally exploratory and ubiquitously discomforting dramatist of Irish social situations and postures, exposing how cycles of hatred are perpetuated by vested political and economic interests, and how this is internationally tragic and blackly farcical.

See: Lawley, P., in Berney (1994), pp. 499–504.

MOTTON, Gregory (1961– ), b. London. Motton's early plays trace the unpredictable dealings of social derelicts, and his middle period work shows him to be more of a politically incisive surrealist than a social realist. *Cat and Mouse (Sheep)* (1995) is his fiercest excoriation of the degradation of the British national character and political rhetoric. Like much of his recent work, it was premiered in France. Motton is a wildly original dramatist, apparently too discomforting for his native land to accord him the honour he deserves.

MURPHY, Tom (1935– ), b. Tuam, educ: Vocational Teachers' Training College, Dublin. Apprentice fitter and welder, 1953–5; engineering teacher, 1957–62; actor and director, 1951–62. After his bleakly compulsive portrait of the Irish combative impulse, *A Whistle in the Dark* (1961), Murphy's frequently intrinsically rambling and meandering plays portray representative protagonists, benighted by self-perpetuating circuits of self-preoccupation.

See: Cave, R. A., 'The Plays of Tom Murphy', in Acheson (1993), pp. 88–102.
O'Toole, F., *The Politics of Magic* (1987).

NEILSON, Anthony (1967– ), b. Edinburgh, educ. Welsh College of Music and Drama. A dramatist-director, Neilson explores the entwined compulsions of sexuality and violence through predominantly naturalistic drama, which nevertheless presents the most unguarded of impulsive actions played out with challenging immediacy, best exemplified by *The Censor* (1997) and the film *The Debt Collector* (1999).

NICHOLS, Peter (1927– ), b. Bristol, educ: Bristol Old Vic Theatre School. Served in RAF, 1945–8; actor, 1950–55; teacher, 1957–9. Rec: *Evening Standard*, John Whiting, Ivor Novello, Tony and New York Critics Circle awards. Nichols's dramas of multiple perspective subvert familiar theatrical forms, yet can also (re)confirm the tenacity of what they are satirising, suggesting that reiteration is more compulsive and attractive to the English than change. In 1984, he published *Feeling You're Behind: An Autobiography*.
See: Jones-Owen, K., in DeMastes (1996), pp. 257–267.

ORTON, Joe (1933–67), b. Leicester, educ: Royal Academy of Dramatic Art. Orton's murder, by his partner, curtailed the career of this most profoundly mischievous comic dramatist.
See: Charney, M., *Joe Orton* (1984).
Shepherd, S., *Because We're Queers: The Life and Crimes of Kenneth Halliwell and Joe Orton* (1988).

OSBORNE, John (1929–94), b. London, educ: Belmont College, Devon. Journalist, 1947–8; repertory actor and stage manager, 1948–9; actor-manager, Ilfracombe Repertory, 1951. Co-Director, Woodfall Films, from 1958. Rec: *Evening Standard*, New York Drama Critics Circle, Tony, Oscar, Writers Guild awards. The most (in)famous spokesman for vehement, if generalised, male frustration of his age. His two volumes of autobiography, *A Better Class of Person: An Autobiography 1929–1956* (1981) and *Almost a Gentleman: An Autobiography 1956–1966* (1991), are observant on theatre and culture of their period, and an artful disclosure of the experiences which ostensibly informed his drama.
See: Banham, M., *John Osborne* (1969).
Carter, A., *John Osborne* (Edinburgh 1969, 1974).
Dixon, G.A., 'Still Looking Back: The Deconstruction of the Angry Young Man in *Look Back in Anger* and *Déjàvu*', *Modern Drama* XXXVII, 3 (Fall 1994), 521–9.
Sierz, A., 'John Osborne and the Myth of Anger', *New Theatre Quarterly* XII, 46 (May 1996), 136–146.
Taylor, J. R. (ed.), *John Osborne: 'Look Back in Anger': A Casebook* (1968).
Trussler, S., *The Plays of John Osborne* (1969).

O'ROWE, Mark (1970– ), b. Dublin. Rec: George Devine, Rooney and Irish Times/ESB awards. O'Rowe has developed McPherson's storytelling momentum into areas beyond the latter's neo-Chekhovian dwelling on the poignance of accommodation. O'Rowe's frankly, energetically non-naturalistic dramatic hurtles through gangland alliances and betrayals manifest a disturbing energy and sense of possibility.

PENHALL, Joe (1967– ), b. Surrey. Rec: John Whiting award. *Some Voices* (1994) traces the human costs and consequences of government mental health legislation to release schizophrenics into so-called 'community care' of a society predicated on business and consumer interests. His subsequent plays are astutely drawn examples of modern social realism, depicting the plight of the dislocated outsider, but also their dislocating effect on those around them, as their unconventional responses to a coldly rapacious society call its promises of identity, success and progress into question.
See: Sierz (2001).

239

PINTER, Harold (1930– ), b. Hackney, educ: Royal Academy of Dramatic Art. Conscientious objector: no national service. Actor, 1949–60, and occasionally since; also a director. Rec: *Evening Standard*, Italia, New York Film Critics, Tony, Whitbread, Cannes Film Festival, New York Drama Critics Circle, BAFTA, Writers Guild, British Theatre association awards. Perhaps the most influential of living British dramatists, Pinter is a theatrical poet of the nuances of power in social interaction. He frequently depicts the crushing of defiance, and the disturbing eroticism which may accompany this. *Various Voices* (1998) is an illuminating collection of his prose and poetry writing, particularly strong on his later political campaigning.

See: Billington, M., *The Life and Work of Harold Pinter* (1996). (Journalistic biographical profile, but usefully documents shift in self-definition as a political spokesman.)

Cahn, V. L., *Gender and Power in the Plays of Harold Pinter* (Basingstoke, 1994). (Sound consideration of early and mid-period thematic terrain.)

Quigley, A. E., *The Pinter Problem* (Princeton, 1975). (Detailed readings of selected plays, with informative introductory overview on allegory-seeking shortcomings of much previous critical work on Pinter.)

Raby, P. (ed.), *The Cambridge Companion to Harold Pinter* (2001).

POLIAKOFF, Stephen (1952– ), educ: King's College, Cambridge. Rec: *Evening Standard*, BAFTA, Venice Film Festival, Bergamo Film Festival awards. In his work for major British subsidised theatres (RSC, RNT) and for film and television, Poliakoff has developed an unpredicable form of social realism, examining issues of loyalty, betrayal, implication and selective memory.

See: Bull, J., in Berney (1994), pp. 583–586.

Demastes (1996), pp. 326–334.

RATTIGAN, Terence (1911–77), b. Kensington, educ: Trinity College, Oxford. Served in Coastal Command of Royal Air Force, 1939–45. Rec: Ellen Terry, New York Drama Critics Circle awards, CBE. A determinedly and deliberately popular dramatist, Rattigan's best work nevertheless testifies to the contradictions between social reason and individual passion.

See: Darlow, M. and Hodson, G., *Terence Rattigan: The Man and his Works* (1979).

RAVENHILL, Mark (1966– ), b. Haywards Heath, educ. Bristol University. Self-styled 'post-gay' dramatist and director, whose casually, fluently ironic dramas of shocking developments puncture the moral superiority of various forms of political correctness. His combination of postmodern irony and social satire is deliberately discomforting and provocative.

See: Sierz (2001).

RIDLER, Anne (née Bradby) (1912–2001), b. Rugby, educ: King's College, London (diploma in journalism), worked in editorial department of Faber and Faber publishers. Extensive work as a poet, translator, librettist and editor. Ridler's plays emerge from the post-war genre of Christian verse drama for church performances. *The Shadow Factory* (1946) importantly anticipates Orwell's *1984* (1949) in its imaginary extrapolations and interrogations of postwar industrial initiatives of social integration.

See: Smith, in Berney (1994), pp. 610–613.

Spanos, W. V., *The Christian Tradition in Modern British Verse Drama* (1967).

RIDLEY, Philip (1964– ), b. Bethnal Green, educ. St. Martin's School of Art. Rec: *Evening Standard* awards. Author of three novels for adults (*Crocodilia, In the Eyes of Mr Fury, Flamingoes in Orbit*) and nine for children (*Mercedes Ice, Dakota of the White Flats, Krindlekrax, Meteorite Spoon, Kasper in the Glitter, Scribbleboy, Zinderzunder, Vinegar Street, Mighty Fizz Chilla*); also three children's plays (*Fairytaleheart, Sparkleshark,*

*Brokenville*). Ridley has also written screenplays for the films *The Krays* (1990), *The Reflecting Skin* (1990) and *The Passion of Darkly Noon* (1995), the latter two of which he also directed. Also exhibited as a painter. His stage work is an artful blend of extravagance and enclosure, in which characters alternate between self-mythologisation and regression, but are often ultimately subjugated to forms of restriction and actions of withdrawal, in ways which recall early Pinter.

See: Sierz (2001).

RUDKIN, (James) David (1936– ), b. London, educ: St. Catherine's College, Oxford. Served in Royal Corps of Signals. Assistant master of Latin, Greek and Music, Bromsgrove, 1961–4. Rec: *Evening Standard*, John Whiting, Obie, New York Film Festival, European Film Festival awards. The most darkly romantic of contemporary dramatists, Rudkin works through complex poetic language and stage directions to create moral landscapes that uniquely externalise inner turmoil. He explores what constitutes human identity and the terms of its manifestation in social crisis, with characteristic references to imperialism, religion, the animal savagery of instinct, and the darkest recesses of sexuality. Recently, and frustratingly, his imagination has been restricted professionally and sidelined into screenplay adaptations and translations, though he continues to write unperformed drama for a British stage which predominantly lacks the capacity of courage to engage with his work.

See: Rabey, D. I., *David Rudkin: Sacred Disobedience* (Amsterdam, 1997). (Complete and fully authorised critical study of all work to that date.)
Wilcher, R., 'The Communal Dream of Myth: David Rudkin's *The Triumph of Death*', *Modern Drama* 35 (1992), 571–84.

STOPPARD, Tom (1937– ), b. Tom Straussler in Zlin, Czechoslovakia; moved to Singapore, 1939, Darjeeling, 1942, and England, 1946. Educ: Nottinghamshire and Yorkshire. Journalist, 1954–63. Rec: John Whiting, *Evening Standard*, Italia, Tony, New York Drama Critics Circle awards, CBE. Stoppard's self-conscious, potentially disarming ludic explorations of the relativity of truth have proved popular implicit defences of middle-class *status quo* values.

See: Kelly, K. E. (ed.), *The Cambridge Companion to Tom Stoppard* (2001).

STOREY, David (1933– ), b. Wakefield, educ: Slade School of Fine Art. Professional rugby player, 1952–6. Rec: Rhys Memorial, Maugham, *Evening Standard*, New York Drama Critics Circle, Obie and Booker awards. Has published eight novels and a collection of poems, *Storey's Lives* (1992). Storey moves through social realism (*In Celebration*, 1969) to photographic naturalism (*The Contractor*, 1969; *The Changing Room*, 1971) to naturalised absurdism (*Home*, 1970) and the consideration of transgressive performance (*Life Class*, 1974). However, his drama often resembles exercises within a chosen form, rather than the developments of form (as achieved by Mercer, Beckett and Griffiths).

See: Hutchings, W., in Demastes (1996), pp. 382–398.

TAYLOR, C(ecil) P(hilip) (1929–81), b. and educ: Glasgow. Author of nearly eighty plays, many for regional, community and youth theatres in Scotland and Newcastle.

See: Elsom, J., in Berney (1994), pp. 673–677.
DeMastes (1996), pp. 399–405.

THOMAS, Ed(ward) (1961– ), b. Abercraf, educ: Welsh College of Music and Drama. Actor. F. and Artistic Director, Y. Cwmni theatre and television production company, 1988; name changed to Fiction Factory, 1998: along with Howard Barker's The Wrestling School, one of only two long-running and regularly funded major British theatre companies dedicated to the premieres and revivals of work by a single dramatist-director. Thomas's imaginatively freewheeling plays dramatise the ludicrousness, necessity and painful dignity of attempting renewal through self-authorisation, consciously and wilfully attempting to become the writer and reader of one's own life. His characters frequently undercut themselves, and each other; but they also manifest a faith that things invisible may nevertheless be possible, significant and attainable.

See: Davies, H. W., (1998).

WALSH, Enda. Artistic Director of Corcadorca theatre company, Cork. Rec: George Devine award for the internationally successful *Disco Pigs* (1996), also performer of *misterman* (1999) and director of *bedbound* (2000). Walsh depicts regressive but wilful characters, struggling to assert an identity from the wreckage of traditional relationships.

WERTENBAKER, Timberlake, educ. France and USA. Journalist in London and New York; teacher of French in Greece. Rec: *Evening Standard*, Olivier, John Whiting, London Theatre Critics Circle, Writers Guild awards. Wertenbaker repeatedly questions the terms and conditions of using language, making moral judgements and being human – all of which are demonstrated to be irrevocably linked. Her plays also depict how public experience, and its individual expression, challenge prescribed social definitions.

See: Rabey, D. I., 'Defining Differences: Timberlake Wertenbaker's Drama of Language, Dispossession and Discovery', *Modern Drama* 33.4 (Dec. 1990), 518–28.
Wilson, A., 'Timberlake Wertenbaker's Recent Drama', in Acheson (1993), pp. 146–61.

WESKER, Arnold (1932– ), b. Stepney, educ: Hackney and London School of Film Technique. Served in RAF, 1950–2. Various jobs including cook in London and Paris, 1954–8; f. and director, Centre 42, 1961–70. Rec: *Evening Standard*, Encyclopaedia Britannica and Goldie awards. The loss or transmutation of idealism persists as a vital issue in both Wesker's career and his drama. The winding up of Centre 42 – an initiative to promote the cultural enrichment as well as the material prosperity of working people – was succeeded by disputes with major British theatres (not dissimilar from Bond's, and Arden and D'Arcy's). His work has been increasingly dependent for visibility upon performances in regional British theatres or overseas. As Wilcher notes, Wesker chooses to dramatise and explore failure rather than success, in order to emphasise the resilience required to confront disappointment, without the dangers of facile optimism and nihilistic despair.

See: Dace, L., 'Two East End Playwrights', *Adam* 401–403 (1977–8), 86–7. (Pithy contrast of Wesker and Pinter.)
Leeming, G., *Wesker the Playwright* (1983).
Wilcher, R., *Understanding Arnold Wesker* (1991). (The most thoughtful and complex consideration of Wesker's work.)

WHITING, John (1917–63), b. Salisbury, educ: Royal Academy of Dramatic Art. Served in Royal Artillery. Actor in repertory and in London, 1936–8, 1944–52. Drama critic, *London Magazine*, 1961–2. Rec: Festival of Britain award, 1951. Whiting deliberately wrenches the comic and melodramatic forms he inherited away from the conventional ideal of pleasurable comprehensibility, preferring to foreground 'the remote, isolated figure neither giving nor asking for understanding or love' (*At Ease*, 94). His dramatisations of self-conscious abjection and existential resolve still anticipate the future rather than seek ingratiation with the present. His essays and reviews are collected in *At Ease in a Bright Red Tie: Writings on Theatre* (1999).

See: Goodall, J., 'Musicality and Meaning in the Dialogue of *Saint's Day*', *Modern Drama* 29 (Dec 1986), 567–79. (Excellent on Whiting's 'dissolution of regularity and poise'.)
——, 'The Devils and its Sources', *Themes in Drama* 12 (Cambridge, 1990, 185–98). (Important detailed reading of the figure of Jeanne.)

Hayman, R., *Contemporary Playwrights: John Whiting* (1972).
Robinson, G., *A Private Mythology: The Manuscripts and Plays of John Whiting* (1988). (Informative and detailed, if occasionally schematic, consideration of repeated themes and motifs in Whiting's *oeuvre*.)
Salmon, E., *The Dark Journey: John Whiting as Dramatist* (1979). (The most detailed work of research on Whiting's drama of 'melancholy desperation', with production photographs.)
Trussler, S., *The Plays of John Whiting* (1972).

WILLIAMS, Heathcote (1941– ), b. Helsby. Associate editor, *Transatlantic Review*. Rec: *Evening Standard*, George Devine, John Whiting, Obie awards. Film actor: *The Tempest* (1980), *Little Dorrit* (1987), *Orlando* (1993). The acclaim won by the wildly inventive *AC/ DC* (1970) suggested that Williams might be an influential dramatist and stylistic experimenter. His other, relatively minor work is inventive and provocative, but he and British theatre drew away from each other, in times when his visceral revolts against indictments of imaginative internalisation of technological consumerism and voyeurism have become ever more timely. The deliberate and purposeful *excess* (both poetic and physical) of his stage work both foreshadows and outstrips most of the 'in-yer-face' drama (*sic*, Sierz, 2001) of the 1990s. His prose work, *The Speakers* (1964), was dramatised by Joint Stock theatre company, and his poetry includes *Whale Nation* (1988), *Falling for a Dolphin* (1988), *Sacred Elephant* (1989) and *Autogeddon* (1991).

See: *Gambit* magazine, nos. 18–19 (1971): Heathcote Williams issue.
Anderson, F. R., in Berney (1994), pp. 738–739.
Also: Cohn (1991), Worth (1972).

WILLIAMS, Nigel (1948– ), b. Cheadle, educ: Oriel College, Oxford. Rec: Somerset Maugham award. Has published ten novels. Television director and presenter. The characters in Williams's early plays demonstrate an artfully performative, alternately self-mocking and mesmeric ability to adopt, and then subvert, stereotypical associations. In his later work, ironic comedy and pathos (rather than tragedy) are separately dominant, to less original effect.

See: Lawley, P., in Berney (1994), pp. 740–743.
Rabey (1986).

WOOD, Charles (1932– ), b. Guernsey, educ: Birmingham College of Art. Served in 17/21st Lancers, 1950–5. Designer, stage manager and scenic artist, Theatre Workshop, London, 1957–9. Rec: *Evening Standard*, Screenwriters' Guild, Prix Italia, BAFTA awards. Wood savagely and eloquently depicts war as a populist sideshow, rigged by those in power, in which soldiers self-consciously perform 'turns' of momentary glamour in a system which promptly consumes them; and entertainment as a reconciliation which barely masks mutual exploitation. His exposure of the postures of conventional entertainment and heroism as symptomatic instruments of self-repression is scathingly, remorselessly, unforgiving.

See: Graham-White, A., in Berney (1994), pp. 753–756.
Worth (1973).

# Index

# Longman Literature in English Series

General Editors:
David Carroll, formerly University of Lancaster
Chris Walsh, Chester College of Higher Education
Michael Wheeler, University of Southampton

**Pre-Renaissance English Literature**
English Literature before Chaucer *Michael Swanton*
English Literature in the Age of Chaucer *Dieter Mehl*
English Medieval Romance *W. R. J. Barron*

**English Poetry**
English Poetry of the Sixteenth Century *Gary Waller (Second Edition)*
English Poetry of the Seventeenth Century *George Parfitt (Second Edition)*
English Poetry of the Romantic Period, 1789–1830 *J. R. Watson
(Second Edition)*
English Poetry of the Victorian Period, 1830–1890 *Bernard Richards*
English Poetry since 1940 *Neil Corcoran*

**English Drama**
English Drama before Shakespeare *Peter Happé*
English Drama: Shakespeare to the Restoration, 1590–1660
*Alexander Leggatt*
English Drama: Restoration and Eighteenth Century, 1660–1789
*Richard W. Bevis*
English Drama of the Early Modern Period, 1890–1940 *Jean Chothia*
English Drama since 1940 *David Ian Rabey*

**English Fiction**
English Fiction of the Eighteenth Century, 1700–1789 *Clive T. Probyn*
English Fiction of the Romantic Period, 1789–1830 *Gary Kelly*
English Fiction of the Victorian Period, 1830–1890 *Michael Wheeler
(Second Edition)*
English Fiction of the Early Modern Period, 1890–1940 *Douglas Hewitt*

**English Prose**
English Prose of the Seventeenth Century, 1590–1700 *Roger Pooley*
English Prose of the Nineteenth Century *Hilary Fraser with Daniel Brown*

**Criticism and Literary Theory**
Criticism and Literary Theory, 1890 to the Present *Chris Baldick*

## The Intellectual and Cultural Context
The Seventeenth Century, 1603–1700 *Graham Parry*
The Eighteenth Century, 1700–1789 *James Sambrook (Second Edition)*
The Victorian Period, 1830–1890 *Robin Gilmour*

## American Literature
American Poetry of the Twentieth Century *Richard Gray*
American Drama of the Twentieth Century *Gerald M. Berkowitz*
American Fiction, 1865–1940 *Brian Lee*
American Fiction since 1940 *Tony Hilfer*
Twentieth-Century America *Douglas Tallack*

## Other Literatures
Irish Literature since 1800 *Norman Vance*
Scottish Literature since 1707 *Marshall Walker*
Indian Literature in English *William Walsh*
African Literatures in English: East and West *Gareth Griffiths*
Southern African Literatures *Michael Chapman*
Caribbean Literature in English *Louis James*
Canadian Literature in English *W. J. Keith*

## Future Titles
English Poetry of the Eighteenth Century, 1700–1789
English Poetry of the Early Modern Period, 1890–1940
English Drama: Romantic and Victorian, 1789–1890
English Fiction since 1940
English Prose of the Eighteenth Century
Criticism and Literary Theory from Sidney to Jonson
Criticism and Literary Theory from Wordsworth to Arnold
The Sixteenth Century
The Romantic Period, 1789–1830
The Twentieth Century: 1890 to the Present
American Literature before 1880
Australian Literature